Understanding Sport

An introduction to the sociological and cultural analysis of sport

- John Horne
- Alan Tomlinson
- Garry Whannel

Spon Press
Taylor & Francis Group

LONDON AND NEW YORK

First published 1999
by E & FN Spon, an imprint of Routledge
2 Park Square, Milton Park, Abingdon, Oxon, OX14 4RN

Simultaneously published in the USA and
Canada
by Routledge
270 Madison Ave, New York, NY 10016

Reprinted 2000

Reprinted 2001, 2002, 2003, 2004, 2005, 2006

by Spon Press

*Spon Press is an imprint of the Taylor & Francis Group,
an informa business*

Typeset in Times by J&L Composition Ltd,
Filey, North Yorkshire
Printed and bound in Great Britain by
TJ International Ltd, Padstow, Cornwall

British Library Cataloguing in Publication Data
A catalogue record for this book is available from
the British Library

*Library of Congress Catologing in Publication
Data*
Horne, John.
  Understanding sport: an introduction to the
sociological and cultural analysis of sport/John
Horne, Alan Tomlinson, and Garry Whannel.
    p.   cm.
  Includes bibliographical references and index.
  ISBN 0–419–13640–1
  1. Sports—Great Britain—Sociological aspects.
  2. Sports—Great Britain—History.
  I. Tomlinson, Alan.   II. Whannel, Garry.
  III. Title.
GV706.5.H664   1999
306.4′83′0941—dc21   98–42126
                                                 CIP

ISBN10: 0-419-25290-8 (hbk)
ISBN10: 0-419-13640-1 (pbk)

ISBN13: 978-0-419-25290-0 (hbk)
ISBN13: 978-0-419-13640-8 (pbk)

101 829 258 6

Understanding Sport

ONE WEEK LOAN

Contents

CONTENTS

Illustrations

Figures

Tables

Acknowledgements

The Authors would like to thank their families, friends, colleagues and former students; and their publisher (particularly Philip Read) in showing such heroic patience in awaiting the delivery of this manuscript.

Introduction

This book is designed as an introduction to the sociological study and cultural analysis of sport in modern Britain. There has been a dramatic growth in sport science, sport studies and physical education at degree level during the last fifteen to twenty years, and the authors – as scholars, researchers, teachers and examiners – have been extensively involved in the development of sociological courses reflecting and exemplifying this growth.

In the late 1970s only a very few colleges or universities offered degree programmes in sport-related subjects. In the handbook of university courses for the academic session 1997–98, over three dozen higher education institutions offered such programmes. In several universities in 1997 first-year intakes of well over two hundred were studying on these courses. Also, in 1996 the higher education funding bodies of Britain (in their research assessment exercise) recognised sport-related subjects as a discrete and distinct area of research activity, and in the later 1990s sports science and leisure studies were due to be evaluated in those bodies' teaching quality exercise assessments.

This growth in the academic study of sport, and the volume of research into specialist aspects of sport, culture and society, has produced a burgeoning literature. There are good books – both readers (collections of seminal or original articles) and textbooks – on sport in the USA and in other societies and countries, and on sport in cross-cultural and political contexts. Research monographs, including detailed and illuminating social historical studies, have also enhanced our understanding of sport in modern society. But, surprisingly, few books have attempted to produce an integrated socio-cultural analysis of sport in modern Britain. This book offers such an analysis, in accessible yet simultaneously rigorous and scholarly form, and is aimed explicitly at the needs of undergraduates. Many such undergraduates will have studied some social aspects of sport in pre-degree study, on A level courses in physical education and sport studies. In this book we invite such students to develop their understanding in greater depth, and to encounter and engage with original sources, and polemic and debate within the field. Although the book takes a predominantly sociological perspective, it draws too upon a number of complementary approaches and frameworks. The authors' own backgrounds embrace critical social science and interdisciplinary humanities, the latter incorporating literary studies, social history, media studies and cultural studies.

Although sport has been a subject for degree level study in its own right for at least twenty years, some still express surprise that the subject is considered appropriate for academic analysis. It is seen by some as too trivial, marginal or epiphenomenal to warrant serious attention. Others view sport as a hermetically sealed world of its own, apart from the rest of society. Indeed, for participants and spectators this perceived apart-ness may well be precisely part of its appeal.

Yet by any standards sport is a set of cultural practices with significant historical and sociological resonances. To give some examples, historically, sport in nineteenth-century public schools was seen as a vital form of moral character training that produced the leadership and team work skills required by the dominant class, both domestically and in governing the Empire. Whilst the structure of amateur sport served the interests of elite groups, nevertheless football, in its professional form, had by the 1920s become a major leisure interest of the male working class, and an important expression of community identity. During the 1930s the government was disturbed enough about the poor physical condition of its citizens to mount a National Fitness Campaign. In post-war Britain, National Sport Centres were established as part of a pursuit of elite-level success, and in the 1990s the first plans were made to establish a National Sports Academy.

Sociologically, sport and fitness loom large in the media. Sport programmes, dedicated sport channels, sports pages and sport supplements in newspapers, and specialist sport magazines have become increasingly prominent. Although only a small minority of the population are active participants, a great many more have some degree of interest in following sport. The images derived from sport play a significant role in constituting our notions of the body and how it should, ideally, look. In both representational forms and in lived practices, sport is one of the cultural spheres that most distinctively marks gender identities and differences. The activities of top sport stars are highly publicised, and debate rages about the extent to which they are role models who have a responsibility to set a good example. Many politicians are fond of sporting metaphors, and former Prime Minister John Major spearheaded a drive to regenerate sport in schools, couched in terms that echo the Victorian confidence in its capacity to train character and instil moral values. Alongside this, sport has consistently provided a forum for the expression of national identity.

Sport studies courses have a strong scientific element – the study of physiology, psychology and bio-mechanics are quite rightly regarded as integral elements in the multi-disciplinary approach characteristic of such courses. But the historical formation of sporting practices and institutions, and their place in the wider social formation, are also of great importance to a full understanding of sport. All the scientific understanding of the sporting body and mind in the world is of little use to sports development unless the nature of the wider social and cultural environment is understood. This book is designed to offer such a complementary source for those seeking an all-round understanding of the place of sport in the modern world.

This book will not offer any simple essentialist definition of sport. An historical and sociological understanding of sport makes clear that 'sport' has no such fixed meaning – it has had different meanings in different societies, and refers to different activities at different historical moments. Most people would not now regard cruelty to animals as a sport, but until the early nineteenth century, cruelty to animals was a central aspect of sport. Hunting and shooting are now seen as rather marginal sporting activities, yet in the eighteenth century they would have been at the heart of the meaning of the term, indeed the very notion of the sporting man referred to the hunting man. The meaning of the term sport, therefore, involves a form of social construction, which can be analysed from a socio-cultural perspective.

The study of sport can still be greeted with scepticism and disbelief. In one of our own universities a para-medical colleague in a very new department in the university recently asked one of us who had been teaching in this area for two decades whether he was joking when telling her that he specialised in the sociology of sport. Mirth turned to puzzlement as it sunk in that the response was serious: 'Sport, sport and sociology . . . ? Do sports players now need social workers?' Well, this level of misapprehension was too extreme to unravel. A hasty retreat was made to check on the admissions figures in the university's most booming area of recruitment.

At A level too, sport studies has been the growth subject of the last two decades, along with media studies. Sociologists and social historians have been demonstrating for some time now that sport's role in society has been an important one, and is becoming still more important within social and cultural formations; that in some important respects the phenomenon of sport can be seen to lead or shape society. Some more prominent cultural commentators have been awakening to this possibility. Martin Jacques, editor of the *Guardian*, former editor of *Marxism Today* and collaborator with Stuart Hall (former Professor of Sociology at the Open University), has recognised that sport is now more than a mere pastime or hobby, that it might be seen as a symbol of a changing society, or even as a pervasive metaphor and rationale for mainstream sections of society such as business and the media, and critical in terms of contemporary conceptions of the body: 'It would be an exaggeration to say that society is being refashioned in the image of sport, but there is a kernel of truth in the proposition' ('Worshipping the body at altar of sport', *The Observer*, 13 July 1997, pp. 18–19). Any such proposition must be subjected to informed evaluation. This introductory book brings together relevant evidence, scholarship and theoretical debate in order to allow such evaluations to take place, and to indicate to the beginning student or the curious sports enthusiast where one might look to find out still more about the social bases and cultural characteristics of the sport phenomenon.

The book is simple to use. The chapters are designed to be read, either in whole or in part, and reviewed in group discussion. They are designed, too, as foundations and introductions, which should stimulate interested and committed students to explore further sources. Some further reading is indicated after each chapter, and all references cited in each chapter are listed at the end of that chapter. We see this as a clearer indication to the reader of the main sources on which the chapters are based, theme by theme; it is also a reminder of some sources that, cited across several chapters, have had a strong, long-lasting and recurrent impact on the development of the sociology of sport. The index, selectively thematic, indicates where key definitions and recurrent and complemetary themes can be located. For broader conceptual and theoretical context, students are also recommended to use, alongside the book, a reputable sociological dictionary such as *The Concise Oxford Dictionary of Sociology* (edited by Gordon Marshall, Oxford University Press, 1994), or *Collins Dictionary of Sociology* (edited by David and Julia Jary, Harper Collins, 1991). Sample essay titles and indicative interpretive exercises are also provided at the end of each chapter. These are included not to recommend the sole emphases that set work might take in the field, but to convey our own view of the expected level of work that can be set at university level, and the interesting tasks that can be accomplished in developing the sociological imagination.

The book has been produced collaboratively, but each chapter is based upon a single authored contribution. Authorial responsibility is as follows: Chapters 1, 2, 3, and 4, Tomlinson; Chapters 5, 7 and 8, Horne; Chapters 6 and 9, Whannel. We are grateful to our publisher, E & FN Spon, for its patience in awaiting delivery of the manuscript, to Philip Read in particular for his commitment to the project, and to three anonymous readers/reviewers for their perceptive comments, which have stimulated a reworking and reshaping of some of the chapters. We would be pleased to receive comments and responses, individually and collectively, on the book, on matters of both accuracy and interpretation.

John Horne, University of Edinburgh
Alan Tomlinson, University of Brighton
Garry Whannel, Roehampton Institute London

July 1998

Chapter one

Industrial society, social change and sports culture

Introduction

Modern sports have exhibited some core characteristics that make them specifically modern, and these can best be understood in contrast to earlier forms of sports. These earlier forms have been described and classified as *popular recreations* (Malcolmson, 1973), *mediaeval sports* (Guttmann, 1978), or *folk sports* (Dunning and Sheard, 1979). To clarify the differences between the older and modern forms of sports it is necessary also to understand the changing nature of the society of which those sports forms are a part. Therefore, in the first two chapters we review important elements of social change and their cultural implications; outline on a general level the primary features and characteristics of those sports forms, comparing the modern forms with older types of games; demonstrate the importance to the emergence of modern sports of athleticism in the British public schools, and its impact in spheres beyond the school, alongside the impact of reformers (Chapter 1); provide case studies of major team sports and individual sports to illustrate the tensions at the heart of the amateur–professional dynamic in those sports, and the working through of these tensions into the late modern period; and review the principal features of and trends in the development of modern sports in contemporary Britain (Chapter 2).

These two chapters are followed by a chapter that covers in more detail the debates about how best to account for and theorise this story of the growth and development of contemporary sports cultures.

Social change and the cultural implications of change

Malcolmson has argued that traditional recreation was rooted in a society that was, in its core features, vastly different to the society produced by the processes of urbanisation and industrialisation. Popular recreations of a traditional kind were features of a society that was predominantly agrarian, strongly parochial, and had a deep sense of corporate identity. The changing society – the inchoate modern industrial society – was very different indeed. It was urban-centred, and generated uniquely congested cities; it was governed by contractual relations, in spheres of life such as work and the family, and increasingly in leisure; it was biased towards individualism, prioritising the unit of the self or the individual rather than the collective or the corporate; it was rooted in factory-labour discipline, rather than the social relations of the community or the inherited relations of the community; and it was based on free enterprise, with all the concomitant volatility that the release of the entrepreneurial spirit implies. Societies so different would obviously generate cultural, leisure and sports forms with very different characteristics. Culture does not change immediately in the wake of social change, though, and Malcolmson recognised an interregnum between popular recreation and the growth of the sports of the industrial society, and suggested that, for many people, this interregnum 'was filled by the public house' (Malcolmson, 1973: 170–171). Indeed, as the 'new world of urban industrial culture' (Holt, 1989: 148) was established in nineteenth-century cities, the role of the pub was far from diminished, and social drinking around sport was an important dimension of male leisure: 'the new generation of publicans seemed to have taken over the role of sporting enthusiasts with as much gusto as the ale-house and tavern-keepers of the past. This was a powerful source of continuity in popular culture' (Holt, 1989: 148). Holt's work shows how 'half-hidden continuities between generations' might be as significant as more dramatic transformations in understanding the growth of modern sport, and stresses the 'gradual shift in cultural attitudes towards popular recreation' as much as 'sudden changes or discontinuities brought about by the onset of industrialization' (1989: 3 and 4). In studying the emergence of a specifically modern sports culture in Britain, and the main effects wrought by the hugely influential process of industrialisation, it is important to bear in mind these insights from Holt's authoritative and sensitive historical analysis.

James Walvin, in the context of his study of the demise of the folk form of football, identified four factors as the main influences upon the decline of the game (1975: 26–27). These were a growth in the policing powers of the state; a tightening of labour discipline, based upon the longer controllable working hours that were possible in the new forms of industrial production in the factory; the take-over of urban space inherent in the process of urbanisation; and the rise of 'a new middle-class mentality', which was to effectively marginalise popular traditional sports and codify some into new forms for the privileged classes, and to encourage the development of forms of rational recreation (those forms of activity deemed to be worthy rather than worthless, and often of potential benefit for self-improvement) for the popular and working classes. It is clear that the new and emerging society did not spawn new sports in any inexorably natural way. These social changes involved sets of interests and forms of cultural brokership in which some activities were deemed as of more value than others. John Hargreaves (1982: 37–39) has provided an outline of the development of modern sports which suggests that the key social changes represent 'organised interests'. He points to five aspects of social change that create the climate in which modern sports emerge. First, the way of life of the majority of people is subjected to attack; second, for many people, time and space is eliminated; third, patrician patronage is the basis of the reconstruction of some sports; fourth, forces of social class affect the way new sports forms are developed, with 'games' being produced for the leaders and 'drill' the physical diet recommended for the subordinate class. Finally, there is an expansion of commercial provision in the new society. For Hargreaves, the social changes in which the modern sports culture emerges are revealing of 'a bringing to bear of pressure on subordinate groups; pressure ranging from outright coercion and the use of material incentives to moral exhortation' (1982: 38). Some of these pressures will be clear to see in the case studies that follow in the next chapter; the full implications of such a theorisation will be considered in Chapter 3.

Whatever the theoretical starting-point, though, there is an interpretive consensus concerning the major aspects of social change that demarcate the limits and possibilities for cultural expression in the sphere of sports. The pre-industrial social order was more based in traditional relationships than in essentially contractual ones. Time becomes more quantified in the new industrial order. Space becomes more rationalised, and functionally defined in ways which are, in their precision, excluding as much as enabling. Social groups are, in industrialising society, defined anew in terms of their position with regard to the newly dominant industrial economy and its division of labour – defined, that is, as social classes. And leisure and sports are seen as important forms of cultural expression, but the basis and expression of their importance are far from shared by the different social classes.

Quoting an Address to the Manchester public during a strike in 1818, a cotton operative known as 'A Journeyman Cotton Spinner' referred to employers and workers as 'two distinct classes', and his address served for E.P. Thompson as remarkable testimony to the grievances of the working people in this formative period of changes in the nature of capitalist exploitation. Such grievances were:

> the rise of a master class without traditional authority or obligations; the growing distance between master and man; the transparency of the

exploitation at the source of their new wealth and power; the loss of status and above all of independence for the worker, his reduction to total dependence on the master's instruments of production; the partiality of the law; the disruption of the traditional family economy; the discipline, monotony, hours and conditions of work; loss of leisure and amenities; the reduction of the man to the status of an 'instrument'.

(Thompson, 1968: 221–222)

Leisure and sports cannot be adequately understood if not contextualised in terms of the sorts of processes, relationships and dynamics identified here by Thompson.

Seminal social historical studies have drawn out some of the cultural implications of these social changes. In his majestic and imaginative study of the centrality of new modes of time keeping, E.P. Thompson (1967) lists the ways in which the new industrial order fundamentally restructures the basis of everyday life. His analysis is premised upon the recognition that 'the transition to mature industrial society entailed a severe restructuring of working habits – new disciplines, new incentives, and a new human nature upon which these incentives could bite effectively', and he then asks 'how far is this related to changes in the inward notation of time?' (p. 57). Thompson reviewed anthropological and cultural sources that indicate how time has been related to 'familiar processes in the cycle of work or of domestic chores' (p. 58). For the Nuer, the cattle clock served the function of a daily timepiece; time was determined by 'the round of pastoral tasks'. Bourdieu's early anthropological work showed how Algerian peasants were nonchalantly indifferent to the passage of time, seeing the clock as 'the devil's mill'. In the Aran Islands, people's sense of time depended upon the direction of the wind. This kind of task-orientation, seen by Thompson as 'more humanly comprehensible than timed labour' and more conducive to the intermingling of 'social intercourse and labour', is less tolerated by those who are ruled by the clock: 'to men accustomed to labour timed by the clock, this attitude to labour appears to be wasteful and lacking in urgency' (p. 60). As the industrial society attaches measurable value to labour and its output, the task becomes less important, and time's value in cash terms becomes dominant: 'Time is now currency: it is not passed but spent' (p. 61). Thompson lists seven ways in which the 'new labour habits were formed, and a new time-discipline was imposed . . . by the division of labour; the supervision of labour; fines; bells and clocks; money incentives; preachings and schoolings; the suppression of fairs and sports' (p. 90). Modern sport, as it was shaped in the context of such cataclysmic changes in conceptions of time and work, must be understood as, if not a directly determined product of, then certainly a cultural corollary of, these major processes and influences. This can be seen in the recognition, within social historical work (Brailsford, 1991), of the importance of shifting conceptions of time in the development of modern sports.

In the early 1880s one contemporaneous critic of the industrial revolution recognised its essence as 'the substitution of competition for the mediaeval regulations which had previously controlled the production and distribution of wealth' (Toynbee, 1967: 1). Its 'facts', as Toynbee called them, were straightforward enough: the rapid growth of population; cataclysmic agricultural changes as the common-field system was destroyed, enclosure of commons and waste-lands was effected, and large farms became the main form of ownership; technological inventions affecting the nature of manufacture; advances in the means of communication with important consequences for the expansion of trade; a revolution in the distribution of wealth, constituting 'a great social revolution, a change in the balance of political power and in the relative position of classes' (p. 5); and the substitution of a 'cash nexus' for the more traditional human tie. All of these six facets had implications for the context and meaning of recreational activity and sports practices.

If industrialisation has been the primary process in the development of modern British society, how then can its consequent societal form – industrialism – be characterised? It has become a sociological orthodoxy that industrial capitalism is 'the conjunction of capitalistic enterprise with machine production' (Giddens, 1982: 16), and sociological analysts have in some detail classified the facts of the societal type produced by the industrial revolution. The capitalist regime, as Aron (1967: 81) dubbed it, is characterised by five features: private ownership of the means of production; piecemeal, pragmatic, market-led and decentralised regulation of the economy; a separation of employer and employees which generates a wage-earning class; the predominance of the profit motive; and volatility in prices and the economy. Similar classifications have been generated (see Turner, 1975: 108), emphasising too the importance of bureaucracies and the alienating nature of work for many. The identification of these features of the new industrial society has an impressive intellectual pedigree, deriving as it does from the classical sociological thinkers of the late nineteenth and early twentieth centuries, Marx, Weber and Durkheim. As Krishan Kumar observes, the 'sociological image of industrialism, in its details' (1978: 63) derives from the work of these founding fathers. Kumar sets out six 'elements of the contemporary sociological model of industrialism' (p. 64): urbanism as a way of life; the demographic transition; the decline of community; a specialised division of labour; centralisation, equalisation and democratisation; and secularisation, rationalisation and bureaucratisation. These constitute not just social influences; they become primary social relations and, as Giddens notes, industrial capitalism's world-wide expansion 'brought about social changes more shattering in their consequences than any other period in the whole previous history of mankind' (1982: 17). It is important to extract the understanding of such a scale of change in the vision – often of loss and anxiety, anger and despair – underlying the analytical and theoretical treatises of the classical sociologists. Kumar reminds us of this, with a warning to textbook scribes thrown in for good measure:

> In the dead prose of a multitude of textbooks on 'industrial sociology' lay buried and congealed the passionate accounts of Marx and Engels on the conditions of the proletariat; Weber's icy and characteristically ambivalent dissection of bureaucracy and bureaucratization; Durkheim's concerned vision of industrial man in the state of *anomie*, impossibly striving after infinitely receding goals.
>
> (1978: 63)

These theorists were seeking to make sense of a new social order, an emerging cultural universe. Peter Burke's brilliant study of pre-modern popular culture (1978) places the end of early modern Europe at the eve of the industrialisation process in Britain, acknowledging 'the enormous cultural changes set in motion by industrialization' (1978: prologue). Kumar argues persuasively that 'in historical perspective industrialism and modernity seemed to be the same thing . . . To become modern was to go through the process of industrialization . . . to arrive at something like the state of society envisaged in the sociologists' image of industrialism' (1978: 111). These social forces, and the cultural forms and practices disrupted or stimulated by them, constitute the context in which the development of modern sports must be understood. Whatever more recent debates about the category of industrialism (and its relationship to the allegedly postmodern, or to the 'new times' heralded by the break up of the 'fabric of Fordism' (Murray, 1989: 41)) there can be no doubt that at key points of its formation cultural elements within it would bear traces of the societal form itself.

We will see in the classifications and case studies covered in the following chapter, and in illustrative material presented in Chapter 3, how important these social changes and their cultural ramifications are for an understanding of the forces shaping modern sport. Peter Bailey's study (1978) of the early industrial period argues that the growth of new forms of leisure and sports in the kind of cultural climate evoked by Thompson should be seen as a form of cultural struggle: the development of rational recreation – the use of sport and leisure activities in 'the creation of a healthy, moral and orderly workforce' (Holt, 1989: 136) should be seen as an element in the contest for control of industrial society's new culture (Bailey, 1978). Bailey's emphasis is an important one, for it warns against any simple reduction of the character of sport to a mere mirror image of the society. At the same time, though, there is no doubt that the features of the newly emergent and dominant sports forms were in many cases close to the core features of the new social order. There was a consonance between the core values of the societal form of industrialism and the sports forms that emerged within that societal form. It is hardly surprising, then, that any classification of the core features of those sports will comprise elements that are also characteristic of the society itself.

The characteristics of pre-industrial and modern sports

Several typologies have been developed offering valuable classifications of the features of modern sports. Allen Guttmann presents a typology of this sort for each of four societal types: primitive society, classic civilisations (Greece and Rome, treated separately in Guttmann's analysis), mediaeval society, and modern society. This is worth presenting in full (Table 1.1).

Reservations might be expressed about the accuracy of some aspects of this classification. There is evidence, for instance, of the prominence of records and of the quantification of performance in the ancient Olympics in Greece (Young, 1984). Also, it has been pointed out (Tomlinson, 1992) that the classification could be seen as championing a relatively linear and evolutionary process, with the sports of a primitive society appearing to be almost completely the opposite of the sports of a modern society. But Guttmann himself has shown full awareness of these implications (1986) and believes that it is a harsh criticism to hold them against him (1992). The main achievement of the Guttmann classification is that it highlights, in an illuminating comparative framework, the specificity of the nature of sport in different and distinctive social contexts. The framework demonstrates how sports cultures and forms vary across time and space, that sport is socially constructed and not some sort of trans-historical and supra-social phenomenon. Guttmann defines sports as 'playful physical

TABLE 1.1 Guttman's characteristics of sports in various ages

	Primitive	Greek	Roman	Mediaeval	Modern
Secularism	Y&N	Y&N	Y&N	Y&N	Yes
Equality	No	Y&N	Y&N	No	Yes
Specialisation	No	Yes	Y&N	No	Yes
Rationalisation	No	Yes	Yes	No	Yes
Bureaucracy	No	Y&N	Yes	No	Yes
Quantification	No	No	Y&N	No	Yes
Records	No	No	No	No	Yes

Source: Guttmann, 1978: 54

contests' which, in the modern age, have come to express an increasingly scientific view of the world. Gruneau has criticised Guttmann's work for what he calls its 'theoretical affirmation of voluntarism and the merits of liberal democracy' (1983: 43), and for its implication that sports, being inherently playful, are also therefore 'voluntary and free' (p. 44). But despite such critical reservations, Guttman's broad perspective is upheld in seminal work on the origins of British sport. All of the characteristics of the Guttmann model bar one – secularism – are stated or implied in Eric Dunning and Kenneth Sheard's path breaking typology of what they call 'the structural properties of folk-games and modern sports'. This classification was developed in the context of Dunning and Sheard's brilliant study of the development of rugby football (1979), but it focuses invaluably upon the general characteristics of sports in the transformative period of industrialisation (Figure 1.1).

'Structural properties', as Dunning and Sheard call the core values of modern sports, do not spring from nowhere: they are cultural constructions, socially shaped. Important economic and social developments in industrialising and urbanising Britain provided the setting in which modern sports emerged. Golby and Purdue (1984: 110) see the transformation of popular culture as strongly influenced by four factors in particular, from the 1840s onwards: the rise of public transport in the form of the railway system; a reduction in working people's working week, providing, by the middle of the century, the Saturday half-day for leisure; an increase in real earnings, particularly in the last decades of the century, providing unprecedented levels of disposable income; and an expansion of commercial provision in leisure, 'marked especially by the growth of the music hall, and of the popular press, professional sport and seaside holidays'. But such influences alone do not in any simple fashion shape the contours of the emerging sports cultures: they are the necessary conditions for certain changes and developments. But for the sociologist of sport, the important task is to identify those social influences and social relations that are the most important in the process whereby some 'structural properties' and values rather than others come to the fore. In the making of modern sport in Britain, it was athleticism – the cultivation of the values of amateur sport – and rational recreation – conceived as a transformative project for the improvement of the masses – that were the most telling (in the case of rational recreation, albeit in unanticipated ways) of such influences. In the rest of this chapter, the nature and impact of these influences are reviewed. In the following chapter, in the context of selected case studies, their relationship to (and in many respects struggles with) other influences such as professionalism and commercialism is illustrated.

Folk games	Modern sports
1 Diffuse, informal organisation implicit in the local social structure.	Highly specific, formal organisation, institutionally differentiated at the local regional, national and international levels.
2 Simple and unwritten customary rules, legitimated by tradition.	Formal and elaborate written rules, worked out pragmatically and legitimated by rational-bureaucratic means.
3 Fluctuating game pattern; tendency to change through long-term and, from the viewpoint of the participants, imperceptible 'drift'.	Change institutionalised through rational-bureaucratic channels.
4 Regional variation of rules, size and shape of balls, etc.	National and international standardisation of rules, size and shape of balls, etc.
5 No fixed limits on territory, duration or numbers of participants.	Played on a spatially limited pitch with clearly defined boundaries, within fixed time limits and with a fixed number of participants, equalised between the contending sides.
6 Strong influence of natural and social differences on the game pattern.	Minimisation, principally by means of formal rules, of the influence of natural and social differences on the game pattern: norms of equality and 'fairness'.
7 Low role differentiation (division of labour) among the players.	High role differentiation (division of labour) among the players.
8 Loose distinction between playing and 'spectating' roles.	Strict distinction between playing and 'spectating' roles.
9 Low structural differentiation; several 'game elements' rolled into one.	High structural differentiation; specialisation around kicking, carrying and throwing, the use of sticks, etc.
10 Informal social control by the players themselves within the context of the ongoing game.	Formal social control by officials who stand, as it were, 'outside' the game and who are appointed and certificated by central legislative bodies and empowered, when a breach of the rule occurs, to stop play and impose penalties graded according to the seriousness of the offence.
11 High level of socially tolerated physical violence; emotional spontaneity; low restraint.	Low level of socially tolerated physical violence; high emotional control; high restraint.
12 Generation in a relatively open and spontaneous form of pleasurable 'battle excitement'.	Generation in a more controlled and 'sublimated' form of pleasurable 'battle excitement'.
13 Emphasis on physical force as opposed to skill.	Emphasis on skill, as opposed to physical force.
14 Strong communal pressure to participate; individual identity subordinate to group identity; test of identity in general.	Individually chosen as a recreation; individual identity of greater importance relative to group identity; test of identity in relation to a specific skill or set of skills.
15 Locally meaningful contests only; relative equality of playing skills among sides; no chances for national reputations or money payment.	National and international superimposed on local contests; emergence of elite players and teams; chance to establish national and international reputations; tendency to 'monetisation' of sports.

FIGURE 1.1 The structural properties of folk games and modern sports

Source: Dunning and Sheard, 1979

Athleticism and its contribution to the growth of modern sports

Many of the core characteristics of modern sports were shaped in the British public schools of the nineteenth century. This is widely acknowledged and useful accounts and discussions abound (Holt, 1989: 74–86; Hargreaves, 1986: 38–45). But the definitive source for an understanding of the nature and impact of the public schools' approach to games, sport and physical activity is the work of J.A. Mangan. In his seminal study of athleticism in the public schools of the nineteenth and early twentieth century Mangan (1981) produced a substantial empirical study of the genesis and impact of what he labelled the 'ideology of athleticism'. Six case-study schools were chosen for the study. Harrow was chosen as representative of the great public schools. Stonyhurst (1873) was the denominational type (though these spread across Catholic, Quaker and Protestant). Proprietary types, with shareholders, were represented by Marlborough (1843). Uppingham (1853) was the selected elevated grammar. The Woodward Anglican middle-class type of school was represented by Lancing (1948). And individually financed and owned private venture schools were represented by Edinburgh's Loretto (1862). In selecting these six types of school Mangan was confident that his case study material would be extensive enough to permit generalisations about the significance of athleticism in the public schools generally. He could then assert with confidence that four educational goals were stressed by physical educators in the public schools. Physical education, it was believed, would cultivate desirable moral values: physical and moral courage; loyalty and cooperation; the capacity to act fairly and take defeat well; and the ability to command and obey (Mangan, 1981: 9). With such an agenda, the public school educators attributed to sports a capacity for character building. As Mangan shows so vividly, riotous and brutal forms of activity by the undisciplined public school youth – such as 'a brutal frog hunt in the school grounds' in the early 1840s at Marlborough, in which the frogs were beaten to death and the bodies piled high (1981: 18) – were replaced by formalised disciplined activity. From around 1870, Bamford notes, 'there was a subtle but organized drive by authority to sublimate the boy's self to a team' (1967: 83); a drive so successful that the rhetoric of athleticism took such a hold that it could resonate across the British Empire (Mangan, 1986; Mangan, 1992; Holt, 1989: 204–211); and early in the twentieth century could be heard from the 'donkeys' (Clark, 1991) in the battlefields of the First World War (Mangan, 1981: 191–196). The discipline of the Victorian upbringing could become a template for conduct, notions of chivalry and decency and the rules of the game dictating an unthinking conformity in battle (Clark, 1991: 174); and when the eighteenth London Regiment lost 1,200 men in a single hour at Loos, they had 'dribbled a football in front of them as they crossed No-Man's Land' (Clark, 1991: 150).

These may be extreme and tragic instances of the wider manifestation of athleticist values, but the particular achievement of the public schools in sport was the development of a vehicle for the transmission of moral values to newly educated generations of upper-class and upper middle-class males. In his 1904 book *Let's Play the Game/The Anglo-Saxon Sporting Spirit* Eustace Miles wrote that cricket could illustrate:

> such valuable ideas as co-operation, division of labour, specialisation, obedience to a single organiser (perhaps with a council to advise him), national character, geography and its influences, arts and artistic anatomy, physiology and hygiene, ethics and even – if the play can be learnt rightly – general educational methods.
>
> (cited in Dobbs, 1973: 28)

There is a clear manifesto here for the production of the disciplined individual with a set of socially acceptable moral values. It would be difficult to overestimate the importance of what Peter McIntosh has noted as the equation of physical education with moral education. McIntosh notes too that the recognition that physical education can contribute to moral education emerged in the late eighteenth century, out of the ideas of French philosopher and educationalist Rousseau concerning the body–mind relationship, and out of pioneering developments in gymnastics on the European mainland. But the public schools were to institutionalise such ideas into powerful sets of principles and a coherent working ideology. As McIntosh puts it:

> It was in the Public Schools during the second half of the (nineteenth) century that two basic new theories were developed. The first was that competitive sport, especially team games, had an ethical basis, and the second was that training in moral behaviour on the playing field was transferable to the world beyond.
>
> (1979: 27)

Lest one might think that such theories have been long discredited, consider how much they have in common with the declarations of then Conservative prime minister John Major in his introduction to the policy document *Raising the Game* (DNH, 1995). Framed as 'ideas to rebuild the strength of every level of British sport', and claimed as 'the most important set of proposals ever published for the encouragement and promotion of sport' (p. 1), the policy document was rooted in the founding principles of the morality of athleticism. *Raising the Game* argued that sport should be cherished for its capacity to bond and bind people together across ages and national borders and, 'by a miraculous paradox', also to represent 'nationhood' and 'local pride'. In doing this, sport is claimed to (DNH, 1995: 2):

- through competition, teach lessons which last for life;
- be a means of learning how to be both a winner and a loser;
- thrive only if 'both parties play by the rules', and accept the outcome 'with good grace';
- teach how to live with others as part of a team;
- improve health;
- create friendships.

The vehicles for the inculcation of these values were 'our great traditional sports – cricket, hockey, swimming, athletics, football, netball, rugby, tennis and the like' (DNH, 1995: 3) – an explicit acknowledgement of the moral values long attributed to the playing field and above all to team games.

Compare the Major eulogy for sports with celebrations of the values of games from a century earlier. Mangan reported the beliefs of an early apologist for public school games who believed that these games could help produce 'a manly straightforward character, a scorn of lying and meanness, habits of obedience and command, and fearless courage. Thus equipped, he goes out into the world, and bears a man's part in subduing the earth, ruling its wild folk, and building up the Empire' (cited in Mangan, 1981: 9); well prepared by his grounding in the 'institutional wars on the playing field . . . The alliance between character-building and games promoted self-restraint and cooperation without wholly destroying a competitive sense of struggle' (Wilkinson, 1964: 30). In 1909 the captain of the Cambridge University cricket team of twenty-five years before could still write, in the *Empire Annual for Boys*, that to play the game was to exhibit a 'supreme standard of excellence'. From such a perspective, three main sporting values were worthy of cultivation: 'to aim high, to never lose heart, and to help your neighbour' (Kanitkar, 1994: 187). Cricket, rugby and football were the sports that featured most in this kind of rhetoric. Arthur Mee, too, famous in mid-century as the author of his *Children's Encyclopaedia*, stressed the importance of the playing field for the laying down of the 'laws of honour'. Belief in the importance of games and sport was deeply rooted in the schools, and practice matched rhetoric throughout the twentieth century. In the mid-1960s, most (boarding) public schools still allocated three or more half-days per week to organised games (Kalton, 1966: 110); in 1963 sporting activities could still serve as a primary form of 'ritualistic symbolisation of the social values on which . . . the public school system rests' (Wakeford, 1969: 124); in the academic year 1993/4, 83 per cent of 11-year-old pupils in independent secondary schools had more than two hours of physical education per week, compared to 48 per cent in state schools, and weekend, lunch time and after-school sport was reported to have further decreased in the state sector (Secondary Heads Association, 1994: 8). The legacy of athleticism was still being widely preached in the pedagogy of the privileged close to a century and a half on from its inception.

Belief in the appropriateness of sport and physical activity as a means of developing moral values was not exclusive to male educational establishments. At the end of the nineteenth century the institutional foundations were laid for several influential colleges of physical education for women. Although the existence of these colleges did not guarantee radical feminist outcomes – Hargreaves observes that the profession idealised the role of the woman within the family, and 'the colleges reproduced the structure and ideologies of the "perfect" Victorian home, thus reinforcing conventional sexual divisions in society' (1994: 78) – they nevertheless established a parallel character-building agenda to that of the public schools and their university counterparts. The pioneering Swedish educational gymnast Madame Osterberg opened a college in 1895 in Hampstead, North London, and this moved to Dartford in Kent ten years later. Dartford College 'offered the first full-time specialist course in the theory and practice of physical education in England' (Hargreaves, 1994: 74) and was the exemplar for other innovative initiatives of the late Victorian and early Edwardian period. Anstey College (1907), Chelsea College (1898), Bedford College (1903) and Liverpool College (1904) followed the pioneering model of Osterberg's Dartford.

Dorette Wilkie was the 'Founder' of the Chelsea College, which became the Chelsea School in the University of Brighton in 1992. She initially founded a Gymnastic Teachers' Training Department in connection with a Day College for Women and associated with the Chelsea Polytechnic in London – this was launched in 1898, with six pioneer students and Dorette Wilkie as 'Headmistress'. Wilkie, an 18-year-old Prussian immigrant to England in 1885, had suffered from a spine condition and came to England to seek a cure, entering the Training School of Adolf A. Stempel's gymnasium. Benefiting directly and dramatically from the curative effects of gymnastics she made physical education her career, anglicising herself still further on naturalisation by dropping the title 'Fraulein' and adding an 'i' to the Prussian name Wilke. Establishing a Saturday afternoon games session for the deprived children of Battersea Park, south London, she saw sport and physical activity as a form of escape, declaring that 'the time for fairyland is half-past two till four pm, and the only condition of entrance is a desire to play and be happy' (Webb, 1979: 45). In a fin-de-siècle lecture Miss Wilkie preached the philosophy of sports values and physical education, specifying three core aims in physical education training (Webb, 1979: 57). First, the development of 'a body as hard as steel' would help 'to bear up against our many difficulties'. Second, the physical educator should help students cultivate 'a mind as clear as crystal, to see and understand all that is good and noble and beautiful in the world, and also to distinguish the true from the false'. Third, Miss Wilkie recommended an emphasis on empathy, in nurturing 'a heart as warm as sunshine, so that we may feel and sympathise with the ways and troubles of our fellow creatures'. In 1903 Miss Wilkie confirmed her feminine if not feminist mission: 'it is no use setting a man to drill girls. He does not understand them as does a woman. His place is to drill an army; we do not want our women for the Army' (Webb, 1979: 59). In terms of gender, such institutions were to pursue separatist missions until the last quarter of the twentieth century, with important implications for the nature of generations of girls' (and so of course boys') experience of sport and physical education in school.

The realities of the character-building claims in the public schools were rather different to the rhetoric. T.C. Worsley's reminiscence of his time at Marlborough in the early 1920s shows how the status attributed to those with prowess in sports and games could lead to tyrannical regimes within the school. Worsley 'got into' the school cricket team early and, given Marlborough's particular celebration of athletics, he found himself promoted above his peers to the school's Prefecture. His main job was to police the Upper School, a 'cold, barbarous barn . . . a brutal, junior hell':

> And it was barbarous. For the only supervision came from one athletics master and his six Junior Prefects chosen for their athletic ability. The only law was a jungle law of force; and the special sufferers were the individualists and the non-conformers.
>
> Such a one, for instance, was John Betjeman who was in the same form as I was for several years, and was already distinguished for his aesthetic tastes and somewhat bizarre manner and appearance. He, like many others, paid the supreme penalty of the 'basket'.
>
> (Worsley, 1985: 45)

The 'basket' involved having one's head and face immersed in a large receptacle of waste paper and refuse, and a mix of ink and treacle applied to the body, particularly the face and the neck. To reconstruct this scene – the most privileged and athletically excellent males of a generation subjecting the future Poet Laureate to this form of ritual abuse – is to reveal the contradictions at the heart of the athleticist rhetoric: the celebration of the crudely physical; the denigration of rival qualities and values; the triumph of sheer force. Mangan has documented how, at Marlborough, these 'Victorian values of virile muscularity' came under attack from the 'high aesthetic band' (1981: 216). Yet later in his life Worsley could sound like one of the ideal products of the athleticist code. After a teaching spell at Wellington College he taught for a single term at Kurt Hahn's Gordonstoun, having been attracted by Hahn's visionary lectures delivered in

London in the mid-1930s. In the austere reality of the Firth of Moray, Worsley's idealism and respect for Hahn soon faded:

> He revealed himself as having a fierce temper, a strong hand with a cane and a temperament which hated being crossed. Especially damaging to my very English view, was his dislike of being defeated at any game. Hahn was an avid tennis player. But was it an easily forgivable weakness that his opponents had to be chosen for being his inferiors or else, if their form was unknown, instructed not to let themselves win?
>
> (1985: 186)

In summary, public school sports and games were not conceived as some innocent pastime. They constituted a vehicle for powerful and prestigious social actors, for the transmission of preferred values and for the generation and perpetuation of a particular form of culture, stressing the moral responsibilities of an elite and the manly virtues (Maguire, 1986) that were seen as the basis of the execution of such responsibilities. And the conception of sports fostered in those schools closely matched the political agenda of sports-reared politicians, many of whom were the products of the schools themselves. A.J. Balfour, for instance – prominent Scottish landowner, Cambridge philosopher and golf zealot as well as Conservative prime minister – was a tireless proponent of the benefits of sports:

> My firm conviction is that there is no public interest of greater importance than the public interest of providing healthy means of recreation for all classes in the community . . . I earnestly hope that everybody interested in the game (of golf) will do their best to extend it not only to the class who chiefly enjoy it now, but to every class of the community who has the opportunity and advantage of having a Saturday half-holiday which he would like to spend in the open air in one of the healthiest and most delightful methods of enjoying the beauties of nature and the pleasure of exercise that the wit of man has yet contrived to invent.
>
> (1899 and 1909, in Balfour, 1912: 276 and 278)

Balfour preached his gospel widely. In an 1897 edition of *Fortnightly Review* (LXI, new series) he spoke before a university audience in Edinburgh to extol the virtues of the sporting life. The feeling of community in university life was, he reminded his audience, fostered by education, lectures and study,

> but no influence fostered it more surely and more effectively than that feeling of common life which the modern athletic sports, as they had been

developed in modern places of learning, gave to all those who took an interest in such matters, whether as performers or spectators.

(de S. Honey, 1977: 117)

Educators, industrialists, priests and soldiers – as well as politicians – emerged from these institutions with a belief in and a commitment to spread the gospel of athleticism. This was accomplished in their own universities as they became undergraduates, and in their professional lives in the institutions of the new industrial communities. The clerical sponsorship of weekend football, for instance, was 'promoted as a wholesale alternative to drink' at certain points during the nineteenth century, and many churches at the turn of the nineteenth and twentieth centuries 'were energetic pioneers of new popular pastimes' (Harris, 1993: 162). This contrasted with their equivalents in mid-Victorian Britain, 'when clerics were more often engaged in "rationalizing" or repressing the archaic pleasures of the poor' (ibid.).

As the nineteenth century progressed, the gospel of athleticism was made manifest in the institutional form of amateur sport. The process of ascendancy of this model of sports can also be linked to the desire to produce a modern healthy model of the physical. The cultural historian Bruce Haley has captured the importance of this health rationale, and its interconnectedness with established sets of interests, in the rise of organised games:

The institutionalization of games in the later nineteenth century made them more healthful – worklike. Sport moved toward an external 'vital centre', the center of culture, and derived its meanings from that. The center it sought to identify with was . . . merely the social code, and very often only the code of a particular class, or even of a particular school. Therefore, in playing the game, the moral faculty took over entirely from the cognitive. The healthy body was an instrument not for understanding the ineffable, but for ritualizing an obedience to the reasonable.

(1978: 259)

It was in the public schools that much of this thinking took hold, framing the beliefs and practices of the privileged and the powerful. In this sense, as Hargreaves (1986: 38) states, the 'importance of the public schools in the development of sporting forms and in articulating them on the power network in this period can hardly be exaggerated'; concluding that the athleticist ideology actually permeated the country's political culture and had 'long-lasting effects on the character of sport in Britain' (p. 45).

'Teaching the poor how to play' –
rational recreation and the
struggle over sport

As noted above, rational recreationists saw some forms of sport as a means of moral education, a source, as Holt (1989: 136) observes, for the cultivation of a 'play discipline' capable of 'teaching the poor how to play'. And although early and more zealous campaigners exhibited a messianic zeal in their quest to stamp out long-established popular cultural practices, whilst (as Harris noted) their successors at the end of the nineteenth century were keen promoters of new sports, the effects of rational recreationist initiatives should be understood on the basis of an understanding of the combined and sustained effects of such approaches over a long period. Golby and Purdue summarise this change in form, but consistency of intent, of rational recreation. Early in the nineteenth century, they observe, new industrial workers experienced a reduction in leisure time. But 'religious, humanitarian and educational bodies' became concerned, as the century progressed, that the labouring classes should be provided with 'as many accepting and improving activities as possible':

> these should cater for all age groups and be dispensed through a wide variety of agencies, from Sunday Schools to Mechanics' Institutes. It was only by this method, so reformers claimed, of providing 'improving' and 'rational' pastimes in place of debasing and degrading ones that the lower orders could be weaned away from drinking and gambling and other excesses and could develop as members of a culturally harmonious society. However, as the century progressed, it was increasingly recognised that by no means all working men wished to spend their leisure time in chapels, class rooms or reading rooms and that other more attractive alternatives needed to be provided which would combine both instruction and amusement. So what was meant by 'rational' changed during the century. By the 1850s and 1860s the educational content of many rational recreations had diminished and given way to activities which in the 1820s and 1830s would not have been acceptable.
>
> (Golby and Purdue, 1984: 92)

Forms of activity may have changed, then, but not the overarching objective of the reformers, whether targeting the middle class itself early in the century or the working classes much more widely as the century progressed. Throughout the century 'Rationality implied both order and control' (Cunningham, 1980: 90). The spirit, intent and impact of the rational recreationists can be seen clearly in a wide range of cases and initiatives. For illustrative purposes, five such cases are outlined here: developments in the culture of the London working class; football in the urban industrial cities of the Midlands and the North of England; physical drill for the working classes in schools; the provision of open space, in the form of parks, within cities; and the visionary ambitions of Dr W.P. Brookes, proponent of an 'Olympian Games' in Much Wenlock, Shropshire (England).

Stedman-Jones (1983) has shown how in the last three decades of the nineteenth century a conservative (in the sense of forgoing political activism) working-class culture was established. At the beginning of the century it could be said that, even though social distinctions might be clear, 'there was no great political, cultural or economic divide between the middle class and those beneath them' (p. 185):

> Culturally, there were certainly greater affinities between these groups than were to exist later. All classes shared in the passions for gambling, theatre, tea gardens, pugilism and animal sports. All except the richest merchants lived within a short distance of their work, if not at the place of work itself. The pub was a social and economic centre for all and heavy drinking was as common among employers as among the workmen.
>
> (Stedman-Jones, 1983: 185)

In the first half of the nineteenth century political and religious/evangelical concerns, and a move to the suburbs of the propertied classes, fuelled a separation between the classes. The working class became more and more widely perceived as a problem, and three waves of anxiety consolidated this: in the 1840s/50s around the political activism of the working classes and the European revolutions; between 1866 and 1872 around the Second Reform Bill and revolution in Paris; and in the later 1880s around high unemployment, urban overcrowding and ethnic immigration into London. At each point the 'respectable and the well-to-do' were concerned that the working class would pose a threat to the social order, and a succession of organisations were founded 'to hasten the work of christianizing and "civilizing" the city' (p. 191). This was the basis for the rational recreational initiative aimed at the London working class. This constituted a project to 'create a physical and institutional environment', via legislation, which would undermine working-class habits; and the inculcation of 'a new moral code' through private philanthropy. Stedman-Jones (1983: 194–195, 202–203) catalogues the successes of such a project. By the end of the century the following popular cultural practices had all but disappeared from the public life of London: gin palaces, cock fighting, bear baiting, ratting, rat-baiting, bird singing competitions, street gambling. In their place there emerged 'a growing number of parks, museums, exhibitions, public libraries and mechanics' institutes' which 'promoted a more improving or innocuous use of leisure time' (p. 195). Without doubt, the institutional and everyday environment of the

London working class was altered by these interventions, but the new working-class culture was itself distinctive:

> it was clearly distinguished from the culture of the middle class and had remained largely impervious to middle-class attempts to dictate its character or direction. Its dominant cultural institutions were not the school, the evening class, the library, the friendly society, the church or the chapel, but the pub, the sporting paper, the race-course and the music hall.
>
> (Stedman-Jones, 1983: 207)

Rational recreationists were important figures in the formation and early development of many football clubs which were to feature in the formation of the professional game. Public school and Oxbridge educated enthusiasts for the game, middle-class missionaries seeking to reform the populations of the new cities, may well at times have provided an important basis for the growth of the game. Aston Villa, Bolton Wanderers, Wolverhampton Wanderers and Everton (from the north-west of England and the West Midlands, the cradle of the professional game) were all associated originally with religious organisations (Cunningham, 1980: 127). Other clubs, in Preston and Sheffield for instance, were initiated by local employers or industrialists. Between 1870 and 1885 in Birmingham, around one in four football clubs and around one in five cricket clubs were connected to religious organisations (Holt, 1989: 138). But the initiative in some cases came from the ordinary people themselves, and the development of spectatorship was hardly the stuff of which the rational recreationists' dreams were made. In the last year of the century, one commentator could observe that 'football in the North is more than a game. It excites more emotion than art, politics and the drama, and it awakes local patriotism to the highest pitch' (Mason, 1996: 50). Aston Villa may have been founded by young male members of a Wesleyan Chapel in 1874, but its pitch was provided by a local butcher and a local publican provided the dressing room. Cunningham points out that any working men wanting to play football would not have been worried about the motives of their providers:

> the working class, for lack of any alternative, was prepared to accept for as long as necessary, the fact of middle-class sponsorship, but not its ideology . . . working people wanted simply to enjoy what was being offered, and as soon as financial constraints allowed they shook off what they perceived as heavy-handed patronage.
>
> (1980: 128 and 129)

Rational recreationists in the middle class might have promoted football as one of several means geared towards the bringing together of classes, the goal of class conciliation, but working men made the sport their own and the development of the professional game with its boisterous and visible public culture both on the field and off defied the worthy objectives of the moral improvers of the time.

In schools, the working classes were denied any potential benefits of organised games' moral worth until after 1908, when trainee teachers began to be trained in physical education, giving some substance to the 1902 Education Act, which had recommended a wider programme of physical education for elementary schoolchildren (Holt, 1989: 139) – not unconnected to the concern felt by the state at the poor levels of health and fitness of conscripts during the Boer War campaigns. The 1870 Education Act had permitted, though not required, the instruction of schoolchildren in drill: 'Military drill fleshed out with some general exercise was considered to be all that the ranks required' (Holt, 1989: 139). Reformers like Chadwick, Hargreaves (1986: 50) points out, promoted drill, not sports, for the working class, and consequently physical space in state schools was minimal. Consequently, some priests or schoolmasters – or 'dedicated improvers of the young' as Holt calls them – devoted their own time to organising extra-curricular initiatives, sometimes prompting developments on a more formal level, such as the formation of Schools' Football Associations. Here, the interventions of the rational recreationists can be seen to have at least loosened the stranglehold on working-class children's schooling of a restricted form of physical activity.

If middle-class reformers saw disorderly public sports as desirable, they argued the need for and benefits of appropriately designed and constructed open spaces in urban areas, which it was believed would both contribute to the reduction of crime, drunkenness and immorality, and check the spread of infectious diseases (Golby and Purdue, 1984: 102). Britain's legacy of municipal parks stems from such concerns, along with the desire of local notables and dignitaries to inscribe themselves in the history of their locality by gifting land to the town for the public good (Cunningham, 1980: 94–95). A public meeting in Manchester in 1844 recommended the provision of parks in the town, as they would 'contribute to the health, rational enjoyment, kindly intercourse and good morals of all classes of our industrious nation' (Golby and Purdue, 1984: 102). Although initially many such spaces were educational – providing a guide to nature, and a source for healthy exercise, walking (Cunningham, 1980: 95) – the space secured by them provided a vital long-term resource for the playing of sports. Rightly – as a stroll through any town or city in the country will show over a hundred years on, with the town's parks laid out in mosaics of bowling greens, football pitches and tennis courts – the establishing of municipal parks can be seen as the most important and long-lasting achievement of the rational recreationists.

England's little-known but resilient champion of the Olympian Games, Dr

William Penny Brookes, had a less direct influence upon everyday sports cultures, but provided an intriguing footnote to world sports history in his own brand of rational recreationist intervention (Hill, 1992: 9–15). A gentleman and a surgeon, Brookes believed that the expansion of the political franchise, after the 1832 Reform Act, demanded new measures. In 1841 he founded the Agricultural Reading Society, intended for all classes and with the purpose of encouraging literacy, so that people could read if they were to have the vote. In 1850 the Society established an 'Olympian' section, to encourage games, as a way of keeping the population of Much Wenlock out of the local drinking places. The Olympian section spawned the Olympian Society, which organised annual games which came to be more athleticist and national in profile. Brookes, as medic, sports enthusiast and rational recreationist, had strong views on the necessity of providing physical education in state schools, and welcomed the 1871 Act in which instruction in drill for up to two hours a week and no more than twenty weeks a year could count as school attendance. In the late 1870s Brookes argued for the introduction of Swiss-style gymnastics in schools, and was a vigorous advocate of the values of athletics for the masses:

> The encouragement of outdoor exercise contributes to manliness of character. I say contributes, for true manliness shows itself not merely in skill in athletic and field sports, but in the exercise of those moral virtues which it is one of the objects of religion to inculcate.
>
> (cited in Hill, 1992: 10)

Some low-profile Games had taken place in Greece in 1859 – Brookes' Wenlock Olympian Society donated a prize of £10 for one of the races – and Brookes urged the Greek government to revise the ancient Games. He also exchanged letters with Baron Pierre de Coubertin, French founder of the modern Olympic movement in 1894, and de Coubertin even visited Much Wenlock in 1890. It is fascinating to observe that in the figure of Brookes and his moral mission the tenets of an avowed athleticist were blended with the driving zeal of a rational recreationist, and that this combination could have had some effect upon the origins of the modern Olympic Games.

Overall, then, the rational recreationist project – in Hargreaves' summary, 'the attempt to spread bourgeois mores concerning the use of free time', in promoting activities 'that would be "improving", educational, respectable and more refined than the boisterous and dissolute pursuits of popular culture' (1986: 22) – was far from successful in its primary goal of cultural transformation, for those at whom it was aimed could use facilities for their own purposes, could appropriate them for their own ends and imbue them with their own meanings. Nevertheless, as examples as wide apart as the Wenlock Olympian Games and the cultural transformation of the London working class show, the influence of the reformers was widespread. It created spaces, facilities and resources for new ways of playing, even if the meanings of that play for the poor and the popular classes could not be dictated and controlled by the reformers.

Conclusions

Modern sports in Britain emerged as the cultural products of a rapidly industri- alising society undergoing unprecedented levels of change. But that is not to say that the sports simply reflected the characteristics of the society. Rather, they were – and are – a product of the social relationships within that changing soci- ety. The conflict of the gospel of athleticism and the rational recreation project, with emerging forms of professional sport and commercial forms of sport and leisure provision, is the central dynamic at the heart of the process of the growth of many modern sports, and is critical to any understanding of particular case studies of their emergence. Core principles of amateurism – fair play, working for others in teams with character-building benefits – have in many respects been admirable, and certainly long-lasting. Fabled hero of the 1981 movie *Chariots of Fire*, the 1924 Olympic gold medallist and athletics writer Harold M. Abrahams could write, in 1948, of the forthcoming London Olympic Games:

> First and foremost we must really get away from the point of view of regarding only the *winners* of Olympic events as those who are worthy of praise. It is this very narrow point of view which is so wrong and unfair . . . I was lucky enough in 1924 to win an Olympic title, and I realise to the full that the praise showered upon me was out of all proportion to the occasion. I am not going to pretend that I did not train extremely hard, but I realise to the full that luck played an enormous part.
>
> (Rivers, 1948: 14)

Here, immediately post-Second World War, the amateur-based spirit of athleti- cism still prevailed. And into the last decade of the century, a prominent fig- ure in sports broadcasting, cricket commentator Brian Johnston, could call upon the central themes of athleticism as a driving force, offering lessons for life more generally and not just sport. From his background at Eastbourne Col- lege, Eton and Oxford University, and then the BBC establishment, Johnston could comment:

> All that time spent on just a game! Or is it something more than that? Many of us believe that it is. More than anything else in my life it taught me to try and work and play with others, and to be a member of a team. I

was taught the importance of improving my own performance by practice, dedication and discipline; and to accept the umpire's decision, to win or lose gracefully and to take the inevitable disappointments with a smile. These are the ideals and I am not boasting or pretending that I have ever lived up to them, but they do explain the phrase 'it's not cricket.'

(1990: 1)

Generations schooled in such an ethos sought to offset the rising influences of professionalism and commercialism in sport (whilst, ironically, in the cases of both Abrahams and Johnston, gaining a good living from the rising cultural profile of sport), acting in their own way as latter-day rational recreationists. But veiled in hypocritical notions such as effortless excellence, the values of athleticism could became tarnished and, in the British example, could come to operate as a conservative and discriminatory force, effecting the marginalisation of much talent. But the legacy of athleticism could resurface in some surprising spheres. US social scientist Amitai Etzioni – with a far from negligible influence upon the British prime minister Tony Blair – in his book *The Spirit of Community* has argued for 'a new moral, social, public order – without puritanism or oppression', and based upon shared values, the renewal of social bonds and the reform of public life. It was to extracurricular activities, in the form of school games and team sports, that Etzioni turned when seeking an example of how the values necessary to such an order might be cultivated. Sports, he recognised, could be abused if coaches focused upon winning as the sole object of the activity and neglected:

to instill learning to play by the rules, teamwork and camaraderie. 'Graduates' of such activities will tend to be people who are aggressive, maladjusted members of the community . . . If parents see the importance of using sports to educate rather than to win, sports can be a most effective way to enhance values education . . . they generate activities that are powerful educational tools. Thus, if one team plays as a bunch of individuals and loses because its adversary plays as a well-functioning team, the losing players learn – in a way that no pep talk or slide show can – the merit of playing as a team.

(1994: 103)

From the playing fields of Rugby, and elsewhere, to the policy chambers of the White House and 10 Downing Street – athleticism and its related ideologies, seeing moral education in physical activity, will go down as more than a mere footnote in the history of Britain; the struggles over the meaning of different conceptions of sport as more than a sideshow to mainstream political and cultural life. These central tensions and dynamics in the making of modern sport are explored in more detail in selected case studies in the following chapter.

ESSAYS AND EXERCISES

Essays

Discuss the main changes, accompanying the industrial revolution, that reshaped the social basis of popular recreation.

How successful was the character-building project of athleticism/organised games in the nineteenth- and early twentieth-century public schools?

Apply *either* the Guttmann *or* the Dunning/Sheard classification of the features of modern sport to the analysis of one sport that you know well.

Exercises

Make a list of the municipal sports facilities in your home town, from parks to playing fields to swimming pools. Find out how old they are, who founded and funded them and how they might have connections with the rational recreation initiatives of the nineteenth century. Compare your findings with those of classmates, making urban/rural and any other comparisons.

Drawing upon your personal history of involvement in sport, consider how and when you might have embodied the values of athleticism in your own sporting practice. Has sport, for example, been good for the character?

How important are social conceptions of time and space for the formation of modern sports?

FURTHER READING

Allen Guttmann, *From Ritual to Record – The Nature of Modern Sports*, New York, Columbia University Press, 1978, provides a provocative discussion of the comparative characteristics of sports in different types of society and at different points in history.

J.A. Mangan, *Athleticism in the Victorian and Edwardian Public School – The Emergence and Consolidation of an Educational Ideology*, Cambridge, Cambridge University Press, 1981, is a seminal study in the field, illustrating the nature of the formative influences upon modern British team games.

References

Aron, R. (1967) *18 Lectures on Industrial Society*, London: Weidenfeld and Nicolson.

Bailey, P. (1978) *Leisure and Class in Victorian England – Rational Recreation and the Contest for Control 1830–1885*, London: Routledge & Kegan Paul.

Balfour, A.J. (1912) *Arthur James Balfour as Philosopher and Thinker – A Collection of the More Important and Interesting Passages in his Non-political Writings, Speeches and Addresses 1879–1912*, selected and arranged by Wilfrid M. Short, London: Longmans, Green.

Bamford, T.W. (1967) *Rise of the Public Schools – A Study of Boys' Public Boarding Schools in England and Wales from 1837 to the Present Day*, London: Nelson.

Brailsford, D. (1991) *Sport, Time and Society – The British at Play*, London and New York: Routledge.

Burke, P. (1978) *Popular Culture in Early Modern Europe*, New York: Harper and Row.

Clark, A. (1991) [1961] *The Donkeys*, London: Pimlico.

Cunningham, H. (1980) *Leisure in the Industrial Revolution c.1780–c.1880*, London: Croom Helm.

De S. Honey, J.R. (1977) *Tom Brown's Universe – The Development of the English Public School in the Nineteenth Century*, New York: Quadrangle/The New York Times Book Co.

DNH (Department of National Heritage) (1995) *Sport – Raising the Game*, London: Department of National Heritage, DNHJ0096NJ.July 1995.70M.

Dobbs, B. (1973) *Edwardians at Play: Sport 1890–1914*, London: Pelham Books.

Dunning, E. and Sheard, K. (1979) *Barbarians, Gentlemen and Players: A Sociological Study of the Development of Rugby Football*, New York: New York University Press.

Etzioni, A. (1994) *The Spirit of Community – The Reinvention of American Society*, New York: Simon Schuster/Touchstone.

Giddens, A. (1982) *Sociology – A Brief but Critical Introduction*, London: Macmillan.

Golby, J.M. and Purdue, A.W. (1984) *The Civilisation of the Crowd: Popular Culture in England 1750–1900*, London: Batsford Academic and Educational.

Gruneau, R. (1983) *Class, Sports, and Social Development*, Amherst: University of Massachusetts Press.

Guttmann, A. (1978) *From Ritual to Record – The Nature of Modern Sports*, New York: Columbia University Press.

Guttmann, A. (1986) *Sports Spectators*, New York: Columbia University Press.

Guttmann, A. (1992) Personal correspondence with Alan Tomlinson.

Haley, B. (1978) *The Healthy Body and Victorian Culture*, New Haven: Harvard University Press.

Hargreaves, Jennifer (1994) *Sporting Females – Critical Issues in the History and Sociology of Women's Sports*, London and New York: Routledge.

Hargreaves, John (1982) 'Sport, Culture and Ideology', in Jennifer Hargreaves (ed.), *Sport, Culture and Ideology*, London: Routledge & Kegan Paul.

Hargreaves, John (1986) *Sport, Power and Culture – A Social and Historical Analysis of Popular Sports in Britain*, Cambridge: Polity Press.

Harris, J. (1993) *Private Lives, Public Spirit: A Social History of Britain 1870–1914*, Oxford: Oxford University Press.

Hill, C.R. (1992) *Olympic Politics*, Manchester: Manchester University Press.

Holt, R. (1989) *Sport and the British – A Modern History*, Oxford: Oxford University Press.

Johnston, B. (1990) *It's Been a Piece of Cake – A Tribute to My Favourite Test Cricketers*, London: Mandarin.

Kalton, G. (1966) *The Public Schools – A Factual Survey of Headmasters' Conference Schools in England and Wales*, Longmans, London.

Kanitkar, H. (1994) '"Real True Boys" – Moulding the Cadets of Imperialism', in A. Cornwall and N. Lindisfarne (eds), *Dislocating Masculinity – Comparative Ethnographies*, London: Routledge.

Kumar, K. (1978) *Prophecy and Progress – The Sociology of Industrial and Post-industrial Society*, Harmondsworth: Penguin Books.

McIntosh, P. (1979) *Fair Play – Ethics in Sport and Education*, London: Heinemann.

Maguire, J. (1986) 'Images of Manliness and Competing Ways of Living in late Victorian and Edwardian Britain', *British Journal of Sports History*, vol. 3, pp. 191–215.

Malcolmson, R. (1973) *Popular Recreations in English Society 1700–1850*, Cambridge: Cambridge University Press.

Mangan, J.A. (1981) *Athleticism in the Victorian and Edwardian Public School – The Emergence and Consolidation of an Educational Ideology*, Cambridge: Cambridge University Press.

Mangan, J.A. (1986) *The Games Ethic and Imperialism: Aspects of the Diffusion of an Ideal*, London: Viking.

Mangan, J.A. (ed.) (1992) *The Cultural Bond – Sport, Empire, Society*, London: Frank Cass.

Mason, T. (1996) 'Football, Sport of the North', in J. Hill and J. Williams (eds), *Sport and Identity in the North of England*, Keele: Keele University Press.

Murray, R. (1989) 'Fordism and Post-Fordism', in S. Hall and M. Jacques (eds), *New Times – The Changing Face of Politics in the 1990s*, London: Lawrence and Wishart.

Rivers, J. (ed.) (1948) *The Sports Book 2 – Britain's Prospects in the Olympic Games and in Sport Generally*, London: Macdonald.

Secondary Heads Association (1994) *Enquiry into the Provision of Physical Education in Schools 1994*, Secondary Heads Association.

Stedman-Jones, G. (1983) 'Working-class Culture and Working-Class Politics in London, 1870–1900: Notes on the Remaking of a Working Class', in *Languages of Class – Studies in English Working-Class History 1832–1982*, Cambridge: Cambridge University Press.

Thompson, E.P. (1967) 'Time, Work-Discipline, and Industrial Capitalism', *Past and Present*, no. 38, pp. 56–97.

Thompson, E.P. (1968) *The Making of the English Working Class*, Harmondsworth: Penguin Books.

Tomlinson, A. (1992) 'Shifting Patterns of Working-class Leisure: The Case of Knur and Spel', *Sociology of Sport Journal*, Volume 9, pp. 192–206.

Toynbee, A. (1967) 'The Classical Definition of the Industrial Revolution' (1884), in P.A.M. Taylor (ed.), *The Industrial Revolution in Britain – Triumph or Disaster?*, Boston: D.C. Heath.

Turner, B. (1975) *Industrialism*, Harlow: Longman.

Wakeford, J. (1969) *The Cloistered Elite – A Sociological Analysis of the English Public Boarding School*, London: Macmillan.

Walvin, J. (1975) *The People's Game – A Social History of English Football*, London: Allen Lane.

Webb, I. (1979) 'The History of Chelsea College of Physical Education', unpublished doctoral thesis, Department of Education, University of Leicester.

Wilkinson, R. (1964) *The Prefects – British Leadership and the Public School Tradition: A Comparative Study in the Making of Rulers*, London: Oxford University Press.

Worsley, T.C. (1985) *Flannelled Fool – A Slice of a Life in the Thirties*, London: The Hogarth Press.

Young, D. (1984) *The Olympic Myth of Greek Amateur Athletics*, Chicago: Ares Publishers Inc.

Chapter two

Case studies in the growth of modern sports

Case studies can illustrate clearly how particular sports have manifested the features pointed to by Guttmann, and Dunning and Sheard, how such features have been more or less characteristic of the amateur and professional forms of those sports, and how they must be located in their social and social-historical context. As John Bale has put it: 'Sport, bound by rules, precision, quantifying, record-seeking and under bureaucratic control, increasingly came to mirror society at large' (1989: 42), and in this process the 'transition from folk game to sport typically followed five stages': (i) the folk game stage; (ii) the formation of clubs; (iii) the establishment of a rule-making national bureaucracy; (iv) the diffusion and adoption of the sport in other countries; (v) the formation of an international bureaucracy. In this chapter we offer four case studies cast in terms of this type of stage analysis, recognising its general applicability, but adding a more sociological and British-based emphasis, rather than Bale's international and geographical dimension, in the consideration of later phases.

Athletics is the first case study, in recognition of its 'key role in the development of amateurism' (Whannel, 1983: 43). Two prominent team sports – association football and cricket – and one individual sport – golf – comprise the other case studies. The football case study is the fullest one, for several reasons: there is a wide range and real depth of scholarly work and sources available; it became established as the most popular spectator and (male) participant sport remarkably quickly; and it provides the opportunity for fleshing out contextual detail on, for instance, the growth of cities and the rise of consumerism in sport – the context in which the commodification of sport (the intensifying production of sport and sport-related goods for the market, for sale and for profit) is established and promoted.

Athletics

Whannel has summarised the pre-modern form of athletics in Britain, which had existed for centuries:

> The rural festivities of the sixteenth and seventeenth centuries featured running races. A tradition of rural athletic meetings in the eighteenth century became particularly strong in the north of England and Scotland with events like the Highland Games and the Border Games. Pedestrianism and the running of head-to-head matches for gambling was well-established before the nineteenth century. In the nineteenth century it is known that there were both open professional athletic events, with prizes, and open meetings that were mainly middle-class affairs, with low-value prizes.
>
> (1983: 43–44)

The amateur form of athletics superseded these established practices, in the context of class disputes and tensions, as upper-class, middle-class and working-class enthusiasts struggled to gain control of the emerging institutional base of the sport. If the traditional forms can be seen as the first phase in any periodisation of the historical development of the sport, then the succeeding phases were (i) the formation of clubs and the struggle to lead the sport, rooted in class-specific tensions over the amateurism issue; (ii) the dominance of the amateur ethos, during which time women's athletics also developed; (iii) a period of athlete power in which the premises of athleticism were questioned, disputed and opposed, and which also coincided with the high point of 'shamateurism'; and (iv) the impact of commercialism and of open professionalism, in intensifying forms as media interests and sponsors effected a commodification of the athletic event and its champions and stars, with the production of the athletic event and the construction of the athletic celebrity (and associated goods and products) in increasingly uncompromising market terms.

Whannel argues persuasively that 'the rigid distinctions erected between the amateur and the professional were in the end rooted in class domination' (1983: 53), and the consensus among specialist historians of the later nineteenth century confirms this emphasis upon class: 'many historians of different ideological persuasions have identified the last quarter of the nineteenth century as the period in which the tentacles of class became all-embracing, in which all other social and cultural attributes became reducible to class categories' (Harris, 1994: 6). Sport, resonant of the new and rooted in the social relationships of the time, could hardly be immune from this. Definition of amateur status was commonly based upon forms of privilege and power rooted in class position and relations. The AAC (Amateur Athletic Club, formed in 1866, later to become the three As, when 'club' was changed to 'association') formulated an influential definition of the amateur (Bailey, 1978: 131) which affected a range of sports in its deliberations on the issue. The Club was formed to enable 'gentlemen amateurs' to practise and compete among themselves 'without being compelled to mix with professional runners'. The AAC offered an elitist and excluding definition of 'amateur':

> Any person who has never competed in an open competition, or for public money, or for admission money, or with professionals for a prize, public money or admission money, and who has never, at any period of his life, taught or assisted in the pursuit of athletic exercises as a means of livelihood, or is a mechanic, artisan or labourer.
>
> (Bailey, 1978: 131)

So, just in case any non-elitist athlete might qualify for membership, the AAC came clean in its last clause, and expressed the class basis of its constitution.

The Amateur Rowing Association and the Bicycling Union also barred such workers from membership, on the rationale that workers who worked physically so much would enjoy an unfair advantage in competition with the more sedentary professional, and were really in need of more mental exercises away from work. In golf, too, similar emphases were articulated concerning the material gains that might accrue from playing or providing services for sport (Cousins, 1975: 39), though the English Amateur Athletic Club's definition did not explicitly exclude on the basis of social class or type of work. But generally, professionals were defined as an unacceptable other, on the basis of criteria of exclusion – if you were characterised by X, then you could not be included in category Y. The organisation and administration of athletics was shaped by such excluding principles.

The modern form of athletics was modelled on the Amateur Athletic Club's first championship, held in the mid-1860s. Clubs were formed within the networks of the public schools, the universities, the professions and business (Crump, 1989). The notion of the club was critical, providing 'an element of collective endeavour' (Crump, 1989: 44) which fuelled the team spirit characteristic of organised games, and marked the new sport off from the competitive individualism of pedestrianism, the established form of running races. The Amateur Athletic Association (AAA), formed in 1880, was the initiative of three former Oxford University athletes, and successfully united amateur athletics in England, at least until the British Olympic Association was established to organise the 1908 Olympic Games in London, and the Women's Athletic Association was established in 1922. The AAA campaigned against professionalism and illegal payments to athletes, defending the purity of the amateur ideal, which was bolstered in the 1890s by the formation of the Olympic movement by the French aristocrat Baron Pierre de Coubertin. We have seen that the Amateur Athletic Club's 1866/7 definition of amateur ruled that no mechanic, artisan or labourer could be accepted as an amateur, reasoning that manual labour would give such people an unfair advantage in athletic competition. This definition was loosened in 1868 but still stated that 'An amateur is a gentleman who has never competed' (Crump, 1989: 51). The AAA revoked this 'gentle-man' clause, but fought a long-term offensive against professionalism. Pro-fessional athletics continued to flourish, nevertheless, especially in regions such as the north of England, and in the Scottish Highlands. The AAA excluded pro-fessionals from other sports, such as cricket and football, in 1883 and 1899 respectively, and funded the prosecution, for fraud, of those breaching the ban, some offenders even receiving prison sentences. In 1899 the AAA authorised payment of travel expenses to athletes, and it appeared that the leadership and shape of the sport were by then well established, in class-based and amateur form; so much so that in the 1920s the gentleman amateur dominated British athletics, and the national team was made up in most part of members of the Achilles Club, which had been established by and for Oxbridge graduates.

Women's athletics developed separately from men's. The first women's athletics club to be formed in England was the London Olympiads Athletic Club, formed by women returning from the Women's Olympiads in Monte Carlo in 1921 and Paris in 1922 (Hargreaves, 1994: 130). Most of these women were from the Regent Street Polytechnic and, with others who ran and played netball for England, they provided the basis for the formation of the Women's Athletic Association (WAA). Women's athletics, Hargreaves argues (1994: 131), was less exclusively middle class than many other female sports as it was considered to be unladylike. Indeed, the administrators of the WAA commis-sioned a medical report in 1925 which argued that 'even if one does not see any ill results at the time from too strenuous devotion to athletics, the final result may be very deleterious to the girls' health and natural functions' (Hargreaves, 1994: 133). The report claimed that child-bearing could be adversely affected by participation in athletics, and the WAA accepted the report without question. Although some women may have challenged class dominance in developing women's athletics, prejudices about the female body continued to inhibit the sport's development. Fragmentation in the organisation of British athletics was such that when the Scottish Amateur Athletic Association complained to the International Amateur Athletic Federation about the power and nature of the AAA, the British Amateur Athletics Board (BAAB) was set up in 1932. In 1981, the Minister of Sport Neil MacFarlane was shocked to find that nineteen organ-isations could claim to control some aspect or other of British athletics (Crump, 1989: 49).

The final phase in the growth of athletics saw it break free from the stranglehold of the amateur ideal and open the door more widely to the forces of commercialism, and to open professionalism. In this, a form of athlete-power was important, when the International Athletes Club was formed in 1958, developing out of the dissatisfaction felt by non-university athletes during and after the 1956 Olympics in Australia, and disputes concerning the payment of pocket money to athletes. A confusing period of 'shamateurism' – with underhand payment to so-called amateurs, hand-in-hand with manufacturers such as Adidas – was followed by the introduction of the trust fund in 1982. This fund enabled athletes to keep all appearance, sponsorshoip and advertising income for the purposes of subsistence, training and retirement, whilst retaining the status of amateur. The BAAB retained the right to authorise arrangements for any trust funds.

Reports and committees in the 1960s and the 1980s were to warn that unless British athletics united, increasing sponsorship income could be misdirected. These reports were shown to be timely when the boom years of athletics in the 1980s were followed by the bust years of the 1990s and, ignominiously, the BAAF plunged into financial crisis with little explanation as to what had happened to the huge income flowing into the sport during its prosperous years. Emblematic of such mismanagement was the famous race between Zola Budd and Mary Decker-Slaney in 1985 (Crump, 1989: 56; Channel 4, 1986).

Decker-Slaney had raced against Budd in the final of the 3,000 metres at the 1984 Los Angeles Olympics, blaming Budd for a collision and a fall which she claimed lost her the race. The rematch, at Crystal Palace in July 1985, attracted £200,000 sponsorship from a US television company. Budd, a South African running at the Olympics by claiming British citizenship, was paid £90,000; Slaney received £54,000. It was widely perceived that Decker-Slaney was the superior athlete, with a personal best 8 seconds faster than Budd's. Budd herself commented at a pre-race press conference that 'I certainly don't think I can win', but that 'anything can happen in a race'. The stadium was far from full, as the meeting had been stretched into a second day in order to accommodate Saturday coast-to-coast coverage of the race in the USA. Many spectators at the first day were therefore disgruntled at the changed schedule and the unpredictability of the line-up in other races, as Sebastian Coe, Steve Cram and the Brazilian Cruz were annnounced as running in separate races, or not at all. Meanwhile, behind the scenes the sponsor of the event, Peugeot Talbot, entertained its 900 key customers in its hospitality suite, the company's director Tod Evans welcoming these clients as family and friends. Peugeot was also taking advantage of a new regulation which permitted sponsors to advertise during programme breaks of programmes that they were themselves sponsoring. Cavalcades of Peugeot's new model were filmed on the track, and a special advertisement had been made for broadcasting over the two days of the meeting. Peugeot's John Russell could draw analogies between his own company's values and those of athletics, the latter described as clean, lively, full of integrity and dynamic. Professional commentators were less fulsome in their praise. Steve Goldstein, print journalist from Philadelphia, commented that 'this is one of the biggest showbiz extravaganzas that's ever taken place in sport', comparing it to soap opera and the televison audience expectations for a mix of drama and celebrity. Sports journalist Colin Hart (of the *Sun*) described the contest as 'an event not a race, no contest, a mismatch . . . they're selling advertising, it's money'. Alan Pascoe, of Alan Pascoe Associates, the man responsible for guaranteeing British athletics a sponsorship income of £3 million over five years, labelled the event as 'one of the big personality races of the century'. Created for television, this 'head-to-head that had to happen' was a complete mismatch, heralding an era of event management in the sport, in which entertainment and celebrity would become as important as competitive realities. New alliances between the sport, sponsors and television – brokered in important ways by marketing figures such as Pascoe – established a financial bonanza for British athletics. But as Decker-Slaney strolled to her victory at Crystal Palace, British athletics proceeded down the road to its eventual insolvency. Individual athletes such as Daley Thompson, Linford Christie and Sally Gunnell would benefit greatly, but athletics itself failed to disseminate its newfound riches, with entrepreneurial opportunists doing little for the wider development of the sport (Downes and Mackay, 1996). In this process, too, the *esprit de corps* of the amateur ideal and national pride has given way to a more individualistic ideal: 'the athlete's effort and dedication are directed at least as much to self-realisation and to the peer group of athletes as to the national team and the wider public' (Crump, 1989: 59).

Such self-realisation has been driven as much by financial motive as by performance aspiration. Downes and Mackay see the Budd versus Decker-Slaney event as pivotal in the transformation of athletics, a process which they label as a 'loss of innocence' based upon the perceived market value of individuals:

> In athletics' first ten years of professionalism, a strange, arcane system of 'subventions' had grown up, mainly about the sport's continuing coyness about paying large sums of money to its leading performers. Under this subvention system, star quality was recorded, but not actual performance. The meeting promoters would decide on an athlete's worth, and agree a fee with the competitor or their agent in advance of the meeting. Athletes were being paid to appear, not to compete. The sport's values soon began to warp.
>
> (1996: 18)

Such warping or distortions would include not just made-for-tv fiascos such as Budd versus Decker, but a range of examples corrupting the values of fair competition. British athletics promoter Andy Norman, for instance, ensured that top stars were not present and offered payment to a runner not to win in the 'carefully orchestrated event' that was Alan Pascoe's last race, in front of a capacity crowd at Crystal Palace in 1979 (p. 91). In 1995 Kenyan Moses Kiptanui, running in Sweden, deliberately avoided breaking his own world record in the 3,000 metres steeplechase World Championships final, so that he could reap all the benefits on offer at the meeting in Zurich later in the week – where, as the first man to run under 8 minutes, the Kenyan's bonuses and fees amounted to around £130,000 (pp. 114–115). Corrupt officials would con-tribute to fixed outcomes. International Amateur Athletics Federation president Italian Primo Nebiolo built an extra lane and bent the rules to get the host nation into the final at the Rome World Cup in 1981; and was implicated, in the cover-up at least, when long-jump measurements were fixed in the computer at the 1987 World Championships in Rome, so guaranteeing an Italian competitor a medal (pp. 133–135). Nebiolo is also reported to have rigged the voting in the poll for World Athlete of the Year in 1995, so robbing English hurdler Sally Gunnell of a second successive such honour (p. 140); and to have covered up a positive drug test on an Italian hammer thrower at the 1984 Los Angeles Olympics (p. 135). The systematic use of drugs has also distorted the record books, especially up to the point at which Canadian Ben Johnson set his steroid-aided all-time 100 metres record at the Seoul Olympics: 'in the doping control clampdown that followed the Johnson scandal, there was not one world-record set in a women's Olympic event for five years' (p. 158). Not just state-centred regimes such as East Germany and Bulgaria were prominent in the administra-tion of performance-enhancing substances. A sudden emergence to prominence of Italian distance runners in the mid-1980s has been attributed to doping by steroids, and blood transfusions (p. 223). In Britain, top performers such as Linford Christie and Sally Gunnell have achieved great performances in the post-clampdown period – though they have not always been available when drug-testing teams have sought to administer random tests at the athletes' home base.

Athletics – in its basic form, the glorious epitome of sporting competition – has emerged as a celebration not merely of individual athletic talent, but as a sport increasingly vulnerable to exploitation by individual performers, adminis-trators, and political and market forces. The riches that poured into British ath-letics in the boom years of the 1980s and the early 1990s – redistributed at times 'in a brown paper bag' and 'a stack of used notes' (Downes and Mackay, 1996: 108) by Andy Norman – did little to secure the longer term prosperity of the sport. The case of the Chafford Hundred Athletics Club is a revealing one, related by Downes and Mackay (pp. 104–111). This club was created in 1991, and became, overnight, the richest athletics club in Britain, though entering and competing in no team competitions: 'Chafford Hundred AC was established purely as a marketing ploy, a one-stop shop for sponsors wanting to become involved in one of Britain's most successful sports' (p. 104). Top British athletes – including Christie, Gunnell and John Regis – could wear the vest of this fictional club on the international Grand Prix circuit, plastered with whatever logo the elite group agreed to display from the favoured sponsor. Income into the sport would thus flow into the individual accounts of a few stars, bypassing the development programmes of the grass roots of the sport. The Chafford Hundred Club – named after an Essex housing development close to Andy Norman's home, and managed by Fatima Whitbread, former javelin world champion and Norman's fiancee – diverted potential income away from the sport's federation and real conventional clubs, and was 'just the latest manifestation of the greed and money motive that threatens to corrupt athletics forever' (ibid.). In the light of marketing initiatives such as this, and the collapse of the financial infrastructure of British athletics, it is no surprise that Peter Radford, former Olympic sprinter and erstwhile head of the British Athletics Federation, has argued that sport is too important to be left to the sports organisations and other agencies, and that a degree of state involvement and direction is now necessary if sport is to fulfil its true potential (BBC Radio 4, 1998).

Football

The social history of the game of association football in England can be divided into seven distinct phases: the folk game; the formalisation of the athleticist-amateurist codes in the public schools; the split between association football and rugby football, and then later within rugby football itself – bound up with the emergence of the professional game; the insularity of the British game in the inter-war years of the twentieth century; the post-war years of austerity; the years of further commercialisation of the game in the 1960s, 1970s and 1980s; and the more recent phase based upon the creation of a breakaway elite Premier League and sponsorship and media influences upon the game.

Accounts of the early game of football in Wales (Dunning and Sheard, 1979: 29–30) and in Derby, England (Malcolmson, 1973: 37) evoke the image of a rough and ready, sometimes riotous and certainly loosely structured activity, unrecognisable in terms of any modern form of the game. Malcolmson's reconstruction of an example of the folk game, and the social and cultural context of that particular example, is extracted below, and is followed by another extract describing the game in the north-west of England:

> In many places the principal football match of the year was on Shrove Tuesday. During the earlier nineteenth century there were still scores of Shrovetide games, many of which were played through the streets of town.

Among the recorded holiday matches were the ones at Alnwick, Chester-le-Street, Sedgefield, Derby, Ashbourne, Nuneaton, and Corfe Castle; Twickenham, Teddington and Bushey Park in Middlesex; and Dorking, Richmond, Kingston-upon-Thames, Hampton Wick, East Mousley, Hampton and Thames Ditton, all in Surrey. 'From time immemorial', observed *The Times* of 6 March 1840, 'it has been the custom in most of the parishes and places in the western portions of the counties of Middlesex and Surrey, for the inhabitants on Shrove Tuesday in every year to devote the greater part of the day to the *manly sport* of foot-ball, which has not been confined to the open spaces of the respective towns and villages, but the ball has been pursued by hundreds through the most public thoroughfares, the shops and houses of which were customarily closed, and the windows barricaded with hurdles, to prevent their being broken'. In some places the contests were associated with other holidays. Devonshire games were often on Good Friday; at Workington and Eakring, Nottinghamshire, the main match of the year was on Easter Tuesday; and at Kirkham, Lancashire, it was customarily played on Christmas Day.

Since each holiday match had its own special customs and playing arrangements, no one case can be regarded as completely typical; however, we can at least examine one of them, the well documented Derby game, both as an interesting case in its own right and as an illustration of the general character of a Shrovetide match. In theory the Derby competition was between the parishes of St. Peter's and All Saints, but in practice the rest of the borough was allowed to take part, and the townsmen were usually joined by a large influx of holidayers from the countryside. Business was suspended for the afternoon and play began at two o'clock from the marketplace. The objective of each team (there were 500 to 1,000 a side in the early nineteenth century) was to carry the ball to a goal about a mile outside the town, St. Peter's the gate of a nursery ground towards London and All Saints the wheel of a watermill to the west. In most matches the St. Peter's side tried to get the ball into the River Derwent and swim with it, a circuitous approach to their own goal but a tactical removal of the ball in the opposite direction from the All Saint's watermill. If the Peter's men could overpower their rivals in the water, the ball was landed at a point near their goal and carried home; if the defence was too strong it would be hidden until dark, sometimes to be relieved of its cork shavings and the covering smuggled in under someone's smock or petticoat. Occasionally, when one side had uncommon muscle, the offence was straight overland, but this strategy obliged the Peter's team to cross the brook which led to their opponent's goal, an approach which could easily backfire. New ploys for attack or defence were warmly received: on one occasion, for instance, an enterprising fellow was reputed to have escaped with the ball into a sewer and passed under the town, only to be surprised as he surfaced by a party of opponents. Towards the finish of the match, when the drift of the contest was clear, the climax centred on the stratagems around one goal, such as starting up the All Saints' water-wheel. The player who ended the game was chaired through the winners' home territory and was given the honour of throwing up the ball at the start of the next year's play. A similar match for the youth of the town was staged on Ash Wednesday under the supervision of their elders.

Although the Derby game probably attracted an unusually large following, many of the other holiday matches would also have been recreational highlights in their own, usually smaller communities. The entry for Shrove Tuesday 1767 in William Cole's Bletchley diary mentioned 'Football playing on the Green', and in a case like this a significant proportion of the able-bodied men in the parish would have had to turn out just in order to make up the teams.

(Malcolmson, 1973: 37–38)

Bannister (1922) writes of the folk form in the north-east Lancashire town of Colne:

Football matches were very popular, not so frequent but more exacting than the modern type, because every man had to join the game. The game was played between all the men of Trawden or Winewall, and the men of Colne, or Colne Waterside. The ball was kicked off at some place midway between the townships, say at Cowfield or Doughty, and each party tried to get it to their own place. There were no rules of the game and no time limit. The play was very rough at times, bruises and serious wounds being made, while when they came to the river it was not unusual for men to be doused in the water. At one such game, when Big Joany had kicked off at Cowfield on Christmas Day, the play lasted till evening, and had ultimately reached the Trawden Valley near the watercourse. Then did Joany lift the ball above his head, and dare anyone to touch him or the ball, as he carried it off in triumph to Trawden.

The verses called 'Blueberry Cake' . . . were said to have been written as a sequel to this famous football match.

The folk game was clearly a distinctive activity and event, bearing little resemblance to the more formal forms of football that were to be developed. It expressed local and community affiliations, and accounts such as the ones above have provided the basis for the descriptions of the general characteristics of folk games or popular recreations such as that of Dunning and Sheard. The accounts portray what is also an essentially male-based activity. In no substantive account are women prominent as players. A Scottish source from 1891 has indicated an exception to this: 'the fisherwomen of Musselburgh are reported to have played golf and the fisherwomen of Musselburgh and Inveresk football' (Tranter, 1994: 28). But this is an unconfirmed account, an isolated sighting, not paralleled in the English or indeed wider European literature. No doubt women swelled the ranks of the onlookers and the crowd, indistinct at times from the players, but the marginalisation and exclusion of women seems well established in the history of pre-modern football.

The folk form was obviously perceived as undesirable by elements in the expanding industrial communities. Anthony Delves has explored the social relations underlying the decline of folk football in Derby, identifying a 'largely middle-class consensus over the need to abolish football and contain popular recreation' (1981: 106). There were three grounds for this, he argues. First, popular recreation was seen as 'inconvenient to, and probably incompatible with, the requirements of a rapidly-industrializing economy'. Boarded up banks and shops did not make good commercial sense. Second, popular recreation was seen as 'a source of general moral regression', not only slowing down the momentum of the market economy, but also 'obstructing attempts to turn savages into civilized men'. Many aspects of popular recreation, pubs especially, were seen as corrosive of moral and social standards, seen too as generative of social problems such as crime and poverty which were associated with working-class culture. Third, the social tensions of the 1840s led many in the middle classes to seek ways of incorporating the working class, and such an aspiration was incompatible with the continuation of specifically working-class cultural activities.

Folk football, then, was not conducive to the mores, values and aspirations of an expanding commercial and industrial culture. Opposition to it was not new in the nineteenth century. The gathering of large numbers of people for such forms of popular leisure was viewed with 'long-standing suspicions', as Brailsford puts it:

> Large gatherings meant rowdiness, tumult or worse. Arranging football matches to attract enough of the disaffected to pull down enclosure fences, stop fen drainage, or demolish mills, was not unknown – it happened on at least three occasions in the middle years of the [eighteenth] century in the Eastern counties.
>
> (1992: 48)

So it was unsurprising that in the evolving urban context opposition would intensify. At exactly the time that popular recreational football was opposed in the ways described by Delves, football codes were emerging in the public schools in the 1840s, laying the foundations for a later 'struggle between public schoolboys to be "model makers" for the game on a national level' (Dunning and Sheard, 1979: 99).

Mason describes this process of codification, as between 1845 and 1862 staff and pupils at seven leading public schools consigned the rules of their various codes and games to print. Games continued to be robust, but a redefinition of the acceptable limits of physicality was under way, what Mason calls 'a process of reconciliation . . . between spontaneity and vigour on the one hand and control and moderation on the other' (1980: 14). Public school recruits to the Universities of Cambridge and Oxford continued to play football, and in 1848 – the year of the revolutions that swept across mainland Europe, and of the publication of Marx and Engels' *The Communist Manifesto* – and on to the 1860s 'formal and informal experiments finally produced a body of rules that appeared to have a fairly wide acceptance' (Mason, 1980: 14). By 1871 rules appeared to be sufficiently standardised for the southern-based Football Association (FA) to travel to play a game against the Sheffield Football Club, the latter having been formed in 1857 around a nucleus of former pupils of the Sheffield Collegiate School, in all likelihood inducted into the game by ex-public school men, and playing a version of the Cambridge rules of 1856. Public school and university-based interpretations of and disputes over rules and codes were clearly, as observed by Dunning and Sheard above, explicit in the wider society at the key points in the development of football. In 1871, too, the Rugby Football Union (RFU) was founded, marking formally the separation of the association and the rugby codes of football. Dunning and Sheard point to three factors that led to this initiative. First, the formation of the FA in 1863 was followed by a spurt of popular support for soccer, at rugby's expense. Second, without any central body for the making and monitoring of rules, rugby could not be systematically developed. And finally, and most importantly, there was growing disapproval of the violent dimensions of the rugby code as evident in the practice of 'hacking', increasingly perceived as 'barbarous' (1979: 111–112). With the two codes formally separate, and increasing commonality of purpose within the association code, by April 1877 'one set of laws was finally achieved', with the London FA accepting some of the Sheffield Club's ideas, an arrangement which 'did much to strengthen the position of the Football Association in London as the game's leading authority' (Mason, 1980: 14). Other growing associations across England now affiliated to the FA. But there was to be no smooth process in the growth and expansion of the game. As football took root in the new urban communities of the industrialised society its popularity in terms of both participation and spectatorship produced the conditions for the emergence of the professional form.

The conditions for the emergence of professionals were forged by the new industrial culture in which players without extensive leisure time and the administrators of those players and their sports turned a game into work, and when a new sports industry around the teaching of sports and spectating and playing developed. Traditional amateurs (for some of whom the tradition was a relatively recent and new one) were very concerned that the basis of their own game would be threatened by the development of professionalism. Indeed, Tischler has argued that:

> the professional game reflected English society in the critical area of labour relations. Working-class fans could follow both on-the-field heroics and the player–director struggles of their favourite teams . . . [the introduction of] admission fees at matches revolutionised numerous aspects of football. The sport became less a gentleman's pastimes and more a commercial enterprise when played at its highest levels. Relationships among teams increasingly came to resemble the relationships among ordinary competitive business firms. Indeed, the debate over professionalism was a by-product of the commercialization of football.
>
> (1981: 36 and 41)

Responses to commercialism from traditionalists were widely critical of professional sport. One writer in the *Birmingham Daily Mail* (4 November 1881) observed that the 'creeping' development of 'gate money exhibitions' would be accompanied by the 'inevitable tendency' towards the lowering of the game's character. The intrusion of money into the game was, for this writer, anathema to the spirit of the amateur code, 'giving a sordid aspect to the contests which, if carried on at all, should be for the honour of victory alone without any ulterior thought as to how much the "gate" is worth' (Tischler, 1981: 41). Mason has documented the nature of this debate and shown more fully the respective arguments used by the opponents of professionalism. The two main ones were premised on a view of the nature of leisure itself, and an opposition to the potential scale and scope of commercialised sport. First, it was said that the nature of a 'voluntary leisure activity' would be corrupted by turning it into a business. Second, it was alleged that professionalism would undermine the survival of all but larger, wealthier clubs and so threaten 'essentially local rivalries' (Mason, 1980: 72). Three further arguments were used in this debate. It was believed that professionalism would destroy amateurism because the latter would not be able to compete on equal terms with the former; that professionalism would produce an overemphasis on winning, at any cost; and that the football professional was no true 'professor' anyway, for he had no teaching responsibilities (Mason, 1980: 230). Against this trend of professionalism, the middle classes believed that the amateur code of the game 'was good for the physique, it helped to build character, it perhaps led to diminution in drinking, it brought the classes together' (Mason, 1980: 229).

Despite such arguments the momentum towards the formation of professional football was sustained. The professional Football League was founded in 1888, with twelve members: Accrington, Aston Villa, Blackburn Rovers, Bolton Wanderers, Burnley, Derby County, Everton, Notts County, Preston North End, Stoke, West Bromwich Albion and Wolverhampton Wanderers. The roots of this professional League lay in the emergent industrial communities of the nineteenth century, in the quintessential expanding industrial regions of the north-west and the Midlands. Entrants to the FA (Football Association) Cup were from very different social and regional roots. The Football Association, 'formed by the representatives of a small number of mainly southern clubs in 1863' (Mason, 1980: 15) was, initially, an agreement between those clubs to stage matches based on the same rules. By 1868 there were thirty member clubs, and the nature of these sorts of clubs can be gleaned from the list of entrants to the first FA Cup in 1871–72. Thirteen of the fifteen entrants came from London or the Home Counties and many had names resonant of the public schools or the professions. The thirteen southern entrants were Barnes, Civil Service, Clapham Rovers, Crystal Palace, Great Marlow, Harrow Chequers, Hampstead Heathens, Hitchin, Maidenhead, Reigate Priory, Royal Engineers, Upton Park and Wanderers. The two teams from beyond the south were Donington School from Spalding in Lincolnshire, and Queens Park Glasgow. The regional, cultural and class-based roots of these different branches of the game were to have long-lasting effects on how football was to develop, as much in rivalry as in co-operation over the following century (Tomlinson, 1991). But there was little doubt that the emerging working-class, embryonic professional clubs would prove the prophets of the amateurist crisis to be right. In the first eleven years of the FA Cup the trophy was won by just four clubs: Wanderers, Old Etonians, Old Carthusians and Clapton Rovers. In 1882 Blackburn Rovers reached the final but lost. The following year, though, its local rival toppled the toffs. When Blackburn Olympic won the FA Cup in 1883 the Blackburn side spent a week in Blackpool for preparation and training before the semi-final against Old Carthusians. The Blackburn side's local newspaper listed the occupations of the players: clerk, master plumber, licensed victualler, dentist, iron-foundry workers (labourer and dresser), gilder, loomer and three weavers (Mason, 1980: 54). The *Athletic News* of the time provided an editorial on the clash of cultures symbolised in this semi-final, characterising it as a meeting of 'patricians and plebians', with educated gentlemen/undoubted swells pitted against rough and ready workers. Blackburn won easily, on the basis, it was widely acknowledged, of skill and technique rather than brawn or strength. Football was clearly making a strong impact in the regional and local cultures of the industrial working-class communities, helped in many cases by local business sponsors aware of the advantages of the game for class harmony. Blackburn Olympic was supported by the local iron founders (which seems to have provided at least two of the cup-winning side) and Mr Sydney Yates told the players that 'although they were merely working lads they might, if they could stick together in the future, and with the assistance of people of influence, soon be able to reach the top of the tree' (Mason, 1980: 33).

A sport with the profile of professional football was able to express in important ways the new 'urban loyalties' (Holt, 1989: 170) of the local population, albeit primarily the male population. In Manchester, these loyalties were still being forged in the inter-war years of the twentieth century when the young Matt Busby first arrived from the Scottish coalfields to begin his English professional football life. Manchester's phenomenal growth in the nineteenth century – by 1831 the city had a population of 142,000, an increase of nearly 40 per cent in ten years (Briggs, 1968: 89) – had established the city as an unusually cosmopolitan one, in which, as the century progressed, 'the outsiders, first or second generation Catholics, Jews, and Italians shared common ground' (Dunphy, 1991: 94). Manchester was, Dunphy adds, 'fertile ground for the planting of new roots. For the Busbys, Roccas and McGraths as for the Jews, there was a sense of place, of belonging' (p. 95). Along with entertainment and the arts, sport contributed to the creation of a culture expressive of a community and its emerging identity. Whether we look to the fictional cosiness of Priestley's Bruddersford, as depicted below (p. 45–46), or to the documented community of Busby's Manchester, the central point holds. Football forged, not just reflected, a sense of place, belonging and identity in an uncertain world, lending a real seriousness of intent and expression to an apparently trivial pursuit (Tomlinson, 1993).

It is important to grasp the enormity of the social and cultural changes underlying the growth of the new industrial society, and the meanings surrounding new cultural institutions such as sport in such a context of change. In Middlesbrough's case, this sort of growth was phenomenal in the nineteenth century and 'no other English town', Asa Briggs records, had a more dramatic growth rate: 'Within the reign of Queen Victoria itself, Middlesbrough grew from a very tiny rural community to a very large town of over one hundred thousand people' (1968: 141). In 1801 Middlesbrough comprised twenty-five inhabitants living in four houses; in 1831 the census recorded 154 inhabitants, and in 1841 5,463 inhabitants were testimony to planned growth around the coal-shipping port. On this basis, and despite its location on a 'turbulent urban frontier' (p. 245), in the 1840s the town's 'first complex of urban institutions' (p. 246) were established. These included a Wesleyan Methodist Chapel, a Primitive Methodist Chapel, a Mechanics' Institute, an Oddfellows' District and school buildings. The demographics of this growth were, as iron and steel became the industrial mainstay of the town in its later phases of growth, predominantly working class and male, and Briggs compares this with Australian demographic history. It was a potent mix, utterly conducive to the flowering of a cultural institution such as football. The legendary Middlesbrough footballer Wilf Mannion emerged as a product of this culture, football his expression of both community identity and the possibility of change. Raised in a quintessentially working-class neighbourhood of the town, and nurtured by football-loving schoolteachers, Mannion became a Golden Boy of the English game. Initially learning his art on the streets and the schoolyards of his childhood – playing with a sixpenny ball, a ragball, a paperball, a pig's bladder, whatever was available – he rose to star in the memorable post-Second World War match in front of 134,000 at Hampden Park, Scotland, when Great Britain beat the Rest of Europe 6–1. One informant to a revealing BBC regional documentary on Mannion could claim, thirty years after the event, 'he was more important to Middlesbrough than any J. Arthur Rank stars' (BBC North East, 1978). Mannion, a modest and in some senses apparently naive man, did not seek the trappings of stardom. But in inter-war Middlesbrough and the immediate post-war period, however reluctantly, a star is what he was.

In the inter-war period English professional football consolidated its place in a male-dominated urban and industrial twentieth-century culture. Women's football had been developed by women workers in munitions factories during the First World War (Williams and Woodhouse, 1991), and by factory and charity teams from both working-class and middle-class backgrounds. Most women players were working class, though, and peacetime conditions and the concomitant return of women to traditional roles and positions of subordination undermined the basis of the women's game. Also, as Hargreaves tellingly states, male organisational power was turned on this development, the FA declaring in 1921 that 'the game of football is quite unsuitable for females and should not be encouraged', so demonstrating 'the power that men had to impede the smooth progress of women's sports and the way in which they did so when the success of the women's game seemed to be threatening the enactment of traditional masculinity' (1994: 142 and 143). Later examples of the development of women's football were determined by regional and class influences, with its impact greater in the middle-class areas of southern England (Bale, 1980), where traditional male prejudice was perhaps less deeply entrenched.

It has been argued that the inter-war years of the twentieth century were a time in which the present character of English football began to be shaped (Wagg, 1984: 21). Wagg points to five elements in this shaping: connections between football and politics; developments in the football-based media event; intensifying commercialisation of the game; the increasing grip of a technicised, expert's view of the game; and the development of the more public visibility of the football manager. Certainly matches became even more prominent public rituals in the life of the urban community and stadia were established as central landmarks in the urban cultural landscape. The stability and poetry of this was captured by J.B. Priestley in his picaresque novel of working-class life and culture *The Good Companions*. In evoking the cultural institutions of his typical West Riding (of Yorkshire) industrial town of Bruddersford he mentions the mills and mill chimneys, the railways, the canals, the lorries, the town hall, the chapel. In the 1920s the Bruddersfords were experiencing economic downturns and some of the mills and factories were already 'like monuments of an age that has vanished' – 'perhaps because fashionable women in Paris and London and New York have cried to one another, "My dear, you can't possibly wear that!" (Priestley, 1976 [1929]: 12–13). But bad trade or not, 'grim and resolute' as Bruddersford looks, on this late September Saturday afternoon its citizens and the town are 'not thinking about the wool trade', and 'the thoroughfare to the west of the town . . . Manchester Road . . . cannot be seen at all. A grey-green tide flows sluggishly down its length. It is a tide of cloth caps' (p. 13). Here Priestley goes on to depict the cultural resonance and impact of professional football in communities such as Bruddersford:

> These caps have just left the ground of the Bruddersford United Association Football Club. Thirty-five thousand men and boys have just seen what most of them call 't'United' play Bolton Wanderers. Many of them should never have been there at all. It would not be difficult to prove by statistics and those mournful little budgets (How a Man May live – or, rather, avoid death – on Thirty-five Shillings a Week) that seem to attract some minds, that these fellows could not afford the entrance fee. When some mills are only working half the week and others not at all, a shilling is a respectable sum of money. It would puzzle an economist to know where all these shillings came from. But if he lived in Bruddersford, though he might wonder where they came from, he would certainly understand why they were produced. To say that these men paid their shillings to watch twenty-two hirelings kick a ball is merely to say that a violin is wood and catgut, that *Hamlet* is so much paper and ink. For a shilling the Bruddersford United A.F.C. offered you Conflict and Art; it turned you into a critic, happy in your judgement of fine points, ready in a second to estimate the worth of a well-judged pass, a run down the touch line, a lightning shot, a clearance by back or goalkeeper; it turned you into a partisan, holding your breath when the ball came sailing into your own goalmouth, ecstatic when your forwards raced away towards the opposite goal, elated, downcast, bitter, triumphant by turns at the fortunes of your side, watching a ball shape Iliads and Odysseys for you; and, what is more, it turned you into a member of a new community, all brothers together for an hour and a half, for not only had you escaped from the clanking machinery of this lesser life, from work, wages, rent, doles, sick pay, insurance cards, nagging wives, ailing children, bad bosses, idle workmen, but you had escaped with most of your mates and your neighbours, with half the town,

and there you were, cheering together, thumping one another on the shoulders, swopping judgements like lords of the earth, having pushed your way through a turnstile into another and altogether more splendid kind of life, hurtling with Conflict and yet passionate and beautiful in its Art. Moreover, it offered you more than a shilling's worth of material for talk during the rest of the week. A man who had missed the last home match of 't'United' had to enter social life on tiptoe in Bruddersford.

(1976 [1929]: 13–14)

The professional game in the inter-war period was a prominent form of working-class cultural expression. As Priestley's paean to its cultural virtues in the 1920s indicates, it was expressive of local identity; it was a vehicle for collective social relationships; it was separate from other spheres of social life; it was compensatory for the bad times; it was generative of interpretive and discursive reflection; it was heavily masculinist; it animated urban life. Most of all, it was culturally important, not just on the periphery of everyday or community life but a focal point of it. Professional sport and the cultural relationships around it had achieved an institutional weight in the new industrial communities that was comparable to other public and collective expressions of that culture such as the trade union, the co-operative movement or the political party – part of what Williams described as the social institutions of a distinctly working-class culture, not as collectively democratic perhaps as the more explicit political forms, but nevertheless an element in what Williams referred to as 'a very remarkable creative achievement' (1963: 314). New sports and leisure forms were integrated elements of an industrial culture: 'In many industrial towns football clubs, brass bands, works outings and church-going were all part of a densely woven culture centring on the local pit or factory', in an 'intermingling of work and pleasure' (Harris, 1993: 139).

One historian of the period has even been tempted to describe 'the football grounds of England' as 'the Labour Party at prayer' (Fishwick, 1989: 150). Fishwick's study of English football from just before the Great War until just after the Second World War traces the growth and consolidation of the game in the national culture. The average crowd at (an English) Football League First Division game in the 1927–28 season was 25,364; the all-time peak of attendance was achieved in the 1949–50 season, 40,702 per game. Throughout the period local elites (often with middle-class entrepreneurial roots) continued to own, organise and administer the sport at its club and league levels, patrician classes continued to administer the game at the level of the overarching body of the Football Association, and the professional players and the crowds comprising the consumers of the professional games continued to be drawn predominantly from the working classes. The junior game, at local amateur level, expanded from 12,000 registered clubs in 1910 to 35,000 in 1937. There were strong philanthropic and reforming motives behind the teaching of and provision for the game at this level. In Sheffield and Oxford co-ordinating bodies for school recreation were set up, and in Sheffield Corporation Physical Training Department's Annual Report of 1928 the belief was expressed that 'manly vigorous play in healthy surroundings [is] the antidote to cramped home and school conditions; is the preventive treatment of ailments', and that recreation could make boys fitter for the industrial life (Fishwick, 1989: 4). Fishwick identifies four driving motives behind the provider's support for sport, recreation and football:

> There was . . . a Chadwickian belief in the economy of spending to prevent ill health; a Corinthian faith in the desirability of the values sport supposedly inculcated; a desire to broaden the recreation of the poor; and a desire to bring parents and teachers together through shared interest in their children's sporting fortunes.
>
> (1989: 4)

Away from the school setting, at the junior level football was 'controlled at the top by a form of middle-class gerontocracy' and 'established on its basis of popular participation and elite control' (pp. 18 and 19). In this, the class dynamics of the junior game replicated those of the professional game.

The professional game was also a crucial contributor to the legitimation of gambling, through the football pools, in which fortunes could be won predicting the outcome of matches (Fishwick, 1989). And the contribution of professional soccer, and the profile of top players, to an expanding sporting press reinforced its prominence in both local and national cultural life (Mason, 1989 and 1990). Players could not realise the full potential of their talent and application – top 'stars like Tommy Lawton saw themselves as inadequately paid professional entertainers', whilst others saw themselves 'as better paid working men' (Fishwick, 1989: 90). In football's increasingly commercialised phase things would change, and Halsey has noted this in the context of fundamental changes in status associated with an increase in the 'affluence and mobility of the working class' which 'provided the material base for new and less dependent status positions'(1986: 58). Halsey cites movie stars and pop stars as examples of such status positions, but most fully develops his point through a commentary on football:

> A history of football heroes would sharply illustrate the point: it would run from Eddie Hapgood of Arsenal and England in the 1930s, with short back and sides, deferential to the manager, Mr Chapman, proud to play for his country, paid the wages of a skilled manual worker, and leaving Wembley or Highbury to return home by bus or train. By the 1970s the archetypal hero had become George Best of Manchester United, idolized

by teenagers, forever flouting the authority of referees and trainers, fre-
quenting boutiques and nightclubs, practising widely publicized sexual
promiscuity, driving a Jaguar, and catching planes to Los Angeles.

(1986: 58–59)

One wonders whether Halsey, from the tranquility of his college rooms, saved
the worst for the last in this list! But his portrait of the game points to a strong
traditional football culture, its culture and heroes not infrequently embodying
regional values (Holt, 1996; Mason, 1996). The professional game continued in
the post-Second World War years in much the same vein as in the
inter-war period. Players continued to have the same identity and status as the
Hapgoods, and at an organisational level the game was confident in itself, arrogant about the rest of the world (Walvin (1975: Chapter 6) has described the inter-
war game as 'the insular game'), and unaware of the impact that the growing
consumer society would have on patterns of leisure and associated sports cultures.

However widely popular the professional game was, not all of the local
population could afford to attend the live professional football match, and not
all were welcome: 'the sport still excluded women and many men despite its
capacity to draw massive crowds' (Davies, 1992: 38). Andrew Davies' pene-
trating work on Salford working-class culture in the first forty years of the
twentieth century demonstrates the sustained importance of the local and neighbourhood base of sport. Based in Salford pubs, teams would compete, and bet a
few pence on their own performance, in games played on waste ground in the
most deprived areas of the city:

these contests aroused passions as strong as any professional encounter.
Mr Lomas described contests between pub teams in the Adelphi:

They used to play football on the (Adelphi) croft for a shilling a man,
which was quite a good sum of money. And they used to play different
pubs. The Adelphi pub would play the Rob Roy or the Olive Branch.
Would anybody watch these games?
Oh yes, it was quite a Sunday afternoon entertainment. The teams had
followers, gangs, and chaps that went in the pub that didn't play football.
They'd come down, twenty or thirty strong ... And they'd all be round the
croft and they used to shout the team on. They'd nothing else to do.
Did they wear a kit in those pub games?
No kit, no studs, they just turned out in the ordinary day clothes.
What would they have on their feet?
Ordinary boots or shoes.

At this level, football was informally organized, and provided a free spectacle.

(Davies, 1992: 38–39)

Davies' researches reveal what Cunningham (1980: 127) has called 'the continuous history of football as a popular sport', his Salford poor playing essentially the same game as had young miners on the wastelands of the West Riding coalfields half a century or more earlier. More organised forms flowered in local amateur leagues, inspired perhaps by the success of professional sides. Crag Road United, of Shipley, won several cups in the Bradford Amateur League of the 1920s. Kitted out in smart, full playing gear and proudly immaculate in its team photo, the side had been 'founded in 1921 by a bunch of lads "wi' nowt to do"', and 'won the support and sponsorship of local publican, George Ricks' (Firth, 1989: caption to photograph 31). The local publican thus assured himself of regular trade and, if the presence of a dozen or so Sunday-suited non-players in the team photograph is anything to go by, some prestige within the local sporting community. At all these different levels, then, football was established as a major leisure pursuit and competitive activity. And by the inter-war years of the twentieth century the professional game had unquestionably taken a strong hold within the working-class urban industrial communities. Several influences disrupted this established – and some would say ossified – culture of the professional game, and ushered in the sixth phase in the game's development. The impact of the car and television on established forms of leisure, culture and consumption can hardly be overestimated (Philips and Tomlinson, 1992). In professional football itself, old constraints on players were removed. Legal action in the famous George Eastham case (see Mason, 1989: 161–162) led to the abolition of the retain and transfer system in 1963. And the maximum wage – which had stood at a maximum of '£8 a week for most of the inter-war years and gradually rose after 1945 to reach £20 per week during the playing season and £17 in the summer by 1961' (p. 160) – was abolished in 1961, after a 'new and publicity-conscious chairman' of the Professional Footballers Association, Jimmy Hill, had 'organised a successful strike ballot' (p. 161). As Polley (1998: 115) puts it: 'social, economic, and cultural changes in the professional sport settings from the 1960s onwards established a new phase of industrial relations'. Stars could now bargain for their market value and in the expanding consumer industries seek forms of sponsorship external to the game; television could offer the game new forms of subsidy, but in return for changes to the format of the game itself. Some of these changes are best captured by looking at the changes in the profile of the top professional player.

Chas Critcher has offered a typology of this changing player-profile in the post-war period, showing the marked contrasts of the modern game with its pre-war form, which 'was an integral part of that corporate working-class culture rooted in the late nineteenth-century' (1979: 161). He offers a typology of four styles of player. The traditional/located player – a post-war version of Halsey's Eddie Hapgood – is typified in the figure of Stanley Matthews, on the basis of his rootedness in the working-class context of his origins, whatever his

transcending talent. Matthews nevertheless became 'the first professional footballer to appear in the New Year's Honours List: on 2 January 1957 he became
a Companion of the British Empire' (Mason, 1990: 159). In 1965 Matthews
became 'Sir Stanley', whilst still playing at the age of 50 – the only football-
playing knight until his contemporary Tom Finney was knighted by New Labour
in January 1998. For a third of a century, from 1932 onwards, Matthews was
a prominent player in English League football, and throughout this time
he 'appeared to represent skill as against force' (Mason, 1990: 160). Bobby
Charlton represents similar playing values, but different social ones – the
transitional/mobile type of player, in Critcher's terms, who, however many
forms of fame or success or celebrity accrue to him, continues to evoke the
image of the working-class gent. Alan Ball, buzzing workhorse of England's
1966 World Cup victory, represents an incorporated/embourgeoised type. The
fourth of Critcher's types – the superstar/dislocated type – is best embodied in
the figure of George Best. A fifth type – rationalised/cosmopolitan perhaps –
might be identified in the well-adjusted successes of soccer millionaires such as
Kevin Keegan, Gerry Francis and Trevor Francis. The key influences on the evolution of such types has been the changing material and economic bases of the
sports and leisure industries, the transformation of the basis of the player's cultural identity, and the relationship of star players to followers of the game.
Mason sees in Keegan 'the arrival of the modern footballer-businessman', the
more well-adjusted side of the status shift that Halsey depicted so pessimis-
tically in his portrait of George Best. Keegan, – a player for Scunthorpe,
Liverpool, Hamburg, Southampton and Newcastle United:

> signed contracts to promote Faberge Toiletries, Harry Fento suits, Mitre
> Sports Goods, Patrick (UK) Ltd., Boots, Nabisco Shredded Wheat and Heinz
> Baked Beans. He formed companies registered in tax havens such as the Isle
> of Man: Kevin Keegan Investments Ltd., Kevin Keegan Enterprises Ltd., and
> Kevin Keegan Sport and Leisure Ltd. He also had a four-year contract with
> BBC Television worth, it was reported, £20,000 . . . more players were
> participating in soccer than ever before and they were buying £23 million
> worth of football boots each year. *Sports Trader* has characterised the 1980s
> as a 'veritable soccer boom'. It was a boom which enabled Bryan Robson
> to sign a contract for £25,000 a year to wear Balance Boots and Gary
> Lineker to endorse a boot for a 3 per cent royalty on sales which, his
> accountant hopes, will net one million pounds. In 1951 Stanley Matthews
> received £20 per week for endorsing football boots made by the CWS.
>
> (Mason, 1989: 163)

As well as changes to the economic infrastructure of the game, public order concerns in the wake first of the prominence of football hooligan subcul-

tures and then tragedies such as those at Bradford, Heysel and Hillsborough in the mid- and late 1980s have also hastened changes, and have led to the seventh distinct phase in the social development of the game. By the early 1990s the Taylor Report (consequent upon the Hillsborough disaster of 1987, in which 96 Liverpool fans died at the FA Cup semi-final game with Nottingham Forest at Sheffield Wednesday's ground (Taylor, 1991)) had led to a reshaping of the physical environment of the sport. Modernised all-seater stadia were demanded of top clubs, and in the summer of 1992 a new Premier League (the top division of the old 104-year-old Football League) broke away from the old league structure. Lucrative deals were immediately struck with Rupert Murdoch's BSkyB network, costing 'BSkyB £304 million over five years (about six times more than the previous arrangement with terrestrial TV)' (Williams, 1994: 384). ITV (Independent Television) had offered £200 million over four years, or £262 million over five years. Evidence suggests that the bidding was not taking place on the most even of playing fields. At the meeting of the Premier League chairmen to consider the offer it was decided to adjourn for half an hour, reading time for the offer. One of the club chairmen, Alan Sugar of Tottenham Hotspur Football Club, did not spend, according to reports (Mullin, Henry and Thorpe, 1992: 3), all of that time reading. Instead, he went to a telephone and rang BSkyB where, reportedly, his telephone call to a Sky contact was 'overheard by Trevor East, executive director of ITV football, the man who had just submitted the ITV bid. Mr Sugar's call 'included details of ITV's new bid. Mr Sugar was said to have ended with the words "Blow them out of the water"' (Mullin, Henry and Thorpe, 1992: 3). Mr Sugar also owned the company Amstrad (derived from 'Alan Michael Sugar Trading), whose satellite discs, it was anticipated, would sell in millions if the most popular game in the country was on satellite rather than universally available television (Tomlinson, 1992: 40).

In the third season of the new Premier League several controversies raised football's profile in the moral discourses of the moment. At Arsenal Football Club the England player Paul Merson admitted to gambling, alcohol and cocaine addictions. The Arsenal manager George Graham was under investigation by the Premier League/FA in the 1994–95 season, for allegedly accepting over a quarter of a million pounds as a gift during the transfer of a Scandinavian player to the club a few years before. Documentation revealed the sum at issue to be in fact more than £400,000. Graham was dismissed from his post in February 1995, still protesting his innocence and declaring that these monies (which he returned to Arsenal, with interest, in the autumn of 1994) were unsolicited gifts from the Norwegian agent at the heart of the transfer deals taking Scandinavian players to English professional clubs. The Newcastle United player Andy Cole was transferred to Manchester United for a controversial new record fee of £7 million. And in January 1995 the French player Eric Cantona (captain of his national side and current player of the year in England, and idol of the Manchester United fans whose club he had inspired to two successive championships) was suspended by his club for the rest of the season, for assaulting a fan who was taunting him after he was dismissed from a Premier League match with Crystal Palace for violent conduct against another player. His memorably acrobatic and athletic attack, kung-fu style with flying feet, upon the fan on the spectator's side of the perimeter fence precipitated an extraordinary depth of response in every niche of the media. It was ironic that at that very time the moral values of traditional English games were being espoused by the Conservative prime minister John Major (Holt and Tomlinson, 1994). His political rival, Labour Party leader Tony Blair, was soon to take the opportunity to make populist milage out of the sports issue. After the Andy Cole transfer, Blair commented on the crisis of the professional game for the smaller clubs,

> often against a background of falling gates and rising costs. The bigger clubs, and the game itself, must not lose sight of their responsibility to the smaller clubs, not just as a breeding ground for new players but as part of the general health of the game, and our cultural heritage. The TV deal struck recently suggests a worrying trend as far as the smaller clubs are concerned.
>
> (In interview with Ian Ridley, *Independent on Sunday*,
> 22 January 1995, p. 8)

This breakaway phase in the history of football might have revitalised the economic fortunes of the top clubs. In the season 1993–94 Manchester United's turnover was £43.8 million, a 74 per cent increase even before the club opened its superstore. In 1994 merchandising at the club generated £14 million income. The sum had been only £2 million in 1990. Arsenal's turnover for 1993–94 was 40 per cent up to £21.4 million, Newcastle's 50 per cent up to £18 million, and that of Tottenham Hotspur at £17.7 million (Haylett, 1995: 38). But, as predicted by some commentators (Tomlinson, 1991; Tomlinson, 1992), it also threatened the very fabric of the national game. In his article in *The Independent* (12 January 1995, p. 38) Haylett also cited Gerry Boon, of Touche Ross accountants: 'Manchester United has always been a very powerful brand name, and now they have the people there able to convert that into good profits which are then ploughed back into the club.' This enabled Manchester United to inflate the transfer market on 10 January 1995 in the club's swoop for Newcastle's Cole.

By the middle of the 1990s football embodied the central features of a modern high-profile sport, as much a mediated spectacle and vehicle for insatiable consumerism as a forum for physical pleasures, cultural affiliation and playful creativity. New breeds of entrepreneur had moved into the game, making fortunes in share and property deals as top clubs became public limited companies, and the football business expanded to meet the needs of shareholders and accountants rather than members and administrators (Conn, 1997). At the end of the 1997–98 season Premier League chairmen voted against the introduction of pay-per-view coverage on Murdoch's Sky Sports operation. Their motives were less likely to be with issues of universal access than with bargaining strategies for clinching the best economic package. The people's game had become a lucrative global commodity (Sugden and Tomlinson, 1998: Chapter 4), and the Premier chairmen were clearly not prepared to sell themselves short in the global market-place.

Cricket

Cricket's development has been traced, by Brookes, across five phases (1978: 7). These are the pre-1660 folk game; a period of aristocratic patronage of the game; the prominence of the professional XIs in the mid-nineteenth century; the rise and dominance of amateurism as the basis for the game; and the commercial and business years, which Brookes takes up to the mid-1970s, on the brink of the years of the widespread influence of the Australian magnate Kerry Packer's World Series Cricket initiative. A sixth phase can be added: one of intensifying spectacularisation and commodification of the cricket product, especially in its televised form. Williams comments: 'Throughout the twentieth century cricket has been inseparably intertwined with the class system and its history does much to make clear the changing nuances of social relationships within Britain' (1989: 116). The same can be seen to be true of the longer term history of the game. In this case study – particularly as more modern phases in the history of the game will feature in some of the specific themes covered in later chapters, but also because 'by 1840 it had more or less crystallized into the form into which it is still being played today' (Sandiford, 1994: 1) – it is the earlier phases of the game that are concentrated upon.

The first two phases in the game's development must be understood in the context of the social class dynamics of a changing society, and the inherent game form would evolve in tandem with the sorts of social changes discussed at the beginning of the chapter. Brookes summarises the three main sorts of folk games prominent in the society of the early seventeenth century (1978: Chapter 2). First, a collective team game involved players on the move (using hands, feet or an instrument such as a stick to control the ball) seeking to score by hitting the ball towards a goal. Second, direct competition between individuals involved a stationary player hitting the ball away from the body with an implement, and using the strokes to direct the body towards a hole or across a course. Third, a team game involving co-operation, with one side pitching its individuals against the collective opponents: in this form, a stationary player struck a ball or piece of wood away from his or her person, and registered scores by running between two or more fixed points. Cricket in its folk form was this sort of game, along with stoolball, tip-cat, trap-ball and cat and dog. Football, as we have seen, exemplified the first type. Golf, as we shall see, was an example of the second type.

The folk form of cricket was a relatively unorganised form, fluid in form and therefore difficult to police, and played by the popular classes and the peasantry in the typically unstructured and varied ways. Cricket's second phase is really a story of appropriation of the popular recreational form by the aristocracy. Brookes identifies 'four main reasons why the aristocracy patronized and played the game' (1978: 38). The first reason was, by mixing with a wide range of people through the game, to impose or at least reassert local authority over the people living on the landowner's estates. A second reason was social, with cricket providing the opportunity to reaffirm or establish friendship networks. The way that Brookes describes it, the cricket match was a gossip shop and a plotting cabal as well as a game. Third, the aristocracy could sustain a public declaration of personal rivalries safely, without the risks of duelling. Finally, it was a cultural form and ritual ideally suited to the lifestyle of a powerful and privileged leisure class, providing 'a source of entertainment, exercise and excitement for a group of people who possessed almost infinite amounts of time and money to devote to the cause of leisure' (Brookes, 1978: 40). The implications of the aristocracy's involvement in the game were profound. Matches became organised in more elaborate forms, it was recognised that rules needed to be standardised, and the rivalries between individual aristocrats bred the game's first professionals, and the consequent improvement in playing levels (Brookes, 1978: 45). In this phase of the game two forms of organisation predominated: country house cricket and London-based matches among the aristocracy, and local village contests involving the gentry, shopkeepers and craftsmen as well as the aristocracy. Sir Horatio Mann, Member of Parliament for Sandwich for thirty-three years and extensive landowner in Kent, was the quintessential aristocratic patron of the game. His 1814 obituary in *The Gentlemen's Magazine* emphasised the importance of leisure in a life 'rather dedicated to pleasure than to business . . . he was much attached to gymnastic exercise, especially cricket' (Brookes, 1978: 46). By the plate depicting this man of leisure in post-hunt repose, Brookes reports on his reputation as 'agreeable, gay and affable', noting too that 'he once staged a match in which both teams played on horseback' (1978: plate opposite p. 114). In those forms of cricket involving groups from across the community it was 'the bond of communal sympathy which motivated both players and spectators' (Brookes, 1978: 53). The famous Hambledon Club represented this form of the game. In the 1770s crowds of 20,000 would watch the team, costs for players could be covered, and 'bonds of birth and residence' (Brookes, 1978: 60) provided the framework for the club's prosperity. The Marylebone Cricket Club (MCC), formed in 1787, was to surpass the influence of the Hambledon club and help usher cricket into the emerging industrial society. In the nineteenth century cricket was remoulded under the influence of the middle classes and the working classes. From the turn of the century and up to the middle of the nineteenth century cricket was remade, from 'an aristocratic diversion . . . on the way to becoming a sport, an occupation and a career' (Brookes, 1978: 83).

League, club and county cricket had established a sound foundation and organisation in England by the last quarter of the nineteenth century, but the

> vast bulk of first-class cricket during 1845–70 had been provided by the great All England and United professional touring teams, led by William Clarke, George Parr, the Lillywhites and John Wisden, who popularized cricket by taking it virtually to every nook and cranny of the kingdom.
> (Sandiford, 1994: 58)

Clarke had formed the first all-England XI in 1846 and, helped by the new transport infrastructure of railways and communications infrastructure of popular media, established a successful initiative which was continued by his successors and which 'demonstrated that there was an almost insatiable demand for cricket of high quality and generally showed how that demand could be met' (Sandiford, 1994: 59). The impact of the professional XIs was undeniable, but they were in effect a travelling circus and, as Brookes succinctly puts it, they 'lacked all but the vaguest geographical identity about which supporters could rally' (1978: 116), and the XIs' strength meant that the matches were inherently uncompetitive. In the 1860s and the 1870s public school, university, North vs. South, Gentlemen vs. Players and inter-county games (Sandiford, 1994: 59) captured centre stage in the unfolding drama of cricket's contribution to Victorian culture. The county game became the essence of English elite cricketing culture, W.G. Grace its personification.

County cricket grew in 'haphazard fashion', as Sandiford puts it, but by 1873 nine counties played in the first-class competition: Derbyshire, Gloucestershire, Kent, Lancashire, Middlesex, Nottinghamshire, Surrey, Sussex and Yorkshire. Five further counties – Derbyshire, Essex, Hampshire, Leicestershire and Warwickshire – joined in 1895, and Worcestershire joined in the last year of the century. 'The sporting press . . . played the leading role in determining the champion county' (Sandiford, 1994: 60) by logging performances, and also catapulted W.G. Grace into the centre of the celebrity culture of the time.

Grace, with his 'modern scientific batsmanship . . . did much to modernize cricket during the 1870s' (Sandiford, 1994: 130 and 131). Grace dominated the sporting press, doing 'most to transform Victorian cricket into a full-scale spectator entertainment' (Sandiford, 1994: 131). He was also renowned for his gamesmanship, and for his manipulation (despite his avowedly amateur status) of every commercial opportunity – Midwinter (1981: 156) estimates that Grace pocketed an income equivalent to a million pounds in 1980s values. Early women's cricketing initiatives were frowned upon by Grace, who (drawing somewhat dubiously perhaps upon his professional medical background) pronounced women as 'not constitutionally adapted to the sport' (Sandiford. 1994: 46). Just as his middle-class status placed Grace in a bridging position between upper class and lower class adherents to cricket (Midwinter, 1981: 9), so it allowed him to bend the codes of amateurism in what were really ungentlemanly and rather professional practices – 'his attempts practically to instruct umpires in their duties bordered on the unfair and the autocratic' (Midwinter, 1981: 157). But whatever these failings – or perhaps aided by them – his achievements in first-class cricket, mostly for his county, Gloucestershire, were legion and fabled: 54,896 runs and 2,876 wickets. In one eight-day spell in August of 1876 his feats led one journalist of *The Saturday Review* to conclude that he was 'wholly indifferent to atmospheric influences' (Midwinter, 1981: 61). Throughout all this he sustained his medical career.

Cricket was seen as contributing to health by strengthening physique, but was also seen as valuable for producing mental alertness and spiritual adequacy (Sandiford, 1994: 171). It shared the core values of the ideology of athleticism. Grace's career and impact show both the centrality of that ideology in the formative phase of development of one of England's major sports, and the rhetoric and hypocrisy at its core. These latter were to persist right through the first three-quarters of the twentieth century, until what became known as the 'Packer Revolution' effectively challenged the old order, when the cream of English cricketing talent ignored appeals to traditional loyalties and joined Australians, South Africans, Indians, Pakistanis, West Indians and New Zealanders in the Australian media magnate Kerry Packer's World Series Cricket initiative. It had not been until 1953 that the England cricketing side was captained by a professional, the Yorkshire player Len Hutton, and some traditional inequalities persisted still later, such as separate entrances for amateurs and professionals, and different ways of listing their names. It was not until 1963 that the MCC abolished the distinction between (amateur) gentlemen and (professional) players.

Asked in June 1993 what the legacy of Packer's late 1970s initiative was for cricket in general and cricketers in particular, the English wicketkeeper-batsman and Packer recruit Alan Knott was in no doubt about its benefits:

> It was the best thing that ever happened to cricket. It gave the player a different position in terms of respect as well as being financially better off. The game has gone forward regarding TV coverage; fitness is far more important; and it showed the appeal of one-day cricket. Over here the administrators are trying to kill one-day cricket which is ridiculous. I can

see one-day cricket becoming the major world game; if you travel the world, people don't go to Test Matches but they flock to one-day cricket.

(Luckes, 1994: 151)

Interviewed in January 1993 another WSC recruit, former England fast bowler John Snow, commented how the world's top players from the West Indies, Australia and England

were frustrated by the workings and attitudes of those running the game and were quite happy to go to Packer in order to change the game. It was like coming up against a brick wall all the time . . . the dead wood needed to be cut out . . . Something had to shake the game up, Packer went in in a commercial way and why not – if someone comes with a lot of money you don't tell him to bugger off: you see what he can do for you and you for him.

(Luckes, 1994: 155)

Ironically, the great amateur W.G. Grace's actions – if not his expressed principles – concurred with such a philosophy.

Without doubt, though, and after a century's stability in English cricket, the Packer intervention heralded a new phase in which it became clear that 'social standing and a sense of heritage' were 'ill-equipped to resist a concerted and determined assault by an entrepreneur backed by the crucial factor of commercial funding' (Luckes, 1994: 1). Sponsorship of tournaments and individual players, and new television deals with broadcasters such as Sky Sports, heralded the new age of the cricketing product, with rule changes designed to produce exciting spectacles, sometimes played under floodlights by sides clad in colourful costumes rather than the traditional all-white kit.

Golf

The origins of the modern form of golf (rather than of golf *per se*) can be identified in its folk-game form in Scotland, and a second phase in which the sport became more organised, codified and institutionalised. A third phase in its development is its growth within the context of the expansion of modern suburban Britain, as a sporting element in the expanding leisure cultures of the middle classes. The amateur–professional dynamic in golf revealed the social class dimensions that have had and continue to have such a widespread influence on the formation of modern sports. In the same way that high-profile team games were affected by processes of commercialisation linked to professionalisation, golf in the second half of the twentieth century continued to grow within the context of the expanding sports industries. In this vignette of the sport's development we concentrate upon the phase of the game's expansion in England.

It has been commented that the story of the growth of golf is one of expanding opportunities, that in the light of the success of figures such as Tony Jacklin 'a boy [*sic*] with great potential can break through in any circumstances . . . nowadays any keen boy [*sic*] can learn golf in an organised way, can receive help in equipping himself, and be encouraged by school authorities and county unions' (Cousins, 1975: 146 and 148). A more rigorous review of the social historical development and sociological and cultural profile of golf is not commensurate with Cousins' interpretation, and a more critically informed appreciation of its history and contemporary form shed light not just on sports history, but upon, as John Lowerson so insightfully puts it,

> a number of major strands in modern British society – the tension between spare time and active recreation, the frequent confusion between the idea of a game and the assumptions of a sport, and the parallel strands of exclusiveness and extension which the development of sophisticated signs of social class has necessitated.
>
> (1989: 187)

Golf's Scottish pedigree has been acclaimed by some cultural historians, and more recently disputed by dispassionate historians (Lowerson, 1994). Whether or not the roots of the game stem from Scotland or the Netherlands or elsewhere, its impact in late nineteenth-century England was remarkable. The suburban roots of golf have indicated its importance as an expression of the public culture of a newly suburbanised middle-class community. Lowerson captures the scale of the game's impact between the middle of the nineteenth century and the First World War: 'England boasted one ancient club, the Blackheath, at mid-century, possibly a dozen by the 1870s: but by 1914 there were almost 1200 clubs playing over 1000 courses' (1993: 125). This English sporting boom had very precise social nuances, for 'golf became *par excellence* a fine instrument of social differentiation' (p. 126). Case studies can flesh out the skeletal outlines of the general trends, and Richard Holt has provided just such a case study of the Stanmore Golf Club, in the northern suburb of England.

The Stanmore club was founded in 1893 by a member of the Gordon family (owners of the world's largest hotel chain) and the Blackwell half of the Crosse and Blackwell entrepreneurial partnership. Gordon had built his own railway link to the golf course and had the course laid out for family fun. A number of golf courses were laid out in Middlesex in the preceding and succeeding years, so that by 1907 *Golfing Year* listed the number of clubs in the county as 51 (though only 17 of these had their own courses). The boom in both

Scotland and England was, according to Lowerson, 'triggered' by the anxieties of the middle classes:

> Newer sections of the middle class found themselves sufficiently affluent, with disposable time and income, but insufficiently secure socially. They sought healthy, ethically acceptable recreations which would strengthen their class perceptions, provide attainable targets for aspiration and control over those with whom they wished to mix. With their selection procedures, and the possibility of blackballing for exclusion, golf clubs fitted the moment admirably.
>
> (1994: 80)

Holt describes the simple pleasures of the golf club:

> Pleasure and competition, companionship and rivalry, striving against others and the private contest with the course itself . . . Golf clubs provide an interlude and a space between office and home, work and family . . . a cheerful and comfortable place to be . . . a busy place, a social and sporting centre for a thriving new suburban community.
>
> (1993: 9 and 35)

In the early years of the twentieth century the Stanmore club had 400 members, never closed and allowed Sunday play – in line with the views of the Scot Balfour but not Lloyd George, with his 'Welsh non-conformist constituency to think of' (Holt, 1993: 35). Women's involvement in the club was encouraged, initially along separatist lines in the form of the Ladies Club, which made up a third of the club's overall membership before the First World War. One day of the week – Tuesday – was specified as the competition day for the Ladies Club, and the Ladies Golf Union, dating from 1893 too, appointed handicap managers so that equanimity of competition was assured from the beginning. However middle class and, in terms of core members, single-woman based, the impact of the Ladies Clubs and their counterparts across the land should not be underestimated:

> The Stanmore Ladies were part of a pioneer movement for women's sport which developed in the girls' public schools with hockey or gym and spread into the suburbs through the tennis club – conveniently attached to the Club in Stanmore's case – and the golf course.
>
> (Holt, 1993: 90)

Striking images of this pioneering yet privileged women's sporting involvement persisted through to the immediate post-Second World War period, when the legendary American Babe Zaharias (double Olympic gold medallist in track and field in Los Angeles in 1934) beat Stanmore Ladies member Jacqueline Gordon in the 1947 final of the British Open at Muirfield. Gordon, scion of the founding family of the club, made a lasting impression upon one contemporary commentator, arriving 'for the British Girls' dressed in silk stockings and white, buckskin shoes – all from Bond Street' (Holt, 1993: 99). Middle-class women actually had less access to the club than did non-middle class males. Even school*teaching* was not enough, in 1932, to be approved as a member. In that year, applications for membership were received and rejected from a labourer, a railway clerk and a schoolteacher – you could join as a full member, though, if you were a *graduate* school*master*. Those denied full membership could aspire to play in the Artisan's Club, set up at Stanmore in the 1920s. In 1928 this had forty members, and a small building to the side of the main clubhouse. The inequalities of English society were vividly expressed in the microcosm of the suburban golf club. The 'artisan' members were tolerated for as long as they knew their place, but by 1964 their status could be questioned by a Committee member asking 'what contribution the Artisans made to the club in view of the fact that there seems to be a certain amount of affluence in the Artisan section in the shape of cars?' (Holt, 1993: 116). By the early 1970s the Artisan Club had been discontinued. The Club was no longer willing to subsidise it, and the less well-off were to lose their opportunity for 'cheap golf'.

In the last quarter of the twentieth century professional golf developed as a major spectator sport and advertising medium, linked to 'high levels of commercial sponsorship' (Lowerson, 1989: 211). Sponsorship was not new. Equipment manufacturers had for a long time sponsored the professional, alert to the benefits that would accrue from the association of their products with top performers. The Master's tournament in America had been sponsored by Dunlop from 1946–1972. But the entry of tobacco and drink companies into the sponsorship game, coupled with increasingly sophisticated marketing and television opportunities, moved golf into the sphere of high-profile consumer leisure and media industries.

On the participation front it could be argued that in the age of affluence, noticed by the Stanmore member applying the powers of observation to the club car-park, the barriers of exclusion were being challenged: figures from the Golf Foundation suggested that from 1954 to 1963 there was a rise in active golfers in Britain from 450,000 to 750,000, with a situation close to saturation in some areas (Nicholls and Massey, 1972). Evidence from the 1970s shows conclusively, though, that the increase in participation was not evenly spread throughout different social groups. An on-site survey of 1000 golfers in the summer of 1974, balancing public and private courses and regions in the sample (739 interviews in England, 220 in Scotland and 41 in Wales) revealed that 83 per cent of golfers were male, 81 per cent were married and their average age was 43. And 'the higher social classes were disproportionately represented: 47% of golfers were of classes AB, 29% of class C1 and only 24% of classes C2 DE' (MEW, 1975). The male domination of golf also showed clearly in research on golf in England's northern region in the 1970s (Northern Council for Sport and Recreation, 1977); the same report also identified the main areas in need of further provision as the heavily urban and industrial areas of Middlesbrough, Sunderland and Newcastle.

Golf provided a public – if exclusive and self-selecting – culture in newly constructed social settings. In many ways golf in middle-class suburbs can be claimed to have been generative of and not merely reflective of its social context. John Bale has noted that sport's development beyond its folk-game origins 'had a number of effects upon the landscape. In some central areas of cities and in some suburbs it is fair to say that sport has been the dominant factor influencing the character and shape of the landscape' (1989: 173). Certainly the prominence of football stadia, cricket grounds and golf courses in the contemporary English landscape bears witness to this perceptive evaluation of the influential impact of modern sports upon the landscapes of recent and contemporary everyday culture. Golf also developed as an attractive sport for potential sponsors, in its televisual presentation of global superstars playing in beautiful outdoor settings, watched live and on screen by affluent consumers. Early sponsors emphasised the place of their product in a game of the elite, in the case of the Dunlop Masters tournament, which ran from 1946 to 1972. Cigarette manufacturers – banned from television advertising – soon followed the cricket example, with Silk Cut sponsoring the event from 1973 to 1978, and Dunhills from 1979 onwards (Polley, 1998: 75).

Modern sport: the nature of contemporary sports culture and the social influences upon it

We have seen how several mainstream sports can be analysed in terms of shifts and continuities in the social context in which they have emerged, prospered or declined. Their fate has been determined by essentially material social and economic factors, and the human cultural response to those influences. The pull between the past traditional practice and the novelty or the necessities of the present has often been a tense dynamic, a feature far from exclusive to sports. The whole period of the last third of the nineteenth century and the decade and a half up to the Great War has been characterised as a volatile one. Changes and collapses, as Harris has put it, were widespread across social institutions and cultures, with 'many countervailing pressures of locality and custom', and 'in the last resort patterns of employment, settlement, taste, consumption and value were all subordinate to the pursuit of "comparative advantage"' (1993: 5).

Britain's free trade policy allowed home producers no protection against American wheat and this led to the 'consequent collapse of archaic rural communities, an explosion of migration to great cities, a rapid rise in living standards for those in secure employment, and an invisible revolution in the structure of class power' (Harris, 1993: 5). These processes constituted the infra-structural base of the society in which the parameters of modern sport were set. Harris goes on to depict the material and the mental pressures and contradictions of this society in the making, which she sees as exhibiting 'a certain latent in-stability' characteristic of the industrial world. In this society 'change was a norm of life in a way that had not been true in past ages' (1993: 5). New forms of sport could both reflect that change and offer sources of cultural identity that might calm the seas of such tempestuous changes.

The making of modern sports has, too, been a predominantly masculinist narrative, with women marginalised or disenfranchised at most stages of the narrative. We have reconstructed the developmental histories of what became the dominant forms, recognising too the experiences of women when these were integrated in or contiguous to that dominant form, as in golf, or were threaten-ing to and opposed by men, as in football. Women's involvement in cricket, too, was margimalised early on, and Sandiford notes that cricket was seen as too much a 'manly sport' even for the tennis and hockey playing women students at the Universities of Cambridge and Oxford in the late nineteenth century (1994: 44). It was not until 1926 that the British Women's Cricket Association was founded, by hockey and lacrosse players from Malvern College (Hargreaves, 1994: 123). It thrived speedily, in the institutionalised context of schools, colleges, universities and clubs, away from the more public face of cricket, which remained 'a traditional bastion of male chauvinism' (Hargreaves, 1994: 123). Evidence of *some* cricketing initiatives among women in working-class areas, or of informal cricketing games between young boys and girls, remains evidence of a marginalised and widely scorned activity. Even in 1993, when the English women's cricketing team became World Champions – at precisely the time when the English men's team was plummeting towards new lows of per-formance in international competition – press coverage of this tremendous achievement was tinged with a patriarchal hue. The persistence of such situa-tions is explored in more ethnographic detail in Chapter 4.

The major English sports have developed as male-dominated activities, and most female involvement in those traditional sports forms has been in middle-class sports such as golf and tennis. A balanced social history must recognise the dominance of the male form and the persistence of the male-dominated sports culture that was established in key formative phases in the growth of sport.

It is also important to recognise that those dominant forms have not appeared overnight, sweeping lived cultures aside and striding forward unopposed. Cultures are more complex, stubborn and sturdy than that. Social change and cultural development intermingle in varied and complex ways. Robert Graves, when he moved into the Oxfordshire village of Islip in the late summer of 1921, encountered and lived out some of these complexities:

> Every Saturday during the winter months I played football for the village team. We ex-soldiers reintroduced the game at Islip after a lapse of some eighty years. The village nonagenarian complained that football was not so manly now as in his boyhood. He pointed across the fields to a couple of aged willow trees: 'Them used to be our home goals,' he said. 'T'other pair stood half a mile upstream. Constable stopped our play in the end. Three men were killed in the last game – one kicked to death; t'other two drowned each other in a scrimmage. Her was a grand game.' I found Islip football, though not unmanly, ladylike by comparison with the Charterhouse game. When playing centre-forward, I often got booed for charging the goalkeeper as he fumbled with the shot he had saved. The cheers were reserved for my inside-left, who spent most of his time stylishly dribbling the ball in circles round and round the field until robbed of it; he seldom went anywhere near the goal. But the football club was democratic, unlike the cricket club. I played cricket the first season, but resigned because the team seldom consisted of the best eleven men available; regular players would be dropped to make room for visiting gentry.
>
> (1960 [1929]: 255)

Here in this social exchange between the rural local and the academic and chronicler of the Great War several codes of football are referred to: the popular recreation of the 1840s, the public school code in which Graves was versed (with some reluctance) in the years preceding the First World War, and the more modern game reintroduced by the soldiers in the Oxfordshire village, not so physically assertive it seems, and stressing personal skills.

Harris has observed that as a consequence of economic and financial changes at the turn of the century,

> British society was having to adapt to new forms of economic life and thought, long before it had fully absorbed the social consequences of industrial change and agricultural decline. One result was increasingly a society in which rootlessness was endemic and in which people felt themselves to be living in many different layers of historic time.
>
> (1993: 5)

Harris cites a Surrey villager's observation of 1912:

city commuters and weekenders who formed the fashionable advance guard of the metropolitan England of George V were living cheek by jowl with cottagers who were scraping a living from residual common land, and whose way of life and mental horizons had changed very little since the reign of George III.

(1993: 5)

This was to produce a turbulent and at times bemusing cultural mix, as Graves' football reminiscence testifies. Social change does not take place overnight, with neat beginnings and ends or smooth transitions. Professional forms of competitive activity had well-established and deep cultural foundations by the middle of the twentieth century. Yet fans of top professional football could still, in the late 1950s and early 1960s, receive a set of rules on becoming a life-member of Charles Buchan's Boys' Club which echoed the mission of the public schools and the philosophy of amateurism. The 'Rules' for membership of this club were:

1   to improve your skill to the best of your ability;
2   to support your team in good times and bad;
3   to play the game as a true sportsman;
4   to be modest in victory and cheerful in defeat.

In a time a third of a century on when the basis of affiliation is television sport and Premier League merchandise, this set of rules seems quaint and rather innocent, yet it also represents a central paradox that has run through the social history of sport in the modern period – the tension between, on the one hand, the amateurist model of participation based, at its peak, in apparently effortless excellence and, on the other, the professional model of hard work, professionalism and winning as the priority.

This is a reminder that sport's place and meaning in everyday life is negotiable and is culturally created, not simply socially imposed. The working through of social and cultural change is a complex and uneven process. In this sense, any socio-historical periodisation of phases in the growth of sports is vulnerable to the criticism that it simplifies social and cultural realities. But without any such periodisation the history of sport risks becoming what has been called a Book of Genesis version of history (Tomlinson, 1984) or an internal inventory of the features of a particular sport (Hall, 1986). Both of those methodological warnings are reminders that the deeper meanings of a sport cannot be found outside of an understanding of the relationship of a sport to its society. This is not to say that a sport is merely the reflection of a society; rather that sport has social meanings and, despite senses in which it can be seen as relatively autonomous (Hargreaves, 1986; Gruneau, 1983), is in itself a social product.

Social historians, sociologists and cultural researchers are united on this final point, and the analysis of the tensions between the social determinants of sport and its cultural location and context are the recurrent themes of researchers in the field. In this chapter we have focused upon just four case studies to exemplify and explore selected themes. A wider sample of case studies would identify comparable interpretive themes. In Mason's very valuable collection (1989) the contributors were asked to concentrate on the themes of competition, physical activity and spectacle in examining ten sports, and to 'give some idea' of each sport's 'origins, the power structure within it, the relationship between the participatory mass and the spectacularly eminent' (1989: 9). Though looking specifically at British sports, contributors were also encouraged to consider gender, Gaelic and global aspects of the case studies. Extracting major themes from the case studies as a whole confirms the centrality of a number of themes to the sociological and cultural analysis of modern sport:

- A decline in live attendance levels in the later twentieth century.
- An intensification of commercialism in sport, in close connection with professionalisation.
- An increasingly sophisticated technological base to sport, affecting sport as a mode of production.
- A rise in individualism in sport (in squash and running, for instance) constituting a new mode of consumption articulated around fashion and narcissism.
- The explosion of media sport – television-made events impacting upon established sports phenomena such as national leagues and, more globally, the football World Cup and the Olympic Games.
- The competition to sport of emerging alternative modes and forms of leisure consumption.
- Moral and political debates about the significance of sport and popular culture.
- The contestation of space, and the aspiration to and desire to acquire or provide space for new types of cultural expression.
- Americanisation and its impact upon more localised and traditional sports cultures.
- The gendered nature of sports – sport as an element within more general forms of male domination, but simultaneously a focus for women's challenge to established forms of male dominance.
- The reluctance to excel – in traditional British sports, a wariness about producing top-quality players in the professionalised and increasingly globalised sports arena.
- The invisibility or marginalisation of race within sports cultures.

Any broad trend data on participation rates in sport need to be understood and interpreted in the light of these twelve themes. One overview of survey data on participation (Minten and Roberts, 1989: 318), drawing from the General House-hold Survey, identifies some changes in participation in the 1970s and 1980s – a swing towards more indoor leisure and sports activity, for instance, and some increase in overall participation. But long-established differences in and con-straints upon participation have persisted. The data on indoor sport activity showed that from 1977 through to 1986 the rate of increase was slightly higher for women than for men, but that nevertheless 'only 37 percent of females par-ticipated in indoor or outdoor sport compared with 57% of males' (Minten and Roberts, 1989: 318). Socio-economic groups exhibited great variations in participation, rates being 'higher among non-manual than manual workers, with professional workers having the highest, and semi-skilled and unskilled manual workers the lowest overall participation rates' (ibid.). Some sports broke with this pattern: football, snooker and darts had higher participation rates among lower non-manual grades and manual grades. Age was also identified as a critical variable affecting participation, rates being highest among 16–19 year olds and then declining – apart from walking, squash, bowls, golf and keep fit/yoga – with age. The Allied Dunbar Fitness Survey carried out in 1990 also identified age as critical. The survey attributes the label 'Activity Level 0' to those who did no activity of 20 minutes' duration in the previous four weeks and noted that 'activity declines markedly with increasing age – less than 10% of 16–24 year olds were in Activity Level 0 compared to 40% of 65–74 year olds' (Allied Dunbar, 1991: 6). Minten and Roberts could conclude at the end of the 1980s that 'the inequalities in sports participation associated with age and socio-economic status in Britain remain as wide as ever' (1989: 319). Patterns of participation as evident in the General Household Survey data available from the early 1990s were similar to those identified for the 1980s, and these are reported more fully as a prelude to further discussion of inequalities and power in Chapter 4.

At the level of high-profile and top-level competitive sport the last third of the twentieth century has seen some radical changes. Whannel has argued that this has amounted to 'a period of transformation which constitutes a remaking of British sport' (1986: 129). The key influences in this remaking have been television and sponsorship, between them producing a 'cultural transformation' when 'the traditional amateur, benevolent paternalism of sport's organisation came under pressure from entrepreneurial interests as the contradiction between sport's financially deprived organisations and its commercial potential widened' (Whannel, 1986: 130). The characteristics and contours of this transformation have been signalled in the case studies in this chapter, and are examined in more detail in later chapters. Two points are worthy of note, though, at the end of this review. First, Whannel's emphasis on the idea of transformation reminds us of the essential features of the traditional organisations of sport: undemocratic, elitist in class and gender terms, yet dedicated often in a voluntarist way to service and resource distribution. Second, a thrusting entrepreneurialism brought more money into sport and released its meritocratic and democratic potential. But this was to focus resources more exclusively at the elite level. Thus were the fears of the nineteenth-century paternalist defendants of amateurism borne out. And thus is shown the importance of the understanding of history, for the crises and contradictions in late twentieth-century English sport have deep roots in a complex social and cultural history.

ESSAYS AND EXERCISES

Essays

'The amateur and professional dynamic in the formative phase of modern sports was an expression of class power and class rivalry.' Discuss.

Taking one sport of your choice, consider the ways in which its post-Second World War history has been shaped by new economic forces.

Discuss the changing status of the sports 'star' during the second half of the twentieth century.

Exercises

Talk to three of your colleagues/peers from different sports specialisms and ask them to summarise their view on the *social* values of sport. Do these vary from sport to sport? Are there echoes of old debates in the responses?

Interview a sports administrator of the sport in which you are most involved and consider whether he or she represents the trend towards entrepreneurial rather than patrician forms of provision of and involvement in sport.

Consult some of the main sources on sports participation (for example, the General Household Survey and the annual Social Trends in which different sources are summarised) and consider why, in terms of participation, an activity of such minority significance has such a high profile.

FURTHER READING

T. Mason (ed.), *Sport in Britain – A Social History*, Cambridge, Cambridge University Press, 1989, provides lucid and informed accounts of the social history of Britain's most prominent sports.

Richard Holt, *Sport and the British – A Modern History*, Oxford, Oxford University Press, 1989, is an elegant, scholarly and accessible account of the influences upon and the context of the growth of sports in modern industrial Britain.

References

Allied Dunbar (1991) *Allied Dunbar National Fitness Survey – A Summary of the Major Findings and messages from the Allied Dunbar National Fitness Survey*, London: Allied Dunbar/Health Education Authority/Sports Council, undated but probably 1991.

Bailey, P. (1978) *Leisure and Class in Victorian England – Rational Recreation and the Contest for Control 1830–1885*, London: Routledge & Kegan Paul.

Bale, J. (1980) 'Women's Football in England and Wales: A Social-Geographic Perspective', *Physical Education Review*, Volume 3, pp. 137–145.

Bale, J. (1989) *Sports Geography*, London: E & FN Spon.

Bannister, F. (1922) *The Annals of Trawden Forest*, Colne: R. Hyde and Sons/*Colne and Nelson Times* Office.

BBC Radio 4 (1998) *Analysis* (presented by David Walker), 1 June.

BBC Television North East (1978) *Wilf Mannion*, written and produced by John Mappledeck, BBC Productions.

Brailsford, D. (1991) *Sport, Time and Society – The British at Play*, London and New York: Routledge.

Brailsford, D. (1992) *British Sport – A Social History*, Cambridge: The Lutterworth Press.

Briggs, A. (1968) *Victorian Cities*, Harmondsworth: Penguin Books.

Brookes, C. (1978) *English Cricket – The Game and its Players through the Ages*, London: Weidenfeld and Nicolson.

Channel 4 (1986) *Take the Money and Run*, in *Open the Box* series, Programme Researcher Garry Whannel, Producer Michael Jackson, Director Mike Dibb, Beat Productions and BFI Education for Channel 4, Channel 4 Television Co., Ltd, broadcast 2 June.

Conn, D. (1997) *The Football Business: Fair Game in the 1990s?*, Edinburgh: Mainstream Publishing.

Cousins, G. (1975) *Golf in Britain – A Social History from the Beginnings to the Present Day*, London: Routledge & Kegan Paul.

Critcher, C. (1979) 'Football Since the War', in J. Clarke, C. Critcher and R. Johnson (eds), *Working Class Culture – Studies in History and Theory*, London: Hutchinson.

Crump, J. (1989) 'Athletics', in T. Mason (ed.), *Sport in Britain – A Social History*, Cambridge: Cambridge University Press.

Cunningham, H. (1980) *Leisure in the Industrial Revolution c. 1780–c. 1880*, London: Croom Helm.

Davies, A. (1992) *Leisure, Gender and Poverty – Working-class Culture in Salford and Manchester, 1900–1939*, Buckingham: Open University Press.

Delves, A. (1981) 'Popular Recreation and Social Conflict in Derby, 1800–1850', in E. and S. Yeo (eds), *Popular Culture and Class Conflict 1590–1914: Explorations in the History of Labour and Leisure*, Brighton: Harvester.

Downes, S. and Mackay, D. (1996) *Running Scared – How Athletics Lost Its Innocence,* Edinburgh: Mainstream Publishing.

Dunning, E. and Sheard, K. (1979) *Barbarians, Gentlemen and Players: A Sociological Study of the Development of Rugby Football*, New York: New York University Press.

Dunphy, E. (1991) *A Strange Kind of Glory – Sir Matt Busby and Manchester United*, London: Heinemann.

Firth, G. (1989) *Victorian Yorkshire At Play – A Pictorial History of Yorkshire Sports and Pastimes*, Nelson: Hendon Publishing.

Fishwick, N. (1989) *English Football and Society, 1910–1950*, Manchester and New York: Manchester University Press.

Graves, R. (1960) [1929] *Goodbye to All That,* Harmondsworth: Penguin.

Gruneau, R. (1983) *Class, Sport and Social Development*, Amherst: University of Massachusetts Press.

Hall, S. (1986) 'Popular Culture and the State', in T. Bennett, C. Mercer and J. Woollacott (eds), *Popular Culture and Social Relations*, Milton Keynes, Open University Press.

Halsey, A.H. (1986) *Change in British Society*, 3rd edition, Oxford: Oxford University Press.

Hargreaves, Jennifer (1994) *Sporting Females – Critical Issues in the History and Sociology of Women's Sports*, London and New York: Routledge.

Hargreaves, John (1986) *Sport, Power and Culture – A Social and Historical Analysis of Popular Sports in Britain*, Cambridge: Polity Press.

Harris, J. (1994) *Private Lives, Public Spirit: A Social History of Britain 1870–1914*, Harmondsworth: Penguin.

Haylett, T. (1992) 'Premier Gate Blow', *The Independent*, Tuesday, 22 September.

Haylett, T. (1995) 'No Turning Back for the Money Men', *The Independent*, 12 January.

Holt, R. (1989) *Sport and the British – A Modern History*, Oxford: Oxford University Press.

Holt, R. (1993) *Stanmore Golf Club 1893–1993*, Stanmore, Middlesex: Stanmore Golf Club.

Holt, R. (1996) 'Heroes of the North: Sport and the Shaping of Regional Identity', in J. Hill and J. Williams (eds), *Sport and Identity in the North of England*, Keele: Keele University Press.

Holt, R. and Tomlinson, A. (1994) 'Sport and Leisure', in D. Kavanagh and A. Seldon (eds), *The Major Effect*, London: Macmillan.

Lowerson, J. (1989) 'Golf', in T. Mason (ed.), *Sport in Britain – A Social History*, Cambridge: Cambridge University Press.

Lowerson, J. (1993) *Sport and the English Middle Classes 1870–1914*, Manchester and New York: Manchester University Press.

Lowerson, J. (1994) 'Golf and the Making of Myths', in G. Jarvie and G. Walker (eds), *Scottish Sport in the Making of the Nation – Ninety-Minute Patriots?*, Leicester, London and New York: Leicester University Press.

Luckes, D. (1994) 'Cricket, Commercialism and the Media, with Particular Reference to the Effects of the Packer Revolution of 1977', unpublished M.Phil. thesis, Chelsea School Research Centre, University of Brighton.

Malcolmson, R. (1973) *Popular Recreations in English Society 1700–1850*, Cambridge: Cambridge University Press.

Mason, T. (1980) *Association Football and English Society 1863–1915*, Brighton: Harvester.

Mason, T. (ed.) (1989) *Sport in Britain – A Social History*, Cambridge: Cambridge University Press.

Mason, T. (1990) 'Stanley Matthews', in R. Holt (ed.), *Sport and the Working Class in Modern Britain*, Manchester and New York: Manchester University Press.

Mason, T. (1996) 'Football, Sport of the North?', in J. Hill and J. Williams (eds), *Sport and Identity in the North of England*, Keele: Keele University Press.

MEW (Marion E. Wertheim Research) (1975) 'Report on the study of Golfers in Great Britain', unpublished report, London: Sports Council.

Midwinter, E. (1981) *W.G. Grace – His Life and Times*, London: George Allen & Unwin.

Minten, J. and Roberts, K. (1989) 'Trends in Sports in Great Britain', in T.J. Kamphorst and K. Roberts (eds), *Trends in Sports: A Multinational Perspective*, AJ Voorthuizen: Giordano Bruno Culemberg.

Mullin, J., Henry, G. and Thorpe, M. (1992) 'Late Winner leaves ITV Sick as Parrots', *Guardian*, Friday, 22 May.

Nicholls, D.C. and Massey, D.W. (1972) 'Golf Course Provision in Britain', unpublished manuscript, London: Sports Council.

Northern Council for Sport and Recreation (1977) *Golf in the Northern Region*, Newcastle: Northern Council for Sport and Recreation.

Philips, D. and Tomlinson, A. (1992) 'Homeward Bound: Leisure, Popular Culture and Consumer Capitalism', in D. Strinati and S. Wagg (eds), *Come on Down?: Popular Media Culture in Post-war Britain*, London: Routledge.

Polley, M. (1998) *Moving the Goalposts – A History of Sport and Society since 1945*, London: Routledge.

Priestley, J.B. (1976) [1929] *The Good Companions*, Harmondsworth: Penguin Books.

Sandiford, K.A.P. (1994) *Cricket and the Victorians*, Aldershot: Scolar Press.

Sugden, J. and Tomlinson, A. (1998) *FIFA and the Contest for World Football – Who Rules the Peoples' Game?*, Cambridge: Polity Press.

Taylor, I. (1991) 'English Football in the 1990s: Taking Hillsborough Seriously', in J. Williams and S. Wagg (eds), *British Football and Social Change – Getting Into Europe*, Leicester: Leicester University Press.

Tischler, S. (1981) *Footballers & Businessmen – The Origins of Professional Soccer in England*, New York: Holmes & Meier.

Tomlinson, A. (1984) 'Physical Education, Sport and Sociology: The Current State and the Way Forward', in I. Glaister (ed.), *Physical Education, Sport and Leisure: Sociological Perspectives*, London: NATFHE (National Association of Teachers in Further and Higher Education).

Tomlinson, A. (1991) 'North and South: The Rivalry of the Football League and the Football Association', in J. Williams and S. Wagg (eds), *British Football and Social Change – Getting Into Europe*, Leicester: Leicester University Press.

Tomlinson, A. (1992) 'Whose Game is it Anyway? The Cultural Analysis of Sport and Media Consumption', *Innovation in Social Science Research*, Volume 5, pp. 33–47.

Tomlinson, A. (1993) 'Culture of Commitment in Leisure: Notes towards the Understanding of a Serious Legacy', *World Leisure and Recreation Association Journal*, Volume 35, pp. 6–9.

Tranter, N. (1994) 'Women and Sport in Nineteenth Century Scotland', in G. Jarvie and G. Walker (eds), *Scottish Sport in the Making of the Nation – Ninety-Minute Patriots?*, Leicester, London and New York: Leicester University Press.

Wagg, S. (1984) *The Football World: A Contemporary Social History*, Brighton: Harvester.

Walvin, J. (1975) *The People's Game – A Social History of English Football*, London: Allen Lane.

Whannel, G. (1983) *Blowing the Whistle: The Politics of Sport*, London: Pluto Press.

Whannel, G. (1986) 'The Unholy Alliance: Notes on Television and the Re-making of British Sport 1965–1985', *Leisure Studies*, Volume 5, pp. 22–37.

Williams, J. (1989) 'Cricket', in T. Mason (ed.), *Sport in Britain – A Social History*, Cambridge: Cambridge University Press.

Williams, J. (1994) 'The Local and the Global in English Soccer and the Rise of Satellite Television', *Sociology of Sport Journal*, Volume 11, pp. 376–397.

Williams, J. and Woodhouse, J (1991) 'Can Play, Will Play? Women and Football in Britain', in J. Williams and S. Wagg (eds), *British Football and Social Change – Getting into Europe*, Leicester: Leicester University Press.

Williams, R. (1963) *Culture and Society 1780–1950*, Harmondsworth: Penguin Books (in association with Chatto & Windus).

Chapter three

Interpreting the growth of sports: Debates in history and theory

History and sociology: a creative tension?

In this chapter we consider debates within and between different theoretical frameworks and traditions that have been utilised in the analysis of the social and cultural roots and contexts of modern sport. In the previous chapter several case studies established some major common and recurrent themes in the social history of sports in England, and to a lesser extent, Britain. We sought in that chapter, and to a limited extent also in Chapter 1, to blend the historical with the sociological, led by a simultaneous concern with both the past and the present, and the relationships between them. Too often a sociological approach has nodded in tokenistic fashion in the direction of the historical, given some space to the portrayal of an historical backcloth, and then proceeded to offer sociological analysis *detached* from that historical basis. A critical analysis concerned with history as process and society as product must avoid this.

The chapter is, as in any exercise of academic analytical judgement, selective, and concentrates upon the sorts of themes introduced in the Introduction to this book. The task of critical sociology and cultural studies involves demanding theoretical questions. It is on this level of theory that sometimes the sociological and social historical agendas have differed. It is this issue that is the concern of the first section of the chapter. A particular case – the political suppression of folk football in the mid-nineteenth century – is then considered as a common reference point for the evaluation of a range of theoretical perspectives that have been brought to bear upon the social history of sports in modern England and Britain.

Three of the most distinguished and prominent social historians of British sport have raised important issues concerning the respective character and merits of the social historical and the sociological approaches. Robert Malcolmson's contribution to the inaugural edition of what, reversing contemporary trends in political and economic history, was *The British Journal of Sports History* but soon became *The International Journal of the History of Sport*, raised broad thematic and conceptual issues central to the analysis of sports in society. Tony Mason, in his book on *Sport in Britain* (Mason, 1989), reviewed a couple of prominent sociological theories under the label of 'Theory'. And Richard Holt, after, rather than in his magisterial study *Sport and the British – A Modern History* proffered an Appendix comprising 'some observations on social history and the sociology of sport' (1989: 357–367).

Malcolmson – specialist scholar of popular recreations in the pre-industrial period – prefaced his contribution to the inaugural issue of *The British Journal of Sports History* with a reaffirmation of what he described as a 'contextual approach to the history of sports' (1984: 60). By this, he referred to the recognition that there are 'conditioning influences of the wider society . . . upon the practice and character of sporting activities' (ibid.). Such influences, for Malcolmson, include the distribution of property in a society and the structure of power and ideologies characteristic of that society. From this perspective of social influences, it can be seen that sports are in many respects '"determined" forms of conduct' (ibid.). Malcomson exemplified his approach to the social history of sports in early modern England by concentrating upon three themes: first, the links between popular sports and forms of work; second, how sports patronised by the privileged social groups were connected to a concern for 'social discipline, popular quiescence, and theatrical display'; and finally, the embeddedness of sporting activities in processes of social and cultural conflict. Malcolmson laid out and prioritised here a clear set of working assumptions and themes for enquiry. They sound very much in common with those of many sociologists, a point which will be returned to in the concluding section of the chapter.

Mason, recognising that 'serious thinkers' no longer 'ignore sport' and that 'the sociology of sport has become a vigorous sub-discipline' (1988: 69), offered some discussion of 'two sociological theories of sport and its place in society' (1988: 77). The first of these was the seminal work by Thorsten Veblen on the place of conspicuous consumption in the leisure cultures of the privileged social groups in late nineteenth-century USA, *The Theory of the Leisure Class* (1899). No critical evaluation was offered of this famous text. Mason then took as representative of a critical neo-Marxist approach the work of Bero Rigauer, summarising his forceful critique of sport, in which it is trenchantly argued that sport is structurally analogous with work. Mason acknowledges the strength of Rigauer's argument but, citing intra-class disputes in British sport over the respective merits of amateurism and professionalism, comments that Rigauer 'has little patience with such niceties' of historical reality (1988: 73). Sympathetic as Mason is to some of the forceful and persuasive ideas of Rigauer, he remains critical of what he sees to be a theoretical inflexibility:

> It is the rigidity of Rigauer's theory, however, which eventually undermines it. In the end there seem too many empirical objections.
>
> (1988: 75)

> Rigauer sees society as domination by one set of values which are largely unquestioned. But such a view does not seem to fit the complexities of the actual world.
>
> (1988: 77)

The empirical realities of historical actuality, then, disturb the coherence, for Mason, of any 'comprehensive critical theory of contemporary sport' (1988: 73). Mason has also referred somewhat condescendingly to the conceptualisation and theorisation of contemporary social trends in his work on football in Latin America. In his postscript to the study he discusses the possibility that variety in styles of play in world football has given way to a standardised approach to the game:

> Caution is the watchword; the game is not to lose. Perhaps this is an aspect of that globalization or homogenization of the sporting world about which sociologists excitedly chatter ... if the homogenization theory is true something which made football vital and attractive will have been lost.
>
> (1995: 157)

Here in an implied critique of social science theorising, the sociologist is reduced to a figure of fun, a naive gossip. But it is a bogus critique, and ultimately disingenuous – for Mason then proceeds to contextualise his own specialist analysis and interpretation within the framework of the theoretical issue about which he is initially so sceptical. Despite his expressed reservations concerning sociological theorising, Mason seems to find (some of) them interesting enough to use.

Richard Holt's appendix to *Sport and the British* begins with a succinct presentation of the source of dispute between the historian and the sociologist, and of some awareness of the respective need the one has for the other. This is worth quoting in full:

> Sociologists frequently complain that historians lack a conceptual framework for their research, while historians tend to feel social theorists

require them to compress the diversity of the past into artificially rigid categories and dispense with empirical verification of their theories. In truth both disciplines need each other, and distinguished authorities in both areas have recently emphasized the interdependence of sociology and history in the identification and pursuit of common problems in social science.

(1989: 357)

Yet immediately following on from this statement Holt writes that the 'apparatus of theory' can weight down history in a crude fashion, and that enjoyment of a subject can be spoiled by the use of 'specialist language' that does nothing to enhance the understanding of the subject. Railing, then, against theory, Holt lists what he calls 'some highly abstract formulations' up against which 'few stay the course and the gap between the new theorists of sport and the ordinary historian can seem unbridgeable' (1989: 357). He then goes on to cite an excerpt of social theory, 'an excruciating sentence' (p. 358), to describe it as 'pretentious and incomprehensible' and then to offer his own interpretation (presumably a comprehension) of the incomprehensible! There is a tension running throughout Holt's discussion in this appendix, between his recognition of the value of social theory and his irritation at the obscurantisms and neologisms characteristic of the forms of expression of such theory. For both the historian and the sociologist, he believes, 'the crux of the matter . . . is the perception of sport and the varying cultural meanings that are attached to games – sometimes to the same game – by different social groups or by different forces within the state that command our attention' (p. 360). At the same time, if the sociologist gets too theoretical about this, he or she is seen as reducing, erroneously, varied realities to a 'single essence' (p. 362):

What may seem conceptually confused and unacceptable to the theorist may be appropriate and right to the historian drawing on different theories to illuminate different aspects of what is in reality not a single phenomenon but a set of loosely related activities shifting their forms and meanings over time. Eclecticism is justified provided it is reasoned and critical.

(Holt, 1989: 362)

Variety, reality, these are what the historian often asserts to be trampled underfoot by the standardising and homogenising sociological theorist. Not just sociologists are adjudged by Holt to be guilty of missing the critical historical point. In an essay on the Scottish footballer Denis Law 'Cultural analysis' is dismissed as 'impenetrable jargon', 'left too much to the Left Bank' and 'at its worst [it] airily dismisses the need for evidence, experience and even clarity of expression' (Holt, 1994: 58). The charge is obscurantism, then, plus finding the facts to fit the theory. John Hargreaves' seminal *Sport, Power and Culture* (1986) comes in for particular criticism here, the 'theoretical neatness of this account' leading 'to problems when dealing with the complex historical reality' (Holt, 1989: 363). What Hargreaves stands accused of here is a selective use of evidence in the construction of a sophisticated and all-embracing theoretical analysis.

The problem of any historically insensitive sociology is that the theory will predetermine the empirical task and that a rigid and prior interpretation will lead the analysis, and this can lead to distortions and misrepresentations of historical realities and complexities. But history without adequate conceptualisation or theorisation can be little more than a form of antiquarianism – an important retrieval of the past, but decontextualised, an academic and anodyne version of the heritage industry. Some sociologists should certainly do more careful and more rigorous historical work, sensitive to the methodological demands and possibilities of detailed historical scholarship. But at the same time, it would be unwise for social historians of sport to ignore the central theoretical debates of the social sciences, for this could consign important scholarship to the margins of academic debate. It could also constitute a lost opportunity, in that the historically sensitive study of the place, role and nature of sport in modern societies has the potential to enhance the analysis and understanding of the wider society and culture. For example, the study of sport spectacle and the ceremonial and ritual around a global phenomenon such as the Olympic Games (Tomlinson, 1996) can illuminate our understanding not just of sport itself, but of international relations, and media-based and cultural dimensions of globalisation itself. Such a study of sport can contribute to the generation of a fuller theoretical understanding. An adequate socio-cultural approach to the understanding of sport needs, therefore, to be receptive to the potential contribution of a variety of theoretical frameworks.

In the next section of this chapter, a descriptive case study of football during a key transitional phase in its history is provided, and this is followed by illustrations of how the case study might be interpreted from some such theoretical perspectives.

Football in transition – the folk form in Derby

This case study is derived from the work of Anthony Delves. We offer a purely descriptive account of the culture of the Derby game in the early nineteenth century, the social context in which it thrived and then was increasingly less prominent in the local culture, and the sporting developments that took place as football's prominence decreased. We are aware, of course, that the case study is dependent upon the historical scholarship of Delves, and that his decisions as to the importance of a source were informed by some conceptual preoccupations. We will make his theoretical tendencies explicit at the beginning of the following section. In this section, we present as objectively as it is possible to do – without having buried ourselves in Delves' primary sources – the empirical realities of the story of football in Derby in the mid-nineteenth century.

As the account offered in Chapter 2 has indicated, the popular recreational form of football bore very little resemblance to more modern forms of football. The game of football in its pre-modern form – street football, as Delves chooses to call it – was 'highly popular, rowdy and controversial' (1981: 89). There was little demarcation between players and supporters. Not much kicking took place either, and, as another name for the activity – 'hugball' – indicates, the primary mode of possession was manual. Numbers were flexible and uncontrolled, hundreds and sometimes more than a thousand on each side. The game was characterised by hours of 'rough horseplay and brawling, leaving a trail of physical injuries, petty vandalism, assaults and much heavy drinking' (Delves, 1981: 90). The all-male playing cast, reflecting the 'masculine republic' (Harrison, 1971: 46) of the pub and the drinking place, was complemented by women spectators. Women were not in merely passive roles, but at critical moments could be instrumental in defence of the game and defiance of those who sought its suppression. In the mid-1840s, at one point a woman was reported in the local press to have smuggled the ball into the market-place to enable play to begin.

This form of football attracted holidaymakers from far afield, and as such operated not just as a contest, but as a popular participatory festival. Attempts at suppression of the game had not succeeded in 1731, 1746 and 1797, and active opposition was rekindled and fuelled from the 1830s onwards. By 1845 representation, claimed to emanate from many working-class as well as middle-class quarters, was made to the Mayor of Derby. In this the game was alleged to cause:

> the assembling of a lawless rabble, suspending business to the loss of the industrious, creating terror and alarm to the timid and the peaceable, committing violence on the persons and damage to the properties of the defenceless and poor, and producing in those who play moral degradation and in many extreme poverty, injury to health, fractured limbs and (not infrequently) loss of life; rendering their homes desolate, their wives widows and their children fatherless.
>
> (*Derby Mercury*, 29 January 1845, in Delves, 1981: 90)

Accurate or representative or not, this appeal had an immediate impact: the Mayor pronounced the game illegal. Players were threatened with prosecution, and offered alternative outlets. Cash prizes were offered for organised competitive athletic sports and cash inducements also offered to players to play outside the town. Some defied this and tried to play in the town centre, leading those in authority to cancel the alternative sports. This left people without either football or the planned alternatives. A vigorously contested game then took place (on Ash Wednesday), following which a few players were made an example of, being prosecuted and fined. The following year, 1846, saw those opposed to football increase the pressure against the game. Magistrates issued warnings against playing the game, and some negotiation took place. When some footballers handed over a ball to the Mayor in a public meeting, he promised to negotiate with local employers for time off for workers, and to subsidise a free railway excursion instead of football.

This negotiation came to nothing though, with employers asked *not* to release workers for the holiday, no alternative sports arranged and several hundred local citizens recruited as special constables. The Mayor and magistrates also arranged for a troop of cavalry to be brought in for the holiday. On Shrove Tuesday 1846 the streets were full of spectators and roving groups of youths. A ball appeared at the customary hour in the town-centre market-place and the crowds started to play, in the event taunting and physically provoking the special constabulary. Hit by a missile, seeing the riot as 'dangerous and appalling' and concerned at the highly charged atmosphere, the Mayor read the Riot Act and called in the troops. The footballers were chased and the crowds broken up, regrouping to play the game beyond the borough boundary. Local moral outrage condemned the game. In the *Derby and Chesterfield Reporter* of 8 May it was alleged to be 'of so low and degrading a nature that it should be swept away from our land as bull-baiting, cockfighting and other brutal sports had been of late years' (Delves, 1981: 95). Legal charges were taken against fifteen of the football organisers, for obstruction or for playing the game or for enticing other players to play it. Five of these were prosecuted and bound over to keep the peace. In succeeding years, the calendar of the traditional game continued to stimulate elaborate public order alarms, with special constables dispersing crowds, troops on the alert and, in 1848 – that most cataclysmic of revolutionary years – another alternative sports arranged and subsidised from the public purse, for the Thursday following Ash Wednesday. Preparations to counter any revival of street football were still being made towards the middle of the following decade.

Football was popular for the way in which it symbolised a two-day holiday for mill and factory workers whose annual holidays totalled only eight days. The game focused forms of reunion, too, for family and friends. It could also serve as a vehicle for other forms of organisation, so that for insecure framework-knitters in 1845 the holiday, the large crowds and the game could provide a possibility of social protest, as they planned and projected trade union organisation.

Interpretations illustrated

How, then, do we go beyond the mere telling of the story or the detailed portrayal of the event? The facts of the matter are undeniable. Though the representation of any historical fact outside the pure context of the historical source can always be claimed as an interpretation or as a selective telling, the facts of this particular matter are surely undisputed. Ideally, we would know more about the main players in the story. Who were the five ringleaders, prosecuted successfully but not sentenced with severity? Who were those who most actively campaigned against street football, in the cause of 'rational recreation' and in opposition to traditional popular cultures perceived as dangerous, threatening and unrespectable? And what is the overall picture that emerges of the society and culture of the time, and the place of popular recreations in that society and culture?

Nevertheless, with the picture provided by Delves we are in a position to outline major theoretical approaches to historical analysis, to consider the impact and value of the concept of hegemony in its emphasis upon how power relations are accepted and consented to, and to articulate the methodological principles and theoretical preoccupations that we believe most usefully inform critical work on both the social history and sociology/cultural analysis of sport. The three influential interpretations selected for consideration are:

1   Developmental/figurational sociology (exemplified in the work of Elias and Dunning).
2   Critical materialism (as in the work of Bailey, Hargreaves, and Clarke and Critcher).
3   Weberian interpretation (for instance, Guttmann).

Other approaches – in liberal history, feminist theory and postmodernist theory – could be used in the same way. But this chapter is not an attempt at any comprehensive review of the social history, sociology and social theory of sport. Jarvie and Maguire (1994) have provided such an overview, concentrating upon social thought and social theory and their application to the analysis of sport and leisure. The selection of approaches covered here is more modest in intent, designed to transmit, to the newcomer to the field, some of the spirit and liveliness of the debates that characterise humanities and social science-based approaches to understanding sport.

Developmental/figurational sociology

The impact of the work of Eric Dunning and others following him in the advancement of developmental, figurational sociology and its application to the history and sociology of sport and leisure has been immense. This work has been a running collaboration and debate with Norbert Elias, revolving around the nature and application of his contribution to social theory and cultural analysis. Prior to summarising the theoretical and conceptual features of Dunning's approach, it is useful to consider some of the main thrusts in the work of Elias himself. For this purpose, we consider here two of his works – *The History of Manners – The Civilising Process*, first published in German in 1939, and in English in 1978, and *What is Sociology?*

The History of Manners (Elias, 1978b) is a dazzling combination of empirical research and theory, depicting the developing inhibitions in social conduct that characterised the period in Western Europe of the emergence of the bourgeoisie and the modern nation-state. From eating habits to sleeping patterns, from breaking wind to urinating, Elias shows how behaviour became more rigidly conditioned throughout the sixteenth, seventeenth and eighteenth centuries. It is argued that these social influences are internalised to the extent that adults act *as if* they are restraining themselves in purely personal terms, that is, the bourgeois personality presents a social code *as if* it is a matter of individual initiative. But, Elias argues, drives are modelled in terms of a particular moment of social structure and personality structure:

> The pattern of affect control, of what must and must not be restrained, regulated and transformed, is certainly not the same in this stage as in the preceding one of the court aristocracy. In keeping with its different interdependencies, bourgeois society applies stronger restrictions to certain impulses.
>
> (1978b: 152)

The overriding theme of Elias' study is the proposition that affect control (what amounts to the increasing tendency of the modern individual to de-primitivise all aspects of human behaviour) is a central feature of the historical development of western societies. Elias' method can make the most impressive interpretive connections on the basis of this emphasis. Thus the discussion of the fork can become a prelude to the description of the modern individual's notion of the body:

> What was lacking in this *courtois* world, or at least had not been developed to the same degree, was the invisible wall of affects which seems now to rise between one body and another, repelling and separating, the wall which is often perceptible today at the mere approach of something that has been in contact with the mouth or hands of someone else, and which manifests itself as embarrassment at the mere sight of many bodily functions of others, and often at their mere mention, or as a feeling of

shame when one's functions are exposed to the gaze of others, and by no means only then.

(1978b: 4)

The construction of such a wall included the intensification of provision of facilities and objects for a more privatised existence. Individuals were to have their own plates, their own beds, and articles such as the handkerchief became *de rigueur*. The toilet claimed its own room, so enclosing the individual in the most privatised of settings for the most natural of acts. For Elias, the 'pattern of affect control, of what must and must not be restrained, regulated and transformed' (p. 152) pervades the whole of social life.

Interested in a sociology of processes rather than of states (pp. 228–235), the exploration of 'the figuration, a structure of mutually oriented and dependent people' (p. 261), and the impact of forms of affect control within the long-term civilising process, the Elias of this majestic study offers an attractive framework for sociological analysis of historical (or developmental) processes. It is cross-cultural and comparative in scope; it stresses the processual dimensions of social reality, striving for a balance between historical and structural levels of analysis; it is innovative in the analysis of empirical phenomena; and it treats culture and social consciousness (sentiments, feelings, attitudes) as objects worthy of rigorous sociological attention.

In *What is Sociology?* (1978a) Elias reiterates some of these principles, and in his joint work with Eric Dunning (Elias and Dunning, 1986) these central points are reaffirmed. There has been considerable, and lively, critique and counter-critique on figurational sociology and its application to sport and leisure (for instance, Horne and Jary, 1987; Horne and Jary, 1994; Dunning, in Rojek, 1989), but undeniably the contribution of the figurational approach to understanding sport has been formidable. How, then, would the sociologist working within this framework make sense of the story of street football in Derby in the middle of the nineteenth century?

The key point in Elias' figurational sociology for the investigation of the developmental history of sport is the contention that affect controls intensify within sport as the civilising process advances. The uninhibited physicality, therefore, of street football, its inherently uncontrolled and anarchic form, becomes subject – to paraphrase the words of Elias – to forms of restraint, regulation and transformation. The popular recreational form is out of tune with the refrains of the marching band of the emergent classes which are at the centre of the civilising process. The key features of the traditional form of street football – its disorderliness, violence and open-endedness – are anathema to these newly powerful social groups and the alliances of interest that bind together some of those groups, and sectional interests within and between those groups of 'mutually oriented and dependent people'.

Street football or the folk antecedent of modern forms of football involved, for the figurational sociologist, 'wild and, according to modern notions, savage brawls. Their violence probably constituted one of the sources of enjoyment' (Dunning and Sheard, 1979: 25). Such folk games 'were rough and wild, closer to "real" fighting than modern sports' (Dunning and Sheard, 1979: 30). It is, effectively, the lack of affect controls that becomes, logically, the major analytical emphasis for the figurational sociologist: 'folk games retained a distinct family likeness determined . . . above all, by the fact that, correlative with the stages in a "civilising process" through which pre-industrial Britain passed, they were rough and wild' (Dunning and Sheard, 1979: 32). Dunning and Sheard recognise the importance of changes in time in the industrialising context, and of the decline in the availability of open space in which to engage in activities like street football. But the 'more deeply-rooted "social forces"' to which they point transcend, for instance, social class differences:

> Englishmen during the early stages of industrialization underwent a 'civilizing' change . . . this period (1780–1850) formed a watershed, a stage of rapid transition in which there occurred a 'civilizing spurt', an advance in people's 'threshold of repugnance' with regard to engaging in and witnessing violence acts.
>
> (Dunning and Sheard, 1979: 40)

The street football of Derby, from this perspective, became an unacceptable form of public spectacle. Its suppression was accelerated by new and more effective forms of social control, and by the lack or withdrawal of local patronage (the Mayor explicitly opposed the game in Derby; his counterpart in 1866 in Kingston 'refused to comply with the old custom of kicking off at the start of the Shrovetide match' (Dunning and Sheard, 1979: 43)). But, despite the range of elements recognised as important by Dunning and Sheard in the decline of folk football, the central influence, they argue, is 'the demand for greater orderliness and more "civilized" behaviour characteristic of an advanced industrial society' (1979: 44). The key conceptual emphasis in figurational sociology is upon 'different degrees and types of regulation' (Elias and Dunning, 1986: 190) in the evolution of modern sport forms from their folk-game predecessors.

Critical materialism

In this section we consider the major interpretive emphases of two prominent social historical works on the nineteenth century, and of two studies by sociologists to whom the analysis of the process of history is paramount. The work of E.P. Thompson – and of the radical analysis and cultural Marxism of other prominent figures in the English new left of the 1950s and 1960s, such as Stuart Hall and Raymond Williams – has been important to this approach. Thompson's stress on the lived experience and everyday culture(s) of the popular classes, on the creative dimensions of cultural life, and his concern with the fundamental transformations wrought by industrial capitalist society (and the concomitant cultural struggles and class conflict) have inspired generations of critical materialist scholars. Malcolmson's groundbreaking work on popular recreations was undertaken under the supervision of Thompson, who suggested 'early lines of enquiry, frequently offered advice on source materials, on several occasions suggested further, and fruitful, approaches to the subject' (Malcolmson, 1973: ix). Thompson's works on the emerging class dynamics of early industrialism, and on the features of the new industrial order, feature in significant ways in the work of Bailey, Hargreaves, and Clarke and Critcher. Indeed, for the latter co-authors, his classic work *The Making of the English Working Class* 'marks the emergence of cultural history':

> Everyday life became more than the cold indices of the standard of living; class consciousness was understood to take forms other than political or trade union organization; and perhaps most importantly, ideas about class conflict were extended beyond the issues of economic and political power to encompass struggles over the cultural legitimacy of images, definitions, meanings and ideologies embedded in social behaviour.
>
> (Clarke and Critcher, 1985: 49)

This is not to say that Thompson's work is all-embracing, and Clarke and Critcher list four reservations about Thompson's pioneering approach and the historical work inspired by it (1985: 49–50). First, its concentration on working-class leisure is at the expense of the leisure histories of other classes and strata. Second, the historical research focuses selectively upon '*institutional* forms of leisure practice', marginalising in our understanding the unorganised or the informal. Third, its history is primarily that of '*male* leisure'. And fourth, the approach has not generated historical material of high quality on the more recent periods of British history, such as the post-Second World War period of the twentieth century. Nevertheless, they reassert, the work of the cultural historians has been of great value. How, then would scholars working within or out of this framework account for Delves' Derby case study?

Peter Bailey's study clearly states its primary themes in its title, *Leisure and Class in Victorian England: Rational Recreation and Contest for Control, 1830–1885*. His core case study is of the Lancashire industrial town of Bolton. Impromptu holidays (at the time of political elections) and lively street entertainment were features of a 'public and gregarious . . . working-class leisure' in the 1830s, based around the social setting of the pub, or the public space of the street. The basis of this leisure culture and its sports corollaries was undermined by, as Bailey puts it, paraphrasing the classic work of the Hammonds, 'the curtailment of time and space, and the hostility of the superior classes' (1978: 11). Factory employers and middle class evangelists combined in the first third of the nineteenth century 'to police the amusements of the poor', their 'principal targets' being 'animal cruelty, Sabbath breaking and intemperance' (Bailey, 1978: 17 and 18). In Bolton in 1844, for instance, local authorities responded to the urgings of such constituencies, the local clergy lobbying the magistracy to prohibit Sunday performances at the Star Museum and Concert Hall, the town's leading singing saloon. This was not an all-embracing opposition. Some elements – licensed victallers, for instance – objected to the constraints, clearly putting business concerns before moral outrage. But there was no doubt that the new officers of the police were having a widespread effect on the nature of popular recreational practice. Peel had reformed the metropolitan police in London in 1829 and parallel forces were established around the country. These officious and at times zealous bobbies enforced the law against blood sports and 'were also effective in curtailing other wild sports, such as the Shrove Tuesday game in Derby' (Bailey, 1978: 21). The police force in Bolton was far from universally popular in Bolton and its locality, in its early days even among the middle classes. But the forces soon began to operate more effectively in the name of respectability: they 'invaded the daily occasions for recreation as well as the popular festivals of the fair and the race meeting' (Bailey, 1978: 21). The middle classes had less and less time for the theory that the street games and public recreations of 'a hard-driven working people' acted as a safety valve for their frustrations and discontents (Bailey, 1978: 22). And certainly, the profile of an activity like the Derby street football was a symbol to the local middle classes of a lack of public order. Bailey captures vividly this clash of cultures:

> The hostility of the reform associations and local authorities was only the most forceful expression of a general middle class impatience with the intractable crudities and excess of so much of popular recreation. The respectable citizens of Bolton who demanded police action against street games were not just concerned to criticize the efficiency of a distasteful new service, but were genuinely affronted by what they saw and heard of. In an age of progress and rationality it was frankly incomprehensible that people should amuse themselves by eating scalding porridge with their fingers or stripping the wicks from a pound of candles with their teeth, all for the sake of a wager and the applause of an audience of like-minded boobies. These folk pleasures were popular contests at the yearly Halshaw Wakes held near Bolton, but similar feats took place all year round – eight pounds of treacle consumed in twenty minutes by a butcher's assistant (the commonest of participants) provides a ready example. Such displays

were generally attended by a great deal of drinking and gambling. The gentry and respectable middle classes recoiled from such uncouth congenialities and, like the clergy, no longer appeared as patrons of the local fairs and feasts.

(1978: 21–22)

In this metaphor of recoiling Bailey evokes the tensions between the social classes of the time, and demonstrates the cultural incompatibilities that were manifest in disputes over the acceptability of recreational activities and folk pastimes. Documenting the 'language of resistance' of many working people to the marginalisation and undermining of their culture, he indicates the political basis of sports and popular culture in the class dynamics of this formative period. Street football in Derby could be, from such a perspective, a major symbol of the social tensions and cultural struggles at a time when the social order and the new modern society was in the making; and at a time, it is well worth recalling, when popular revolutions were sweeping away old hierarchies across Europe, and collectivist political agitation in England (the fight for trade unionism, the Chartist Movement) rendered the privileged classes paranoid at the prospect of a popular uprising. It is in such a climate that the reformist interventionists framing new forms of leisure and sport developed their initiatives. The 'voices of improvement', as Bailey puts it, of the rational recreation movement had more in mind than merely the calming of the crowd. Reform of popular recreations would be 'a constructive contribution to the general drive for social amelioration or "improvement" . . . improved recreations were an important instrument for educating the working classes in the social values of middle-class orthodoxy' (1978: 35). Policies developed for the regulation of amusements, albeit in sympathy with the need and conditions of the urban masses, constituted, in Bailey's terms, the implementation of a 'rationale of social control' (ibid.).

Hugh Cunningham's careful scholarship has reminded us that despite the reformist interventions, the practitioners of many popular recreations were resilient. Street football in Derby was not wiped out overnight, and the immediate impact of official action was not always translated into long-term importance. Cunningham describes how a reformist curate, the Reverend Grimshaw, arrived in the West Yorkshire village of Haworth in 1742. Praying strategically in opposition to local folk games, and serendipitously helped by adverse weather, he succeeded in ending local horse racing and other activities. But soon after Grimshaw's time, regular Sunday football with neighbouring parishes was back on the agenda. Cunningham's insight holds for the case of street football in Derby – the resilience in the face of hostility and the resistance to reformist campaigners was widely characteristic of working people's responses. Cunningham recognises the main hope of the interventionists as, through the management of acceptable forms of leisure, the achievement of 'a reconciliation of classes, a recreation of community and a reassertion of paternalism' (1980: 123). For four reasons, he points out, this was an overoptimistic 'hope'. First, many of the events that were claimed as testimony to class conciliation, and where this principle was preached, were in fact one-offs: they were a-typical, exceptions to a rule of cultural separatism. Second, whilst claims were made for class conciliation in leisure, the intensification of labour discipline and the consolidation of new forms of labour relations had the opposite effect, and 'work is of primary importance in determining class relationships' (1980: 125). Third, when social classes 'did meet in leisure they often interpreted the meaning of the meeting in different ways' (1980: 125). And fourth, aspirations to achieve a mingling of the classes in leisure did not include a mingling of the sexes. Male liberal rational recreationists left their wives at home. Cunningham shows how alliances formed in opposition to activities like street football were not inexorably to succeed, and indeed, quoting Delves, he points out that some liberal recreationists were opposed not so much to the practice of popular recreation, but to the form it took and the way in which it was organised: for them, a more entrepreneurial approach could have economic spin-offs as well as moral credibility (1980: 78). And on a wider point, reviewing the inter-class dynamics of the early stages of football in England, he makes the astute observation that in certain circumstances 'the working class, for lack of any alternative, was prepared to accept for as long as necessary, the fact of middle-class sponsorship, but not its ideology' (1980: 128). 'Give me the resources and facilities, and stuff your sermons' might have been the motto of such a response.

In a conclusion which is really a conceptual and methodological appendix rather than a summative review of his study, Cunningham acknowledges his debts to the work of E.P. Thompson, Raymond Williams and the Italian Marxist theorist Antonio Gramsci. Such sources are important too to the work of Hargreaves, and Clarke and Critcher.

John Hargreaves' social and historical analysis of popular sports in Britain stresses the interconnectedness of three elements which form the title of his book – *Sport, Power and Culture*. The examples of street football that he cites are the Derby game (for which the source is Malcolmson) and (quoting Storch, 1976) the banning of football in Leicester in 1847. For Hargreaves, the Derby story is primarily one of suppression, with agencies of repression – the police, the troops – brought in as, in Storch's phrase, 'domestic missionaries of the bourgeoisie'. These initiatives, perceived by working-class communities as outright attacks on their traditional freedoms and on their right to assemble, were examples of blatant ruling class oppression of an exploited working class. The story of street football in Derby and the attempt to construct more acceptable alternatives is evidence, from a perspective such as that of Hargreaves, of how sport was seen as either playing a part or having the potential to play a part 'in the pattern of working-class accommodation to the new social order' (Hargreaves, 1986: 26).

Clarke and Critcher identify violence and brutality as 'major features of popular culture' in the early 1800s, when 'life, on or off the streets, was often nasty, brutish and short' (1985: 53). Yet still, at the turn of the eighteenth and nineteenth centuries, prominent popular cultural forms were, as they note, endorsed by powerful groupings, by the aristocracy and the gentry. Economic, political, religious and cultural cum consumerist forces were, Clarke and Critcher emphasise, to change that. From such a perspective, the concerted strategy to outlaw street football in Derby was part of a wider trend across the industrialising, modernising society:

> looking overall at the trends evident by the 1840s, the clearest impression is of the wholesale changes in the rhythms and sites of work and leisure enforced by the industrial revolution. It was during this period that what we have come to see as a discrete area of human activity called 'leisure' became recognisable. But, contrary to the account offered by sociological orthodoxy, it did not develop in any simple linear fashion, as an aspect of industrialised progress. It was enforced from above as a form of social control, by magistrates, clergymen, policemen, millowners, poor law commissioners. Its rationale was in the end, despite religious and moral camouflage, that of the economic system. It concerned, most simply, the taming of a workforce.
>
> (Clarke and Critcher, 1985: 58–59)

This is not to say that the suppression of street football is a mere reflection of the economic order, rather that the cultural resonance of such an activity was inimical to the expressed values and priorities of that order – regular and anarchic folk forms were not the sort of non-work recreational activities of which factory owners and local authorities would approve, in a climate in which older patterns of life were being reorganised 'under new moral and social auspices' (Hall, 1986: 24). Avoiding any crude economic explanations Clarke and Critcher (1985: 227) propose that the concept that 'provides a model for analysing culture as creation from below and appropriation from above' is hegemony, for it addresses the dynamics of contested power and recognises the importance of negotiation as a form of contestation within power relations. And certainly the notion of hegemony helps account for how sports cultures in particular circumstances can contribute to the manufacture of consent.

We have called the framework of the writers covered in this sub-section a critical materialist one. By materialism we mean the *historical materialism* of the great multi-disciplinary social scientific thinker Karl Marx, through which the mode of production of a society and the labour process can be seen as having a primary role in the development of human history (Bhaskar, 1993: 372) and upon the nature of social relations. By critical we mean (following Marx's *Theses on Feuerbach*) the recognition that analysis and theory might also have the capacity to affect, if not effect, change, in both comprehension and practice.

A Weberian approach

Guttmann's ambitious classification of the characteristics of sports in different socio-historical ages was included in Chapter 1 (p. 7). It is informed by what he 'refers' to 'in shorthand as a Weberian view of social organisation', which is 'motivated partly by convenience' and very much derived from 'Max Weber's analysis of the transition from traditional to modern society' (1978: 80). The seven characteristics that make up his classification are 'interdependent, systematically related elements of the ideal type of a modern society'. Six of these – secularism, equality, specialisation, rationalisation, bureaucratic organisation, quantification – are seen by Guttmann as characteristics of both the macrocosm (modern society) and the microcosm (modern sports). Along with the quest for records, more marked he observes in sports than in the wider society (though the prominence of the Guinness Book of Records might suggest otherwise), these characteristics 'derive from the fundamental Weberian notion of the difference between the ascribed status of traditional society and the achieved status of a modern one' (1978: 81).

Weber believed that modern societies were increasingly characterised by rational forms of social action, in which traditional or emotional bases of action gave way to means-end or value-rational action, in which the driving force of any action was the calculation about how best to achieve the required outcome.

How, then, would Guttmann's application of Weber's ideas help interpret or theorise the case of street football in mid-nineteenth century Derby? It is clear enough. It would be classified as a pre-modern, mediaeval sport sharing none of the characteristics of modern sports – except perhaps, and only to a limited extent, the characteristic of secularism. The game was played by people in terms of 'in Max Weber's classic formulation, ascription rather than achievement' (Guttmann, 1978: 26), that is, the ascribed characteristics of class, status, strength and sex determined the nature of the individual's involvement. Equality was not a feature of the street game. The specialisation so characteristic of modern sports was not a feature of street football. Guttmann, citing the seminal analyses of Eric Dunning, makes much of this point:

> Among the peasantry, specialization probably went no further than the selection of the physically powerful to represent the group at wrestling or

lifting. The undifferentiatedness of mediaeval sports is especially clear in the village game which eventually became modern soccer.

> In mediaeval football, there was room for everyone and a sharply defined role for no one. The game was played by the entire village or, more likely still, by one village against another. Men, women, and children rushed to kick the ball and the devil took the hindmost. From the vantage point of a church tower, the players must have looked like a swarm of bees as they battled fiercely for possession of the ball.
>
> (1978: 38)

It is likely that Guttmann overestimates the role of women in this free-for-not-quite-all, but the principle holds, and there is no doubt that the streets of Derby during the Shrovetide game were not witness to specialised forms of input to the game.

Guttmann's Weberian approach would also emphasise the irrational dimensions of the street game. In modern sports the nature of rules is that they are rationalised 'in Max Weber's sense of *Zweckrationalitat*, i.e. there is a logical relationship between means and ends . . . the rules of the game are perceived by us as means to an end . . . The rules are cultural artefacts and not divine instructions' (Guttmann, 1978: 40). In the street version of football in its pre-modern form rules were not formalised, practices were customary, traditional and relatively unchanging. Weber is again Guttman's inspiration for highlighting the nature of bureaucratisation in sport, for his 'analysis of the distinctions between a primitive hierarchy of prescribed behaviour and a modern bureaucracy of functional roles' (1978: 45). The street game in Derby had the character of such a 'primitive hierarchy'. And its participants were certainly less interested in 'the numeration of achievements' (Guttmann, 1978: 50) and the 'modern mania for quantification' (Guttmann, 1978: 51) as manifest in sports records, than in the elemental passions of the spectacle.

In short, the pre-modern phenomenon of football is, for Guttmann, defined by that very state – its inherent pre-modernness. What leads to the supersession of this form by the more formalised, sophisticated form of modern sports? For Guttmann, the answer is not the explanatory factor of industrialisation, offered in his view by the economic determinism of some forms of Marxism. Ranging wide in cross-cultural scope, citing the Bulgarian and Cuban achievements in sport, he pithily asserts that 'Industrialism no longer seems to be the key, if it ever was' (1978: 81). For Guttmann, then, the explanatory factor accounting for the rise of modern sports is the set of values that frames the mores and dominant value-systems of a society – not, as in Weber's own monumental analysis of the rise of capitalism, the Protestant Ethic, but the scientific world-view: 'The emergence of modern sports represents neither the triumph of capitalism nor the rise of Protestantism but rather the slow development of an empirical, experimental, mathematical Weltanschauung' (1978: 85). To such a world-view, street football could seem only barbaric and, perhaps worse, uncontrolled and unsystematic, a kind of public anti-science. One can imagine the bourgeois of Derby fretting over the threat contained in street football to their ordered universe, looking to make alliances with similarly concerned groups in other social classes. In this sense the traditional recreational activity embodies the clash in core values typical of a turbulent transitional social and cultural climate. A Weberian approach can illuminate street football as a form of traditional action, inevitably incompatible with the more rationalised forms of purposive-rational action characteristic of the modern society and its framing world-view, and effectively captured in Ritzer's (1993) evocation of contemporary production processes (including sport) as evidence of the 'McDonaldization' of modern society.

Conclusions

Other theoretical frameworks could be instanced. Liberal historians have disputed the analyses of critical materialists, seeing in the concept of hegemony 'a brilliant attempt to span the chasm between the evidence and an unsatisfactory theory' (Golby and Purdue, 1984: 13). They argue that nineteenth-century popular culture may well have expressed 'the aspirations and desires of most men as most men are' (ibid.). From such a perspective, the demise of street football could be seen as a kind of popular progressivism, the more orderly conception of sport representing an emerging consensus. Feminist scholarship would point to the absence of women from the street football ritual as an indication of its deep-rooted patriarchal nature, and to its endemic violence and physical roughness as an elemental form of masculinity.

The beginning sociologist or cultural analyst of sport might wonder how it is that scholars and writers sharing so much in common – after all, aren't they all sociologists or social historians? – can spend so much time at loggerheads. But one of the main sources of excitement in the social sciences is the challenge of interpretation, and debates over the respective merits or validity of different concepts and theories are central to this challenge. To recognise this is to debate the nature of history and its legacies, to assess the impact of relations between dominant and subordinate groups in a particular society, and to illuminate the place of a cultural form such as sport in history and society. Jarvie and Maguire have also stressed the commonality of different approaches, pointing to three core 'common hallmarks of good sociology': the examining of the nature of 'structured processes understood to be concretely situated in time and space'; the recognition of unintended as well as intended outcomes of social processes; and an awareness of the interrelationships between individual lives and the structural context of those lives (1994: 256).

Some of the most influential sociologists of the modern age have been at pains to emphasise such common preoccupations. Mills (1970) argued for the development of a sociological imagination in which self and structure, individual and history, were understood together. For Giddens (1982), the sociological imagination is at once critical, anthropological (or comparative) and historical. Though there may be theoretical disputes over the balance between and emphases of competing conceptualisations, the broader sociological agenda should be acknowledged and the crafts of social history absorbed. But if the nature of historical scholarship is not recognised, then sociologists run the risk of theorising in a vacuum. In interpreting the growth of modern sports, and seeing the respective possibilities, merits and deficiencies in theoretical and conceptual approaches to that growth, sociology needs history, and history can benefit from a partnership with sociology.

ESSAYS AND EXERCISES

Essays

With reference to one sport other than football, discuss the contribution that figurational sociology can make to an understanding of the sport's growth.

In what ways might sport be said to have become 'McDonaldized'?
Make illustrative reference to at least two sports.

'Contestation is a central dynamic of sports cultures.' Evaluate this claim with reference to critical materialist accounts of sport.

Exercises

Review one journal article on the history of sports, summarising its argument, listing the types of sources upon which it is based, and evaluating its theoretical stance (300 words).

Interview, for 20–30 minutes, one person aged 70 years or more who has had an active life in sports, asking him or her to comment upon how the meaning of sport has changed. Make notes of the main points of the interview, and speculate upon how you might theorise the account, and the changes in meaning documented in it.

List the different kinds of documentary and oral sources upon which the social historian and the sociologist draw. Write down any differences in how they use those sources, and draw out any interpretive or theoretical implications.

FURTHER READING

G. Jarvie and J. Maguire, *Sport and Leisure in Social Thought*, London, Routledge, 1994, provides an overview of leading social theories and schools of thought, and their relevance for the analysis of sport and leisure.

R. Holt, *Sport and the British – A Modern History*, Oxford, Oxford University Press, 1989, includes, in the appendix, a provocative discussion of the difference between historical and sociological styles and approaches.

References

Bailey, P. (1978) *Leisure and Class in Victorian England – Rational Recreation and the Contest for Control, 1830–1885*, London: Routledge & Kegan Paul.

Bhaskar, R. (1993) 'Materialism', in W. Outhwaite and T. Bottomore (eds), *The Blackwell Dictionary of Twentieth Century Social Thought*, Oxford: Basil Blackwell.

Clarke, J. and Critcher, C. (1985) *The Devil Makes Work – Leisure in Capitalist Britain*, London: Macmillan.

Cunningham, H. (1980) *Leisure in the Industrial Revolution c. 1780–c. 1880*, London: Croom Helm.

Delves, A. (1981) 'Popular Recreation and Social Conflict in Derby, 1800–1850', in E. Yeo and S. Yeo (eds), *Popular Culture and Class Conflict 1590–1914 – Explorations in the History of Labour and Leisure*, Brighton: Harvester.

Dunning, E. and Sheard, K. (1979) *Barbarians, Gentlemen and Players: A Sociological Study of the Development of Rugby*, New York: New York University Press.

Elias, N. (1978a) *What is Sociology?*, London: Hutchinson.

Elias, N. (1978b) [1939] *The History of Manners: The Civilising Process 1*, Oxford: Basil Blackwell.

Elias, N. and Dunning, E. (1986) *Quest for Excitement – Sport and Leisure in the Civilizing Process*, Oxford: Basil Blackwell.

Giddens, A. (1982) *Sociology: A Brief but Critical Introduction*, London: Macmillan.

Golby, J.M. and Purdue, A.W. (1984) *The Civilisation of the Crowd – Popular Culture in England 1750–1900*, London: Batsford Academic and Educational.

Guttmann, A. (1978) *From Ritual to Record – The Nature of Modern Sports*, New York: Columbia University Press.

Hall, S. (1986) 'Popular Culture and the State', in T. Bennett, C. Mercer and J. Woollacott (eds), *Popular Culture and Social Relations*, Milton Keynes: Open University Press.

Hargreaves, John (1986) *Sport, Power and Culture – A Social and Historical Analysis of Popular Sports in Britain*, Cambridge: Polity Press.

Harrison, B. (1971) *Drink and the Victorians: The Temperance Question in England 1815–1872*, London: Faber.

Holt, R. (1989) *Sport and the British – A Modern History*, Oxford: Oxford University Press.

Holt, R. (1994) 'King across the Border: Denis Law and Scottish Football', in G. Jarvie and G. Walker (eds), *Scottish Sport in the Making of the Nation – Ninety-Minute Patriots?*, Leicester: Leicester University Press.

Horne, J. and Jary, D. (1987) 'The Figurational Sociology of Sport and Leisure of Elias and Dunning: An Exposition and a Critique', in J. Horne, D. Jary and A. Tomlinson (eds), *Sport, Leisure and Social Relations*, London: Routledge & Kegan Paul.

Horne, J. and Jary, D. (1994) 'The Figurational Sociology of Sport and Leisure Revisited', in I. Henry (ed.), *Leisure: Modernity, Postmodernity and Lifestyles*, Eastbourne: Leisure Studies Association (Publication No. 48).

Jarvie, G. and Maguire, J. (1994) *Sport and Leisure in Social Thought*, London: Routledge.

Malcolmson, R.W. (1973) *Popular Recreations in English Society 1700–1850*, Cambridge: Cambridge University Press.

Malcolmson, R.W. (1984) 'Sports in Society: A Historical Perspective', *The British Journal of Sports History*, Volume 1, pp. 60–71.

Mason, T. (1988) *Sport in Britain*, London: Faber and Faber.

Mason, T. (1995) *Passion of the People? Football in South America*, London: Verso.

Mills, C.W. (1970) *The Sociological Imagination*, Harmondsworth: Penguin.

Ritzer, G. (1993) *The McDonaldization of Society*, London: Sage.

Rojek, C. (ed.) (1989) *Leisure for Leisure?*, London: Macmillan.

Storch, R.D. (1976) 'The Policeman as Domestic Missionary: Urban Discipline and Popular Culture in Northern England 1850–1880', *Journal of Social History*, Volume 9.

Tomlinson, A. (1996) 'Olympic Spectacle: Opening Ceremonies and Some Paradoxes of Globalization', *Media Culture & Society*, Volume 18, pp. 583–602.

Chapter four

Social stratification and social division in sport

Introduction

Sport is often seen as the domain of fair play in which opportunity is said to be open to all. From such a perspective, the legacies of the values of athleticism as established in the nineteenth century – playing to the rules, honouring one's opponent for instance – blend with the meritocratic rhetoric of modern sport. Yet throughout modern history sport participation and its meanings have been differentiated and diverse, rooted in social inequalities and divisions. Sport has been developed and sustained in a modern society characterised by deeply embedded forms of social stratification; it is hardly surprising, therefore, that sports forms and practices are themselves indices of such differences. In this chapter we consider the primary sources of stratification in sport – social class, gender and ethnicity – in illustrative detail, and signal other sources of division in examining how social inequalities and divisions have been variously and recurrently manifest in sporting forms and practices.

The term 'stratification' derives from the technical geological word for the different layers of the earth's crust. Figuratively, in sociology, it has come to refer to the way in which a society comprises layered groupings, separate yet interconnected within a totality – the organic power of the metaphor has persisted. By the second half of the nineteenth century the term was beginning to be applied specifically to society. As the German Baring-Gould could put it in 1879: 'The stratification of the German classes, and of the aristocracy, is most peculiar' (OED, 1979: 3084). It has become a central concept in the analysis of societies:

> In all complex societies, the total stock of valued resources is distributed unequally, with the most privileged individuals or families enjoying a disproportionate amount of property, power or prestige . . . most scholars . . . identify a set of 'social classes' or 'strata' that reflect the major cleavages in the population. The task of stratification research is to specify the shape and contours of these social groupings, to describe the processes by which individuals are allocated into different social outcomes, and to uncover the institutional mechanisms by which social inequalities are generated and maintained.
>
> (Grusky, 1993: 610)

A classic formulation of stratification in American society points out that it is in societies in which success, equality and classlessness are claimed as central social values that many people are blinded to 'the contours, and the pervasiveness of social stratification' (Hodges, 1964: x):

> ours is in fact a multi-layered society, a hierarchical society in which whole classes of people are quite commonly accorded low, middling or high social esteem, power and material wealth . . . Complex societies are everywhere and always *stratified* societies: this is inescapable fact. It is a fact as true of today's United States – and of contemporary Japan or the Soviet Union or Thailand or Paraguay – as it was of medieval Europe, classical Greece, or ancient Mesopotamia.
>
> (Hodges, 1964: x–xii)

Although sport has in some cases offered opportunities for dramatic and spectacular social mobility – sports stars earning money and accruing status undreamt of in the social and cultural milieux of their origins – sports have, at most levels of commitment and performance, exhibited the differentiations and divisions of the wider, stratified social context. This is not to say that sport is always no more than a mere reflection of the society: sporting practices and cultures can break the mould of inherited inequalities, or challenge an existing order of division and inequality. In such ways, a particular sporting form can exhibit a complex mix of the residual, dominant and the emergent (Williams, 1977a; Williams, 1977b) within a society and a culture. But for the most part, sport cultures have contributed to the reproduction of existing patterns of social stratification and division. Sugden and Tomlinson (1999) have summarised thus:

> It was the American novelist and popular historian, James Michener (1976) who suggested that for most of this century a glance at the boxing rankings in the American sports press was a reasonably accurate gauge of which social groups were situated towards the bottom of that country's social

order. When Jewish, Italian and Irish names began to appear less frequently, this could be taken as a clear indication that these groups had become socially mobile and that boxing was no longer considered to be an appropriate sport for those on a higher social plane. If this relationship between sport and social standing pertains for the lower orders, then it can be applied equally to social élites and gradations in between. For instance, in the context of British society, involvement in a polo match in the grounds of Windsor Castle, participation in Henley's boating regatta or a trip to the grouse moors of Scotland can be taken as clear signals of high social status. Similarly, playing golf at Royal St Andrews, attending Twickenham for a rugby international, having a season ticket for a Premier Division football club, turning out in the park for the local pub's football team, and keeping and racing pigeons, all convey messages about the social location of the participants.

Stratified sport: sources of division in modern sport

The case studies presented in Chapter 2 demonstrate the importance of the athleticist code, and the definitions and disputes concerning amateur and professional forms of involvement in sport. These are examples of a sports ethos and culture in which the particular set of sporting values are the product of a society based upon rigid distinctions of status, that is, a stratified society in which social class and gender in particular determine the sporting life-chances of the individual. And it is worth recalling the etymology of the terms 'amateur' and 'professional': amateur derives from the Latin word for love – the amateur engages in a particular activity for the love of it; professional derives from the Latin term for a confession, but came to mean a statement of one's driving motives or beliefs, and to refer to a vocation or a calling. The very categories, then, evoke different sets of social circumstances and the cultural forms in which they became expressed represented distinctive assumptions about social status and position in society. Whannel has summarised, in trenchant fashion, such a nineteenth-century legacy for British sport:

> The rigid distinctions erected between the amateur and the professional were in the end rooted in class domination. The formation of these institutions on the base of public school and university sport made them also an expression of the domination of social life by men. This does not mean that no women or working-class people were involved in sport during this period. But such involvement was always within the bounds of authority exercised by men of the bourgeoisie.

> (1983: 53)

97

The evolution of sporting institutions involved forms of alliance between the culture of dominant and emergent social classes, so that the 'aristocratic leisure site' of 'the gentleman's club, became the model for the social organisation of virtually all sporting activity involving the middle classes' (Blake, 1996: 67) and acted as a form of protection for the ethos of amateurism. Simultaneously, amateur forms of sporting practice were forms of conspicuous consumption (Veblen, 1953), in which those who occupy the apex of a system that depends absolutely on the success of industrial enterprise choose to express their social standing by distancing themselves completely from those activities that in any way resemble work, while engaging in the conspicuous display of dilettante forms of leisure which are premised on an infrastructure of labour and capitalist production. This is the kernel of Veblen's *The Theory of the Leisure Class* (subtitled 'An Economic Study of Institutions'), his analysis of the social consequences of the workings of capitalism in late nineteenth century United States of America, published in 1899.

Veblen makes the astute observation that, once established through 'pecuniary emulation' (making money), the ruling class sets itself apart from lower gradations by recreating the imagined lifestyles of the elites of previous eras. An exemption from work is a key feature of this imagery:

> From the days of the Greek philosophers to the present, a degree of leisure and of exemption from contact with such industrial processes as serve the immediate everyday purpose to human life has ever been recognised by thoughtful men as a prerequisite to a worthy or beautiful, or even a blameless human life. In itself and in its consequences the life of leisure is beautiful and ennobling in all civilised men's eyes.
>
> (1953: 42)

For Veblen, status was not passively linked to wealth. On the contrary, 'wealth or power must be put in evidence, for esteem is awarded only on evidence' (ibid.), through the 'non-productive consumption of time'. In short, in order to maintain their status, the ruling class had to be seen to be busy, spending both time and money, doing nothing. In this regard, 'a life of leisure is the most conclusive evidence of pecuniary strength, and therefore of superior force' (ibid.). Suitable 'evidence' for a life of leisure comes in rich variety and includes styles of dress, modes of travel and tourism, appreciation for and possession of art and literature, honorary titles and ensignia, and all other attributes of exclusiveness and 'good taste' in a wide variety of cultural products.

In Veblen's hands class and caste merge in the ways through which ruling elites, once established through economic success, bond and can be identified through shared participation in categories of activities that are exclusive and generative of high status. It is in this context that Veblen pays special attention to sport which, after war, he views as an ideal medium through which the ruling class can display its physical superiority; recreate the imagined conditions of a more barbarous and yet, simultaneously, more 'chivalrous' past; provide socialisation and character development for its children; and, finally, offer a proving ground for *parvenus* who would seek to join its ranks:

> Hence, the facility with which any new accessions to the leisure class take to sports; and hence the rapid growth of sports and of the sporting sentiment in any industrial community where wealth has accumulated sufficiently to exempt a considerable part of the population from work.
>
> (1953: 176)

Moreover, given the prohibition on work, other than war, sport, argues Veblen, is the only legitimate terrain where the ruling class (males) can engage in public displays of physical prowess:

> From being an honourable employment handed down from the predatory culture as the highest form of everyday leisure, sports have come to be the only form of outdoor activity that has the full sanction of decorum.
>
> (1953: 172)

Veblen saw sport in his day as one of the 'modern survivals of prowess' (ibid.). He believed that the warlike temperaments, actions and nomenclature associated both with field sports (hunting) and athletics, legitimated ruling class participation in them. Veblen recognised that sports provided elite groups with the perfect opportunity to define their boundaries, both from within and in the eyes of outsiders. But he was acerbic in his condemnation of the posing and posturing that accompanied many of these activities:

> It is noticeable, for instance, that even very mild mannered and matter-of-fact men who go out shooting are apt to carry an excess of arms and accoutrements in order to impress upon their own imagination the seriousness of their undertaking. These huntsmen are also prone to a histrionic, prancing gait and to an elaborate exaggeration of the motions, whether of stealth or of onslaught, involved in their deeds of exploit. Similarly in athletic sports there is almost invariably present a good share of rant and swagger and ostensible mystification – features which mark the histrionic nature of these employments . . . The slang of athletics, by the way, is in great part made up of extremely sanguinary locutions borrowed from the terminology of warfare.
>
> (1953: 171)

Veblen's thesis concentrates almost exclusively on the activities of society's uppermost strata. However, in his work there are hints that he understood that the overlap between class and status operated at all levels of a social hierarchy which, as capitalism developed, became increasingly differentiated and complex. Stratified sport offered established or dominant, and emergent classes, especially, vital sources for the generation of cultural identity and social status. This can be seen in the examples of fox-hunting in early nineteenth-century Britain, in the growth of tennis clubs in middle-class life and in the importance of hobbies in working-class culture at the end of the nineteenth century and in the first half of the twentieth century.

In the middle of the nineteenth century certain sporting events and practices bestowed and confirmed the status of privileged and elite groups in British society. Such sports were part of the formal life of British 'society', which took place in private locations and according to rigid convention. Davidoff describes how the formation of such a social life 'embraced by aristocratic and middle classes in both town and country' made it possible for upwardly mobile individuals and parts of families to gain access to new groups if they had the necessary qualifications: 'The whole basis of social relations was family (or pseudo-family) ties between equals in the elite, or patronage across well-defined hierarchical lines' (1986: 27). Yachting at Cowes, grouse-shooting in Scotland and partridge-shooting in country houses were famous examples of the 'extra, semi-sporting rural or artistic events' by which elite society exhibited its cultural distinctiveness and superiority. The activity *par excellence*, as Davidoff puts it, that illustrated the capacity of sport to display forms of conspicuous consumption, combined with public declarations of some openness and social integration and harmony was hunting – bringing together local people and people from London Society:

> It had all the elements of aristocratic patronage and deference masked by a male equality in sports. But the cost of maintaining the horses and dogs, the beaters and coverts, meant that it also provided an unsurpassed sphere of social aggrandisement for the new rich. Hunting, too, allowed a limited amount of class mixing in the field: that is, local farmers, doctors and similar people could hunt along with the great as long as they were sufficiently keen and skilful . . . also . . . hunting and riding were the only outlet for physical activity allowed even mid-Victorian girls and women. And when out in the field, the very strict rules of chaperonage had to be relaxed.
>
> (1986: 28–29)

In the example of hunting (see, too, Elias, 1986 and Itzkowitz, 1977), sport provided the ideal vehicle for a blending, in public ritual masquerading as long-

established tradition, of the interests of the dominant culture and the emergent culture – framed mainly in terms of a cultural identity associated with
the accommodating dominant culture of the aristocrat. Elias has demonstrated
the specifically modern nature of English fox-hunting as it evolved in the
eighteenth century as part of 'the 'sports ethos' . . . of wealthy, sophisticated
and comparatively restrained leisure classes who had come to value the tension and excitement of well-regulated mock battles as a major part of their
pleasure' (1986: 168). In the nineteenth century hunting continued to carry
'the greatest *social cachet*', whilst also 'looked to by many merely in search
of social advancement' (Itzkowitz, 1977: 29) and retaining a popular presence
in the calendar of rural life. The sport combined the image of an earlier
period with an openness of access which could bestow status and cultural
pedigree upon newly emergent groups with no direct connection with that
earlier age:

> In the hunting field, the old England of squires and tenants, of mutual
> dependence and deference lived on unchanged, unmindful of the growth
> of cities, of the appearance of new men, and of the establishment of new
> relationships. It was this that constituted hunting's appeal for so many
> who hunted and others who merely watched. It was this that made hunt-
> ing so natural a part of the life of a country gentleman, for in the hunting
> field as indeed at the rent-day dinner or the agricultural show, he was ful-
> filling the natural destiny of his order. It was this that made hunting so
> attractive to the newly-rich city man who saw it as a quick, simple way of
> entering the life of that old England.
>
> (Itzkowitz, 1977: 178)

More modestly, and perhaps a little less conspicuously, sports provided important cultural outlets for the emerging middle classes. At the turn of the nineteenth and the twentieth centuries, sport offered a site for the public expression
of the new suburban culture. As Davidoff notes: 'Very often a tennis or other
club would be used as the social centre where a mini-season of activities including the presentation of local girls took place' (1986: 74). Established in
its modern form in the 1870s, (lawn) tennis was promoted in society magazines and assumed such popularity that Oscar Wilde wrote to a friend, from
Nottinghamshire: 'We have had some very pleasant garden parties and any
amount of lawn tennis' (Walker, 1989: 147). The game's popularity among
middle- and upper-class society had faded by the early 1890s, but it became
very popular among the new suburban middle classes, particularly women.
Tennis clubs (and golf clubs and courses, as described in Chapter 2) became
elements integral to the planning of suburban developments and estates.
Reviewing the impact of tennis and golf during the inter-war period, Howkins

and Lowerson conclude that 'the frontiers of exclusiveness expanded slightly. . . . Both sports often influenced the siting of the more affluent suburbs' (1979: 42). Golf contributed to 'the reinforcement of a complex series of overlaps within social elites', whilst tennis 'went further down the social scale and involved a greater female following' (ibid.). But both sports expressed the distinctiveness of middle-class suburban life.

Certain team sports – notably, football – provided new industrial populations with a focus for the collective expression of community. Tin-miners migrating from Cornwall in the south-west of England to, for instance, Burnley in the north-west of England could express a cultural and regional identity, and a collective status, by supporting the local football side. But other sporting practices also provided opportunities for the expression of a distinctive working-class status and identity. Hobbies, as argued by McKibbin (1991: 102), could be freely chosen, required regular commitment, organisation and discipline of an intellectual and/or physical kind, required knowledge and sustained interest, and usually involved the expression of a mental or physical tension. From the 1880s onwards, hobbies became increasingly popular. One writer, Paterson, on London working-class adolescents of 1911 talked of a 'genius for hero-worship' in the sport talk of the boys, which went beyond just cricket or football:

> Boxers or wrestlers, runners and cyclists, weight-putters and dog-fanciers . . . are in the sweetstuff shop assumed to be national celebrities, their times, weights and records stored away in minds that seem capable of containing little else.
>
> (Cited in McKibbin, 1991: 147)

Hobbies were an important form of cultural activity in new working-class settings. They provided an autonomy in working-class life, often in collectively based forms of administration in pigeon, dog or canary breeding, or in the formation of football clubs, and provided a forum for an intense intra-class public competitiveness (McKibbin, 1991: 161–163). In working-class culture, sports-related hobbies became established as significant sources for the allocation of public esteem (overwhelmingly, for men) in newly emergent industrial communities.

Stratified sports cultures were generated in a stratified and hierarchical society, and even in the cases where the sport might have had some impact as a form of social bonding, in bringing social classes together for the hunt for instance, the distinctions of status were ultimately reaffirmed. There is no doubt that sports have in some circumstances a capacity to articulate a new social and cultural order, but the historical record illustrates the differentiated and stratified character of such developments.

Social class

Social class has been a central concept in the social sciences, 'one of the best established approaches for analysing data on social structure' (Wesolowski and Slomczynski, 1993: 82). This has been accomplished by looking at how social classes differ according to the share of unequally distributed goods, their varied opinions and attitudes, their group actions and political beliefs and behaviours, and the extent to which they are socially mobile (that is, able to move between classes). Different theoretical approaches have emphasised particular aspects of class stratification. A functionalist approach suggests that people occupy different positions according to their suitability and society's need to place appropriate people in functionally important – but differently rewarded – positions. From this perspective, everybody contributes to the overall functioning of the society, but individuals are differentially rewarded. Such an approach has been widely criticised as neglecting the nature of power and privilege, and the capacity of powerful social actors to mould society in their own image. A Marxist approach to class stratification, at its simplest, places the conflict relation between classes at the centre of its concerns. In this approach, industrial capitalism produced groups whose economic interests were at loggerheads with the capitalist owners exploiting, for economic profit, the labour of the workers (the proletariat). The general nature of the society, from such a Marxist perspective, was a product of the fundamental antagonism and conflict that defined the relationship between the main social classes. Although Marx recognised the complexity of class groupings in particular historical circumstances, it is the nature of the economically derived conflict and division between the main social classes that is stressed. Looking beyond the Marxist formulation, Max Weber proposed that social class affiliation is more negotiable, for the class situation of the individual was an outcome of that individual's opportunity to sell professional skills and goods. For Weber, too, status and power could stem from sources beyond just the economy. On a general conceptual level, functionalist, Marxist and Weberian conceptions of social class, and the application of such conceptions to the understanding of sport, have been reviewed by Sugden and Tomlinson (1998). Here, their outline of the work of Bourdieu – conceived as combining the strengths of both a Marxist and a Weberian framework in illuminating the social class and status dimensions of contemporary culture – is drawn upon as the framework most appropriate to understanding the ways in which sport has been stratified along social class lines.

As a starting point for his discussion of the relationship between sport and social class, Bourdieu notes that the emergence of

> sports in the strict sense . . . took place in the educational establishments
> reserved for the 'elites' of bourgeois society, the English public schools,

> where the sons of aristocratic or upper-bourgeois families took over a number of *popular* – i.e. *vulgar* – *games*, simultaneously changing their function.
>
> (1978: 823)

He connects the rationalisation of games into modern sports forms with a class-based philosophy of amateurism: 'the modern definition of sport . . . is an integral part of a "moral ideal", i.e. an ethos which is that of the dominant fractions of the dominant class.' (1978: 825). To play tennis or golf, to ride or to sail, was, as Bourdieu argues, to bestow upon the participant *'gains in distinction'* (1978: 828). Sports in which lower middle-class or working-class adolescents participate develop 'in the form of spectacles produced for the people . . . more clearly as a mass commodity' (1978: 828). For Bourdieu, then, sport acts as a kind of badge of social exclusivity and cultural distinctiveness for the dominant classes, for the social elite, and as both a means of control or containment of the working or popular classes and a potential source of escape and mobility for talented working-class sports performers. Sports, therefore, are not self-contained spheres of practice:

> class habitus defines the meaning conferred on sporting activity, the profits expected from it; and not the least of these profits is the social value accruing from the pursuit of certain sports by virtue of the distinctive rarity they derive from their class distribution.
>
> (1978: 835)

From this perspective, then, sports participation is not a matter of personal choice, of individual preference. It depends upon the financial resources available to the potential participant, the social status of those prominent in that activity, and the cultural meaning of a sport and the individual's relationship to those meanings. The recruitment and induction processes into, say, golf and tennis clubs, bear testimony to this. Take the apparently open-minded and egalitarian basis of a newcomer playing him or herself in at a tennis club. In order to do this the aspirant must communicate competently with the gate-keepers of a club; read the social interactions and etiquette and conventions of a club; comply with the dress code; be equipped with relatively sophisticated technology (he or she would be unlikely to get far with a wooden Dunlop Maxply in the 1990s); and be able to play at a level of acceptable competence. This apparently open choice is in reality a possibility or trajectory based upon what Bourdieu recognises as the power of economic and cultural capital:

> Class variations in sporting activities are due as much to variations in perception and appreciation of the immediate or deferred profits they are

supposed to bring, as to variations in the costs . . . Everything takes place as if the probability of taking up the different sports depended, within the limits defined by economic (and cultural) capital and spare time, on perception and assessment of the intrinsic and extrinsic profits of each sport in terms of the dispositions of the habitus, and more precisely, in terms of the relation to the body, which is one aspect of this.

(1986: 212)

The notion of the habitus is central to the Bourdieuian framework: 'different conditions of existence produce different habitus – systems of generative schemes applicable, by simple transfer, to the most varied areas of practice' (1986: 170). The habitus embodies both that which is structured and that which is structuring: 'As a system of practice-generating schemes' it 'expresses systematically the necessity and freedom inherent in its class position and the difference constituting that position' (1986: 172). Rojek provides a useful summary of the concept:

Habitus refers to an imprinted generated schema. The term 'generative' means a motivating or propelling force in social behaviour. The term 'schema' means a distinctive pattern or system of social conduct. For Bourdieu, the socialization process imprints generative schemata onto the individual.

(1995: 67)

Generally, habitus refers to those patterns of behaviour, thought and taste which link social stuctures to social practice or social action (Marshall, 1994: 209).

The concept of habitus reminds us of the boundedness of sports cultures. Far from sport being an open sphere of limitless possibilities, it is a social phenomenon and cultural space that can operate, in Weberian terms (Parkin, 1976) as a form of social closure, in which potential entrants are vetted and excluded as suits the incumbent gatekeepers, and the inner world of the sports culture is tightly monitored and controlled. The same processes may be at work in golf club membership committees and in other sports institutions in which entry requirements – written or unwritten – operate as potential barriers to open participation. The bounded social class basis of participation in such sports is clear from empirical evidence in large-scale national surveys in the UK. Data from the 1983 General Household Survey indicated clearly that 'apart from walking, participation in sports, games and physical activities is low, declines across the social classes (class 1 stands out as most active) and is higher among men than women' (Reid, 1989: 383). The same pattern was evident a decade later:

Generally, professionals, employers and managers were more likely to participate in out-door sports than those in other groups. The same cannot be said for indoor sports and activities. Those in the skilled manual and own account non-professional groups had the highest participation rates for cue-sports and darts. There is clearly still some class distinction in some sports and games. Those in the professional group were much the more likely to play squash and golf, for instance.

(Central Statistical Office, 1993: 147)

Figures from surveys conducted in the UK in 1986/7, 1990 and 1994 corroborate this, demonstrating – despite changes in interviewing technique that produced higher reported participation rates after 1987 – continuities in the embeddedness of the class habitus of sports. Table 4.1 illustrates this in the case of golf.

The rigidity of class boundaries may have diminished in some ways, and sociological debates have raged on the 'mounting evidence that societies like Britain are more open than they had believed' (Saunders, 1997: 282), but in contemporary sports cultures class categories – in terms of socio-economic classifications, in which the combined influence of economic, status and cultural factors have persisting influence and impact – continue to influence participation and activity. The figures in Table 4.1 also suggest that, with the largest fall-off in participation rate among the best and less well-off social group, such trends are connected to economic cycles of boom and recession. But the broad parameters of the sporting milieu remain unaltered. More generally, 82 per cent of people in professional occupations 'had taken part in at least one physical activity in the previous four weeks in 1993–94 compared with only 48 per cent of those in the unskilled manual groups' (CSO, 1996: 224).

Class cultures in which the meanings of sport are rooted do not disappear overnight. Even in the traumatic context of the mid-1980s coal dispute in northern England, it was traditional cultural, leisure and sporting strategies that continued to 'shape family life, social relationships and leisure' (Waddington *et al.*, 1991: 104). And 'Sports and social clubs, pubs and churches seemed to

TABLE 4.1 Participation in golf, in percentages, by socio-economic group, 1987, 1990 and 1993

Year	Professional	Employers and managers	Intermediate and junior non-manual	Skilled manual, own account non-professional	Semi-skilled manual and personal service	Unskilled manual	Total
1987	11	12	8	5	5	4	7
1990	13	10	4	5	2	1	5
1993	9	10	5	6	2	2	5

provide most of what local adults wanted' (p. 103). Further qualitative, ethno-graphic work in sociological community studies, anthropology and cultural studies illuminate the deep-rootedness of such cultures. The social and economic conditions that formed the basis of the place of rugby league in the community life of an early post-Second World War northern English mining village (Denis *et al.*, 1995) may have undergone dramatic change. But the values of working-class community that were at the heart of that culture were still important influences upon the game where it survived in the mid-1990s: 'the working class maleness that forms part of the values of the Sudthorpe social networks of the imaginary community of "the game" is in tension with the expressions of masculinity in Australian league, and the discourses around the Superleague' (Spracklen, 1995: 116). In their participant observation studies of working-class male youth groups in the early 1970s, in the West Midlands and north-east England respectively, Paul Willis (1977) and Paul Corrigan (1979) demonstrated the cultural resistances of working-class males to formal institutional structures and official cultures of school and sport. The studies gave prominence to the views and voices of their respondents.

Willis' study of twelve secondary-aged male working-class pupils in an English West Midlands school in the early 1970s identified the intensely hostile attitudes of 'lads' to an official culture of the school. Lads who may have begun secondary school with what teachers saw as a positive outlook to educational life are drawn into what Willis calls a process of *differentiation* from formal school life, a process whose 'dynamic is opposition to the institution which is taken up and reverberated and given a form of reference to the larger themes and issues of the class culture' (Willis, 1977: 62–63). To the institutional leader, as Willis puts it, the teacher, this is an individual pathology, a personal failure. The following report on the pupil Spansky captures both the process and the institutional response:

> (Spansky) in the first three years was a most co-operative and active member of school. He took part in the school council, school play and school choir in this period and represented the school at cricket, football and cross-country events.
>
> Unfortunately, this good start did not last and his whole manner and attitude changed. He did not try to develop his ability in either practical or academic skills . . . his early pleasant and cheerful manner deteriorated and he became a most unco-operative member of the school . . . hindered by negative attitudes.
>
> (Willis, 1977: 62)

For a working-class pupil such as Spansksy, the street culture, the commercial dance and the prospect of the excitement of the evening against the mundanity of the daytime offer more meaningful cultural values than the dubious promise of schooling. And sport becomes widely associated with the formal, official school culture.

Corrigan's ethnography of the school and leisure lives of 14 to 15-year-old boys in Sunderland, north-east England, makes still more explicit this incompatibility between the expressed class culture of the boys and the sports culture of the school. Corrigan notes that sociologists had recorded previously the reluctance of such kids to play school sport or represent the school at sport, but adds a fresh layer of interpretation, exploring what he calls the *mode* of sport offered by the school and the alternative mode of playing preferred by the kids away from the school:

> School sports are not simply an attempt to allow the boys a chance to enjoy themselves, they are meant to instil a certain attitude to sports as their prime reason for being on the timetable. Playing football for the school represents a certain form of 'playing football' which by no means represents the 'normal' way of playing football for the boys in this study . . .
>
> *Question* Do you like football?
>
> *Bert* Yes, a lot. I used to play for the school team only you had to turn out every Saturday, and you had to buy a bag so I dropped out.
>
> *Question* Where do you play football around here?
>
> *Bert* Used to play outside the metalwork shop. But the coppers came and said 'Next time we catch you here you're gonna get summoned'. He took the ball away in his panda.
>
> (1979: 101)

Corrigan shows that there is a number of different games of football – modes of involvement and commitment – for the boys in his study and that 'for most of them the activity of playing football was not that of the structured game' (1979: 102). This complex relationship between class cultures, or habitus, and formal sports institutions has been further analysed, at a theoretically more sophisticated level, by John Hargreaves. He shows how the practices and technologies of schooling and sport have served as instruments of class domination, and have contributed to the cultural reproduction of class difference and social inequality. This has occurred on the basis of the capacity of physical education and school sport to divide working-class children:

> far from there being a clash between working-class culture as such and the school, there are in fact, in important respects, linkages between the school culture and the culture of a significant proportion of the working class, which means there is also pressure and demand for competitive

sport from the more achievement-oriented pupils and their parents . . .
Voluntary involvement of male working-class pupils in school sport and
relative compliance with models of behaviour promoted in the PE programme then, need not imply a one-way imposition of school or middle-
class values. What it does mean is that a process of accommodation is
going on, which draws the middle class, as represented by the school, and
the upper working class, closer together and which produces a quite sharp
division among working-class pupils in the school.

(Hargreaves, 1986: 175)

Social class, therefore, can act as a force for modification to established social
relations, allowing for some degree of social mobility and the realignment of
class fractions. In this sense, sport can contribute – as in the example of the
dynamics of the amateur–professional relation in sport in the modern period –
to processes of class formation and the reproduction and reformation of class
categories. The work of Willis and Corrigan shows how class is an objective
feature of social relations, a dynamic framing the lived realities of their subjects.
Hargreaves reminds us that the analytical tool of class can also identify a wider
range of class dynamics.

Urry (1989: 87–88) has summarised major trends in social class in Britain
on the eve of the century's final decade, listing six points:

- The traditional working-class has shrunk, as manufacturing industry and
  manual work have employed fewer people.
- Social inequalities between the 'have-nots' and the 'have-lots' have
  increased.
- Limited chances for upward social mobility have been evident, mainly for
  white men.
- Middle-class groupings have become differentiated in more complex
  ways.
- Occupations are not wholly patterned by the capital/labour relationship.
- The 'institutionalisation' and 'internationalisation' of capital has become
  more advanced.

To take Urry's points one by one. First, traditional and often collective working-
class sports may persist in some regions, but the community and urban base for
such sports has been to a large extent eroded. Second, sports participation data
do corroborate the existence of inequalities, with 'issues of access and exclusion' (Tomlinson, 1986) still at the heart of Britain's sports cultures. Third, it
is clear that some sports professionals' careers provide dramatic evidence of
income and status-based forms of social mobility, and some sports audiences
are also testimony to the shifting boundaries of life-chances and cultural

opportunity. Fourth, and relatedly, *nouveau* elements within the class structure (and particularly the newer middle classes, or relatively unskilled income-earners who see themselves as middle class rather than working class) have more opportunity to play sports such as golf, tennis or squash than in earlier generations. Fifth, on the level of sports workers and occupations, the expansion of public sector sports provision, the continuing buoyancy of clubs and voluntary sports bodies and institutions, and the growth in the private-sector sports industry have all contributed to a growth of far from easily classifiable forms of work and occupation in sport. Finally, sport has become more and more internationalised as multinational capital and international media and marketing have fundamentally reshaped traditional sporting institutions and practices and sought to import sporting cultural products (such as American football, basketball and sumo). Rather than indicating the 'end of class', these trends and exemplars of trends point to a complex repositioning of some traditional social class groupings and sub-groupings, and the continuing importance of sport as a barometer of social change and continuity.

Gender and sport participation

Gendered differences in sport participation have been, and remain, marked, despite well-intentioned interventions by bodies such as the Sports Council (London, UK), which have aimed policies at women. But participation data point to continuing differences in level and type of involvement in sport and physical activity by men and women. One of the most interesting of these differences relates to outdoor and indoor sports: 'In outdoor sports, women's participation rates remain well below men's. These fell from 25% in 1983 to 24.3% in 1988, representing a reduction of about 100,000 participants' (Sports Council and Women's Sports Foundation, 1992). Where women did appear to be participating in higher numbers was in those sports that could be undertaken in the safety of an indoor venue, and that could be seen to combine health and self-image benefits. Swimming and keep-fit/aerobics emerged, after the doubtful category of walking, as the top participatory sports for women in 1990 (Sports Council and Women's Sports Foundation, 1992):

Walking	38%
Keep fit/aerobics	16%
Swimming	13%
Cycling	7%
Snooker	5%
Darts	4%
Badminton	3%

Ten pin bowls	3%
Golf	2%
Jogging/cross country/road running	2%

Despite the decrease in women's participation in outdoor sports, and even allowing for the change in mode of questioning for the General Household Survey, the increase of 2.5 million in women's weekly participation in a sports activity between 1987 and 1990 is revealing. Jogging had increased significantly from a negligible base a decade earlier, and the overlap between the cultural and fashion industries and the sports culture encouraged the expansion of activities such as aerobics. Yet even here, increased participation is no simple index of a move towards gender equality. Researchers have pointed to the vulnerability of women in settings such as the aerobics class:

> the body is exposed to the gaze of others . . . The great fear of aerobics is to be caught under the gaze of others . . . most participants are most comfortable at the back of the class, anonymous, where they can see and not be seen, follow the movements of others and not be seen.
>
> (Flintoff *et al.*, 1995: 98 and 99)

Sport and the physicality embodied in sport render it a major source for the re-affirmation of traditional gender relations, in some cases in public spheres where initially and potentially women's sport constitutes a progressive intervention in, and sometimes a challenge to, dominant male assumptions concerning the place of sport and women's relationship to traditional forms of sport. Three striking examples of this are available: the research of Prendergast on women's stoolball in the south of England; Middleton's work on the gender dynamics and struggles surrounding the use of a (cricketing) sports facility in a Yorkshire village; and Carr *et al.*'s analysis of sport policy and facility provision in the south of England.

Prendergast studied the stoolball case during 1977, when she was living in a rural parish in the Kent/Sussex Weald. She was astonished that 'the playing of stoolball was surrounded by a whole mythology of meaning and explanation, in the minds of men particularly, that simply did not occur in the equivalent male game, cricket' (1978: 15). Her study illustrates the way in which sporting practices can be determined by and implicated in wider issues of sexuality and gender identity. Modern changes in work patterns and labour opportunities meant that village households have become much more dependent upon the women of the locality continuing to live, and to work, in or within the vicinity of the village. The stoolball team in the village was also a catalyst for wider aspects of village life, and connected in important ways with women's involvement in community issues, child-rearing and work in the fields. Prendergast argues that this strong combination of interests was threatening to the males in the village, and to their sense of masculine identity. Women's stoolball practices were characterised by banter, joking, gossip, physical exuberance and display, and some male reactions – of young men on cycles and motorbikes, old men with their lifelong assumptions – were to disrupt the women's activities by riding through the practice area itself, or to label the women as promiscuous, as feminine failures:

> The remark of an older man, a shepherd, perhaps serves to illustrate the particular combination of explicit sexual meanings of the game, as read into it by men, with its corollary, the suggestion that men could easily control this display if they so wished. 'I'd be in two minds as to send me old dog down there and get 'em all up for the tup' . . . He was saying in effect, that the women were like the ewes that were, on the word of the farmer, brought up from the marshes and mated with the rams, in order to lamb in the Spring.
>
> (Prendergast, 1978: 19)

The stoolball game, Prendergast argues, is seen by the village males – young and old, around the village and in the pub – 'as a manifestation of the strength of women when they act as a group, rather than their "ideal" state of division and isolation in the home' (1978: 22). In this context, the abusive joking of the males is a means of attempting to reposition and reassert control over women's behaviour. Women with a firm economic base and financial independence, and a public and confident sports culture, are doubly threatening to the males of the village, whose main response is to abuse, harass and vilify the women.

Middleton's study identifies a village sports institution – the cricket club – as a revealing instance of how social boundaries are established and re-affirmed. She is concerned with the economic and the political boundaries that constrain women (Imray and Middleton, 1983), but also with the ways in which the boundaries between public and private operate in practices like sport, in the rhythms of everyday village life. Her fieldwork was carried out between 1979 and 1982 in a village in the English county of Yorkshire, and she questioned the assumption that men and women experience 'the village' in the same way: 'social movement in all its aspects – travel, employment, mobility, social contact and, most tellingly, use of village space – is consistently curtailed for women' (Middleton, 1986: 121). The institutions of the village to which women were seen to have access – the village hall, the shops, the school, for instance – were those in which they were expected to fulfil a public dimension of their domestic, household roles as parent, wife/partner, family carer or household manager. Their access to certain resources was limited. As Mary put it, with reference to the family car: 'I can't have it just when I want it – not for too flippant a reason' (1986: 125). Mary's last daytime use of the family car had been to take a son to hospital; shopping was seen, by her partner, as in the 'flippant' category. As Middleton (1986: 125–127) observes, for women:

> role-sets become frozen while their husbands' are extended . . . Women have only limited entry to places of leisure; they may be tolerated in these but with restrictions. They are in fact kept on the fringes of community space . . . much public space is off-limits to women.

Women alone, 'manless' as Middleton puts it, using public leisure spaces such as the river and its surroundings, or the pub, were seen as 'asking for it', or offering themselves as 'fair game'. The overall picture painted by Middleton is of a village life in which public space is dominated by men, and 'the two sexes have distinct lives and inhibit different domains' (1986: 132). When women sought to make inroads into public sporting space in the village, they were seen as a threat to established male activity and territory.

Imray and Middleton describe in detail the way in which the men of the village discriminate against women, using their labour to support their own sporting institutions and practices, and generating ritualistic forms of affirmation of their own superiority and dominance over women. The village cricket team – comprising males of both working-class and middle-class backgrounds, from the ages of 14–60 – were the prima donnas of village life, expecting widespread support for their own activities, but giving no support to other village activity. They dominated the bar space of the sports and social club and forbade other forms of activity on what they saw as exclusively their playing pitch. The space around the clubhouse, the seating arrangements and the playing area were seen as spaces for men: 'But in the private sphere, women are hard at work producing leisure for men', washing whites, providing teas, activities vital to the 'production of a cricket match' (Imray and Middleton, 1983: 23). Women prepare drinks for players, but can go no further than the edge of the cricket pitch, where a man takes over the carrying duty and takes them to the square at the centre of the pitch. The men's changing room was off a corridor which linked the bar to the kitchen. Women working in catering who needed to go from the kitchen to the bar had to go outside and round the building. Once a year, on a weekday evening, men played women. The club fielded a young inexperienced male side. The women wore badminton skirts, tan tights, men's long sweaters and plimsolls. On the club veranda, segregated spectators comprised male cricketers on one side, women on the other. Veteran players yelled obscene comments at women during the play. The young men played with the cricket bat weaker-hand-round. The ritual end was a victory for the women by one run. In this apparently harmless and playful annual event is inscribed a deep-rooted male-dominated power and status structure:

> Once a year, then, members of the private sphere are allowed onto the 'square' where they are encouraged to flaunt their femininity and where inexperienced cricketers are defined as 'women', being beaten by them . . . a calendrical rite of status reversal . . . (which has) . . . the long-term effect of emphasising the strength and permanence of the usual order.
>
> (Imray and Middleton, 1983: 24)

Going beyond the role of uninvolved, detached observer/researcher, Middleton became secretary of the sports and social club, and attempted to organise the space for women to play seriously in team hockey. The cricket club offered initial support for use of the outfield of the cricket pitch for winter-season hockey, but, seeing the seriousness of the proposal, did not sustain the support: 'if women are allowed on the cricket pitch, this village will fall apart' (p. 25) was the masculinist view that prevailed.

Even when women are targeted as the beneficiaries of particular sports policies, the inequalities of gender can limit the effects of the policy intervention. Carr, Tomlinson and White (1997) have shown how this can occur at the level of facility management of innovative forms of provision. Their study evaluated the impact of the provision of three artificial turf pitches in the south of England at the turn of the 1980s and the 1990s, by focusing particularly upon the dynamics of women's participation, and the ways in which policy and practice impacted upon women's use of the new facilities. Two out of three of the artificial turf pitches were seen by the Sports Council Regional Officer involved as 'good "Sport for All" facilities' and 'he "hoped" the pitches would play a role in furthering Sports Council participation objectives, particularly in terms of promoting use among the target groups of women and young people' (Carr *et al.*, 1997: 185). But there was no indication that an adequate strategy had been evolved, at any level, for the realisation of such 'hopes'. Consequently, the local management of the facilities tended to favour established users and entrenched forms of participation, and facility aims, rather than people aims, were emphasised in the provision process. Carr *et al.* note (1997: 188):

> Whilst community recreation and welfare-oriented values, such as promoting women's participation, were held by some agents involved in policy formulation at the local level, they lacked the power to ensure these values guided practice.

The analysis of the case studies confirmed Talbot's (1988) assertion that provision for sport and recreation, particularly within the voluntary sector, is based on an ideology of consumer control. In practice, this meant that incumbent users continued to assume ownership in the sphere of new facilities, and in most of these cases the incumbent users were men. Managers of the facilities, rather than recognising that constraints on women's participation might derive from management structures and practices, implied that it is the target group that should change its behaviour. In this way the blame for women's user patterns was apportioned to women themselves, for not wanting to become involved in particular types of activity occurring on artificial pitches, and for not making more effort themselves.

Communal space for stoolball in the locality; space for organised sport in a voluntary sector club; and publicly provided facilities for multi-purpose use – three contexts across time and space. But the interpretive messages have much in common, and the three cases illustrate the importance of several themes in understanding the gendered basis of sports practices and institutions. First, the social space in which sports occur is to a great extent characterised by gender inequalities. Second, time itself is less flexible and malleable for women than for men. Third, sports as institutions are widely – both formally and informally – controlled by men, at the levels of management and policy, and supported and serviced by women. Fourth, sports continue to be seen as affirming of stereotypes of masculinity and femininity, and as spheres in which gender prejudice can be confirmed, even to the point of abuse.

Sexuality and the dimensions of power and status associated with sexual identity are important persisting influences upon the making and remaking of sports cultures. Women's initial experiences of sport, in school-based physical education, have been shown to be a source of girls' resistance to involvement in sport, for the culture of femininity so important to schoolgirls did not fit with:

> what they perceive as on offer from PE:
> (a) the development of muscle
> (b) sweat
> (c) communal shower/changing facilities
> (d) 'childish', asexual PE kit
> (e) low status activities.
>
> (Scraton, 1995: 125)

Forms of out-of-school involvement in sports clubs have also been male-dominated at the level of administration and management (White *et al.*, n.d.), and in terms of an organisational sexuality that can render girls and young women vulnerable to a range of forms of harassment and abuse (Tomlinson and Yorganci, 1997). In a number of key sites of social life – the family, the school, the community, the club, the local authority facility – forms of prejudice, discrimination, harassment, and sometimes abuse, curtail the scope and level of women's involvement in sport.

More generalised accounts of women's sport and leisure activities and experiences (Deem, 1986; Wimbush and Talbot, 1988; Green *et al.*, 1990) confirm the widespread persistence of such gendered inequalities. Quantitative signs (in participation figures) that women's participation in sport has increased in the final quarter of the twentieth century must be contextualised within an understanding of the nature of the particular activities or sports. Some 'new sports' as Bourdieu called them (1986) – windsurfing, surfing, fitness activities – have offered new possibilities to those women with the available resources in time and money. But aerobics, however potentially empowering, appears to have confirmed rather than challenged traditional and established models of femininity (Hargreaves, 1994: 160–162; Tomlinson, 1997; Flintoff *et al.*, 1995). Where other inroads have been made into traditional male territory – as in sports presentation within the broadcasting media – parallel paradoxes are evident. Although the Channel 5 presenter Gail McKenna's career profile from aspirant nun to tabloid page 3 girl, through pantomime and soap opera *Brookside*, was hardly typical of the emergent women's presence in sports broadcasting, it is clear that in large part the women's contribution is seen, even by the presenters themselves, as complementary to rather than challenging of traditional modes of presentation by men (Thompson, 1997).

There have been important critiques of the gender order in sports, fuelled by feminist scholarship and activism. Hall (1996: 101) has acknowledged, in this context, a 'notion of sport as a site of cultural struggle', a sense of the 'history of women in sport' as 'a history of cultural resistance'. Apparent increases in the number of women participating in sport can veil the basis and nature of women's participation, which is often reaffirming of the established structures and stereotypically treats 'women as unitary subjects' (Hargreaves, 1994: 241). Citing a Sports Council pamphlet on 'Sport for all Women', Hargreaves points to the consequences of this:

> One million more women have been attracted to sport in the last five years BUT the benefits of increased participation are not being shared by all women. Particularly under-represented are: black and ethnic women, girls and young women, housewives, single mothers, unemployed women, those on low incomes, and women with disabilities.
>
> (1994: 241)

The newly active women participants are, then, affluent, middle class, able bodied, white and adult. Gender inequalities are compounded by other dimensions of stratification and sources of social and cultural division. The mode of participation in sport – its location and frequency – continues to set women's sport cultures apart from those of men. The sociological evidence indicates clearly that in the sphere of sports, a hegemonic masculinity – 'defined as the configuration of gender practice which embodies the currently accepted answer to the problem of the legitimacy of patriarchy, which guarantees (or is taken to

guarantee) the dominant position of men and the subordination of women'
(Connell, 1995: 77) – continues to prevail. Such gendered values as masculinity
are not innate, as Connell (1983) also notes: sport is not a vehicle for the
articulation of an inherited manliness. Rather, a sphere such as sport provides a
regular and routinized forum for the promotion and expression of a learned
and generated masculinity, as is considered in more detail in Chapter 5 (on
socialisation). This point is developed by Salisbury and Jackson:

> School sport doesn't just play a part in shaping boys' emotional and social
> lives. It also locks many boys into an aggressively virile culture through
> the masculinizing of their bodies ... Boys are born with male bodies
> (biological characteristics) but quickly develop a gendered sense of
> masculinity in their bodies through the social meanings and relations they
> meet in a world that is organized in the interests of male power ... what
> many boys are learning in playing rugby, cricket, football, all the year
> round ... (is) ... to suggest the menacing promise of power through the
> way they hold their bodies.
>
> (1996: 208)

Despite the values that may be claimed for sport as a form of egalitarian or
meritocratic physical practice; or the social and health benefits that some sports
undeniably generate; or the innocently framed pleasure, fun and enjoyment that
accrue to participants from many sports – despite the importance of these meanings of sport, it would be an incomplete sociological and cultural reading of the
meaning of contemporary sport that failed to recognised the large degree to
which it acts as a source of and an expression for stratified status based upon
gender. Such gendered status is fiercely and cunningly defended within the
institutional structures of sport. It can sound ridiculous how this occurs. Two
examples within the context of English and Welsh golf clubs show how
entrenched the gendered practice and attitudes can be.

In spring 1997, at a South Wales golf club, a member was asked to leave
the club because he was sporting an ear-ring. The outraged authority from the
club, who voiced the official line of disapproval to a bemused and equally
amused media, muttered unconvincing words about dress code and standards:
the subtext was that anything traditionally non-masculine was unacceptable to
the conservative core of the membership. In July 1997 Johnny Briggs, Mike
Baldwin in British soap opera *Coronation Street*, wrote in a magazine that
women golfers were: 'an abomination ... take liberties, don't know the rules
... and take over everything like cockroaches' (cited in Jojo Moyes, 'The Fairer
Sex takes a Swing for Golfing Equality', *The Independent*, Friday, 11 July
1997, p. 5). Reports confirmed the male domination of British golf clubs, where
women were voteless, excluded from bars, offered inferior membership status

and widely restricted to off-peak playing hours. 'A lot of these clubs seem to work on the basis that women will play on weekdays after they've done the housework', said golf writer Liz Kahn (ibid.). In examples such as this, it is clear how traditional structures of sport can close ranks to defend traditional privileges. Sports clubs – private, unaccountable, excluding rather than including – can be used as powerful and effective tools for the reinforcement and reaffirmation of difference, hierarchy and division.

Race, black identity and sport

Ethnicity and black identity have been identified as important areas of research into the social and cultural role of sport in modern Britain. It has been established that black people are disproportionately under-represented in participation patterns across sport, but over-represented in certain elite levels of sports such as athletics and football. Sport policy makers and providers have at times seen the problem of participation as a general one, 'with no clearly articulated understanding of the issues relating to ethnic minorities and sport . . . initiatives seem largely to have been aimed at the general community in the vague hope that minority groups would join in' (Kew, 1979: 29). Alongside such ethnocentric provider philosophy, limited examples of black people's high profile in sport (as documented in Cashmore, 1990: 84) and the negative effects of stereotyping black people as 'naturally' good at certain sports (and so restricting opportunities in other spheres of life) (Cashmore, 1982) have provided the basis for a complex picture and pattern of participation. Fleming (1995) reminds us of the essential heterogeneity of South Asian cultures and of the varying place of sport in the wider ethnic culture. Participation rates vary across ethnic groups and between genders within ethnic groups. As Verma and his collaborators reported (1991: 335), males in all ethnic groups participated in sport more than did females. This gender pattern pervaded the findings:

> the difference in participation levels between the most active group of males – Chinese – and least active – Pakistani – was much smaller than the difference between the most active females – Chinese – and the least active – Bangladeshi. The differences between Chinese, White British and Caribbean males and females were quite small whereas those between Indian, African, Pakistani and Bangladeshi males and females were significantly greater.
>
> (Verma et al., 1991: 335)

Some black sports stars such as footballers achieve their goals against a backdrop of racial harassment and abuse (Fleming and Tomlinson, 1996), which has persisted, if more muted, despite the well-intentioned development of anti-racist initiatives (Garland and Rowe, 1996). It is well established that ethnically based forms of sport have often flourished as a means of asserting a distinctive identity, in response to discrimination. For instance, 'Bermudian blacks responded to segregation by forming their own clubs, mainly for sports and recreation', and also for arts, charity work and fashion (Manning, 1973: 29). Similarly, some responses within the black British community have prioritised a cultural autonomy in sport. The Muhammed Ali Sports Development Association, in the 1970s, stressed 'the importance of having black leaders in institutions and of designing projects specifically for black youngsters' (Kew, 1979: 30). Twenty years later, the all-black Accra Football Club in Brixton represented the pride of black identity and was seen by one of its organisers as 'a valuable social institution which can help prepare young black men for the difficulties they are likely to encounter in a racist society' (Tomlinson and Fleming, 1996: 93). One response to racism has been, therefore, to turn inwards. Carrington's study of the Caribbean Cricket Club illustrates the rationale for and nature of such a response.

The Caribbean Cricket Club was formed in Leeds in 1947, by West Indian Second World War veterans who had settled in the city. Both a social and sporting club, it offered a black community space for the following half century and a means of achieving at a high level in the local sports culture. Carrington (1997) emphasises the importance of the Caribbean Club and its ground and clubhouse (dating from the 1980s), The Oval, on the edge of the Chapeltown area, as a 'discursively constructed black social space':

> (In) the discussions and interviews . . . the club is mentioned as a 'black space', by which is often meant a place where black people can 'be themselves', free from the surveillance imposed by the 'white gaze' . . . In this sense the club's significance goes beyond merely being a cricket club and assumes a heightened *social* role as a *black* institution within a wider white environment. This can operate on a number of related levels, from being a space removed, albeit not entirely, from the overt practices of white racism; as a social and cultural resource for black people; and an arena that allows for black expressive behaviour.

Carrington's interviewees recall the importance to them of the club, as a focal and survival point. One 17 year old who played for other sides where he was one of only two blacks described how he could face racial abuse there, whereas no opposing side would abuse a Caribbean side that was predominantly black. As the club expanded in achievement and, concomitantly, profile, more teams were established and its junior teams comprised a wider ethnic mix of white, Asian and Chinese players. Its gender complexion remained exclusively male, with women's inputs being support-based and marginal, and talk of the development of a women's team never leading to action. The achievement of the Caribbean Cricket Club has been, nevertheless, to prosper and diversify, by adopting a strategy of the affirmation of cultural identity and therefore difference. This has shown the capacity of sport to both confirm yet challenge the sources of social division and stratification, to challenge racist stereotyping and prejudice by positive action and achievement. Sport provides a forum in which communal identity can be expressed and – in the case, for instance, of the northern English rugby league – some stereotypes challenged: 'at the symbolic level at least, the increased participation of . . . Asian players in the "hard white working class culture" of rugby league would make the stereotyped claims about Asian passiveness and fragility all the more difficult to sustain' (Long *et al.*, 1996: 13). On a more global scale, sport can also act as a forum for the assertion of black identity, in cases such as black athletes, basketball players and American footballers, and in sports not so usually associated with ethnic heterogeneity, such as tennis and golf: witness the case of the US golf star Tiger Woods.

Woods shot to prominence in the USA in 1996, voted *Sports Illustrated* man of the year, and globally early in 1997 in the build-up to and the aftermath of his victory in the US Masters' grand slam tournament at Augusta. He won that title, at the age of 21, by a 12–shot margin, watched by a record US television audience. Pitched into international superstardom, he signed further contracts, with American Express and Rolex, played one-day professional-amateur (pro-am) matches at a fee of $350,000 per day, spurned invitations from President Clinton and became embroiled in high-profile debates concerning his ethnic identity and his responsibility as a role model (Andy Farrell, 'Tiger back in his Natural Habitat', *Independent on Sunday*, 8 June 1997, p. 13). Woods had already earned more than $40 million in the year before his victory.

Woods shot to prominence early in life, with a remarkable pedigree of achievement as an amateur – the only player ever to win three successive American Amateur titles, from 1994 to 1996 – on the back of a golf scholarship to the elite Stanford University, California. The range of his golfing drive threatened to dwarf the traditional fairways, and potential sponsors wooed him before he accepted a Nike deal for $40 million, along with a $3 million deal from Titleist, the golf ball manufacturer. Most marketable of all, in Woods, were his ethnic roots: African-American origins via his father and Asian origins via his Thai mother, mixed with Chinese, Cherokee and European influences from more distant relatives. His mother could call him 'The Universal Child', his father hail him as 'The Chosen One', with the power 'to impact nations' (Andy Beckett, 'Tiger, Tiger Burning Bright', *Independent on Sunday*, 23 February 1997, pp. 6–9). Behind such messianic rhetoric, the global marketing possibilities for a black prodigy in the world sport of the middle classes, marketed by IMG (International Management Group), were beyond estimate. This sort of profile could also provide a forum for an interventionist cultural politics. Although Woods himself could say, on the one hand, that he wanted to be the greatest golfer ever, not the greatest black golfer ever, in his famous television advertisement for Nike he could state: 'There are still some courses in the United States that I am not allowed to play on because of the colour of my skin.' Woods and Nike also established a foundation – in Woods' name – to establish golf clinics for young urban blacks; 'Echoing Bill Clinton, he began to say in public that he wanted the sport to 'look like America'' (Beckett, ibid., p. 8). Criticised from many sides – from a black community for using the race issue to give such publicity to a multinational sponsor; from a pseudo-neutral sports community for 'bringing politics into sport'; from a white constituency for challenging its liberal assumptions – Woods nevertheless illustrated the power of sport and its major figures to address important social and cultural issues of the day, and the potential of a sport to challenge some central assumptions concerning stratification and social division.

Conclusions

This chapter has concentrated upon primary aspects of stratification and sources of social division, and some of their interrelationships. Others include age and disability. Obviously a participation profile of a given individual will change throughout the process of a lifetime of activity – perhaps less so if individual sports such as tennis, golf or snooker are played at an early age, than in the case of competitive team sports. But people who do not start to play sport or exercise early in life are highly unlikely to convert to sport later in life. The Allied Dunbar fitness survey concluded that 'people who exercise regularly in their youth are more likely to continue or to resume exercise in later years. 25% of those active when aged 14 to 19 years were very active now compared with 2% active now who were inactive at that earlier stage' (Allied Dunbar, 1991). This suggests that if sport involvement has strongly reflected entrenched forms of social division, then these will be characteristic of the ageing population. Woods (1994: 6) describes the rising life expectancy and the falling birth-rate as combined factors that have produced 'a unique and irrevocable shift in the history of western societies', producing a population in which, it is predicted, by 2031, 38 per cent of the population of the UK will be over 50 years of age. Woods reports shifts in the 1990s in the respective levels of involvement of older people: 'the differences in participation rates (between older and younger groups) are narrowing rapidly in a number of key leisure pursuits (for example, visits to the cinema and sports centre, swimming, participation in team sports and evening classes)' (1994: 9). Without doubt, this expanding population offers much to the sports industry and the sports market has geared up to cater for an increasingly active and health-conscious elderly population. Traditional surveys establishing satisfaction scores as an indication of well-being found consistently that 'older age groups are more satisfied with almost all life domains than younger groups' (Long and Wimbush, 1979: 19), but an expanded range of activities creates possibilities of non-involvement and dissatisfaction. Retirement, for instance, raised a number of problems for the respondents in Long and Wimbush's study – 'nothing to do and inability to cope with the time available' (1985: 122), linked to no purpose to or satisfaction with life, inadequate income, the lack of socialising that was previously provided by work, and attitudes of others towards the retired. Survey data (OPCS, 1995: 151–152) portray an inactive elder population in Britain. Apart from walking, no activity was engaged in by 10 per cent or more of 60–69 year olds. The only reportable participation rates were for 'any swimming' (8 per cent); keep fit/yoga (6 per cent); cycling and 'any bowls' (each 5 per cent); snooker/pool/billiards, and golf (each 4 per cent); darts (2 per cent); and badminton, ten-pin bowls/skittles and fishing (1 per cent). The vast majority of these golfers were men (7 per cent of men and only 1 per cent of women made up the 4 per cent overall participation rate) and only in keep fit/yoga were men less active than women.

Abrams has summarised the financial, ill-health, educational and situa-tional (isolation) factors that act as constraints upon leisure time use by the elderly, and concludes that:

> A population in which nearly 40% of all elderly people live alone and are acutely aware of loneliness had clearly not yet found how, through their leisure activities, to add re-engagement to retirement on any significant scale – except for a small minority with large incomes and with some experience of further or higher education.

> (1995: 87)

Ageing alone – that stealthy thief of able-bodiedness – does not account fully for involvement or non-involvement in sport: in combination with gender, class and ethnic-cultural factors, though, it acts as a major constraint upon participation and involvement.

Disability, too, is a lifelong influence upon those for whom the able-bodiedness so taken for granted in sports cannot be assumed. The everyday assumptions concerning access to and movement in the outdoors can be a source of frustration and trauma to people with disability, as research by Limb *et al.* (1995) has shown.

Sport at all its levels can therefore be seen to express social divisions on the basis of a range of sources of stratification. The social class, gender or ethnic category into which an individual is born will affect the status outcomes of any single individual's life. As Dahrendorf emphasises in his neo-Weberian approach, 'life chances are a function of two elements, *options* and *ligatures*' (1979: 30). In this formulation, options refer to possibilities of choice and ligatures are allegiances, bonds or linkages. The social habitus (Elias, 1993: 32) can also be conceived in this fashion, with the tribe or the community placing the individual in the particular context, and the development of individual strands, at the level of instincts and feelings, indicating options for the future. All social groups feature, in different ways, in the process through which a stratified social order is constructed, maintained and amended. Sporting possibilities and prospects are not immune from these central dynamics of a society and its cultures. Patterns of stratification are not laws of nature: they can be contested. But it would be sociologically naive to ignore their prevalence across time and space, and the persisting influence of forms of habitus and their capacity to effect social closure in sports cultures. Where a dominant sports culture is challenged by an emergent one, negotiated concessions can be made which modify but preserve the basis of privilege and dominance. In such ways can hegemony be sustained. When such a basis is marginalised, the previously dominant culture will often find ways of surviving in a residual form. Sport can encapsulate the contested and shifting dynamics of stratified societies, and can make some contribution towards challenging or reshaping those dynamics, but as a form of contemporary conspicuous consumption, sport has continued to be a major site for the explicit demonstration of difference framed by hierarchy, and of publicly expressed forms of social division.

Three primary dimensions of social stratification have been conceptualised by Turner (1988: 65–67): first, status as a legal-political phenomenon – a sense of entitlement based upon a principle of citizenship within a nation-state; second, the cultural dimension of lifestyle; and third, economically derived class position, referring to the individual's possession and effective control of economic resources. Turner argues that in a postmodern society – 'one in which, among other things, cultural styles become mixed, inter-woven and flexible, precluding any clear maintenance of hierarchical distinctions' (1988: 75) – social differentiation and social evaluation are not eroded, but are expressed in the possibility of 'more fluid cultural styles and the decline of conventional hierarchies' (p. 76): 'The conventional hierarchies within the cultural system appear to be more fragmented and diversified than in any previous period' (p. 77), producing 'an explosion of cultural signs and a cacophony of lifestyles' (p. 78). In the sports cultures of Britain in the late 1990s some trends in sports participation seemed to bear this out. Fashionable new sports such as windsurfing appeared, on the surface, to be class-less and gender-less in comparison with more traditional sports. But research revealed that committed windsurfers were very much middle-class professionals, youths or young adults, able-bodied to the point of conspicuous consumption, and that – despite inroads by highly independent and competitively successful women – the wind-surfing culture was deeply masculinist (Wheaton, 1997). Qualitative research into the sports cultures of crown-green bowls, salmon fishing, sea-angling, golf, football and tennis would be likely to show that at the end of the twentieth century the classic sources of social stratification remained primary determinants of who was involved in what sports culture, and where and why they were involved in that particular way. The meanings of sports are not independent of the social setting, but are an indicator of the forces by which societies are stratified, often reproduced and sometimes changed.

ESSAYS AND EXERCISES

Essays

Discuss the ways in which sport participation statistics reflect the stratified nature of contemporary British society.

With reference to qualitative studies of sport culture, consider the ways whereby gender inequalities are reproduced through sport.

How can sport contribute to challenging prejudice and cultural stereotyping? Discuss with particular reference to issues of women's empowerment through sport, and black identity in sport.

Exercises

Consult data on sports participation for men and women in publications such as *Social Trends* and the *General Household Survey*, and list the possible causes of the different rates of participation recorded.

Interview one person under 25, and one person over 55, whom you know to be active in sport, and list their activity patterns at succeeding stages of their life-cycles. What influences have affected these patterns?

Make some notes on your own involvement in sport. Who do you play with? Where do you play? What do you have in common with those with whom you play? How, if at all, does sport contribute to your own male/female, black/white identity?

FURTHER READING

M. Polley, *Moving the Goalposts – A History of Sport and Society Since 1945*, London, Routledge, 1998, covers the relationship of sport to gender, social class and ethnicity, in Chapters 4, 5 and 6 respectively.

Journal of Sport and Social Issues, Vol. 22, no. 2, August 1998, contains articles on ethnicity and gender, framed in terms of themes of social division, power, domination, resistance and empowerment.

References

Abrams, M. (1995) 'Leisure Time Use by the Elderly and Leisure Provision for the Elderly', in C. Critcher, P. Bramham and A. Tomlinson (eds), *Sociology of Leisure – A Reader*, London: E & FN Spon.

Allied Dunbar (1991) 'Activity Matters – The Facts', in *Allied Dunbar National Fitness Survey – A Summary of the Major Fndings and Messages from the Allied Dunbar National Fitness Survey*, London: Allied Dunbar/Health Education Authority/Sports Council, undated but probably 1991.

Blake, A. (1996) *The Body Language – The Meaning of Modern Sport*, London: Lawrence and Wishart.

Bourdieu, P. (1978) 'Sport and Social Class', *Social Science Information*, Vol. 17, pp. 819–840.

Bourdieu, P. (1986) *Distinction: A Social Critique of the Judgement of Taste*, London: Routledge & Kegan Paul.

Carr, C., Tomlinson, A. and White, A. (1997) 'Facility management: case-studies in policy and patriarchy', in A. Tomlinson (ed.), *Gender, Sport and Leisure: Continuities and Challenges*, Aachen: Meyer & Meyer.

Carrington, B. (1997) 'Community, Identity and Sport: An Exploration of the Significance of Sport within Black Communities', paper presented at the British Sociological Association Annual Conference, 'Power/ Resistance', University of York, April.

Cashmore, E. (1982) *Black Sportsmen*, London: Routledge.

Cashmore, E. (1990) *Making Sense of Sport*, London: Routledge.

Central Statistical Office (CSO) (1993) *Social Trends 23, 1993 Edition*, London, HMSO.

Central Statistical Office (CSO) (1996) *Social Trends 26, 1996 Edition*, London: HMSO.

Connell, R.W. (1983) *Which Way is Up? Essays on Sex, Class and Culture*, Sydney: Allen & Unwin.

Connell, R.W. (1995) *Masculinities*, Cambridge: Polity Press.

Corrigan, P. (1979) *Schooling the Smash Street Kids*, London: Macmillan.

Dahrendorf, R. (1979) *Life Chances – Approaches to Social and Political Theory*, Chicago: University of Chicago Press.

Davidoff, L. (1986) *The Best Circles: Society Etiquette and the Season*, London: The Cresset Library.

Deem, R. (1986) *All Work and No Play?*, Milton Keynes: Open University Press.

Denis, N., Henriques, F. and Slaughter, C. (1995) 'Leisure in Ashton', in C. Critcher, P. Bramham and A. Tomlinson (eds), *Sociology of Leisure – A Reader*, London: E & FN Spon.

Elias, N. (1986) 'An Essay on Sport and Violence', in N. Elias and E. Dunning, *Quest for Excitement – Sport and Leisure in the Civilizing Process*, Oxford: Basil Blackwell.

Elias, N. (1993) *Time: An Essay*, Oxford: Basil Blackwell.

Fleming, S. (1995) *'Home and Away': Sport and South Asian Male Youth*, Aldershot: Avebury.

Fleming, S. and Tomlinson, A. (1996) 'Football, Racism and Xenophobia in England (1): Europe and the old England', in U. Merkel and W. Tokarski (eds), *Racism and Xenophobia in European Football*, Aachen: Meyer & Meyer.

Flintoff, A., Scraton, S. and Bramham, P. (1995) 'Stepping into Aerobics?', in G. McFee, W. Murphy and G. Whannel (eds), *Leisure Cultures: Values, Genders, Lifestyles*, Brighton: Leisure Studies Association (Publication Number 54).

Garland, J. and Rowe, M. (1996) 'Football, Racism and Xenophobia in England (2): Challenging Racism and Xenophobia', in U. Merkel and W. Tokarski (eds), *Racism and Xenophobia in European Football*, Aachen: Meyer & Meyer.

Green, E., Hebron, S. and Woodward, D. (1990) *Women's Leisure: What Leisure?*, London: Macmillan.

Grusky, D.B. (1993) 'Social Stratification', in W. Outhwaite and T. Bottomore (eds), *The Blackwell Dictionary of Twentieth-century Social Thought*, Oxford: Blackwell.

Hall, M.A. (1996) *Feminism and Sporting Bodies – Essays on Theory and Practice*, Champaign, Illinois: Human Kinetics.

Hargreaves, Jennifer (1994) *Sporting Females – Critical Issues in the History and Sociology of Women's Sports*, London and New York: Routledge.

Hargreaves, John (1986) *Sport, Power and Culture – A Social and Historical Analysis of Popular Sports in Britain*, Cambridge: Polity Press.

Hodges, H.M. (1968) *Social Stratification – Class in America*, Cambridge, Massachusetts: Schenkman.

Howkins, A. and Lowerson, J. (1979) *Trends in Leisure, 1919–1939*, London: Sports Council and Social Science Research Council.

Imray, L. and Middleton, A. (1983) 'Public and Private: Marking the Boundaries', in E. Gamarnikow, D. Morgan, J. Purvis and D. Taylorson (eds), *The Public and the Private*, London: Heinemann Educational Books.

Itzkowitz, D.C. (1977) *Peculiar Privilege – A Social History of English Fox-hunting 1753–1885*, Hassocks: Harvester.

Kew, S. (1979) *Ethnic Groups and Leisure*, London: Sports Council and Social Science Research Council.

Limb, M., Matthews, H. and Vujakovic, P. (1995) 'Disabling Countryside: An Investigation of Wheelchair Users' Experiences of Informal Recreation', in S. Fleming, M. Talbot and A. Tomlinson (eds), *Policy and Politics in Sport, Physical Education and Leisure*, Eastbourne: Leisure Studies Association (Publication No. 54).

Long, J., Carrington, B. and Spracklen, K. (1996) 'The Cultural Production and Reproduction of Racial Stereotypes in Sport: A Case Study of Rugby League', paper presented at British Sociological Annual Conference, 'Worlds of the Future – Ethnicity, Nationalism and Globalization', University of Reading, April.

Long, J. and Wimbush, E. (1979) *Leisure and the Over 50s*, London: Sports Council and Social Science Research Council.

Long, J. and Wimbush, E. (1985) *Continuity and Change: Leisure Around Retirement*, London: Sports Council and Economic and Social Research Council.

McKibbin, R. (1991) *The Ideologies of Class – Social Relations in Britain 1880–1950*, Oxford: Oxford University Press.

Manning, F. (1973) *Black Clubs in Bermuda – Ethnography of a Play World*, Cornell: Cornell University Press.

Marshall, G. (ed.) (1994) *The Concise Oxford Dictionary of Sociology*, Oxford: Oxford University Press.

Middleton, A. (1986) 'Public and Private: Marking the Boundaries', in P. Lowe, T. Bradley and S. Wright (eds), *Deprivation and Welfare in Rural Areas*, Norwich: Geo Books.

OED (Oxford English Dictionary) (1979) *The Compact Edition of the Oxford English Dictionary*, London: Book Club Associates.

Office of Population Censuses and Surveys (OPCS) (1995) *General Household Survey 1993 – An Inter-departmental Survey Carried Out by OPCS between April 1993 and March 1994*, Social Survey Division (K. Foster, B. Jackson, M. Thomas, P. Hunter and N. Bennett), London: HMSO.

Parkin, F. (1976) 'Strategies of Social Closure in Class Formation', in F. Parkin (ed.), *The Social Analysis of Class Structure*, London: Tavistock.

Prendergast, S. (1978) 'Stoolball – the Pursuit of Vertigo?', *Women's Studies International Quarterly*, Vol. 1, pp. 15–26.

Reid, I. (1989) *Social Class Differences in Britain – Life-chances and Life-styles*, 3rd edition, London: Fontana Press.

Rojek, C. (1995) *Decentring Leisure: Rethinking Leisure Theory*, London: Sage.

Salisbury, J. and Jackson, D. (1996) *Challenging Macho Values – Practical Ways of Working with Adolescent Boys*, London: The Falmer Press.

Saunders, P. (1997) 'Social Mobility in Britain: An Empirical Evaluation of Two Competing Explanations', *Sociology*, Vol. 31, pp. 261–288.

Scraton, S. (1995) '"Boys Muscle in Where Angels Fear to Tread" – Girls' Sub-cultures and Physical Activities', in C. Critcher, P. Bramham and A. Tomlinson (eds), *Sociology of Leisure – A Reader*, London: E & FN Spon.

Sports Council and Women's Sports Foundation (1992) *Women and Sport – The Information Pack*, London: Sports Council.

Spracklen, K. (1995) 'Playing the Ball, or the Uses of League: Class, Masculinity and Rugby – A Case Study of Sudthorpe', in G. McFee, W. Murphy and G. Whannel (eds), *Leisure Cultures: Values, Genders, Lifestyles*, Brighton: Leisure Studies Association (Publication Number 54).

Sugden, J. and Tomlinson, A. (1999) 'Theorizing Sport, Social Class and Status', in J. Coakley and E. Dunning (eds), *The Handbook of Sport and Society*, London: Sage.

Talbot, M. (1988) 'Their Own Worst Enemy? Women and Leisure Provision', in E. Wimbush and M. Talbot (eds), *Relative Freedoms – Women and Leisure*, Milton Keynes: Open University Press.

Thompson, L. (1997) 'The Girls Done Good', *Guardian*, 2, Monday, 5 May 1997, pp. 2–3.

Tomlinson, A. (1986) 'Playing Away From Home: Leisure, Access and Exclusion', in P. Golding (ed.), *Poverty and Exclusion*, London: Child Poverty Action Group.

Tomlinson, A. (1997) 'Ideologies of Physicality, Masculinity and Femininity: Comments on *Roy of the Rovers* and the Women's Fitness Boom' in A. Tomlinson (ed.), *Gender, Sport and Leisure: Continuities and Challenges*, Aachen: Meyer & Meyer.

Tomlinson, A. and Yorganci, I. (1997) 'Male Coach/Female Athlete Relations: Gender and Power Relations in Competitive Sport', *Journal of Sport & Social Issues*, Vol. 21, pp. 134–155.

Turner, B.S. (1988) *Status*, Milton Keynes: Open University Press.

Urry, J. (1989) 'Social Class in Britain', in M. Cole (ed.), *The Social Contexts of Schooling*, London: The Falmer Press.

Veblen, T. (1953) [1899] *The Theory of the Leisure Class: An Economic Study of Institutions*, New York: Mentor.

Verma, G.K., Macdonald, A., Darby, D.S., and Carroll, R. (1991) *Sport and Recreation with Special Reference to Ethnic Minorities – Final Report* (July), University of Manchester, School of Education/Centre for Ethnic Studies in Education.

Waddington, D., Wykes, M. and Critcher, C. (1991) *Split at the Seams? Community, Continuity and Change after the 1984–5 Coal Dispute*, Milton Keynes: Open University Press.

Walker, H. (1989) 'Lawn Tennis', in T. Mason (ed.), *Sport in Britain – A Social History*, Cambridge: Cambridge University Press.

Wesolowski, W. and Slomczynski, K.M. (1993) 'Class', in W. Outhwaite and T. Bottomore (eds), *The Blackwell Dictionary of Twentieth-century Social Thought*, Oxford: Blackwell.

Whannel, G. (1983) *Blowing the Whistle: The Politics of Sport*, London: Pluto Press.

Wheaton, B. (1997) 'The Changing Gender Order in Sport? The Case of Windsurfing Subcultures', paper presented at the British Sociological Association Annual Conference, 'Power/Resistance', April, University of York.

White, A., Mayglothing, R. and Carr, C. (n.d.) *The Dedicated Few: The Social World of Women Coaches in Britain in the 1980s*, Chichester, UK: West Sussex Institute of Higher Education.

Williams, R. (1977a) *Marxism and Literature*, Oxford: Oxford University Press.

Williams, R. (1977b) 'Literature in Society', in H. Schiff (ed.), *Contemporary Approaches to English Studies*, London: Heinemann.

Willis, P. (1977) *Learning to Labour – How Working Class Kids Get Working Class Jobs*, Farnborough: Saxon House.

Wimbush, E. and Talbot, M. (eds) (1988) *Relative Freedoms – Women and Leisure*, Milton Keynes: Open University Press.

Woods, R. (1994) 'Today's Older Consumers: An Emerging Third Age of Personal Fulfilment or a Wasted Era of Frustrated Possibilities?', in Henley Centre, *Leisure Futures*, Vol. 1, '94, London: The Henley Centre for Forecasting, pp. 5–10.

Chapter five

Socialisation – social interaction and development

Socialisation is a complex developmental learning process that teaches the knowledge, values, and norms essential to participation in social life.

(McPherson *et al.*, 1993: 37)

Through socialisation people learn the values, attitudes and normative behaviour of the society in which they live. Whilst socialisation is a life-long process, it is during the early years that many of the patterns for later life are established.

(Women's Sports Foundation, 1995: 47)

Introduction

This chapter is a little different from those which have preceded it. The first four chapters have discussed the broad social and historical context within which sport has developed and the structural influences on current participation patterns. Structural analysis can sometimes be accused of 'reification' – ignoring the processes involved, the people or agents who attach meanings to, and have specific motivations for, their actions. Structural models – for example Marxists using concepts like 'social reproduction' – suggest that the concept of socialisation is an overly functionalist and even out-dated notion. Yet as is clear from the work of Bourdieu (introduced in the previous chapter) who uses the concept of 'habitus' rather than 'socialisation' but refers to essentially the same phenomenon, structural social scientists recognise the need to be able to explain how and why people become involved, or not, in sport.

This chapter (and the next on the mass media) turn the spotlight on the processes by which people acquire an interest in (or a dislike for) sport. This chapter looks at the development of human beings who do not have 'natures' or instincts for particular types of behaviour – some timeless or fixed set of behavioural characteristics (e.g. aggression, tenderness, nurturance, competitiveness) – but are people who acquire these characteristics through interaction with their social circumstances. The notion of *socialisation* focuses attention on the socio-cultural influences that shape human beings, their patterns of life and biographies. An individual's personal identity is still viewed as a cultural and structural product – the result of the influence of family, friends, educational, neighbourhood, legal and religious institutions and the mass media (the next chapter looks more closely at the last of these institutional influences). In this chapter our approach asks, from the point of view of those involved, what is going on in their participation in sport? It suggests that there is a tendency for sports scientists to operate with an 'over-socialised' conception of human beings and we need to consider a more dynamic model of socialisation into and through sport.

Socialisation and sport – an overview of research

Socialisation is a fundamental concept in many of the social sciences, but most research into socialisation and sport has been developed in the sociological context. The following extract from a recent overview of the field indicates the sort of issues investigated:

> Early research on socialisation and sport was typically grounded in widespread concerns about who participated in sports, how they became involved, why they participated, and how they were changed by participation. Those who asked these questions were often associated with organised sports programs, and they usually had vested interests in recruiting new participants into their programs and promoting programs by linking participation in them to positive developmental outcomes . . . Researchers were also interested in discovering whether . . . there was any truth to pervasive beliefs that participation in sports builds character and shapes people in positive ways . . . in recent years new questions have been asked about sport participation as a social process linked to the larger social world in which it occurs. These questions focus on why sport experiences take the forms they take; how sport experiences are mediated by gender, class, and race relations; how sport participation is tied to identity and

identity formation processes; why sport participation choices are made by people at various points in their lives; and what connections exist between participation choices and the cultural, social, political, and economic contexts in which people live their lives.

(Coakley, 1993a: 169)

This chapter will look at some of this research and consider the changes that have occurred in socialisation theory and the methodological approaches used by social scientists in the past twenty-five years. It will be shown that the focus on socialisation and sport has increasingly been superseded by attention to the role of sport participation in *cultural reproduction* and *cultural transformation* – which links the sport socialisation process with wider structural power relations.

What is socialisation?

Socialisation is often defined as the process by which individuals learn to conform to social norms and learn how to behave in ways appropriate to their culture. The individual internalises these social norms and becomes committed to them and thus internalises the 'social rules' of behaviour. This happens because individuals want to gain acceptance and status from other people. An individual becomes socialised as they learn to act in a way that is in keeping with the expectations of others. In short, *socialisation is the transmission of culture*. The major agencies within society that are involved in the socialisation of individuals are the family, the school and the mass media. These institutions can all influence an individual's socialisation in interacting and sometimes contradictory ways. We will look at the influence of these on sport experience shortly.

Clearly the process of socialisation begins early in life. A distinction has been drawn between *primary socialisation* and *secondary socialisation* to distinguish what happens to young children and what happens as people grow up and move through the life course. Primary socialisation is the first socialisation an individual undergoes in childhood and through which he or she becomes a member of society. Secondary socialisation refers to socialisation after childhood, and in *interactionist* theoretical approaches involves the consideration of careers in adult life.

Human infants spend much time undergoing primary socialisation in a family setting. During primary socialisation a child gains his or her conception of self or personal identity, and learns the rules and norms of society to which the child belongs. The sociological conception of socialisation therefore stresses the capacity of human beings to adapt to their environment through processes of learning. Ideas, attitudes and body movements associated with a given sport, for example, from the physical attributes, skills and techniques of coordination, agility, speed, power and stamina, through to the psychological aspects of play, sport and athleticism, all have to be *socially acquired*. Both the psychological disposition to play particular games and the mentality for competitive sport have to be learned.

As we have seen French sociologist Pierre Bourdieu (1984), using the concept of habitus, has suggested that primary socialisation, via various social experiences prior to involvement in formal sport, can be seen as crucial for sports participation. Habitus refers to a set of acquired patterns of thought behaviour and taste. Continuing involvement in sport through adolescence and later adult life is, he believes, connected to the internalisation of specific manners, deportment and demeanours in childhood (Jarvie and Maguire, 1994: 183ff). The acquisition of particular tastes and dispositions for different sport and leisure activities in the family home is connected to differences in social class and gender habituses.

Ken Roberts and David Brodie (1992) carried out a study of involvement in sport in six inner city areas – Belfast, Camden, Cardiff, Chester, Glasgow and Liverpool. They surveyed approximately 7,000 users at sport centres and conducted panel discussions with participants and non-participants over a two-year period. They provide a useful comment which helps to illustrate the concepts of habitus and the importance of early socialisation in the acquisition of an interest in sport. They note that nearly everybody at some stage of their life is involved in physically active leisure when they are young. The question is often asked: why do some (the majority) drop out shortly afterwards while others persist? Research has often been carried out into the movement from youth to adulthood to try to find an answer. In fact, the answer lies *in individuals' experiences in sport during childhood and youth*. Roberts and Brodie argue that 'provided young people had been given secure foundations in sport the chances were that they would continue into adulthood whatever happened in other life domains' (p. 41). It was not the amount of sport played in childhood and adolescence that provided a 'secure foundation', however, but *the number of different sports* that respondents to their survey had become involved in. In short, early sport socialisation is a major determinant of people's participation in sport. If acquired early on in life, the propensity to be involved in some form of physical activity, although not always the same sport, is more likely to continue throughout the life course.

This propensity is not only related to social class, as the previous chapter outlined, but also gender. Iris Young (1980: 146–147) provides a useful illustration of gender differences in bodily experience:

> Women often approach a physical engagement with things with timidity, uncertainty, and hesitancy . . . Women tend not to put their whole bodies

into engagement in a physical task with the same ease and naturalness as men . . . the whole body is not put into fluid and directed motion, but rather, the motion is concentrated in one body part . . . The woman's motion tends not to reach, extend, lean, stretch, and follow through in the direction of her intention . . . We often experience our bodies as fragile encumbrances, rather than the media for the enactment of our aims.

That this gendered experience of the body is a result of socialisation and not part of natural difference can be illustrated by reference to anthropological research. We will look at this below.

Both the existence of culture and the process of socialisation are distinctive features of human society. The large variations in social life that anthropologists have shown suggest that 'human nature' is highly variable. In language, dress, values and beliefs and in patterns of acceptable and unacceptable behaviour human beings have been shown to exhibit great plasticity. Even in the area of such apparently 'natural' behaviour as sex roles, the division of the human group into males and females, it is clear that cultural definitions of behaviour are vital.

Socialisation is therefore a *learning process*. Human beings are not born to be competitive or co-operative, aggressive or passive, naturally 'good' or 'bad', but behave as they do because of culture. Whatever biology predisposes human beings to be and to do, it is only through socialisation that they become part of their social group and culture. The norms and values that constitute the 'rules' of a social group are therefore culturally specific, that is, different cultures educate and socialise their children differently. A fascinating example of this in sport is the case of the taketak game played by the Tangu tribe of New Guinea (Leonard, 1984: 76).

The dominant social value amongst the Tangu is *equivalence*. The idea of defeating opponents through competition disturbs them, since they believe it fosters ill-will and contempt among the participants. Hence although taketak is a team sport – a game resembling bowling in which teams take turns to bowl a dried fruit at a number of coconut stakes – the aim of the game is not to knock over as many stakes as possible, but for both teams to remove the same number of stakes. Winning is completely irrelevant.

Compare this with Britain and the USA where 'win–loss' tables are vital ingredients of the most popular team sports. Increasingly draws are resolved through 'sudden-death' playoffs or penalty kicks. The axiom, attributed to Vince Lombardi, that 'winning isn't everything, it's the only thing', increasingly reigns supreme. Although there are similarities between the USA and the UK, it is hard to imagine the sports press in the States getting as worked up over a drawn cricket match as British journalists still can. Not only are there cultural differences in the meaning of sport and recreation *between* different societies, there are important differences in the meaning of sport *within* single societies. It is important to account for the fact that although everyone under-goes socialisation, *not everyone undergoes the same socialisation experiences*. Indeed this is what makes people 'individual' according to one theoretical model. As we have seen in the previous chapter there are certain social forces and relationships – most notably social class, gender and ethnicity – that have a reality *sui generis* (literally, in their own right) that affect socialisation. Hence according to social class, gender and ethnic group, people will have different 'ways of seeing' the same event, situation or object. It is useful to examine gender socialisation as an illustration of these ideas.

Gender socialisation

In 1935 the anthropologist Margaret Mead published *Sex and Temperament in Three Primitive Societies*. Based on field work conducted in New Guinea it revealed considerable variability in the behaviour patterns of men and women in three tribes living within a hundred miles of one another. Among the Arapesh tribe both men and women exhibited characteristics associated in the West with femininity – non-aggressivity, gentleness and passivity. In the Mundugamor (formerly headhunters) both sexes were assertive and very aggressive – traits typically associated with masculinity in the West. Finally, amongst the Tchambuli tribe a 'role reversal' was apparent – males appeared to take on feminine qualities and females those of masculinity in the West: 'the men act according to our stereotype for women – are catty, wear curls and go shopping, while the women are energetic, managerial, unadorned partners' (Mead, 1977: ix). Each society had its own 'natural' behaviour patterns, which were in fact products of culture.

Undoubtedly the family continues to play an important role in the gender socialisation process. Research has shown that male and female babies are dressed in different colours, given different toys to play with and treated differently (Bellotti, 1975). Boys are not expected to cry, girls are praised for their appearance. Institutions outside the family contribute to this process through, for example, the different language used to describe the behaviour of boys and girls (Stanworth, 1980). If a child is quiet or withdrawn a girl will be described as 'shy', whilst a boy is a 'strong silent type'; if a child shows emotion freely girls are 'over-sensitive' whilst boys are 'wet', 'cry-babies' or 'softies'; a girl who takes the initiative can be 'bossy' whilst a boy is seen as a 'born leader', and so on.

The writer and broadcaster Garrison Keillor offers another illustration of these processes:

> Girls had it better from the beginning, don't kid yourself. They were allowed to play in the house, where the books were and the adults, and

boys were sent outdoors like livestock. Boys were noisy and rough, and girls were nice, so they got to stay and we had to go. Boys ran around in the yard with toy guns going *kksshh-kksshh*, fighting wars for made-up reasons and arguing about who was dead, while girls stayed inside and played with dolls, creating complex family groups and learning to solve problems through negotiation and role-playing. Which gender is better equipped, on the whole, to live an adult life, would you guess?

(1994: 12)

An important influence on the behaviour of boys and girls are their adult carers – usually biological or social parents. Studies have shown the importance of adult/parental interaction with a child on their development. Adults and parents act differently when they know the sex of a child – they are more likely to prevent a boy from crying; encourage girls to smile; allow boys to crawl more and go further than baby girls; boys are treated 'rougher' especially by their fathers, whilst girls are very soon taught about 'appearance'. Girls are protected more, and given less encouragement, generally, than boys. The implications of these different responses in terms of male and female physicality and emotional displays can be seen at an early age. By the time they are 3 or 4 years old girls and boys start drawing conclusions about who they are and what the world is like – the formation of 'self'. Experience of parents and family life in general helps to shape some of our most important conceptions of self (Coakley, 1994: 233).

The school is another major agency of socialisation (Byrne, 1983). It has both a formal curriculum and an informal 'hidden' curriculum which helps to reproduce the gender order. Whilst overt differentiation on the basis of gender is only rarely practised today, boys and girls are encouraged to take different subjects through more subtle methods, through clashes on the timetable for example. Even if there appears to be an open choice it takes considerable determination for a boy or girl to opt for a subject that is not considered suitable for their gender. Boys and girls are expected to behave in different ways (Stanworth, 1980).

In physical education and sport a form of 'aversive socialisation' occurs for girls and young women – sport is tied up with, and more complementary to, emerging male sexuality and gender identity than female sexuality and identity. For young women it is as if a choice has to be made between female identity and sports involvement (Scraton, 1987, 1992). This is not the case for most young boys, although of course not all boys play and enjoy sports to the same extent, and some girls excel in them (Connell, 1983, 1987, 1995). For girls, however, as they grow up the stakes of staying in sport are far greater. Participation in sport and organised physical activity is associated positively with masculinity and sexual identity and boys respond to this accordingly. The opposite still remains largely true for girls. Not only do girls risk being considered unfeminine if they remain involved in demanding sports and physical activity into adolescence, but they also risk their sexuality being questioned.

The mass media enhance these differences and play an important role in reinforcing socially acceptable norms and values. On television it has been suggested that women are under-represented in action drama series, and when they do appear they are featured in a narrow range of roles – 'the virgin, the madonna or the whore'. Women are more often shown in domestic settings than in paid work and usually shown as incompetent in anything other than domestic roles. Women, far more often than men, are the helpless victims of violence, and are usually rescued by men. It is with some justification that Gaye Tuchman (1978) suggests television performs the 'symbolic annihilation of women'!

The reinforcement of sex-role socialisation through television portrayals of women (and men) is important because of its potential impact upon young children. Research has shown that heavy television viewing is associated with extreme stereotyping of sex roles amongst boys and girls (Gunter, 1986). Sex-role stereotyping occurs in other media beside television, notably in reading material directed at young children and adolescents. Studies have shown the male dominance of many preschool and early school reading books. Girls or female characters are often shown as passive and housebound, whilst boys and male characters are more often seen outdoors and involved in exciting adventures. Comics aimed at young children also play a part in the socialisation process. Many of them are linked specifically to a particular product or television programme (see Dixon, 1977a, 1977b and 1990).

In comics for older age groups the differences between male and female interests has often been accentuated even further (Dunne, 1982). Most boys' comics still feature action-packed adventures, where soldiers or football players lead active and dangerous lives (Tomlinson, 1995). Comics for girls have undergone a change. Whilst they were full of romantic love stories in the 1970s, it was suggested that in the 1980s the almost exclusive concentration on romance and dependency on boys was replaced by a new focus. The practices and rituals of femininity portrayed in the magazines for adolescent girls were presented as being on behalf of the development of a more independent self, not with the singular aim of attracting a 'fella' (McRobbie, 1991: 183; see also Philips, 1995 and Whannel, 1995). In the 1990s, however, it would appear that both emphases can be found in teenage magazines. Regular articles featuring sport and physical activity involving girls are still not as commonplace as those featuring boys and young men.

In their classic study *The Femininity Game*, Boslooper and Hayes (1973) argued that the predominant idea in the USA in the 1960s and early 1970s was that 'feminine' women were not supposed to take any form of strenuous physical activity. Despite the changes that have been taking place throughout the

Western world since then, it is not difficult still to find examples of the sort Boslooper and Hayes cited. The mass media provide stereotypes of what type of body image is beautiful and sexually attractive for males and females. The 'ideal' male shape is *mesomorphic* (muscular) and the 'ideal' female is *ectomorphic* (lean).

Phrases such as 'unfeminine' and 'butch' are flung at strong and competitive women, whereas these attributes serve to mark out the 'real men' from the boys in the school playground and elsewhere. Physical education in school tends to reinforce these cultural stereotypes of body image ideals (Scraton, 1992). The mass media often present female athletes in terms of their sexuality, physical attractiveness, etc. whilst this is rarely, if ever, done for male athletes. Female athletes still face either trivialisation or exclusion from the mass media (Sabo and Curry Jansen, 1992; see also Hargreaves, 1994 on the 'sexualisation' of female athletes). Boslooper and Hayes's (1973: 45) comment with regard to the USA in the 1970s is still applicable to the UK today: 'American society cuts the penis off the male who enters dance . . . and places it on the woman who participates in competitive athletics.'

The physical body holds social meaning. It is not a natural thing, purely physical, but a part of culture. Physical sex differences become cultural – they are used, modified, reinforced and accentuated as part of cultural beliefs about the real and the ideal attributes of men and women. Culture projects certain images and influences ideas about gender difference.

Recognising the central importance of socialisation to the construction of culture enables the sports sociologist to pierce through these cultural preconceptions. Yet it is important to realise that although the mass media do reproduce gender stereotypes, readers and viewers are not simply passive recipients of media messages. It is a mistake to think that people simply absorb media messages uncritically and reproduce what they are told. Not all the girls who read *Jackie* in the 1970s and 1980s, or its equivalent in the 1990s, passively absorbed the idea that their one aim in life was to 'catch a man' (Fraser, 1987). Whilst the television programme, newspaper, comic or magazine may have a *preferred reading* some people may read them in different, more critical, ways (see Chapter 6). Media messages are part of the process of socialisation, but so too is the active involvement of people.

Whilst much research into socialisation has focused upon primary socialisation – in which it is held that the basic values and knowledge essential for living in a social community are acquired by infants and young children – it is now widely recognised that socialisation is a lifelong process. Recognition of the importance of secondary socialisation agencies and experiences, socialisation after childhood and processes of social development in adult life, is largely the product of an alternative approach to socialisation. In the remaining sections of this chapter we will draw upon two excellent 'state of the art reviews' on sport and socialisation produced by Jay Coakley to consider these different approaches to socialisation (Coakley, 1993a and 1993b).

Approaches to socialisation

Jay Coakley identified two broad approaches to understanding socialisation in the sociology of sport and leisure literature. The dominant view until the late 1970s, which Coakley calls *socialisation-as-internalisation*, was based on a model of the human actor as a 'tabula rasa' or blank slate, upon which society writes 'its' messages. The assumption was that people were relatively passive recipients of information and social influences, like 'jugs to be filled'. Human beings were passive learners, 'socialised into, out of, and through sport' (Coakley, 1993a: 191). The alternative approach (*socialisation-as-interaction*) was based upon a different model of the human actor. People were conceived of as more active and interactive, interdependent with others. Socialisation occurs through interaction between active and creative agents – more like 'candles to be lit'. Sport and sport experiences are best understood as social constructions involving dynamic social processes. Table 5.1 summarises the main differences in approach.

In terms of research on socialisation into sport the first, *functionalist*, model – involving the concepts 'social role' and 'social system' as central – inspired considerable research into the ways in which the learning of sport roles is related to encouragement and reinforcement coming from relationships with significant others in the family, peer groups and school. Much of this research involved the use of social surveys of young, white, male athletes who were asked to recall their histories of participation in sport, the events surrounding their participation and the influential people in their sport lives. This research lead to three main conclusions.

TABLE 5.1 Two approaches to socialisation

	Socialisation as internalisation	Socialisation as interaction
Key concepts	Social role-social system	Self-identity
Key theory	Functionalism	Interactionism/cultural studies
Key feature	Socially deterministic	Less/anti-deterministic
Image of actor	Individual receives society's messages A 'scripted actor' Passivity Over-socialised conception of 'man'	Agency Individual interprets & responds to society's messages Individual as 'active' or creative A 'role-taker'

Source: Adapted from Coakley, 1993a: 191.

1   Participation in sport roles is particularly related to the amount of social support coming from significant others.

2   The relative influence of various significant others (e.g. father, mother, brothers and sisters, teachers, coaches, friends, peers) and the extent and type of encouragement received in particular social systems of institutions (the family, peer group, school and community) vary for participants and non-participants in sport by gender, class, 'race', age, place of residence and culture.

3   Socialisation involves reciprocity, or *bidirectional effects*, since children's involvement in sport creates responses among the adults (parents, teachers, coaches, relatives) who support and encourage that involvement (Coakley, 1993b: 574).

This approach to socialisation has been criticised, however, on several methodological and theoretical grounds. It focused on a limited range of respondents, different research projects had inconsistent definitions of participation/non-participation and involvement/non-involvement so that comparisons were difficult to make, and confusion remained about the relative influence of different socialising agents, during various stages in the life course, for athletes and non-athletes from different social backgrounds and with different social characteristics.

As a result alternative conceptual approaches to studies of sport socialisation emerged. Underpinning these studies was the idea that socialisation occurs through interaction, rather than internalisation. Interactionist studies of sport socialisation looked at the social construction of identity, the dynamics of participation decisions and the social meanings underlying sport participation. Additionally, research from this interactionist approach did not view the primary issue as how individuals were socialised 'into sport'. Sport participation was not conceived of as a 'once and for all' type of experience to be explained through traditional quantitative survey methods. Instead this approach viewed initial participation and continued participation in sport as just as 'problematic' (i.e. in need of explanation and investigation) as 'non-participation' and 'dropping out'.

Interactionist approaches to socialisation in sport involve four central assumptions:

1   Becoming involved in sport involves a process of identity construction and confirmation. Involvement is not simply an outcome of exposure to encouragement, reinforcement or opportunities for 'role rehearsal'. Identity formation related to sports participation occurs over time and depends upon a number of processes, including the acquisition of knowledge about a sport, being associated with a sport group, learning the values and

perspectives of the sport group, and earning the acceptance of those in the group so that one's identity as a participant is affirmed and reaffirmed over time. Donnelly and Young (1988) provide a good example of these processes in their study of climbing and rugby football sub-cultures.

2   The process of becoming involved in sport among elite athletes is initiated through a process of recruitment in which first-time participation experiences are supported, coerced or subverted by people who are important in the athletes' lives. Involvement in sport is never established in any final sense (Stevenson, 1990).

3   The problematic nature of the decision to participate or not participate in sport schemes, and whether to maintain participation thereafter, was considered by White and Coakley (1986; and Coakley and White, 1992) in their study of sport participation patterns amongst 60 adolescents in south-east England. The context for the study was the 'Ever Thought of Sport' (ETOS) campaign run by the English Sports Council in the mid-1980s. White and Coakley conducted in-depth interviews with the young people and discovered that the decision to become involved in any sports activity was tied to a complex set of considerations mediated in turn by important social relationships and constrained by access to resources, and other wider economic, political, social and cultural forces. Decisions (about participation in sport) were often linked to considerations of the implications of these decisions for the opportunities it gave them for further extending control over their lives, for becoming adults, and for developing and displaying personal competence.

According to White and Coakley, gender and socio-economic status were directly related to the control young people had or perceived they had over their lives. The establishment of personal identity was a primary factor in their decision-making processes and being an athlete was not an identity that most of the young people perceived as satisfactory or satisfying at this point of their lives. Where sport participation was tied to the process of becoming independent, autonomous and competent adults, then it was seen positively. If not, then it was viewed negatively. Their research called into question the distinction between 'participants', 'non-participants' and 'drop-outs' and that of who is and who is not a participant in sport. Current non-participation in certain sports programmes might not mean non-participation in sport and physical activity altogether. As young people's lives and self-conceptions change, so too can involvement and commitment to involvement in sport.

4   Interactionist approaches to socialisation emphasise the extent to which individuals and groups create and negotiate their involvement in sport. Socialisation is not the primary focus of research: instead it is the struggle associated with the determination of what sport will mean in the lives of

particular groups or categories of people. The focus is upon the *dialectic of control* and *power relations*.

This last aspect of the interactionist approach to socialisation bears a strong resemblance to the cultural studies approach broadly consistent with the one taken by the authors of this book. This approach suggests that the connection between patterns of individual involvement and participation in sport and leisure and wider relations of cultural reproduction, subordination and oppression are more clearly linked through the notion of sport and leisure sub-cultures (see Donnelly, 1985). As Jeff Bishop and Paul Hoggett (1986: 43–44) suggest:

> Sub-cultures can . . . be seen to occupy an intermediate position between the individual or club engaged in a leisure activity and the wider social order. Sub-cultures are often very active elements, deliberately negotiating and restructuring this intermediate position . . . leisure sub-cultures are an aspect of society's internal social organisation which is actually thriving and constitutes a crucial vehicle through which dominant values are transmitted, resisted or negotiated and new sets of values, which may take as their point of origin a different mode of production and social organisation, emerge. In particular, collective leisure offers opportunities rare – if not unique – in our society to reassert values related not to passive consumerism but to production for one's own use and enjoyment.

Sport and character building

Undoubtedly one of the foremost expressions of the relationship between sport and socialisation is the idea of an association between a healthy body and a healthy mind. This goes back at least to the English public schools of the mid-nineteenth century (see Chapter 1). Since then there has been a widely held belief in the advanced capitalist countries – such as Britain, the USA and Canada – about the effectiveness of sport in dealing with various perceived 'social problems', such as the prevention of crime and delinquency amongst adolescent boys and young adult males. 'Mens sana in corpore sano' – the notion that sport was character building – was conveyed through the English public school system and 'athleticism' became a key attribute of 'the proper Christian Gentleman' during the last century. The belief that sport produces disciplined, responsible and self-reliant men has been sustained throughout the twentieth century by being incorporated into the basic principles of physical education in both state and public schooling and on occasion being re-emphasised by leading industrialists, police chiefs, members of the armed forces, politicians of all political persuasions and other members of the 'establishment'. Prince Philip, the Duke of Edinburgh, a forthright advocate of the character building qualities of sport and President of the Central Council for Physical Recreation (CCPR), set up his award scheme in the mid-1950s following his experiences as a pupil under the physical fitness and training regime established by Kurt Hahn at the exclusive public school Gordonstoun, in Scotland.

A number of official inquiries set up at the end of the 1950s to look into the 'problem of youth' in Britain voiced concerns about the state of sport and physical activity in Britain. The Wolfenden Report on *Sport and the Community* (1960) included a concern for how potentially troublesome groups of youth spent their leisure. Their findings, or rather assertions, about the preventive properties of sport and other constructive forms of recreation did much to shape subsequent policy. The Report (1960: 2) noted that: 'It is widely held that a con-siderable proportion of delinquency among young people stems from a lack of desire for suitable physical activity.' A little further on it continued:

> [Although we] are not suggesting it [i.e. criminal behaviour] . . . would disappear if there were more tennis courts and running tracks . . . at the same time it is a reasonable assumption that if more young people have opportunities for playing games, fewer of them would develop criminal habits.

Speaking in the 1980s when there had been several successive years of inner city disturbances involving young people, the chairman of the CCPR pronounced:

> We want people, young people particularly, off the street corners, getting them away from frightening old ladies and breaking windows, and getting them into sports areas where they can participate at their own level, have fun, enjoy themselves and really feel that they are part of something that is totally enjoyable and that is being a Briton and enjoying life in Britain.
> (Peter Lawson, speaking on BBC Radio 4 Programme
> *Children and Sport*, March 1986)

In their study of sport in a divided Ireland Sugden and Bairner (1993: 1) suggest that the British Government, from the 1960s onwards has sought to exert a greater degree of influence over sport in Northern Ireland than anywhere else in the British Isles out of the recognition that sport can play an influential part in an individual's political socialisation. The justification for the inclusion of phys-ical education and games in the school curriculum has largely been based upon their supposed 'efficacy as agents of socialisation' (Stevenson, 1975: 287). An emphasis upon the instrumental rationale for sport provision pervades the growth of state intervention in sport in Britain (see Chapter 7). Iain Sproat, as Conservative Minister at the Department of National Heritage responsible for sport in the mid-1990s, clearly believed that team sport might solve many of the country's problems. 'If we had more organised team games in schools', he told a meeting of sports writers in 1994, 'we'd have fewer little thugs like those who murdered James Bulger' (quoted in the *Guardian, 2*, 1 March 1994; p. 2).

How accurate is it to believe that there is a strong relationship between involvement in sport and PE and the development of good character? Whilst this connection is still widely held to exist, the relationship between physical activity and mental health, and the impact of exercise on psychological well-being, is not so straightforwardly a positive one. The remarkable thing is that whilst the validity of these beliefs has been taken for granted and routinely espoused by those associated with organised competitive sports, it was not until the 1950s that people actually began to use research to subject the belief to a systematic examination (Lee, 1986). A recent textbook on psychology in sport concludes that psychological-based research suggests that physical activity can only promote mental health if 'exercise is kept within certain limits and when the reasons why people exercise are intrinsically healthy to begin with' (Kremer and Scully, 1994: 15).

David Robins (1990) has reviewed the research literature into this question from a sociological and criminological viewpoint. He found some research in the USA pointed to a positive relationship between sports participation and less delinquency. But another author in a major review of fifty studies on socialisation and sport carried out in North America could only conclude that 'to date there is no valid evidence that participation in sport causes any verifiable socialisation effects' (Stevenson, 1975). A more recent piece of work carried out for the Scottish Sports Council concluded that it was not possible to say definitely 'that the correlation high level of sports participation/low frequency of delinquency holds good in the UK' (Coalter, 1987: 2).

Robins (1990: 2) concluded that:

> it is an open question whether participation in sports or the provision of sports facilities have any effect on levels of delinquent behaviour at all, or whether perceived associations can be accounted for in other ways.

He continued:

> A research project which sought to examine and control for *all* possible aspects of the relationship between participation in sports programmes and delinquency is theoretically possible, but it would necessarily be extremely complex and expensive, requiring a large sample and longitudinal design.

Possibly the best that can be said with certainty from British-based research is that sports participation does not make things much worse. There is research in the USA, however, that provides reason to doubt even this rather weak conclusion. A study by Hughes and Coakley (1991) suggests that sport programmes can create a tendency for over-conformity and what they call 'positive deviance' which can be as socially dysfunctional as other forms of antisocial behaviour that sport programmes are usually set up to try and deter. 'Positive deviance' is one way of explaining cheating, the pursuit of gaining an unfair advantage, through for example the use of performance enhancing drugs and other substances. Sports participants become so involved in the desire to achieve and win through competition (the 'sport ethic') that they are prepared to break the spirit of play in order to succeed. We will briefly look at some of these studies of socialisation through sport in more detail in the next section.

Socialisation through sport

Between 1950 and 1980 many studies tested hypotheses based upon a variety of popular beliefs held about the social developmental consequences of sport participation, such as:

- the development of positive character traits;
- producing better academic attainment in young people;
- promoting conformity;
- reducing delinquency rates;
- developing conservative social and political attitudes;
- establishing strong achievement orientations and moral development.

The focus of most of the research was normally on children and young people, rather than adults, which reflects the assumption that adults are no longer in a formative stage of development (a particular view of socialisation) and that adult lives are so complex that the effects of sports participation are minimal compared to the socialisation effects of other experiences. In fact since the 1980s research into the issue of socialisation through sport has dropped off. In an overview of American college athletics Chris Stevenson (1985) suggested this was for two main reasons:

1   There was a long record of inconsistent findings, and most studies found little or no significant socialisation effects of sports participation.
2   Research priorities shifted to focus on how to promote sport involvement, especially among young people with the potential to become top-class athletes.

In short, many researchers no longer anticipated being able to find identifiable 'socialisation effects' and instead became more concerned with more pragmatic questions about the origins of sport participation and the factors related to the development of sport skills, especially high performance sport skills. What research has been done into socialisation through sport and the criticisms of it can be briefly outlined.

Loy and Ingham's (1981: 214) review of research concluded that 'socialisation via play, games and sport is a complex process having both manifest and latent functions, and involving functional and dysfunctional, intended and unintended consequences'. They pointed out that up to 1973 (when their article was originally published) neither theory nor data had established the existence of any specific socialisation consequences inherently tied to the experience of participation in games or sports. They were aware of the large number of assertions made about the supposed socialisation benefits of sport participation, but argued that social science research needed to move beyond rhetoric and investigate the conditions under which various types of learning might be associated with particular types of games and game experiences.

More recently McCormack and Chalip (1988) have provided damaging criticisms of the methodological and theoretical flaws in many of the 'correlational analyses' of sports socialisation effects. Most notably they were critical of the following:

1   The failure to build 'pre-test' and 'post-test' designs which would enable a clear distinction to be made between the 'socialisation effects of participation' and the 'selection effects' of those tested in most of the studies.
2   The failure to clarify what is meant by 'sport participation' – does it refer to informal sport as well as organised competitive sports programmes and other forms of physical activity?
3   The assumptions that sport participation involves a unique and consistent set of human experiences; that these experiences are similarly shared by everyone in sport; and that these experiences facilitate or cause identifiable changes in the characteristics of sport participants (i.e. precisely what the studies are supposed to be testing).
4   The assumption that athletes passively internalise specific norms and moral lessons through sport experiences, and that these character-shaping experiences are not readily available to people in activities outside of sport.

According to Coakley (1993b: 577) these four assumptions overlooked the following factors.

1   Athletes will have different experiences arising from different team sports and situations.

2   Athletes will interpret the same experiences in different ways due to differences in their relationships with significant others.

3   Athletes at different stages of development will be influenced in different ways by sport experiences and significant others.

4   Athletes will apply their interpretations of sport experience in different ways to the decisions they make in the rest of their lives, and they will reinterpret the same experiences and apply them to their lives in different ways as they get older.

5   There is no a priori reason to assume that those who do not participate in organised sports do not gain experiences that overlap with those available in sport from other activities.

In sum, the experience of striving to achieve goals within competitive reward structures can be made available in other adolescent activities sponsored and organised by adults, and therefore competitiveness and values of social achievement can be learned irrespective of participation or lack of it in organised sports.

As we have seen, research into sport participation's socialisation effects has focused on five broad areas: academic achievement and aspirations, social/occupational mobility, deviant behaviour, political orientation, and the development of individual character. Coakley (1993b) considers the first area to have received most attention, possibly for the pragmatic reason that it has been relatively easy to add on questions about sport participation on to large-scale surveys of young people in education. The research suggests that most successful athletes have higher educational aspirations than those who do not participate. Yet sport participation is positively associated with academic achievement and aspirations only when it somehow alters important relationships in a young person's life. In other words, there is no relationship between sport participation and academic achievement or aspirations if a person's important social relationships do not change in academically relevant ways as a result of sport participation. Meaningful, positive, social relationships, not sport itself, are the vehicle for improved academic performance or aspirations.

Sport participation and social/occupational mobility has received the second most amount of attention, but again there is little indication that sport participation leads to greater career success for athletes than for others from comparable social backgrounds, nor do athletes have any clear-cut occupational mobility advantages over non-athletes.

Does sport participation 'keep young people off the streets' and out of trouble? Research has not found higher rates of deviance among athletes than among so-called 'non-athletes', but is is not clear whether these lower rates of deviance are tied to learning experiences within sport itself. Shields and Bredemeier (1995: 183) conclude that it is difficult to draw definite conclusions about the relationship between sport and delinquency:

Are individuals with tendencies toward delinquency less interested in sport and removed from sport teams when they do participate, or does sport itself have an inhibiting factor on delinquent behaviour?

They cite one study, carried out by Trulson (1986), that used a 'pre-test'/'post-test' design in attempting to gain some insight into the relationship. Trulson matched thirty-four delinquent boys in terms of age, social class and test scores on aggression and personality and then divided them into three groups. One group received 'traditional' Tae Kwon Do training, which combined philosophical reflection, meditation and physical practice of the martial arts techniques. The second group received 'modern' martial arts training, emphasising only fighting and self-defence techniques. The third group jogged and played basketball and (American) football. Each group met for one hour three times a week for six months. In the 'post-tests' members of the Tae Kwon Do group were classified as 'normal' rather than delinquent, the martial arts group were less well adjusted than when the experiment began, and the traditional sports group showed little change, although self-esteem and social skills had improved. As Shields and Bredemeier (1995: 184) stated:

> These findings underscore the point that whatever advantages or liabilities are associated with sport involvement, they do not come from sport per se but from the particular blend of social interactions and physical activities that comprise the totality of the sport experience. It is unfortunate that Trulson did not include a group receiving the philosophical training without the practice of Tae Kwon Do physical skills. Perhaps the integration of philosophical training with physical activity is so effective because the physical activity provides opportunities to 'embody' the philosophy.

Robins (1990: 18) suggests that the prevalence of the 'sport as crime prevention' view in Britain can be put down to two main factors:

1   The power of the 'Sports Lobby' which has built up over the past 100 years – those interests that are organised around sport and physical recreation and their active sympathisers and supporters in the British establishment.
2   The instrumental aspects of sport and recreation – sports are massively popular with the overwhelming majority of young people and so can provide 'a useful lowest common denominator of activities designed to hold the attention of groups of young people who may be uncooperative and non-compliant'. The purely instrumental aspects of sports can become the underlying rationale for provision (see Chapter 7).

147

Since the 1970s research into the relationship between sport and political attitudes has not been pursued very vigorously. Instead the growth area has been in the related study of sport and moral reasoning and development. Auto-biographical accounts of 'drop-outs' from professional sport in America in the 1970s (e.g. Meggyesy, 1971) indicated that the ethical nature of organised competitive sport was one of conventional morality. One former wide receiver for the New York Jets speaking about his retirement from professional football wrote:

> The bad thing about football is that it keeps you in an adolescent stage, and you are kept there by the same people who are telling you that it is teaching you to be a self-disciplined, mature and responsible person. But if you are self-disciplined and responsible, they wouldn't have to treat you like a child.
>
> (quoted in Loy and Ingham, 1981: 214)

Similar relationships in professional sport in Britain have been revealed in auto-biographies and research into the occupational culture of football (e.g. Dunphy, 1991; Tomlinson, 1983). Shields and Bredemeier (1995: 195) provide another useful summary of the research field into this issue:

> There is limited evidence that experience in some sports is correlated negatively with moral reasoning maturity, but this is not true for participants of all ages or in all sports. Clearly sport does not automatically build character or characters. The influence that sport has for its participants depends on a complex set of factors tied to the specific sport and social interactions that are present.

Hence sport can be said to be causally responsible for both 'the Gary Linekers' and 'the Gazzas' or neither.

Informal sports and games and socialisation

What about informal games and moral development? These occupy a middle ground between play and organised sport. They are more structured than children's play, but retain some of the elements found in play. Devereux (1976) argued that by the early 1970s organised youth sport programmes in the USA had eroded a once rich culture of children's games. Comparing the USA with observations he made in Japan and Israel led him to conclude that children in those societies still had a rich repertoire of games that they played with little or no adult supervision. His informal observations were buttressed by the work in

Britain of Opie and Opie (1969) who documented more than 2,500 different games spontaneously played by children. By comparison, Devereux (1976) argued, children in the USA suffered from a form of 'game poverty'.

The decline of the informal games culture is significant in part because of the unique social benefits such games provide. Coakley (1983) argued that when children play informal games they are interested primarily in four things: action, involvement, maintaining a close score and opportunities to reaffirm friendships. There are important distinctions between adult-organised and informally organised youth sport and games (Figure 5.1). With adult-organised youth sport the aim tends to be performance-oriented, often involving notions such as dominance over opposing teams, and emphasising toughness and hard, disciplined work (learning skills and rules) over spontaneity, expression and creativity. Young boys tend to learn that manhood equals dominance. In many ways adult-organised youth sport may be seen as a denial of childhood and youth. In adult-organised sport the ethic or ideology of achievement is encouraged through such ideas as 'hard work will lead to eventual success', 'stay on in there', 'no pain, no gain' and 'one big play can turn the game around'. Yet the chances of becoming a professional athlete are thousands to one (see Chapter 8).

At the same time informal play can be alienating for some participants (Coakley, 1994: 107–8). Bigger and stronger children may exploit smaller and weaker ones, methods of team selection can leave less skilled children feeling embarrassed or rejected, and cruel comments can be directed at the unskilled or those who simply differ from local peer group norms. Informal games and organised sports alike can both mirror the prejudices and discrimination of the broader culture.

Hence organised sport and physical education at school can be experienced by some pupils as 'aversive socialisation'. Since adolescence is a period of attempts at developing autonomy, gaining control of their lives, the majority of young people can get turned off sport (White and Coakley, 1986). Adult-organised sport can be perceived of as consisting of many 'degradation ceremonies' as fun is replaced by *performance* as a criterion of participation.

Formal play	*Informal play*
Adult controlled	Player controlled
Rules determined by adults	Action
Plans/strategies	Personal involvement
Settle disputes	Close scores
Results/records	Reaffirm friendships

FIGURE 5.1 Distinctions between formal and informal play
Source: adapted from Coakley, 1994

Boys	Girls
Outdoors	In boys' groups (not vice versa)
Large groups	Smaller groups/creativity
Age mixes	
Competitive/explicit goals	Fewer explicit goals
Team/team formations	Less competitive and indirect competition not face to face
Complex rules for different positions	Few leadership roles

FIGURE 5.2 Differences in boys' and girls' informal play
Source: adapted from Lever, 1978

For girls and young women lessons about their 'proper roles' in sport – emotional supports for boys – are learned through exposure to such phenomena as cheerleaders. The role can be seen as preparation for the 'caretaker' role in later life. Feedback from teachers, boys and other girls can legitimise and reproduce girls' marginal involvement in physical activity and sport. This has been observed through studies of boys' and girls' informal play. Janet Lever (1978) studied play in schools in Connecticut via observation of playground activity during break periods, semi-structured interviews, written questionnaires, and activity diaries kept by a sample of children. Boys' and girls' games were totally different according to Lever (Figure 5.2). Girls were often excluded, given less attention or ridiculed by boys (Lever, 1976; 1978). So organised programmes may still provide a better opportunity for equalising sport involvement and can provide participants with a working knowledge of game models which can be carried over into informal games (Coakley and Westkott, 1984).

Shields and Bredemeier (1995: 216) conclude that sport participation may promote moral reasoning among children in cases where sport programmes have been carefully and explicitly designed and administered to produce changes in moral reasoning. On the other hand they quote the Opies, who concluded, after their extensive research, that 'in the long run, nothing extinguishes self-organised play more effectively than does action to promote it' (Opie and Opie, 1969: 16).

Alternative studies of socialisation through sport

Sport participants encounter a wide variety of socialisation experiences. The meaning of sport participation – and the values thereby encountered – make sense only in the context of the experiences and social relationships of those involved. Hence for some participants sport builds character, for others it does not. There is no single response to sport participation – sport is not a carrier of one single message or set of messages, nor are participants recipients in a deterministic fashion of a single message. Socialisation creates a variety of responses. Some may be more likely than others, some may be privileged or preferred, but values other than 'dominant ones' are also communicated.

In order to understand socialisation and sport properly socialisation has to be understood as a *dynamic process* and not just as a series of constraints imposed upon an unsocial, egotistical self. People make choices and decisions as a result of their past and current experiences. Present needs are influential. Hence adolescence is a period during which people seek out ways of developing their personal competence – displays of competence imply personal control over themselves and their environment. Control is at the heart of personal autonomy, and autonomy is a major developmental task for adolescents (White and Coakley, 1986: 44; Coalter and Allison, 1994).

Yet much of the research into socialisation through sport is based upon the observation of correlations with the assumption that those who participate in sport are passively *shaped* by their sport experiences, a view criticised by the interactionist and cultural studies tradition of research. We shall briefly consider studies in this tradition.

As was noted earlier, interactionist and cultural studies approaches to socialisation focus on:

1   The process of identity development through sport participation.
2   The ways in which sport is connected to the production and reproduction of knowledge, meaning, social practices and power relations at personal, cultural and structural levels.
3   The use of *interpretive methods* of social analysis to carry out research – collecting data (usually 'talk') through in-depth interviews and/or detailed observations, case studies and ethnographies.

Coakley and Donnelly (forthcoming) includes several studies in North America which used this approach. British-based studies adopting this approach include Corrigan (1979), Fleming (1995) and Wheaton (1997). One example of the method of analysis is an article by Birrell and Richter. They studied women's recreational slow-pitch softball leagues in two different towns in the USA. The study was carried out over a period of four years. They found that the softball players attempted to create sport experiences that were 'process oriented, collective, supportive, inclusive, and informed with an ethic of care' (1987: 408). In creating these oppositional meanings for sport they argue that feminists attempted to claim as their own sports territory previously inhabited only by men. In this study, as with others in this tradition, sport is not viewed so much as a product as a '*process of invention*' (1987: 397). As Jay Coakley (1993a: 190–191) remarks:

This invention process is grounded in the consciousness and collective reflections of the participants themselves, and it is shaped by conversations about experiences, feelings, decisions, behaviours, accounts of and responses to incidents, and a combination of individual and collective conclusions about the connections between sport and the lives of the participants. In other words, not only is sport a social construction, but so too are the consequences of participation.

For this tradition of analysis sports participation is a social process with *emergent qualities* that reflect the interests of those involved and the context in which it occurs. Interactionist and cultural studies of sport view it as 'a site for the social construction of people's sense of who they are and how they are connected to the rest of the world' (Coakley, 1993b: 581). For this reason Coakley (1993a: 191) argues that

> it makes more sense to frame discussions of socialisation through sport in terms of human agency, cultural practices, struggles, power relations, and social construction than it does to frame them in terms of specific outcomes manifested through measurable changes in the character traits of athletes and former athletes.

Sport is linked to an emerging process of social development at personal, cultural and structural levels. Sport is part of an overall context of social relations and cultural practices in which social development occurs. The interactionist/cultural studies approach attempts to capture the dynamic of the socialisation process as it is related to sport. In the future it is likely that there will be more studies of socialisation in sport and research into socialisation through sport using interpretive approaches. Sports participation will not be conceived of as a *variable*, so much as a *process* where *social relations* combine for social development. As Coakley (1993a: 191) suggests:

> Research on sport participation and what happens in connection with it matters because sport is highly visible, heavily promoted, and organised in ways that often support long-standing systems of power and privilege. Research is also important, however, because sport can be the site of human agency, resistance, struggle and transformation.

Socialisation – out of sport?

In this final section we will look briefly at research into the termination of sport participation, or socialisation out of sport, since this reflects quite well the change in emphasis in sport socialisation research away from *what sport does to people* towards a research agenda that considers *what people do with sport.*

What social factors explain withdrawal from sport – processes of attrition, selection, and de-selection? In the early 1970s critical analyses and exposés of sport, mainly in the USA, provided one set of explanations. Sport was administered and organised in an oppressive and inhumane way. Autocratic command-style coaches and profit-seeking owners sustained exploitative and alienating conditions in sport (Edwards, 1969; Hoch, 1972; Meggyesy, 1971; Scott, 1971; Shaw, 1972). The athlete was a victim of wider structural forces. People who had been socialised into sport might discontinue participation because of the organisation of sport. This set of criticisms applied equally well to children's sport programmes which overemphasised competition and winning as opposed to play and fun (Orlick and Botterill, 1975). These ideas continue to be debated because of the publicity given to such cases as young athlete 'burn-out' – for example the case of Jennifer Capriati in tennis – and over-ambitious parents who force their athletic children to do too much, too young – for example in association football signing them up to professional clubs at a very early age if they appear to show promise. These debates involve critiques of sports organisations and programmes and challenges to change them, rather than attempts fully to explain socialisation out of sport.

An alternative way of conceptualising the termination of sport involvement considers attrition in a different way – dropping out of sport does not always mean dropping out of all sports forever; it may involve shifting priorities and be a positive decision; it may not involve a decline in life satisfaction or victimisation; and it may involve exposure to new and challenging opportunities. From this approach terminating sport participation involves processes linked to social development – identity formation, shifts in personal priorities, changes in social support, success experiences in sport, access to opportunities in and out of sport, gender relations, and the life course and social definitions of age (e.g. Brown, 1985; Allison and Meyer, 1988; Curtis and Ennis, 1988; Johns *et al.*, 1990; Swain, 1991; and Coakley, 1992).

These studies suggest that the reasons given for participating and not participating in sport may often be the same. These reasons are only understandable in the different *contexts* of people's lives. Contexts are social constructions that can change over time and can only be fully understood in connection with wider social and cultural factors that transcend the immediate control of individuals.

Conclusions

Interactionist approaches to the study of sport have been criticised for not being historical, developmental or processual enough (Dunning *et al.*, 1993: 2). In terms of considering the way in which human beings are involved in making choices, however, within horizons limited by class, gender, ethnic and other influences, some notion of interaction is essential in making sense of sports participation and interest (and uninterest). Most recently researchers have begun to use interactionist approaches to look at risk taking in sport, violence in sport and how athletes deal with injury (Young *et al.*, 1994). To provide relevant information on these matters, and others of contemporary importance, it is necessary to continue to develop a model of the human individual that recognises both the freedom and constraint involved in social action.

ESSAYS AND EXERCISES

Essays

'Sport has as great a capacity for producing bullies and thugs as it has good citizens and saints' (Professor John Evans, quoted in the *Guardian*, 1 March 1994). Discuss.

Why are boys' and girls' play patterns so different?

'The number of sports played when young was the best predictor of whether individuals would continue to play into adulthood' (Roberts and Brodie, 1992). Discuss.

Exercises

Obtain a copy of a current pre-school comic aimed at both boys and girls. Use content analysis techniques* to examine the following issues story by story: (a) numbers of males and females; (b) the characters playing the leading roles; (c) which characters are active and which are passive; (d) what activities are they involved in? Use semiotic analysis techniques* to explore the underlying assumptions about gender and sexuality in one of the stories.
*See Chapter 6 for information about these techniques of media analysis.

Make notes on the salient features of any two sport or leisure sub-cultures with which you are familiar, with particular reference to how personal identity is constructed within those sub-cultures.

The Nobel Prize winning novelist and philosopher Albert Camus has famously noted that all he learned about life, he learned on the football field (he played in goal). Have you learned any lessons in this way, and in what ways has competitive sport prepared you for life?

FURTHER READING

J. Coakley, *Sport in Society: Issues and Controversies,* 6th edition, Boston, McGraw-Hill, 1998, synthesises vast amounts of evidence, from British work as well as USA research.

P. Donnelly and J. Coakley (eds), *Inside Sports*, London, Routledge, 1998, gathers together accounts, discussions and interpretations of identity, experience and interactions within sports cultures.

References

Adler, P. and Adler, P. (1991) *Backboards and Blackboards: College Athletes and Role Engulfment*, New York: Columbia University Press.

Allison, M. and Meyer, C. (1988) 'Career Problems and Retirement among Elite Athletes: The Female Tennis Professional', *Sociology of Sport Journal*, Vol. 5, pp. 212–222.

Belotti, E. (1975) *Little Girls*, London: Writers and Readers.

Birrell, S. and Richter, D. (1987) 'Is a Diamond Forever? Feminist Transformations of Sport', *Women's Studies International Forum*, Vol. 10, pp. 395–409.

Bishop, J. and Hoggett, P. (1986) *Organising Around Enthusiasms: Mutual Aid in Leisure*, London: Comedia/Routledge.

Boslooper, T. and Hayes, M. (1973) *The Femininity Game*, New York: Skein & Day.

Bourdieu, P. (1984) *Distinction – A Social Critique of the Judgement of Taste*, London: Routledge.

Brown, B. (1985) 'Factors Influencing the Process of Withdrawal by Female Adolescents from the Role of Competitive Age Group Swimmer', *Sociology of Sport Journal*, Vol. 2, pp. 111–129.

Byrne, E. (1983) *Women and Education*, London: Tavistock.

Clarke, G. and Humberstone, B. (1997) *Researching Women and Sport*, London: Macmillan.

Coakley, J. (1983) 'Play, Games and Sport: Development Implications for Young People', in J. Harris and R. Park (eds), *Play, Games and Sport in Cultural Contexts*, Champaign, Illinois: Human Kinetics.

Coakley, J. (1992) 'Burnout Among Adolescent Athletes: A Personal Failure or Social Problem?', *Sociology of Sport Journal*, Vol. 9, pp. 271–285.

Coakley, J. (1993a) 'Sport and Socialisation', in John O. Holloszey (ed.), *Exercise and Sport Sciences Reviews*, Volume 21, New York: Williams & Wilkins, pp. 169–200.

Coakley, J. (1993b) 'Socialisation and Sport', in R.L. Singer, M. Murphey and L. K. Tennant (eds), *Handbook of Research on Sport Psychology*, New York: Macmillan.

Coakley, J. (1994) *Sport in Society: Issues and Controversies*, St Louis, Illinois: Mosby.

Coakley, J. and Donnelly, P. (1998) *Inside Sports: Using Sociology to Understand Athletes and Sport Experiences*, London: Routledge.

Coakley, J. and Westkott, M. (1984) 'Opening Doors for Women in Sport: An Alternative to Old Strategies', in D.S. Eitzen (ed.) *Sport in Contemporary Society*, New York: St. Martin's Press.

Coakley, J. and White, A. (1992) 'Making Decisions: Gender and Sport Participation Among British Adolescents', *Sociology of Sport Journal*, Vol. 9, pp. 20–35.

Coalter, F. (1987) 'Sport and Delinquency', unpublished manuscript cited in D. Robins (1990).

Coalter, F. and Allison, M. (1994) *Leisure Preferences of Young People in Wester Hailes*, Edinburgh: Scottish Sports Council.

Connell, R.W. (1983) *Which Way is Up? Essays on Sex, Class and Culture*, Sydney: Allen & Unwin.

Connell, R.W. (1987) *Gender and Power: Society, the Person and Sexual Politics*, Cambridge: Polity Press.

Connell, R.W. (1995) *Masculinities*, Cambridge: Polity Press.

Corrigan, P. (1979) *Schooling the Smash Street Kids*, London: Macmillan.

Curry, T. (1991) 'Fraternal Bonding in the Locker Room: A Profeminist Analysis of Talk About Competition and Women', *Sociology of Sport Journal*, Vol. 8, pp. 119–135.

Curtis, J. and Ennis, R. (1988) 'Negative Consequences of Leaving Competitive Sport?: Comparative Findings For Former Elite-level Hockey Players', *Sociology of Sport Journal*, Vol. 5, pp. 87–106.

Devereux, E. (1976) 'Backyard vs. Little League Baseball: The Impoverishment of Children's Games', in D. Landers (ed.), *Social Problems in Athletics*, Champaign, Illinois: University of Illinois Press.

Dixon, B. (1977a) *Catching Them Young, Vol. 1: Sex, Race and Class in Children's Fiction*, London: Pluto.

Dixon, B. (1977b) *Catching Them Young, Vol. 2: Political Ideas in Children's Fiction*, London: Pluto.

Dixon, B. (1990) *Playing Them False: A Study of Children's Toys, Games and Puzzles*, Stoke-on-Trent: Trentham Books.

Donnelly, P. (1985) 'Sport Subcultures', *Exercise and Sport Science Review*, Vol. 13, pp. 539–578.

Donnelly, P. and Young, K. (1988) 'The Construction and Confirmation of Identity in Sport Subcultures', *Sociology of Sport Journal*, Vol. 5, pp. 223–240.

Dunne, M. (1982) 'An Introduction to Some of the Images of Sport in Girls' Comics and Magazines' in M. Green and C. Jenkins (eds), *Sporting Fictions*, Birmingham: Centre for Contemporary Cultural Studies/ Department of Physical Education, University of Birmingam.

Dunning, E., Maguire, J. and Pearton, R. (eds) (1993) *The Sports Process*, Champaign, Illinois: Human Kinetics.

Dunphy, E. (1991) *A Strange Kind of Glory – Sir Matt Busby and Manchester United*, London: Heinemann.

Edwards, H. (1969) *The Revolt of the Black Athlete*, New York: The Free Press.

Fine, G.A. (1987) *With The Boys: Little League Baseball and Preadolescent Subculture*, Chicago: University of Chicago Press.

Fleming, S. (1995) *'Home and Away': Sport and South Asian Male Youth*, Aldershot: Avebury.

Foley, D.E. (1990) 'The Great American Football Ritual: Reproducing Race, Class, and Gender Inequality', *Sociology of Sport Journal*, Vol. 7, pp. 111–135.

Fraser, E. (1987) 'Teenage Girls Reading *Jackie*', *Media, Culture & Society*, Vol. 10, pp. 407–425.

Gilroy, S. (1993) 'Whose Sport is it Anyway? Adults and Children's Sport', in M. Lee (ed.), *Coaching Children in Sport: Principles and Practice*, London: E & FN Spon.

Guardian 1 March 1994.

Gunter, B. (1986) *Television and Sex-role Stereotyping*, London: Libby/Independent Broadcasting Authority.

Hargreaves, J. (1994) *Sporting Females: Critical Issues in the History and Sociology of Women's Sports*, London: Routledge.

Hoch, P. (1972) *Rip Off the Big Game – The Exploitation of Sports by the Power Elite*, New York: Doubleday Anchor.

Hughes, R. and Coakley, J. (1991) 'Positive Deviance Among Athletes: The Implications of Over Conformity to the Sport Ethic', *Sociology of Sport Journal*, Vol. 8, pp. 307–325.

Jarvie, G. and Maguire, J. (1994) *Sport and Leisure in Social Thought*, London: Routledge.

Johns, D., Lindner, K. and Wolko, K. (1990) 'Understanding Attrition in Female Competitive Gymnastics: Applying Social Exchange Theory', *Sociology of Sport Journal*, Vol. 7, pp. 154–171.

Keillor, G. (1994) *The Book of Guys*, London: Faber and Faber.

Kremer, J. and Scully, D. (1994) *Psychology in Sport*, London: Taylor & Francis.

Lawson, P. (1986) BBC Radio 4 *Children and Sport*, 13 March.

Lee, M. (1986) 'Moral and Social Growth Through Sport: The Coach's Role', in G. Gleeson (ed.), *The Growing Child in Competitive Sport*, London: Hodder & Stoughton.

Leonard, W.M. II (1984) *A Sociological Perspective of Sport*, Minneapolis: Burgess.

Lever, J. (1976) 'Sex Differences in the Games Children Play', *Social Problems*, Vol. 23, pp. 478–87

Lever, J. (1978) 'Sex Differences in the Complexity of Children's play', *American Sociological Review*, Vol. 43, pp. 471–483.

Loy, J. and A. Ingham, A. (1981) 'Play, Games and Sport in the Psycho-sociological Development of Children and Youth', in J. Loy, G. Kenyon and B. McPherson (eds), *Sport, Culture and Society*, 2nd edition, Philadelphia: Lea & Febiger.

McCormack, J. and Chalip, L. (1988) 'Sport as Socialisation: A Critique of Methodological Premises', *The Social Science*, Journal Vol. 25, pp. 83–92.

McPherson, B., Curtis, J. and Loy, J. (1993) *The Social Significance of Sport*, Champaign, Illinois: Human Kinetics.

McRobbie, A. (1991) *Feminism and Youth Culture*, London: Macmillan.

Mead, M. (1977) (1935) *Sex and Temperament in Three Primitive Societies*, 2nd edition, London: Routledge & Kegan Paul.

Meggyesy, D. (1971) *Out of their League*, New York: Coronet Paperback Library.

Messner, M. (1990) 'When Bodies are Weapons: Masculinity and Violence in Sport', *International Review for the Sociology of Sport*, Vol. 25, pp. 203–220.

Meyer, B.B. (1990) 'From Idealism to Actualisation: The Academic Performance of Female Collegiate Athletes', *Sociology of Sport Journal*, Vol. 7, pp. 44–57.

Opie, I. and Opie, P. (1969) *Children's Games in Street and Playground*, Oxford: Oxford University Press.

Orlick, T. and Botterill, C. (1975) *Every Kid Can Win*, Chicago: Nelson Hall.

Palzkill, B. (1990) 'Between Gym Shoes and High-heels – The Development of a Lesbian Identity and Existence in Top Class Sport', *International Review for the Sociology of Sport*, Vol. 25, pp. 221–234.

Philips, D. (1995) 'White Boots and Ballet Shoes – Girls Growing Up in the 1950s', in G. McFee, W. Murphy and G. Whannel (eds), *Leisure Cultures: Values, Genders,*

Lifestyles, University of Brighton, Eastbourne: Leisure Studies Association (Publication No. 54).

Roberts, K. and Brodie, D. (1992) *Inner-city Sport: Who Plays, and What are the Benefits?*, Voorthuizen: Giordano Bruno.

Robins, D. (1990) S*port as Prevention: The Role of Sport in Crime Prevention Programmes Aimed at Young People*, Oxford: University of Oxford, Centre for Criminological Research, Occasional Paper 12.

Sabo, D. and Jansen, S.C. (1992) 'Images of Men in Sport Media: The Social Reproduction of Gender Order', in S. Craig (ed.), *Men, Masculinity and the Media*, London: Sage.

Scott, J. (1971) *The Athletic Revolution*, New York: The Free Press.

Scraton, S. (1987) '"Boys Muscle in Where Angels Fear to Tread" – Girls' Sub-cultures and Physical Activities', in J. Horne, D. Jary and A. Tomlinson (eds), Sport, Leisure and Social Relations, London: Routledge & Kegan Paul.

Scraton, S. (1992) *Shaping Up to Womanhood*, Milton Keynes: Open University Press.

Shaw, G. (1972) *Meat on the Hoof*, New York: St. Martin's Press.

Shields, D.L.L. and Bredemeier, B.J.L. (1995) *Character Development and Physical Activity*, Champaign, Illinois: Human Kinetics.

Stanworth, M. (1980) *Gender and Schooling*, London: Women's Research and Resources Centre.

Stevenson, C. (1975) 'Socialisation Effects of Participation in Sport: A Critical Review of Research', *Research Quarterly*, Vol. 46, pp. 287–302.

Stevenson, C. (1985) 'College Athletics and "Character": The Decline and Fall of Socialisation Research', in D. Chu, J.O. Segrave and B.J. Becker (eds), *Sport and Higher Education*, Champaign, Illinois: Human Kinetics.

Stevenson, C. (1990) 'The Early Careers of International Athletes', *Sociology of Sport Journal*, Vol. 7, pp. 238–253.

Sugden, J. and Bairner, A. (1993) *Sport, Sectarianism and Society in a Divided Ireland*, Leicester: Leicester University Press.

Swain, D.A. (1991) 'Withdrawal from Sport and Schlossberg's Model of Transitions', *Sociology of Sport Journal*, Vol. 8, pp. 152–160.

Tomlinson, A. (1983) 'Tuck up Tight Lads: Structures of Control within Football Culture', in A. Tomlinson (ed.), *Explorations in Football Culture*, University of Brighton, Eastbourne: Leisure Studies Association (Publication No. 21).

Tomlinson, A. (1995) 'Ideologies of Physicality, Masculinity and Femininity: Comments on Roy of the Rovers and the Women's Fitness Boom', in A. Tomlinson (ed.), *Gender, Sport and Leisure: Continuities and Challenges*, Brighton University: Chelsea School Research Centre Topic Report 4.

Trulson, M. (1986) 'Martial Arts Training: A Novel "Cure" for Juvenile Delinquency', *Human Relations*, Vol. 39, pp. 1131–1140.

Tuchman, G. (1978) 'The Symbolic Annihilation of Women by the Mass Media', in G. Tuchman (ed.), *Hearth and Home: Images of Women in the Mass Media*, New York: Oxford University Press.

Whannel, G. (1995) 'Sport Stars, Youth and Morality in the Print Media', in G. McFee, W. Murphy and G. Whannel (eds), *Leisure Cultures: Values, Genders, Lifestyles*, University of Brighton, Eastbourne: Leisure Studies Association (Publication No. 54).

Wheaton, B. (1997) 'The Changing Gender Order in Sport? The Case of Windsurfing Subcultures', paper presented at 'Power/Resistance', British Sociological Association Annual Conference, University of York, April.

White, A. and Coakley, J. (1986) *Making Decisions: The Response of Young People in the Medway Towns to the 'Ever Thought of Sport?' Campaign*, London: Greater London and South East Region Sports Council.

Wolfenden Report (1960) *Sport and the Community*, London: Central Council for Physical Recreation.

Women's Sports Foundation (1995) *Women and Sport: A Syllabus Guide for Teachers and Lecturers*, London: Women's Sports Foundation/Sports Council.

Young, I.M. (1980) 'Throwing Like a Girl: A Phenomenology of Feminine Body Comportment, Motility and Spatiality', *Human Studies*, Vol. 3, pp. 137–156.

Young, K., White, P., and McTeer, W. (1994) 'Body Talk: Male Athletes Reflect on Sport, Injury and Pain', *Sociology of Sport Journal*, Vol. 11, pp. 175–194.

Chapter six

Representation, sport and the media

Introduction

This chapter will trace the development of media sport, offer a brief introduction to media analysis and outline how such analysis has been applied to media representation of sport.

Sport itself has no essentialist, pre-given definition, indeed it is very difficult to arrive at a consensus as to what 'sport' is. Fierce argument can and does rage over whether snooker, darts, cycling, fishing, synchronised swimming, skating and professional wrestling are regarded as sports. Some would wish to exclude 'professional' sport from the category. The task of formulating an adequate definition has eluded philosophers. The term has its own origins, and has changed its meanings regularly. In the early nineteenth century it would have included field sports and cruel sports but not many of the activities we now commonly associate with the term.

The media have come to play a significant role in the constant reformulation of the term 'sport'. Our very sense of the meaning of the category sport has been shaped by the emergence of the sporting press, sports pages, cinema newsreels, and by television sport. If a sport, be it showjumping or snooker, is included within television sport, then it must be a sport, whereas, if, like bare knuckle fighting or badger-baiting, it is excluded, then it implicitly is not a sport. The media play an active role in the process of boundary marking, and boundary shifting. Clearly the media play their part in that complex cultural process whereby particular practices (e.g. competitive team games) become dominant, whilst others (e.g. cruel sports, field sports, boxing) slowly become residual, and other new activities (e.g. hang-gliding, wind-surfing, jet skiing) become emergent.

Media sport: a brief history

Before the era of mass media, the recording of cultural imagery was firmly linked to the power of the church and the aristocracy. Painters were commissioned to celebrate the material wealth of owners. Sporting paintings portrayed the horses and dogs of the land-owners (Goldman, 1983). There were also paintings of scenes of carnivalesque celebration, such as the famous Derby Day painting, and of everyday low life showing cock-fighting or dog-fighting (see Pendred, 1987).

The sporting press began to emerge in the last two decades of the nineteenth century. The 1870 Education Act had helped produce a new reading public. The market for popular fiction had grown. There was a rapid growth in sport magazines. From the 1880s the *Sportsman*, *Sporting Life* and the *Sporting Chronicle* were all selling 300,000 a day. A 1914 bibliography of books between 1890 and 1912 listed at least 19,000 items. The modern era of mass circulation popular newspapers began in 1896 with the launch of the *Daily Mail*. The first sports pages began to emerge (Mason, 1993).

The Edwardian era was a period of coming of age for elite spectator sport. Cricket, football, cycling, tennis, athletics, rugby and golf all found and consolidated their audiences, and their events helped provide the substance of the sports sections (Mason, 1993). Like sport itself sport journalism was predominantly a male controlled and defined domain. By and large the sports pages served to transmit and reproduce the dominance of those sporting institutions established by the public school and Oxbridge-educated male Victorian bourgeoisie.

The growth of cinema from the start of the twentieth century had by the 1920s spawned a whole new cultural habit of regular cinema going. Sound arrived by the end of the 1920s and a whole new generation of spectacular picture palaces was constructed. The newsreel was an important element in the programme, and every newsreel had its sport section. For the vast majority of the audience this provided their first glimpse of moving action from major events like the Cup Final or Derby Day.

If the newsreel provided movement, radio provided immediacy. The BBC was launched as a private corporation in 1922 but vested interests of the newspapers prevented it from broadcasting sporting commentaries until 1926 when it became a public corporation. For the first time major sporting events could be followed, as they happened, in the home. This began the process whereby such sporting events became, in the words of Scannell and Cardiff (1991), national corporate rituals – occasions in which the vast majority of the population seemed to participate and share.

Television was first launched in 1936 but didn't reach a large audience – it could only be received within about 20 miles of Alexandra Palace, the sets were expensive, and only around 20,000 had been sold by the time of television's wartime suspension in 1939. When television was re-launched in 1946 as part of post-war reconstruction, sport slowly became a significant element in the schedules. By the end of the 1950s the regular fixed slots of Saturday afternoon (*Grandstand*), Wednesday night (*Sportsview*) and Saturday night (football highlights) were well established on the BBC.

At the start of the 1960s, though, the British television image was still grainy and black and white, but the medium was on the threshold of a technological revolution. The rapid introduction of video recording and editing (1961), the first communication satellites (Telstar in 1962), action replay (1966), slow motion (1967), colour (1968) and new lightweight mobile cameras (1970) transformed the medium and by the mid-1970s, the audience had come to expect as a matter of course that high quality live pictures in colour could be relayed from virtually anywhere in the world. In effect, by 1970 the modern television era was firmly established.

In the last thirty years, developments in the British press have raised the prominence of sport, heightened the sensationalism of its coverage and shifted the relation of public and private spheres dramatically. Two developments were of especial significance. First, the purchase of the *Sun* by Rupert Murdoch, and its re-launch as a tabloid in 1969 triggered off a tabloid revolution in which the *Daily Mirror* and the *Sun* competed for the working-class reader with more explicit pin-ups, sport and scandal (Murdock and Golding, 1978). Second, the destruction of the power of the print unions in 1986, when Murdoch moved his four titles to Wapping, opened the way to a technological revolution (Goodhart and Wintour, 1986). Full computerisation and colour printing accelerated the drift away from traditional page layout and towards a collage style in which headlines and photo displays came to dominate. This in turn heightened the force and impact of stories about easily recognised star figures.

Advances in telecommunications, from the 1970s, enabling high quality live pictures to be beamed around the world, ushered in a globalised 'universality'. The first communication satellite, Telstar, was launched in 1962. But it was only in the 1970s that a network of satellites covering the globe began to be established. As audiences around the world became accustomed to receiving top quality live broadcasts of major sport events, so the television industry became concerned with uniformity. The conventions already established in the leading television nations of North America and Europe were extended to the rest of the world. The placing of cameras and styles of cutting patterns were universalised. Regional diversity and specificity began to decline and by the 1980s even the

163

internal geography of stadium design was tending towards a universality of style. The specificities of place were becoming much less visible.

Until 1982 there were only three channels available in England – BBC 1, BBC 2 and ITV. There had been no change since the introduction of BBC2 in 1964. The launch of Channel 4 ushered in a new period of expansion. Cable had long been well established in America and during the 1980s cable networks began to flourish more extensively in Europe. However, it was the establishment of satellite channels like Sky and the linking of satellite and cable that really triggered a new transformation. Multiple outlets enabled the establishment of generic channels like the dedicated sports channels. Subscription television was growing rapidly in the early 1990s. Pay-per-view now looms as a key element in sports broadcasting. Digital television, which will enable the establishment of hundreds of new channels, was launched in 1998. Satellite and cable, in short, are playing a key role in the deregulation of broadcasting, the commodification of television and the fragmentation of audiences. There has already been a substantial increase in the amount of sport on television, but this has been in the context of a commodification, whereby a small proportion of the potential audience can be induced to pay for pay-per-channel systems.

Since the mid-1980s the other area of significant development has been in the publishing of magazines aimed at men. Up-market glossy publications *Arena*, *GQ* and *FHM* were challenged in the 1990s by *Loaded*, targeted at the new lads, with a defiant reassertion of beer and breasts culture, only thinly veiled as postmodern irony. Its success in turn forced *FHM* to take a down-market direction. The emergence of new lad culture was indicated by such parameters as *Loaded*, the television series *Men Behaving Badly*, and the growth, inspired by the success of Nick Hornby's *Fever Pitch*, of fan-oriented accounts of football.

Brewster (1993) and Shaw (1989) chart the growth of football fanzines, which have also been analysed as a case in which the dominant values of a sporting world have been contested (Jary *et al.*, 1991). The success of fanzines helped trigger the launch of new mainstream sport magazines like *Four Four Two* and *Sported*. Sports photography has received inadequate attention, although there is an excellent collection of examples (Smith, 1987).

Time and space

In becoming the major mass medium, television as a technology and as a cultural form has transformed our sense of time and space.

From the 1950s onward television increasingly became the focal point of the domestic sphere (Root, 1986). By the mid-1960s television ownership had neared saturation point, with over 90 per cent of households having a licence. The introduction of colour provided a vital boost to the industry, and as sales of colour sets grew, the old black and white sets were often moved to bedrooms, or kitchens. The multiple set household emerged and was to continue to grow in significance as the introduction of video, computer games machines, satellite television and cable television all served to promote multiple set ownership. During the 1950s and 1960s television could be seen as a cultural form that served to bind households and families together in the practice of viewing. By the 1980s, multiple set ownership could be seen as a part of a process of fragmentation of domestic space (see Morley, 1986). Just as the availability of multiple channels fragmented the audience, so multiple set ownership dispersed the audience.

In major developed countries television has remained predominantly a domestic medium, consumed in the private spaces of the home. Conversely, in many countries with a lower proportion of television households the public space – bars, cafes, hotel lounges – is often the space of television, constituting a site of communal, rather than domestic, consumption. The provision of television sport in bars transforms the social space of the bar into a viewing space. It continues to be a public space in which social interaction takes place, but the provision of visual spectacle produces a new set of social relations in which the drinkers become spectators and the spectacle becomes the focal point. It is notable that in England the extension of licensing hours and the acquisition by Sky TV of live rights to Premier League Football have provided a significant boost to the practice of providing television sport in pubs. Several specialised sports bars have also opened in London in recent years. The appeal of both sport and pubs, separately, has always been predominantly male. The combining of two forms in one constructs a public space that is highly gendered – viewing sport in pubs is a heavily male-defined ritual and the sports bar, while a public space, is a masculine space. This rapid growth of a cultural form – collective viewing of sport – not previously a major feature of English social life, is a noteworthy example of the combined impact of television's technology, scheduling and financial deals, gender relations, and government legislation, upon what is sometimes described as 'free leisure time'.

Television has shifted our perception and understanding of geographic space. Technological advances now provide live pictures from all over the world, with seamless switching between events in different places. Australia, Bosnia and California all seem tantalisingly close and real, whereas, perversely, our own closer surroundings become largely invisible. However, our sense of these spaces is, of course, framed by what we are shown. Television sport allows us only a very particular kind of view. Atlanta, Barcelona and San Diego become defined by the physical geography of their sports stadia, along with the limited skyline views offered by telephoto lenses in aerial cameras. We get to see very little that is outside the stadium – hors-champs in Daney's (1978) phrase.

Television has, since its rise to prominence during the 1950s, played a significant role in structuring our sense of time and our use of it. On British television sport rapidly acquired its fixed spots in the schedule – *Grandstand* on Saturday afternoons, football highlights on Saturday night (*Match of The Day*), *Sportsnight* on Wednesdays. The invitational imperative is to structure our lives around these fixed points. The ability to relay live events that are at odd hours in the receiving country, combined with the unique appeal of live sport, means that as well as structuring daily time, television can also break into it, marking and underlining its own power to exert a determining influence. Live sport is one of the few programme forms that on occasion (e.g. the World Snooker Championship final between Steve Davis and Dennis Taylor in 1985) can cause us, in our millions, to stay up late into the night. In addition, generic satellite and cable channels open up a special time–space cluster. Eurosport and the Sky sport channels become the place of sport all the time – sport always available whatever the other channels may have scheduled.

Television sport also plays its role in the structuring of calendar time. There is a recognisable sporting calendar, a list of major events that most people could identify – the Grand National, the Derby, the FA Cup Final, Wimbledon tennis, the Boat Race, Test Matches, etc. This list is characterised by its static and recurrent nature, rooted in tradition (see Peters, 1976), the same events appearing year after year at the appropriate time. There is nothing natural or given about this calendar; it is constructed and determined by a set of factors – the history and organisation of sport, its coverage in the press and broadcasting, and the nature of sporting practices in the education apparatus. In recent years television has been the dominant factor in the construction of this calendar, playing a key role in the invention of tradition. Events that television chooses to feature, such as the World Snooker Championship, rapidly seem to be as long established as the Derby. The World Athletics Championship first took place as recently as 1983, yet somehow now seems to have always been a part of the TV calendar. Conversely, where television drops or marginalises an event like the Horse of the Year Show, it very soon seems marginal and irrelevant to the world of sport.

Media analysis

Basic communication theory makes a distinction between the sender and receiver of a message. This in turn gives rise to a three-part model: sender–message–receiver (see Schramm, 1960). Early media content analysis during the 1950s and 1960s analysed the content of media messages, in both quantitative and qualitative fashion.

When study of the media began to emerge as a distinct academic subject it developed in an interdisciplinary fashion, drawing upon history, sociology, literary theory and semiology (see Hall *et al.*, 1980 and Hall, 1980). A division grew between analysis in the sociological tradition, which continued with content analysis, and semiological analysis, which attempted to develop a more systematic understanding of language and its meanings.

Semiology, literally the science of signs, but more precisely the study of meaning production, examines the process whereby language, whether visual, verbal or a combination of the two, produces meanings (Barthes, 1967). In its early phase it focused upon the message, or text, as the product of the system of language that makes meaning possible. It was the underlying system of a language – its codes and conventions – that were seen as enabling the production of meaning. However, as this system only exists in the form of utterances – speech acts, written language, visual representation – in short, texts, texts were the object of analysis. The main aim of analysis, however, was to uncover or reveal the underlying systems of language that made the production of meaning possible.

There were two significant developments upon this base. First, the text was seen as involving a process of encoding. In order to be intelligible, a message has to be composed according to sets of codes or conventions that the audience can decode (for example the ways in which hats – cloth cap/bowler/top hat – act as signifiers of social class). The text is part of a communicative chain linking the production and consumption of a message – production–text–consumption. This concept was the basis of the encoding–decoding model (Hall, 1980).

Second, developments upon early semiology explored the ways in which language acts to position or interpellate the reader (or audience). The text carries within it subject positions that readers come to occupy. An example of this is the assumption of patriotic identification that commentaries upon international football contain, positioning us, for example, as patriotic subjects who want England to win.

Within this tradition there are complex and competing areas of theorisation that will not be explored in this chapter. However, an understanding of the influence of semiology can provide a useful context for reading the analyses of media sport coverage that this piece outlines.

Media sport analysis

Detailed and systematic study of media sport coverage began to develop during the 1970s with the work of Buscombe and Peters in England, and Birrell and Loy and the contributors to the *Journal of Communication* in the USA.

Football on Television (Buscombe, 1975) drew on film theory, as did similar French analysis (Daney, 1978; Telecine, 1978), and concentrated on close textual analysis along with consideration of political and ideological signification (see also Peters, 1976; Nowell-Smith, 1978). The influence of Buscombe can also be detected in North America during the 1970s, alongside more traditional forms of content analysis (see *Journal of Communication*, summer 1977, special issue on media sport; and Real, 1975).

But further developments were slow and spasmodic (see Birrell and Loy, 1979; Clarke and Clarke, 1982; Whannel, 1982; Bown, 1981) and only in the last few years has the field been more thoroughly explored. Alongside studies of British television sport (Barnett, 1990; Whannel, 1992), there are a range of North American studies (Rader, 1984; Chandler, 1988; Wenner, 1989; Cantelon and Gruneau, 1988; Gruneau, 1989; Real, 1989) and the rapid growth of cultural studies in Australia during the 1980s has spawned several studies of media sport (see Lawrence and Rowe, 1987; Rowe and Lawrence, 1989; Goldlust, 1987). Blain, Boyle and O'Donnell (1993) look at the European media in a cross-cultural perspective, and Critcher (1987) has reviewed the emergent field.

Such analyses contend that television and the other media do not simply reflect the world, but rather construct versions, or accounts, of it. Buscombe's football monograph analyses in detail the way that camera positions, cutting patterns, modes of editing, commentary, title sequences and presentation material all serve to construct a particular image of football. Similarly, Peters analyses the ways that television's visual and verbal conventions serve to relay a particular picture of the 1976 Olympic Games. Birrell and Loy (1979) analyse the ways in which television re-arranges time and space in order to produce sport in televisual form. Buscombe (1975) and Peters (1976) both argued that while television sport claimed to be merely presenting reality, it was in fact constructing a version of it, viewed from the position of an imaginary 'ideal' spectator.

The combination of direct and indirect address in television sport, the use of visual devices like slow motion, and action replay, and the use of graphics, cannot simply be seen as a variant of the realist conventions of narrative fiction. To dissect the complex combination of title montages, presentation, contributors, clips, action replays and actuality, it is more useful to think in terms of conflicting tensions between attempts to achieve transparency and desire to build in entertainment values.

Narratives, stars and spectacle

The contributors to the *Journal of Communication* special issue on sport analysed the ways in which commentaries function to produce drama (see Bryant *et al.*, 1977) Such analysis served to highlight the focus of television coverage around action and spectacle, star individuals and drama. Whannel

(1982) examined the coverage of athletes Coe and Ovett, and argued that television narrativises events, turning them into stories with narrative structures that correspond in some ways to the conventions of literary narrative. Such narratives are used as part of the process whereby readers are addressed and positioned, aiding the winning and holding of audiences.

Television has, since the 1950s, undergone a process of spectacularisation, dramatisation and personalisation. The percentage of close shots in sport coverage has increased dramatically. In the 1966 World Cup Final close-ups amounted to around 13 per cent of all shots. In an analysis of four major matches between 1988 and 1992 close-ups provided between 20 and 30 per cent of the total. The average shot length in 1966 was 20 seconds, while in the 1990 World Cup semi-final between England and West Germany it was 10 seconds, and in the 1990 FA Cup Final replay (BBC), it was around 6 seconds. Television does far more than simply relay an event. It selects, frames, juxtaposes, personalises, dramatises and narrates. In the process space and time are re-composed in order to enhance the entertainment value.

In the television age sport has been turned into mass spectacle, a process that arguably began at the start of the 1960s (Crawford, 1992) and is epitomised in major sport events like the Olympic Games (McPhail and Jackson, 1989; Brennan, 1995) the World Cup (Nowell Smith, 1978; Wren-Lewis and Clarke, 1983; and Geraghty and Simpson, 1986) and the Superbowl (Real, 1989). The English football cup final has been analysed (in two Open University television programmes) as a site on which representations of tradition, ritual and royalty are joined to the tension and drama of 'the people's game' (see also Colley and Davies, 1982). Van de Berg and Trujillo (1989) examine the centrality of winning in American sporting ideology and the ways in which the Dallas Cowboys were represented as a symbol of success. Young (1986) examines media coverage of the Heysel Stadium disaster, charting the various ways in which blame was attributed. Gruneau's 1989 case study of television skiing describes the need of producers to make the event look more dramatic and 'make the course look faster'.

Morris and Nydahl argued that, in the 1980s, television producers designed sport spectacles laced with visual surprises that present a range of dramatic experiences that the live event could not, thus inventing an original form of drama. In particular, slow motion replay offered entirely new events outside of real time and space. Slow motion replay not only altered our perception of the action it reviews, but it also established our expectations (Morris and Nydahl, 1985). The power of television is such that, as Barnett (1990) suggested, stadia are increasingly prepared to adopt the role of a surrogate TV producer, introducing huge TV screens with close ups, slomo and advertising.

Ideology, discourse and the body: competitive individualism

A major impetus behind much of this analysis was to trace the presence and operation of ideology within representation. Ideology is one of the more complex terms in sociological and political debate. Marx states that the class that controls material production also controls mental production and that in any era the dominant ideas are likely to be those of the dominant class. Following Althusser, ideology became seen as an all-pervasive way of seeing that is taken for granted and naturalised. It is a partial view of the world, systematically favouring the interests of dominant groups at the expense of subordinate groups.

In studying individual media texts, it is the case that the terms of which they are made up do not acquire their meanings in isolation. Language is a system, or set of systems, within which terms already have meanings with connotations, according to how they are used and have been used in other contexts. Take words like freedom, fair play, commitment, flair – they are all shaped by the contexts in which we are accustomed to hearing them used. They exist within particular discourses – organised sets of utterances. It is possible, for example, to regard the emergence of fitness chic in the late 1970s as a discourse that linked up a whole set of terms (work, pain, fit, individual) and gave them specific meanings.

Sport inevitably involves forms of body transformation, whether conscious, deliberate and strategically planned, as in elite sport, or as the coincidental by-product of active physical activity, pursued for other reasons. Jean-Marie Brohm regards sport as a form of Taylorisation of the body, an attempt to produce maximum productivity through a sado-masochistic training regime which instils an ability to withstand pain, to train and compete beyond the pain threshold. This concept of sport training is a typical aspect of sport films such as *North Dallas Forty* and *Rocky*. Media stories such as the portrayal of goalkeeper Bert Trautmann continuing playing in a cup final despite a broken neck; tabloid pictures of Terry Butcher playing on after a head injury, his white England shirt red with blood; a colour supplement assemblage drawing of Bryan Robson with his body scarred by all the injuries of his career – all celebrate the toughness of those who push the body through pain.

The rise of Thatcherism was accompanied by the growing prominence of a new competitive individualism in which sport became work, fitness classes became work-outs and the new common sense was constituted by phrases like 'no pain, no gain', 'feel that burn', and 'if it ain't hurting it ain't working'. Going on through the pain signified commitment.

Placing the body in jeopardy, in a position of danger and risk, appears to be a part of the production of sporting spectacle. Certain events signify danger – skiing, boxing, motor racing, mountaineering, American football – and thrills and spills are a major point of appeal. For the television audience, show-jumping, skiing and ice-skating all carry promise that something will go wrong. Risk and the threat of an accident contributes to the spectacle – it is part of what binds an audience to these events – and it underlines the heroic nature of those who compete – they place their bodies, and hence their lives, in jeopardy. The 'celebrated body' is for some the end product. The celebrated body is that body seen at the moment of victory, breasting the tape, receiving the trophy, waving to the crowd, in an image to be recycled a hundred times. The celebrated body achieves recognition and admiration, it acquires immortality, in the words of the song 'Fame' 'I want to live forever . . .'. It is in this sense that we can speak of a discourse of competitive individualism.

Gender

Of all cultural practices sport is, arguably, the one that most prominently serves to demarcate the genders. Boys grow into a world in which sport is a significant component of masculinity. Being sporting provides an ease of entry into masculinity, whilst to dislike sport prompts unease and doubts about whether one is a 'real man'. By contrast interest in sport is aberrant within the confines of conventional femininity. Sport and femininity are set up as conflicting systems so that reassurance has constantly to be offered that despite an involvement in sport a girl is also feminine. Such difference is not, of course, produced by representation alone, lived sporting practices themselves have always had masculinity structured in dominance. As such they are means by which patriarchy has been able to reproduce its power and authority in society.

Of the small proportion of media content that is devoted to women, much of it goes to those supposedly aestheticised sports – such as gymnastics and skating – in which supposedly feminine qualities are to the fore. As the number of women who are active in sport has increased, so the quality of elite performances has risen and the gap between women's and men's performances has shrunk, leading some to predict a continuing process of gap narrowing. However, as Paul Willis (1982) argues, the implication here that women's performances are only valid by comparisons with men's, itself only serves to reproduce women's subordination.

Dunne (1982) found that while magazines aimed at pre-pubescent girls feature positive images of sport, by the teen years, in magazines, sport is something that boys do and girls have little interest in. Leath and Lumpkin (1992) found that as the magazine *Women's Sport and Fitness* switched emphasis towards fitness it featured more non-athletes and fewer athletes on the cover. Females were more likely to be posed rather than performing, aggressive sports were covered less than traditional female-appropriate sports, and female athletes were liable to be described in terms devaluing their sporting achievements. The portrayals of sport and fitness in magazines represented a reworking of femininity that tried to reconcile active women with femininity (see Bolla, 1990; and Horne and Bentley, 1989). Shifflett and Revelle (1994) conducted a content analysis of *NCAA News* and found that 73 per cent of space in *NCAA News* was devoted to male athletes and only 27 per cent to female, and more than three times as much space was devoted to photos of male athletes.

Such gender constructions are structured by power relations: by the subordination of women within patriarchy (see Duncan and Hasbrook 1988). Higgs and Weiler (1994) found that

> although women were given greater coverage in individual sports, that coverage was divided into shorter and more heavily edited segments. In addition, commentators relied on gender marking, biased and ambivalent reporting, and a focus on personalities as opposed to athletic abilities when covering women's sports.

Williams, Lawrence and Rowe (1987) argued that despite any gains that women have made in the struggle to obtain equality in Olympic competition, their participation was limited and their image, as defined by the media, is structured according to prevailing gender stereotypes (see also Yeates, 1992).

Feminist scholarship does not just document the construction of gender difference and the underlying power relations, but also challenges such image production. Halbert and Latimer (1994) have argued that although women have made great strides in sport, their achievements will continue to be meaningless as long as sports broadcasters undermine, trivialise and minimise women's performances through biased commentaries. MacNeil (1988) has argued that leisure is a site of contestation in which women's participation presents new ideas of physicality, but residual patriarchal notions that sport is for men are difficult to alter. She describes the commodification of the feminine style through aerobic classes, sports clothes and videos, and argues that patriarchy is reproduced in a newly negotiated form that attracts women to buy a range of narcissistic commodities. She concludes that this exploits women by creating 'needs' that are in reality only 'wants' – female sexuality and glamour help to sell physical activity to women – and that advertising is a major impetus in the acceptance of the aerobic ritual and its style as 'feminine'. Media representations of active women, in activities such as aerobics and body-building, are aligned with dominant hegemonic relations. They reproduce male dominance by continuing to associate women more with appearance than performance, objects for the gaze rather than acting subjects.

If the discourses of sport have historically served to mark both gender difference and male domination, their contestation has helped open up space for the transformation of images of women in the last twenty years, The rise of feminism and the women's movement has prompted legislative and social change. The fitness chic era has produced a whole new range of imagery in which being physically active and sporting is no longer portrayed as un-feminine. However, as Jennifer Hargreaves (1994) argues, this has also led to a heightened sexualisation of the female body, whereby sporting imagery merely offers another form of objectification of the female body for the male gaze. The stress on work and pain in the discourse of fitness chic in the context of the political ideology of Thatcherism also appears to provide a link between the reformulation of femininity and more traditionally masculine ideologies of work, during the period in which women's employment, both full and part-time, was growing.

So masculine imagery has been at the heart of sporting discourse. Repre-sentations of sport celebrate supposedly male virtues – strength toughness, determination, grit, aggression, commitment and single mindedness (Messner *et al.*, 1993). There are close links between the cultures of sport and dominant con-structions of masculinity (Miller, 1989) It is a world of toughness, competence and heroism which celebrates traditional 'masculine' qualities (Sabo and Jansen, 1992).

However, just as there is no single monolithic femininity, nor is there a single simple homogenous masculinity. There are a range of images of masculinities available within images of sport, although these are typically delimited by the parameters of 'masculinity'. The world of American football is viewed, critically, in the film *North Dallas Forty*, as a tough brutal world in which there is no room for doubt or uncertainty (Whannel, 1993). The terrace sub-cultures of English soccer celebrate a tough, aggressive self-asserting local-ism (Williams and Taylor, 1994). The rise of men's style magazines in the late 1980s marks a distinct commodification of masculine appearance, in which sport iconography plays a significant role.

Yet while male vanities are nurtured in media representations of sport, these still characteristically offer a vision in which emotions are only readily expressed in specific contexts like sporting victory, and in which relationships, feelings, and desires are frequently rendered marginal. Neale (1982) analyses *Chariots of Fire* in terms of male gazes at each other, implying a sexuality the film cannot acknowledge. Scorsese's *Raging Bull*, an antidote to the rather more glorified version of violence in boxing in *Rocky*, is seen by Cook (1982) as por-traying a masculinity in crisis – only able to express emotion through violence.

The rise of feminist scholarship, the growth of an interest in the study of masculinity, and a growing body of work on sexualities has brought the body centre stage as an object of study. Work-outs, weight training and body-building have foregrounded a new masculine muscularity (see Klein, 1990). Gymnasia have become the site of cultural contestation, as the rituals of gay, straight and female users struggle to establish sub-cultural space (Miller and Penz, 1991). Sporting imagery also constitutes one of the few cultural spheres in which women (and men, gay and straight) can legitimately gaze at male bodies, often semi-naked. For much of the history of media sport, this sexual dimension has been repressed and unacknowledged. However, one recent trend is very striking. It is not just women's sporting bodies that are being sexualised but also male bodies. This is not a trend limited to sport – advertising and cinema have prominently featured images of semi-naked male flesh, offered up for the admiring gaze, and this trend is increasingly striking in sport coverage.

Sport stars are often dubbed role models, although what precisely this means is rarely clearly specified (Hrycaiko, 1978). They certainly do function as stars and top level sport has developed an elaborate and marketable star system. Hill (1994) discusses the problems associated with understanding heroes, stars and what they represent (see also Nocker and Klein, 1980). While pundits constantly assert that sport stars can be moral exemplars or bad influences, the relation between these images, morality and the youth market is undoubtedly more complex (Whannel, 1995b). Adherence to heroic figures is socially constructed. It rests also on popular memory, and popular tradition, and thus is historically constructed (see Holt *et al.*, 1996).

There is every reason to hypothesise that young people are very well able to distinguish between Gazza the football genius, Gazza the clown and Paul Gascoigne the man who allegedly beats up his wife. Sport stars are somehow being asked to follow in the footsteps of the Victorian heroes of Empire (see Howarth, 1973) and yet we live in different times when heroes are frequently knocked from their pedestals and the very concept of male heroism is fragile (see Harris, 1994; Hall, 1996; and Izod, 1996).

Class

Class is striking both by its presence and by its absence. Sports themselves are heavily and distinctly class stratified. The distinctive class cultures of Wimbledon tennis, Royal Ascot, rugby league, squash or greyhound racing are very clearly marked. Yet in the media, particularly on television, such differences tend to be down-played and masked. Television rarely alludes specifically to class difference, and in its sport coverage tends to minimise the difference between the rooted cultural contexts of sports and to work to produce more of a unity than is apparent in lived social experience. Indeed, as Critcher (1979) has argued, television itself has exerted a transformative effect on a sport like football, helping to weaken its traditional working-class roots and foster the movement of the game away from shared collective communality towards a modernised commercialised form of individual consumption.

Television's own selection of sports has tended systematically to favour those that neatly fit, or can be made to fit, its own needs. Highly popular sports like badminton, speedway, and greyhound racing have occupied a low place in the hierarchy of television. Of course, this is a complex issue. Darts and snooker became major television sports, and during the same period showjumping declined significantly. However, even in the case of darts, television does little to further accentuate the visible working-class locale, and in the case of snooker, television and the promoters seem to have gone to considerable lengths to diminish the traces of the working-class smoke-filled snooker hall image.

Race

We live, many would argue, in a society in which racism is endemic, deep rooted and pervasive. Images of black people in the media fall largely into two categories – victims and perpetrators. Black people are portrayed in terms of social problems. In this context, at first sight, sport might appear to offer something very positive. Here, uniquely, we see black people as active and successful, achieving goals and receiving popular acclaim. In athletics, football and cricket, black sportspeople have achieved a prominence much greater than their proportion within the population might suggest. Media sport offers a fund of images of black people achieving success and therefore offers role models to young black people. However, the picture is not quite so positive, for two reasons. First, the portrayals of black athletes still serve to reproduce stereotypes that underpin racism and, second, such images offer false hope – like the entertainment industry, sporting success can only provide an escape from poverty for a very small minority.

Whilst purporting to condemn any form of racism in sport, the popular media know that the theme of racism guarantees a good headline and an effective storyline. This was a strong undercurrent in the Cantona affair during the 1994/95 English football season. Cantona, rehabilitated after a suspension for assaulting a spectator, was awarded the title of Footballer of the Year by English football writers in 1996 – the previous footballer of the year was Jurgen Klinsmann. It is revealing to note that both these 'foreign' stars received the English accolade after transforming themselves from the media's portrayal of them as arrogant, ruthless, cheating German, and haughty temperamental Mediterranean Frenchman, respectively, into models of the English gentleman and sportsman (Fleming and Tomlinson, 1996: 95). There is a sense, too, in popular media's reportage of persisting instances of racism in football that the 'good' story will be decoded by the readership in highly specific and ethnocentric forms.

The principal stereotype that is reproduced through sporting imagery, according to Cashmore (1982), is the myth of natural superiority – the concept that black people by virtue of racial/genetic characteristics are especially well equipped to succeed at sports, particularly those requiring speed. The assumption can be detected in the constant references to silky skills, natural rhythms and natural ability to be heard in commentaries. There is little evidence to support the notion of natural ability, especially given the lack of validity of the concept of fundamental differences between racial groups. It has two consequences. First, some teachers, coaches and football managers believe that because blacks are well equipped for sport they are less well equipped for other tasks. Second, black people themselves may tend to accept the stereotype and underachieve in other areas as a result.

In the USA stereotypes held by coaches and others about the ability of black athletes have been detected in the process of stacking, whereby black American footballers are found in disproportionate numbers in some positions, where speed and strength are essential, and not found in positions, like quarterback, where mental abilities are seen as central. Similarly, Maguire (1988) demonstrates the degree to which black soccer players are found in highest proportion in peripheral, as opposed to central, positions. The process of becoming popular, too, is subject to significant limits. Boxer Frank Bruno has become a popular hero by being modest, unassuming, genial and almost Uncle Tom-ish, whereas the more street wise flash and sassy Lloyd Honeyghan never won the hearts of the white public. This phenomenon has been manipulated very successfully by Chris Eubank and his manager Barry Hearn. Together, they have carefully forefronted Eubank's arrogance in order to attain fame and hence marketability using that classic boxing promotion strategy of creating the man they love to hate. Eubank's rather arcane posturing and provocative stylistic pastiche of the clothes of an English country gentleman seem calculated to tease the racist underbelly of the white working class. The contrast between Bruno and Eubank marks vividly the limitations upon this road to black success. (See Gilroy, 1990 on Bruno for comparison and also Fleming, 1991, 1994; and Jarvie 1991.)

Sabo et al. (1996), in a study of American televising of international sport found that producers appeared to make efforts to provide fair treatment of athletes, but that the treatment of race and ethnicity varied across productions. There was little evidence of negative representations of black athletes, but representations of Asian athletes drew on cultural stereotypes, and representation of Latino-Hispanic athletes were mixed, with some stereotyping.

Wonsek (1992) found that the majority of black college athletes were exploited by their institutions. She argued that within a historical and contemporary racist culture some black athletes are elevated to super-stardom while other black athletes do not receive an adequate education. The image of black success in athletics tends to support the stereotypical view that black students' abilities lie with sport rather than academic work. She concluded that the media perpetuates the image of the young black male as athlete only, with advertisements playing a significant role in this process.

Wenner (1995) identified a good guy/bad guy frame of reference that served to mark differences between sport stars like Michael Jordan and Mike Tyson. Crawford (1991) examined the limited range of stereotypes of black athleticism in American movies. Majors (1990) argued that the cool pose adopted by black athletes provided a means of countering social oppression and racism and of expressing creativity, but the emphasis on athletics and cool pose among black males was often self-defeating, and came at the expense of educational advancement. Perversely, the very success of black athletes, generating a fund of 'positive' images, at the same time reproduces a negative stereotype, because of the lack of positive images of black achievement in other areas.

National identities

National identities are complex – analysts have spoken of the production of imaginary coherences (Poulantzas, 1973), imagined communities (Anderson, 1983) and of the invention of tradition (Hobsbawm and Ranger, 1983). Media coverage of sport arguably plays a significant part in the construction of national identities. Our sense of our own national identities and our characteristic stereotypical images of other nations can be traced in the ways in which the media represent sport. Nowell-Smith (1978) has discussed the ways in which World Cup football coverage establishes a difference between the North European and Latin styles of play. The British media typically contrast us with grim humourless East Europeans, happy-go-lucky Africans and over-resourced Americans, suggesting that only the Brits have the balance right (Whannel, 1983).

Blain, Boyle and O'Donnell (1993) analysed over 3,000 press reports from ten countries, taking as their key examples the 1990 World Cup, Wimbledon 1991 and the Barcelona Olympics of 1992. To illustrate the narrative frame through which the European media interpret the relation of the 'small' sporting nations like Cameroon and Costa Rica to Europe, they string together quotes from eight sources to demonstrate a hyper-narrative in which the 'insolent, impudent upstarts' are 'put in their place', 'taught a lesson' and given 'a harsh lesson in realism' by the European powers. At stake here, of course, is not just national identities but the construction of a 'European' identity (see also O'Donnell, 1994).

In this process of construction audiences are characteristically positioned as patriotic partisan subjects. National belonging-ness is inscribed in the discursive practices that seek to mobilise national identities as part of the way in which our attention is engaged with a narrative hermeneutic. We want to know who will win and 'we' hope that it will be our 'own' competitor (see Whannel, 1992).

National identities clearly and visibly have considerable prominence in the process of cultural mapping, yet the internationalist impulse is also a factor in the contested process of representation. Controversy developed over the BBC's choice of Beethoven's 'Ode to Joy' for their Euro 96 Football coverage in the context of heightened political tension around the British relation to the European Union. This was generated by the BSE crisis, in which the more jingoistic British papers and politicians managed to divert attention away from our own farming methods by blaming the Germans for banning 'our' beef. The BBC's internationalism, in selecting the European anthem, was criticised as unpatriotic, doubly so in that it was by a German composer. As if in response, ITV chose 'Jerusalem', to accompany a set of images of the green and pleasant land, and were able to occupy the patriotic high ground.

Yet, later on in the competition, when the *Daily Mirror*, notoriously, ran a front page proclaiming 'Achtung, Surrender: for you Fritz ze Euro 96 is over', the bellicose tone misread the popular mood. The public were enjoying the air of festivity and absence of crowd violence that characterised the tournament, and there was a hostile and critical reaction to the *Daily Mirror*'s use of war-time imagery in its build-up to the England–Germany match. The following day the paper ran a conciliatory shot of the editor presenting German captain Klinsmann with a hamper, with the rather weak 'Peas in Our Time' headline as an attempted apology.

Clearly national identities are constructed upon difference; upon oppositions between 'our' qualities and 'theirs'. British and English images of self in the tabloid press often stress the Bulldog spirit, the willingness to take bruises in the cause of Queen and Country, the love of pageantry and tradition, the honour of playing for the country and the commitment to fair play. In a *Daily Mirror* montage during Euro 96, 'England Expects', an image assembled to demonstrate the composite British sporting character included the nerve of Nick Faldo, the spirit of Brian Moore, the heart of Ian Botham, the legs of Seb Coe, the brain of Lester Piggott and the feet of Bobby Charlton. Such representations serve to produce and reproduce 'common-sense' assumptions about 'our' national character.

The national identities being forged in the English media can be understood in sharper focus by examining the properties and values within national images of other nations in the British press. There are, for example, those, usually Latin, who are too temperamental, such as the 'French firebrand' with a 'typically fiery French temper' (*Daily Mirror*, 20/5/95) the 'temperamental Colombian hitman' (*Sun*, 11/7/95), or the Spaniard 'going through one of his opinionated periods' (*Guardian*, 18/5/95). Then there are those, frequently West

Indian, who have great 'natural' skills, but a too casual attitude to the game. References abound to 'often unfulfilled skills', 'dreamy' (*Guardian*, 20/5/95), to simple instincts, shining smiles, to 'stumps fly to the tune of the calypso beat'. The style of such cricket is 'wild cavalier' with 'thunderous sixes' (*Daily Telegraph*, 17/5/95). Then there are those who, by contrast, take it all too seriously 'The Americans just don't have any idea of what sportsmanship entails' (*Daily Telegraph*, 15/5/95). Often, sport reporting has a strong element of violent language. Violent and militaristic metaphors are common – 'Open warfare', 'verbal volley', 'bitter rival' (*Sun*, 10/7/95). Dutch footballer Ronald Koeman was 'Agent Orange' (*Daily Telegraph*, 27/3/95) There are 'foot soldiers' (*Daily Telegraph*, 27/3/95), 'Aussie hardmen', 'battling Scots'. Sports performers are 'raging for revenge' and have a 'smouldering rage'.

Nations are, in Benedict Anderson's phrase, imagined communities (Anderson, 1983). They are the product not simply of wars or of linguistic communities, but also of symbolic practices – mapping, flag design, emblem construction and so on. Such is also the case with Europe. In such symbolic practices national media systems are part of the constant marking and remarking of difference. As Blain *et al*. (1993) suggest, 'Television and the press need a variety of Europes'. French, German, British and Italian media will construct Europe differently.

There is no single simple or essential Europe – it is an area that has had shifting geographic divisions. The historical legacies – wars between England and France, Napoleon, the rise of Germany, the World Wars – have a continuing resonance. The threat from outside – from the USSR, from the USA, from the Third World – have all featured in the construction of a commonality of interest within 'fortress Europe'. Yet in England the notion of Europe as 'other' is still remarkably strong, reinforced by a legacy of war imagery. Even the liberal *Observer* drew on this and commented at the commencement of Euro 96, 'Will it be V.E. Day on 30 June ?' (*Observer*, 2/5/96).

From a British perspective, of course, the Channel always intervenes as a factor in our imaginary landscape, producing a difference between island and mainland. British teams win and 'get into Europe'. It is deeply inscribed in our sporting language that we are *not* in Europe, that we have to win our way *into* Europe, that we go there, that it is a foreign place, alien. We go there on a trip, as football supporters, like an invading army. You can get *knocked out* of Europe, and then you have to try and get back in next year.

Clearly, in cultural practices and in representations, extensive ideological work is performed producing the construction of the unified patriotic collectivity. Before the quarter final against Spain, the *Daily Mirror* front page proclaimed 'Adios Amigos: Make a Noise for our Boys' (22/6/96). Inside the paper it exhorted us to

Set your watches for 3pm Wembley time! That's when you can strike a mighty blow for England. This morning the *Daily Mirror* is handing out 200,000 free whistles nationwide. And as the England–Spain Euro 96 show-down kicks off this afternoon we want one minute's noise for our boys.

A whole variety of strategies are produced to demonstrate that 'we' are all in this together. Ordinary people are invited to fax in their comments, poems and song lyrics to urge 'our' boys on. Features list the stars who will be watching and cheering along with us. In one *Mirror* feature Liam Gallagher, Julia Carling, Damon Albarn and Anthea Turner all professed their commitment to the England cause.

The attempt to construct a collective 'us' conflicted with the masculine centred-ness of sport following. Men are portrayed as rooted to the television sport, whilst women fume at being deprived of their favourite soaps in their normal slots. An edition of *Woman* asked 'Should soaps make way for football?' and featured stories such as:

Colin taught our baby to chant Ooh aah Cantona.

(Woman, June 1996)

I'm going to learn to drive so that I can escape soccer on TV.

(Woman, June 1996)

In the *Sun*, female journalist Jane Moore announced a campaign to 'have a misleading description removed from the English language – football season . . . It's one long turgid cycle of league matches, championships, friendlies and foreign never-heard-of-them games' (*Sun*, 29/5/96).

The media construction of major events also feature a process of winning over – women begin 'taking an interest' 'get swept along'. Dissenting males become fascinated – even if only as commentators from outside on the phenomenon. Commentary from eminent women is enlisted – Germaine Greer wrote in the *Independent* and A.S. Byatt in *The Observer*. For the *Evening Standard*, Nicola Jeal went to her first match and found that soccer chaps are a terribly nice bunch of chaps. In *Woman* one feature was headed 'Julie planned our wedding around the fixtures'. The tendency of major sporting events to permeate all areas of the media gives them a great momentum and they tend to become the topic that demands comment from anyone involved in social commentary.

The concept of national identity is made more complex by the particular nature of the British state. The United Kingdom is a product of the process of establishing English dominance. The very name of the British state is a source of confusions: British/English/Great Britain/Great Britain and Northern Ireland/ United Kingdom/British Isles – few seem to understand clearly the distinction between these terms. Whilst the British are not unique in having this blurred and confused identity, the particular role of the British in the development of world sport reproduced these confusions on the world stage. The Celtic nations, Wales, Scotland and Northern Ireland, are not independent states, yet do, in many sports, have their own representative teams (see Whannel, 1995a).

Their relation with England is not one of equality, but of dominance and subordination; a process constantly underlined by the sports reporting of the media. The ITV title sequence, with its images of the white cliffs of Dover, was amended for Scottish audiences, but for the most part the Scots are constantly told, of England's performances, that the whole nation is rejoicing or, alternatively, mourning.

The construction of national identities involves a struggle over the power to define – national identities are not fixed but are precisely open to contestation. In the 1994 World Cup there was no team from England, Scotland, Northern Ireland or Wales for the first time since 1938. The British media placed a major focus on Ireland, who became implicitly, 'our team', a construction aided by reference to the Englishness (indeed classic working-class/country gent Englishness) of Jack Charlton, and the non-Irishness of much of the team. Jokes about 'Irish' players who are not really Irish (not knowing their own anthem etc.) have become common currency. This comic sub-text serves to mask the massive economic inbalance in which the English Football League, since its inception, has relied on poaching players from the Celtic nations.

The manager has for some time been a key figure in the representation of football (Wagg, 1984). Attributed Svengali-like powers, managers are the personification of their teams. Jack Charlton constituted a link between the Irishness and hence alien-ness of the team and the largely English audience on British television. Ireland were repeatedly characterised as Jack's team. The football magazine *Match* (11/6/94) referred to 'Jack Charlton's Ireland'. The *Irish Post* (11/6/94) headlined 'Jacks Job: time to make those difficult decisions'. *Reader's Digest* (June 1994) ran a profile headed 'Jack Charlton: Ireland's Man of the Match', and reported that in 1993 he was voted Ireland's man of the year. World cup trainers in the official colours green, white and gold, with a shamrock emblem, were advertised with the slogan 'Support Jack's Team' (*Irish World*, 10/6/94). A tee-shirt of Charlton meeting the Pope with the slogan 'Who's that talking to our Jack?' was a popular seller (*Reader's Digest*, June 1994).

Great play was made of Charlton's down-to-earth countryman image 'the gangling tweed-capped figure with piercing blue eyes . . . and convincing eloquence . . . who declares, "I'm not English, I'm a Geordie"'. The implicit rusticity of the image itself serves to anchor the supposed affinity between countryman Jack and the rural Irish. We are constantly reminded of the nature of the link between him and the Irish: 'The bond between the slope-shouldered 59 year old Englishman and the Republic of Ireland is one of sport's most unlikely love affairs – a heartfelt passion between a man and a nation who came together under the most unlikely circumstances' (*Reader's Digest*, June 1994). He has been declared an 'honorary Irishman', and 'direct talking Charlton soon won over the Irish. His fondness for the country sports such as fishing and shooting is well known . . . he will do his best for the Irish and win, lose or draw, he will be saluted as one of their own'. Indeed, as this happy-go-lucky stereotype has it, the Irish as a whole 'will be profoundly optimistic and will celebrate in good humour, whether they win, lose or draw' (*Match*, 11/6/94).

Entry into this relaxed carnival is, it is implied, his reward; 'Jack Charlton doesn't have to win the world. He has won the heart of Ireland and some might say there's no better prize' (*Reader's Digest*, June 1994). Yet we are also told that Charlton has achieved results by getting Ireland to play in a traditionally English style, and has benefited from Ireland's elastic regulations governing nationality, many of his players speaking with cockney or Yorkshire accents. It underlines forcefully that there is nothing 'natural' about national identities, which are always products of social construction involving complex forms of identity formation and imagining.

Stars in postmodernity

There have been some significant and far-reaching transformations in the forms through which sport has been represented in the media over the past decade. Television's increasing use of montage sequences, with music, overlaid graphics, visual colourisation and dubbed music produces a juxtaposition of surface appearances in which appearance subsumes substance.

The tabloid press has undergone two dramatic revolutions in the last twenty-five years. First, from the start of the 1970s, the new Murdoch-owned *Sun* set the pace in pushing a brasher variant of tabloid style in which larger headlines, more pictures, shorter stories and greater sensationalism were central elements. Second, from the mid-1980s, the defeat of the old print unions and subsequent introduction of new technology had a transformative effect of even greater visibility. The introduction of colour, electronic data handling and computerised page layout meant that sports pages developed a collage style in which the old divisions of content type were less rigid. As stories shortened and photos grew in size, the combination of picture and headline increasingly carried the weight of the meaning, with body text often reduced to caption length. This revolution is also highly visible in the magazine market, especially in that sector targeting the youth market. *Smash Hits*, *Shoot*, *Match* and the burgeoning computer games magazines are all collaged layouts.

However, this collaging of media form is not simply part of the postmodern glissage whereby surface appearances continually float before us in a never-ending process of arbitrary re-juxtaposition. Beneath these forms lie real relations which help to determine in a very direct way the production of images.

The increasingly close links between top sports stars, sports agents, advertisers, sponsors and image producers is a case in point. Take an example from basketball. Michael Jordan became a major basketball star in the USA because of his remarkable talents. His position enabled him to secure lucrative clothing contracts, such as that with Nike. Nike designed a whole range of clothing which traded on his name – Jordan Air – and his image. They produced ads which reified and fetishised the sight of his body soaring into the air to score. This brand name and image then proceeded to catch the imagination of a world-wide youth market, many of whom probably never saw basketball itself, or knew that much about Jordan beyond the image. It was one of the most compelling demonstrations of the power of a well-constructed image in recent years.

Following this well-trod path, the career of Shaquille O'Neill, the new rising star was stage-managed according to the same blue print. On his autumn 1993 visit to London, the capital was saturated with enigmatic ads showing 'Shaq' leaping to a basketball hoop suspended from the Post Office Tower. The highly successful visit led to appearances on a whole range of media, almost all of which mentioned the product being advertised, even where, like Carlton's early evening topical news programme, they were drawing attention to the hype. More than ever, sport stardom can increasingly become disconnected from the sport itself. Jordan and Shaq seem almost to float above the sport, as if basketball itself was rather superfluous.

Gazza: a case study

In the recent history of the England football team, Paul Gascoigne's own story looms large. Present as a motif even when absent in person, he has dominated both peaks (the semi-final against Germany in 1990) and troughs (the failure to beat Holland in 1993). A major issue in the build-up to the Holland game was how to replace Gascoigne. It was taken for granted that he had to be replaced – that it was not just a matter of picking a different team, but of replacing a figure on whom the team had come to rely.

There have been four distinct phases in the story. First, in the second half of the late 1980s, word spread within football of an extraordinary if wayward talent emerging at Newcastle – a Geordie lad whose fondness for beer, hamburgers and Mars bars did not prevent his display of impressive ball control. A transfer to Tottenham added momentum to the popular demand (orchestrated by the tabloid press) that he be picked for England as a regular player. It was in this phase that 'Gazza' was born. God's gift to the gimmick photographer, Gascoigne's own behaviour fed the establishment of the wacky, 'daft as a brush' image that the monicker denoted.

Second, having become established in the England side, only just in time to play in the 1990 World Cup Finals, Gascoigne emerged as one of the stars of the competition. Even more importantly, at a key moment in the semi-final, having had his name taken, which would mean missing the final if England qualified, he broke down in tears. The subsequent picture, anchored with the caption 'There'll always be an England', was reproduced on a big-selling T-shirt. This more than any other single event set the seal on the emergence of Gazza as, in the Barthesian sense, a myth.

Opportunities galore opened up for Gascoigne and his agents, and they opted for the instant cash-in as opposed to slow and careful image-sustaining. In the light of subsequent events, this decision looks a lot shrewder than it did at the time. For a while Gazza was everywhere, on every outlet, selling everything imaginable. Concern expressed at this hyperactivity (not least by that other 1980s icon, El Tel – Spurs manager Terry Venables) were eased by his continuing on-field form, culminating in a cracking goal from a free kick that took Tottenham to the Cup Final.

This final, however, ushered in the third phase, in which Gazza began to move into that rather large lexical category occupied by such players as George Best, Charlie George, Stan Bowles and Jim Baxter. In short, it became evident that we had another wayward genius in whom waywardness was starting to subsume the genius. Chas Critcher termed this category the dislocated superstar, and Gazza seemed tailor-made for the role. Emerging even more hyperactive than usual for the Cup Final, Gazza committed two outrageous fouls, born, as always with him, more from overenthusiasm than viciousness. The second one wrecked his knee, threatening a transfer move to Lazio that was calculated to save Tottenham from financial disaster.

Gazza spent a season in semi-limbo, recuperating, and then moved to Italy, helping to inspire the Channel 4 acquisition of the rights to show live Italian games in England. But the move to Italy was not a success, the Italians were unhappy with his form, stories circulated about weight problems and the Gazza story lurched ominously close to the decline and fall narrative structure.

The fourth phase began with his return to Britain and Glasgow Rangers, and an uneven but ultimately successful return to form. This was followed by alleged involvement in riotous behaviour in a night club and on a plane, immediately before Euro 96, a sensational goal against Scotland and a wedding lavishly portrayed in *Hello!* Just as redemption seemed assured, stories of wife beating hit the popular press, and demands were made that he be dropped by England. Born again Christian and new manager of England Glenn Hoddle ignored the demands, retained Gascoigne, but insisted that he commence counselling.

Sport, even team sport, features individual stars, whose style or behaviour is often in conflict with the demands of the group. Sport stars are often written about as role models, people with broader responsibilities. The build-up to Euro 96 featured highly publicised stories about the behaviour of the England squad – 'Men behaving badly', according to a *Sun* (29/5/96) headline; whilst the *Daily Mirror* (29/5/96) had 'Drunken England Stars plane shame'. This prompted Sir Alf Ramsey, referring to Gascoigne, to announce: 'I will not go to Wembley if this man plays' (headline in the *Daily Mirror*, 1/6/96). The *Sun* announced that 'Paul Gascoigne will be read the riot act by Terry Venables when England players report this weekend for Euro 96' (29/5/96). Constantly it was suggested that Gascoigne (and, on occasion others) were not fit to play for England – their behaviour was incompatible with the demands of group discipline and national representation.

When analysed from the structural perspective, the Gazza story precisely conforms to a very typical pattern in the tabloid coverage of stardom. Clearly stars of all types play a very important part in the world of the tabloid press. In the initial phase they are typically celebrated for their ability or achievements or genuine charisma, or the spectacle of their appearance. Once they are established, further celebration becomes of low news value, whereas any whiff of sensation or scandal has a greatly enhanced news value. So the slide from hero to villain/victim that stars like Ian Botham have drawn bitter attention to is in no small part a logical outcome of the very narrative structure of star coverage. It is partly determined by the changing hierarchy of news values within which such stories come to be written at all. Yet once established as villains, the redemption story becomes an attractive one. So star portrayals have an inbuilt tendency to lurch between positive and negative poles.

Of course, the process of image construction is considerably complex. A Michael Jordan or a Shaq cannot be simply invented by the advertising industry. Gazza is not just a product of the restless media desire for a fresh supply of stars. Such star images succeed because in a particular socio-historic conjuncture they catch the imagination of an audience. To do so, something about the image must address, tap into and mobilise the feelings, moods, aspirations or fantasies of an audience. Stars are stars precisely because they succeed in doing this. Times change and stars of previous eras can come to look archaic as a result. While image analysis is certainly insufficient to understanding the process, it is none the less necessary.

Essays

Discuss ways in which national identities are constructed by the media's coverage of sport.

In what ways have the print media changed their coverage of sport with the advent of live broadcasts of the sports event?

Taking a particular sports star, discuss the ways in which the popular press and other media portray him or her as hero *and* villain.

Exercises

Watch one athletics broadcast and note the commentator's use of language when referring to the gender of the participant.

Take one tabloid and one broadsheet newspaper and compare their style and conventions in their coverage of one event (the same event).

Attend a sports event covered by the media and make your own record of the nature and the highlights of that event. Then compare the coverage in the media. Consider why these accounts might be very different.

FURTHER READING

G. Whannel, *Fields in Vision – Television Sport and Cultural Transformation*, London, Routledge, 1992, is a comprehensive analysis of sport in British television.

N. Blain, R. Boyle and H. O'Donnell, *Sport and National Identity in the European Media*, Leicester, Leicester University Press, 1993, provides cross-cultural analyses of media sport.

References

Althusser, L. (1971) 'Ideology and Ideological State Apparatuses', in *Lenin and Philosophy and other Essays*, London: New Left Books.

Anderson, B. (1983) *Imagined Communities*, London: Verso.

Barnett, S. (1990) *Games and Sets: The Changing Face of Sport on Television*, London: BFI.

Barthes, R. (1967) *Elements of Semiology*, London: Jonathan Cape.

Birrell, S. and Loy, J. (1979) 'Media Sport: Hot and Cool', *International Review of Sport Sociology*, Volume 14, no. 1.

Blain, N., Boyle, R. and O'Donnell, H. (1993) *Sport and National Identity in the European Media*, Leicester: Leicester University Press.

Bolla, P. A. (1990) 'Media Images of Women and Leisure: An Analysis of Magazine Ads 1964–87', *Leisure Studies*, Volume 9, pp. 241–252.

Bown, G. (1981) '2000 Million Televiewers', London: Royal College of Arts (unpublished).

Brennan, C. (1995) 'Lillehammer as Seen by the Media', *Citius, Altius, Fortius*, Volume 3, no. 1, USA International Society of Olympic Historians.

Brewster, B. (1993) 'When Saturday Comes and other Football Fanzines', *The Sports Historian* (The Journal of the British Society of Sports History), no. 13, May, London: BSSH.

Brohm, J-M. (1978) *Sport – A Prison of Measured Time*, London: Ink Links.

Bryant, J., Comiskey, P. and Zillmann, D. (1977) 'Drama in Sports Commentary', *Journal of Communication*, summer 77, USA.

Buscombe, E. (ed.) (1975) *Football on Television*, London: BFI.

Cantelon, H. and Gruneau, R.S. (1988) 'The Production of Sport for Television', in J. Harvey and H. Cantelon (eds), *Not Just a Game – Essays in Canadian Sport Sociology*, Ottawa, Canada: University of Ottawa Press.

Cashmore, E. (1982) *Black Sportsmen*, London: Routledge & Kegan Paul.

Chandler, J. (1988) *Television and National Sport*, Chicago: University of Illinois Press.

Clarke, A. and Clarke, J. (1982) 'Highlights and Action Replays', in J. Hargreaves (ed.), *Sport Culture and Ideology*, London: Routledge & Kegan Paul.

Colley, I. and Davies, G. (1982) 'Kissed by History: Football as TV Drama', in M. Green and C. Jenkins (eds), *Sporting Fictions*, Birmingham: Centre for Contemporary Cultural Studies/Department of Physical Education, University of Birmingham.

Cook, P. (1982) 'Masculinity in Crisis', *Screen*, Volume 23, pp. 39–46.

Crawford, S. (1991) 'The Black Actor as Athlete and Mover: An Historical Analysis of Stereotypes, Distortions and Bravura Performances in American Action Films', *Canadian Journal of History of Sport*, Volume 22, pp. 23–33.

Crawford, S. (1992) 'Birth of the Modern Sport Spectacular: The Real Madrid and Eintracht Frankfurt European Cup Final of 1960', *International Journal of the History of Sport*, Volume 9, pp. 433–438.

Critcher, C. (1979) 'Football Since the War', in J. Clarke, C. Critcher and R. Johnson (eds), *Working Class Culture – Studies in History and Theory*, London: Hutchinson.

Critcher, C. (1987) 'Media Spectacles: Sport and Mass Communication,' in C. Cashdan and M. Jordan (eds), *Studies in Communication*, Oxford: Blackwell.

Daney, S. (1978) 'Coup d'envoi – le sport dans la television', *Cahiers du Cinema*, Number 292, pp. 39–40.

Duncan, M.C. and Hasbrook, C. A. (1988) 'Denial of Power in Televised Women's Sports', *Sociology of Sport Journal*, Volume 5, pp. 1–21.

Dunne, M. (1982) 'An Introduction to Some of the Images of Sport in Girls' Comics and Magazines', in M. Green and C. Jenkins (eds), *Sporting Fictions*, Birmingham:

Centre for Contemporary Cultural Studies/Department of Physical Education, University of Birmingham.

Fleming, S. (1991) 'Sport, Schooling and Asian Male Youth Culture', in G. Jarvie (ed.), *Sport, Racism and Ethnicity*, London: Falmer.

Fleming, S. (1994) 'Sport and South Asian Youth: The Perils of "False Universalism"', *Leisure Studies*, Volume 13, no. 3, pp. 159–178.

Fleming, S. and Tomlinson, A. (1996) 'Football, Racism and Xenophobia in England (1): Europe and the old England', in U. Merkel and W. Tokarski (eds), *Racism and Xenophobia in European Football*, Aachen: Meyer & Meyer.

Geraghty, C. and Simpson, P. (1986) 'Dreams of Reading: Tender is the Night', *ITSC Conference Paper*, London: ITSC.

Gilroy, P. (1990) 'Frank Bruno or Salman Rushdie', *Media Education*, Volume 14, pp. 14–18.

Goldlust, J. (1987) *Playing for Keeps: Sport, The Media and Society*, Melbourne, Australia: Longman.

Goldman, P. (1983) *Sporting Life* (anthology of British sporting prints), London: British Museum.

Goodhart, D. and Wintour, P. (1986) *Eddie Shah and the Newspaper Revolution*, London: Coronet.

Gruneau, R. (1989) 'Making Spectacles: A Case Study in Television Sports Production', in L. Wenner (ed.), *Media Sports and Society*, Newbury Park, California: Sage.

Halbert, C. and Latimer, M. (1994) 'Battling Gendered Language: An Analysis of the Language Used by Sports Commentators in a Televised Co-ed Tennis Tournament', *Sociology of Sport Journal*, Volume 11, pp. 309–329.

Hall, S. (1980) 'Cultural Studies: Two Paradigms', *Media Culture and Society*, Volume 2, pp. 57–72.

Hall, S. (1996) 'Introduction: Who Dares, Fails', *Soundings*, no. 3, pp. 115–118.

Hall, S., Hobson, D., Lowe, A. and Willis, P. (eds) (1980) *Culture Media Language*, London: Hutchinson.

Hargreaves, J. (1994) *Sporting Females – Critical Issues in the History and Sociology of Women's Sports*, London: Routledge.

Harris, J.C. (1994) *Athletes and the American Hero Dilemma*, Leeds: Human Kinetics.

Higgs, C.T. and Weiller, K.H. (1994) 'Gender Bias and the 1992 Summer Olympic Games: An Analysis of Television Coverage', *Journal of Sport and Social Issues*, Volume 18, pp. 234–246.

Hill, J. (1994) 'Reading the Stars: A Postmodernist Approach to Sports History', *The Sports Historian*, no. 14, pp. 45–55. London: BSSH.

Hobsbawm, E. and Ranger, T. (eds) (1983) *The Invention of Tradition*, Cambridge: Cambridge University Press.

Holt, R., Mangan, J.A. and Lanfranchi, P. (eds) (1996) *European Heroes: Myth, Identity and Sport*, London: Frank Cass.

Horne, J. and Bentley, C. (1989) 'Women's Magazines, Fitness Chic and the Construction of Lifestyles', in *Leisure Health and Wellbeing*, Leeds: LSA.

Howarth, P. (1973) *Play up and Play the Game: The Heroes of Popular Fiction*, London: Eyre Methuen.

Hrycaiko, D. (1978) 'Sport Physical Activity and TV Role Models', *CAHPER Sociology of Sport Monograph Series*, Canada: CAHPER.

Izod, J. (1996) 'Television Sport and the Sacrificial Hero', *Journal of Sport and Social Issues*, Volume 20, no. 2, pp. 173–193.

Jarvie, G. (ed.) (1991) *Sport, Racism and Ethnicity*, London: Falmer.

Jary, D., Horne, J. and Bucke, T. (1991) 'Football Fanzines and Football Culture: A Case of Successful Cultural Contestation', *Sociological Review*, pp. 581–592.

Klein, A.M. (1990) 'Little Big Man: Hustling, Gender, Narcissism and Body-building Sub-culture,' in M. Messner and D. Sabo (eds), *Sport, Men and the Gender Order*, Champaign, Illinois: Human Kinetics.

Lawrence, G. and Rowe, D. (eds) (1987) *Power Play: The Commercialisation of Australian Sport*, Sydney, Australia: Hale and Iremonger.

Leath, V.M. and Lumpkin, A. (1992) 'An Analysis of Sportswomen on the Covers and in the Feature Articles of *Women's Sport and Fitness* Magazine, 1975–89', *Journal of Sport and Social Issues*, vol. 16, no. 2, pp. 121–126.

MacNeil, M. (1988) 'Active Women, Media Representations and Ideology', in J. Harvey and H. Cantelon (eds), *Not Just a Game*, Ottawa: University of Ottawa Press.

McPhail, T. and Jackson, R. (eds) (1989) *The Olympic Movement and The Mass Media – Past, Present and Future Issues*, Calgary, Canada: Hurford Enterprises.

Maguire, J. (1988) 'Race and Position Assignment in English Soccer: Ethnicity and Sport', *Sociology of Sport Journal*, pp. 257–269.

Majors, R. (1990) 'The Cool Pose', in M. Messner and D. Sabo (eds), *Sport, Men and the Gender Order*, Champaign, Illinois: Human Kinetics.

Mason, T. (1993) 'All the Winners and the Half Times', *The Sports Historian* (The Journal of the British Society of Sports History), no. 13, pp. 3–12.

Messner, M., Duncan, M.C. and Jensen, K. (1993) 'Separating the Men from the Girls; The Gendered Language of Televised Sports', *Gender and Society*, Volume 7, pp. 121–137.

Miller, L. and Penz, O. (1991) 'Talking Bodies: Female Body-builders Colonise a Male Preserve', *Quest*, Number 43, pp. 148–163.

Miller, T. (1989) 'Sport Media and Masculinity', in G. Lawrence and D. Rowe (eds), *Sport and Leisure*, Australia: Harcourt Brace Jovanovich.

Morley, D. (1986) *Family Television: Cultural Power and Domestic Leisure*, London: Comedia.

Morris, B.S. and Nydahl, J. (1985) 'Sports Spectacle as Drama: Image, Language and Technology', *Journal of Popular Culture*, Volume 18, no. 4, pp. 101–110.

Murdock, G. and Golding, P. (1978) 'The Structure, Ownership and Control of the Press, 1914–1976', in G. Boyce, J. Curran and P. Wyngate (eds), *Newspaper History: From the 17th Century to the Present Day*, London: Constable.

Neale, S. (1982) 'Chariots of Fire: Images of Men', *Screen*, Volume 23, pp. 47–53.

Nocker, G. and Klein, M. (1980) 'Top Level Athletes and Idols', *International Review of Sport Sociology*, Volume 15, pp. 5–21.

Nowell-Smith, G. (1978) 'TV – Football – The World', *Screen*, Volume 19, no. 4, London: SEFT.

O'Donnell, H. (1994) 'Mapping the Mythical: A Geo-politics of National Sporting Stereotypes', *Discourse and Society*, Volume 5, pp. 345–380.

Pendred, G. (1987) *An Inventory of British Sporting Art in United Kingdom Public Collections*, Suffolk: Boydell Press.

Peters, R. (1976) *Television Coverage of Sport*, Birmingham: Centre for Contemporary Cultural Studies, University of Birmingham.

Poulantzas, N. (1973) *Political Power and Social Classes*, London: New Left Books.

Rader, B.G. (1984) *In Its Own Image: How TV has Transformed Sports*, New York: Free Press.

Real, M. (1975) 'Superbowl: Mythic Spectacle', *Journal of Communication*, Number 25, pp. 31–43.

Real, M. (1989) 'Super Bowl versus World Cup Soccer: A Cultural-Structural Comparison', in L. Wenner (ed.), *Media Sports and Society*, London: Sage.

Root, J. (1986) *Open The Box*, London: Comedia.

Rowe, D. and Lawrence, G. (1989) *Sport and Leisure: Trends in Australian Popular Culture*, Australia: Harcourt Brace Jovanovich.

Sabo, D. and Jansen, S.C. (1992) 'Images of Men in Sports Media: The Social Reproduction of Gender Order', in S. Craig (ed.), *Men, Masculinity and the Media*, London: Sage.

Sabo, D., Jansen, S.C., Tate, D., Duncan, M.C. and Leggett, S. (1996) 'Televising International Sport: Race, Ethnicity and Nationalistic Bias', *Journal of Sport and Social Issues*, Volume 20, no. 1, pp. 7–21.

Scannell, P. and Cardiff, D. (1991) *A Social History of British Broadcasting V1 1922–39*, Oxford: Basil Blackwell.

Schramm, W. (ed.) (1960) *Mass Communications*, Chicago: University of Illinois Press.

Shaw, P. (compiled by) (1989) *Whose Game is it Anyway?*, London: Argus.

Shifflett, B. and Revelle, R. (1994) 'Gender Equity in Sports Media Coverage: A Review of the NCAA News', *Journal of Sport and Social Issues*, Volume 18, pp. 144–150.

Smith, C. (1987) *Sport in Focus*, London: Partridge.

Telecine (1978) 'Sport et Television', *Telecine*, no. 229, June.

Van de Berg, L.R. and Trujillo, N. (1989) 'The Rhetoric of Winning and Losing: The American Dream and America's Team,' in L. Wenner (ed.), *Media Sports and Society*, London: Sage.

Wagg, S. (1984) *The Football World: A Contemporary Social History*, Brighton: Harvester.

Wenner, L.A. (ed.) (1989) *Media, Sports and Society*, Newbury Park, California: Sage.

Wenner, L.A. (1995) 'The Good, the Bad and the Ugly: Race, Sport and the Public Eye', *Journal of Sport and Social Issues*, Volume 19, pp. 227–231.

Whannel, G. (1982) 'Narrative and Television Sport: the Coe and Ovett Story', in M. Green and C. Jenkins (eds), *Sporting Fictions*, Birmingham: Centre for Contemporary Cultural Studies/Department of Physical Education, University of Birmingham.

Whannel, G. (1983) *Blowing the Whistle: The Politics of Sport*, London: Pluto.

Whannel, G. (1992) *Fields in Vision: Television Sport and Cultural Transformation*, London: Routledge.

Whannel, G. (1993) 'No Room for Uncertainty: Gridiron Masculinity in North Dallas Forty', in P. Kirkham and J. Thumin (eds), *You Tarzan: Masculinity, Movies and Men*, London: Lawrence and Wishart.

Whannel, G. (1995a) 'Sport, National Identities and the Case of Big Jack', *Critical Survey*, Volume 7, no. 2, pp. 158–164.

Whannel, G. (1995b) 'Sport Stars, Youth and Morality in the Print Media', in G. McFee, W. Murphy and G. Whannel (eds), *Leisure Cultures: Values, Genders, Lifestyles*, Eastbourne: Leisure Studies Association (Publication No. 54).

Williams, C.L., Lawrence, G. and Rowe, D. (1987) 'Patriarchy, Media and Sport', in G. Lawrence and D. Rowe (eds), *Power Play – The Commercialisation of Australian Sport*, Sydney, Australia: Hale and Iremonger.

Williams, J. and Taylor, R. (1994) 'Boys Keep Swinging: Masculinity and Football

Culture in England', in T. Newburn and E. Stanko (eds), *Just Boys Doing Business: Men, Masculinities and Crime*, London: Routledge.

Willis, P. (1982) 'Women in Sport in Ideology', in J. Hargreaves (ed.), *Sport, Culture and Ideology*, London: Routledge & Kegan Paul.

Wonsek, P.L. (1992) 'College Basketball on Television: A Study of Racism in the Media', *Media Culture and Society*, Volume 14, no. 3, pp. 449–462.

Wren-Lewis, J. and Clarke, A. (1983) 'The World Cup – A Political Football?', *Theory Culture & Society*, Volume 1, no. 3, pp. 123–132.

Yeates, H. (1992) 'Women, the Media and Football Violence', *Social Alternatives*, Volume 11, pp. 17–20.

Young, K. (1986) 'The Killing Field: Themes in Mass Media Responses to the Heysel Stadium Riot', *International Review for the Sociology of Sport*, Volume 21, pp. 253–266.

Chapter seven

Sport, the state and politics

Fuelled by Cold War rivalry throughout the 1970s and 1980s, made-for-television Olympic Ceremonies became a major source of audience figures . . . The Los Angeles Olympic Games of 1984 can now be seen as a watershed in this regard, providing spectacular Opening and Closing Ceremonies to assert the superiority of the Western, Capitalist, Free American way over the oppressive Eastern, Communist, Totalitarian, Soviet way.

(Tomlinson, 1996: 585)

Every politician has the same idea. We should be collecting gold medals. We ought to have someone in the top 10 in tennis. Winning the odd Test Match would be nice. It is just that no one has a clue about how to do it.

(Vincent Hanna, journalist, *Guardian*, 9 May 1996)

Support for a football club engenders a particularly intense type of loyalty which goes some way beyond a preference for one supermarket over another. Season ticket holders or regular match attenders should in my view not only have declared an interest but also left the meeting.

(Patricia Thomas, Local Government Ombudsman, ruling that support for a football club was a 'declarable' interest in planning decisions made by local councillors, *Guardian*, 31 May 1997)

As long as people believe the myth that sports and politics are unrelated, they remain at a disadvantage when rules and policies are made and funds allocated.

(Coakley, 1998: 434)

Introduction

Whilst for at least the last 400 years (for example, when King James I published *The Book of Sports*) the state has sought to intervene in sport and recreation through prohibition, regulation or promotion of various athletic pastimes, it is only in the last quarter of the twentieth century that the political dimensions of sport and leisure, at local, national and international levels, have become more widely apparent and discussed. Argument over the connection between sport and politics revolves around two broad viewpoints. There are those who argue that sport is a special form of play and as such should be seen as separate from the 'real world'. Involved in these arguments are ideas such as sport is and should be separate from politics; sport is private and personal rather than public and political; the pursuit of the Olympic ideals is non-political.

Whilst there may still be some people who consider sport and politics to be completely separate entities, it is our view that it is not possible to sustain this belief for long when the historical and contemporary evidence is consulted. Sport (and play) involves rules and regulations which are derived in some way from the 'real world'; sport provides politically usable resources; sport can promote nation-building and international image-making; in fact, modern sport has seldom been free of politics (Allison, 1986, 1993).

A brief consideration of the gap between the Olympic ideals ('Olympism') and the social history of the modern Olympic Games since their founding in the last decade of the nineteenth century demonstrates this well (see Tomlinson and Whannel, 1984). Soon after the conclusion of the first modern Olympics – in Athens in 1896 – the Greeks became involved in a war with Turkey which was fuelled by the pride of hosting the Games. In the aftermath of the First World War (1914–18) and the Russian Revolution (1917) workers' sports organisations were formed which held workers' sports or 'workers' Olympics' in the 1920s and 1930s as an alternative to the official 'nationalistic' and 'bourgeois' Olympics, as they were perceived (Kruger and Riordan, 1996). The politicisation of the modern Olympics took a quantum leap in 1936 with the staging of the 11th Olympiad in Berlin when Adolf Hitler's Nazi regime was at its strongest. Since the end of the Second World War (1945) – being *a nation* in the modern world has come to be signified by two things: belonging to the United Nations and marching in the Opening Ceremony of the Olympic Games. As the opening quotation from Alan Tomlinson suggests the Olympic Games also became part of the Cold War between the capitalist West and the Soviet bloc countries at this time. Since 1968 boycotts on a greater or lesser scale have taken place at each of the summer Olympics. Even at Atlanta in 1996 the North Koreans did not compete.

Lincoln Allison (1986) has suggested that one of the major reasons why sport is intimately linked with politics and power is because sport creates politically useful resources. Sport has been linked with 'building character' in Britain since the nineteenth century, as we saw in Chapters 1 and 5, and so has often been considered as an agency of political socialisation. In the twentieth century national governments of many different political persuasions have not been slow to realise the potential of attempting to harness sports to further their particular interests and values. In addition politicians have increasingly sought to associate themselves and their political parties and policies with the positive image of successful competition often delivered by sports men and women (Monnington, 1993). More generally John Wilson (1988: 149) argues that

> Regardless of political regime, modern societies now routinely use leisure to make claims for nationhood, to establish the boundaries of their nation-state, to establish an identity for their people, to deny the claims of other peoples for nationhood, to integrate existing conglomerates into national communities and to symbolise and reaffirm hierarchies of power and status among the nations of the world.

He adds (p. 150)

> When we think of leisure in an international context we tend to think of sport . . . It is bureaucratised play, or sport, that is used as a weapon in international conflict, not the more amorphous world of leisure.

This chapter does not look in great detail at the organisation and administration of sport. For such information the reader is advised to consult Houlihan (1991, 1994), Henry (1993), Coghlan and Webb (1990), and Torkildsen (1992). We do, however, examine the political sociology of sport with specific reference to the relationship between the state and sport in Britain. First, the question 'what makes sport political?' will be discussed. Then some conceptual clarification will be offered. Next different theoretical approaches to the study of sport and the state will be examined. The final section considers the politics of sports policy in the light of these perspectives.

What makes sport political?

It would be wrong to conclude that the only place to analyse the politics of sport is in central and local government. As suggested already, power exists as much in 'non-political' bodies, such as 'governing bodies' of sport. The very title 'governing body' clearly identifies such an institution as being the context for decision making (or the exercise of power) that affects people connected with a sport. A few of the questions you might ask about governing bodies as political organisations are what qualifies as a sport?; what are the rules of a sport?; who makes and enforces the rules in sport?; who organises and controls games, meetings, matches and tournaments?; where will the sports event take place?; who is eligible to participate in the sport?; and how are rewards distributed to athletes and other organisation members?

This approach to power and politics is important when analysing the internal politics of sport. In much of the literature on the politics of sport, however, sport is considered political because it is *ideologically symbolic*. It is not a pure social activity which in some way remains untainted without any of the hallmarks of its social origins. Two principal aspects of this ideological loading are the relationship between different political ideologies and sport and the relationship between nationalism, national identity and sport. These can briefly be considered.

Political ideologies and sport

Political ideologies in Britain can be analysed in many different ways. Simply to identify ideologies with political parties will not suffice, however. Ideologies refer to broader conceptions of the purpose and aims of political parties. They are also more fluid than established party positions. Coalter *et al*. (1988), Henry (1993) and Roche (1993) have identified a number of different political ideologies and related these to sport and leisure policy. Coalter identifies four 'ideal types' of political perspectives: reluctant collectivism (traditional conservatism and the Liberal Party), Fabianism (old Labourism), anti-collectivism (Thatcherism and the new right) and Marxism. Henry (1993: 48–49) outlines five different political ideologies related to sports policy, largely because he subdivides the Marxist category into the 'new urban left' and 'structural/scientific Marxism'. Roche (1993) provides probably the most convenient threefold distinction within sports policy. First, he identifies the dominant ideology of modern British sport – 'gentlemanly amateurism' – which roughly corresponds with the political ideology of reluctant collectivism and the absence of direct state intervention in sport in Britain for most of the twentieth century. Second, the mid-twentieth-century ideology of welfarism – bringing about a more politicised, professional and bureaucratic approach to sport, especially the creation of the Sports Council – was a hallmark of 'Old Labour' or 'Fabian' policy. Third, in the late twentieth century the twin ideologies of global capitalism and consumerism have influenced sport through ideas such as the free market for sports labour and freedom of contract and these ideas have coincided with the anti-collectivism of the new right or Thatcherism. Roche (1993: 102) concludes:

> with traditions, professions, organisations and personalities representing
> at least these three structural waves all currently involved in the struggle

for power and authority in sport policy, it is not at all surprising that policy is disorganised.

Figure 7.1 illustrates these connections between sports interest, political ideology and political party. In addition to these three ideologies Coalter and Henry also note that Marxist and feminist perspectives on sport policy have been developed that present critical accounts of the role and purpose of sport. These have had much less impact on actual sports policy, but are important to consider in terms of their analytical power.

Nationalism, national identity and sport

The second manner in which sport can be seen as overtly political is in its uses to promote national identity. This is not as straightforward as it sounds in the UK, however, since there are complicating factors. Polley (1998: 36ff.) argues that many sportspeople in the UK can adopt dual or even triple forms of identity in performing their sport. Hence in the UK it is clear that 'sport has historically provided a key focus for the constituent parts to emphasise "separateness and distinctiveness"' (Polley, 1998: 54). Hence one of the gaffes that Tony Banks made soon after becoming Minister for Sport was to suggest that the collapsing of the 'home nations' into a British team would be a good idea. Through the maintenance of distinctive sports cultures and structures in the 'submerged' nations of the UK – Scotland, Wales and Northern Ireland – representative sport has provided these countries with the opportunity to be represented as 'full nations' in the wider world of sport. FIFA, the world governing body of association football, actually recognises these and thirteen other football associations of 'countries' which are not recognised as such by the United Nations. On the international stage or playing field sport can provide countries with a status out of proportion to their economic, military or political significance. As Polley (1998: 62) concludes: 'Sport has offered a popular cultural forum for the power relations between the centre and the margins' in post-war UK politics.

Sports interest	Political ideology	Political party
Gentlemanly amateurism	Reluctant collectivism	Traditional Conservatism
Corporate welfarism	Fabianism/collectivism	'Old' Labour
Market	Anti-collectivism	New right/Thatcherism

Figure 7.1 Sports interest, political ideology and political party in the twentieth century

Power, politics and the state – a conceptual clarification

This chapter is not simply concerned to draw attention to 'big P' politics, that is, with the formal machinery of government and the state, although that is a very important dimension of it. The political sociology of sport is concerned with the use of power in a wider social context. Power here can be defined as:

> the ability of an individual or a social group to pursue a course of action (to make and implement decisions and more broadly to determine the agenda for decision-making) if necessary against the interests, and even against the opposition, of other individuals and groups.
>
> (Bottomore, 1979: 7)

The ability to achieve desired ends despite resistance from others implies that power is best understood as a social relationship. Politics thus involves the clash of values and ideologies and struggles for power between different social groups, as much as formal political party politics. Politics most generally should be understood as the processes through which power is gained and used in social situations. Much of the formal analysis of power and politics is concerned with the actions of government, the opposition parties and the state. A focus on this level of politics alone, however, neglects an important distinction between political *involvement* and political *intervention*. We shall argue that there has been a long-term structural relationship between the state and sport at local, regional, national and international levels. This involvement may not have taken the explicit form of intervention until the latter half of the twentieth century, but it has none the less gone on (see Hargreaves (1986) for the nineteenth century and Polley (1998) for more recent examples of this relationship).

The very idea of what the state comprises changes, as the following quotation from Stuart Hall (1986: 26) indicates:

> The field of action of the state has altered almost beyond recognition over the last three centuries. The eighteenth century state had no regular police, no standing army, and was based on a highly restrictive male franchise. The nineteenth century state owned no industries, supervised no universal system of education, was not responsible for national economic policy or a network of welfare provisions.

The state has shifted from being mainly concerned with force to being involved in processes of persuasion – from coercion as the means of securing the maintenance of social order to consent exercised through democratic institutions. As this has occurred the state has moved since the nineteenth century from being mainly concerned with warfare to welfare and now arguably 'workfare'. McGrew (1992) describes this as the process of the 'civilianisation' of the state. The nature and functions of the state have been transformed during the twentieth century through the large scale of activities engaged in by the state and the expansion of functional responsibilities to include welfare and material security of citizens as well as general security and public order. Given the sheer size and complexity of these tasks it would be oversimplistic to treat the advanced capitalist state (ACS) as some kind of monolithic entity that operates in a unified manner. The state is a highly fragmented and in some senses a decentred apparatus of rule; despite variations in ACSs in terms of political structures, state forms and welfare provision, they also exhibit common features and similar evolutionary patterns.

The most important factors shaping the growth and development of the modern state in advanced capitalist societies are the development of capitalism as a world economic system and war between nation-states. The state has been formed and continues to develop through a combination of endogenous and exogenous forces, that is, both by internal, national or 'local' forces and external, international and 'global' forces. According to McGrew (1992: 91) 'international economic crises are in many respects the equivalent of war'. According to George Orwell sport was 'war minus the shooting' (1970 (1945): 63). The modern state 'has always faced both inwards and outwards; inwards towards society and outwards towards a system of states . . . a complex interplay between endogenous and exogenous processes of change' (McGrew, 1992: 93).

The state in advanced capitalism has to operate in both directions and thus faces decisions about what can be called 'inter-mestic' issues. Simply put ACSs are subject to globalising forces (Giddens, 1989: 520). Whilst the major internal and external tasks of the state remain to maintain social order and to compete with other states, increasingly the room to manoeuvre over issues is influenced by international developments. Whilst the European welfare state was built on the basis provided by American military and economic hegemony after the Second World War, it was restricted in the 1970s and 1980s as a result of the global economic crisis. In the 1990s the conditions essential to the survival of the welfare state in its conventional form have been transformed. In addition international regimes – sets of international rules, norms, procedures and so on – have been established which express the internationalisation of the ACS. Examples of this type of issue in sport include boycotts of international sporting events, spectator control at international football matches and the development of a policy on drugs used to enhance sports performance (see Houlihan, 1991, 1994, 1997). The importance of crowd control at international and domestic football matches can be seen as a good example of where this dual – 'inter-mestic' – focus is required. Crowd trouble at the Italy–England World Cup qualifying match in Rome in October 1997 led to condemnation of the 'mindless hooligans' by some sections of the British and Italian press, but a report critical of the Italian police's tactics by the Football Association met with official agreement. It was probably no coincidence that these events took place as the attempt to establish England as the leading European contender to host the 2006 FIFA World Cup Finals had reached a delicate stage.

It is important to remember that the state is not just 'government'. It refers to a whole apparatus of rule within society – the government, police, the army, judiciary, state-owned industries, etc. It is in essence a public power 'container'. It is the supreme law-making authority within a defined territory. As a result, whilst the relationship between the state, the market and civil society is important to understand, it is not possible to define the precise boundaries as they change over time and between different societies. The state also includes sub-central (local) government and public and semi-public regulatory commissions and corporations (or quangos) including the British Broadcasting Corporation and the Sports Councils. Hence our use of the word 'the state' in this book should be understood as a shorthand for 'state apparatus' or 'state system'. This is important because, as Ralph Miliband (1973: 46) pointed out:

> the treatment of one part of the state – usually the government – as the state itself introduces a major element of confusion in the discussion of the nature and incidence of state *power*; and that confusion can have large political consequences.

Perspectives on the politics of sport

Sugden and Bairner (1993: 131ff.) note that in discussions of the politics of sport and the state the principal debate has been between pluralist and Marxist theoretical perspectives. The main division between these two theoretical positions has largely centred around the relative importance of either force or consent in the political process. The classic Marxist view of the state seems to imply it is a coercive instrument for the dominant class. Pluralists see the state more as a value-free mechanism for balancing conflicting interests operating through consensus. More recent discussions derived from Gramsci in the neo- (or 'revised') Marxist tradition suggest that political power is a product of a balance between force and consent. We will look at these arguments in this section.

Pluralist and Marxist perspectives on the state

Pluralism and Marxism offer two broad perspectives in the study of the state and power. As Sugden and Bairner (1993) suggest they differ over the relative balance of 'force' vis-à-vis 'consent' in the running of society. Both pluralism and Marxism comprise a number of different traditions. Within pluralism it is possible to contrast conservative and critical (or 'neo-pluralist') traditions. The former emphasises the gradual evolution of society, the importance of the existence of large numbers of small interest groups with overlapping member-ships, and the state as a governmental process in which government plays the role of a neutral umpire. The neo-pluralist tradition developed in the 1960s and 1970s. It recognises that interest groups are more divergent, with not so many overlapping members, the power of the state is less balanced and some interests are more powerful, structurally well connected and hence are much more influential than others.

Within Marxism the two most often contrasted perspectives are 'instru-mental' and 'structuralist' approaches to the state. The instrumental view of the state (i.e. viewing the state as an 'instrument' of class rule) is exemplified by Miliband (1973) and is derived from the suggestion in *The Manifesto of the Communist Party* that 'The executive of the modern State is but a committee for managing the common affairs of the whole bourgeoisie' (Marx and Engels, 1973 (1848): 44). According to Houlihan (1991) this view can be summarised as follows: (i) the state and policy are controlled by the capitalist class, which does not rule directly but controls by government, which rules on its behalf and interests; (ii) capitalists, state bureaucrats and political party leaders are unified by common social origins, educational experiences, social background and lifestyles; and (iii) the state thus maintains capitalism and in terms of sport would develop policy that creates opportunities for profit, for example through compulsory competitive tendering, and also aims to keep control of young working-class men.

The 'structuralist Marxist' account of Poulantzas (1973) developed out of criticism of the instrumental approach, and in particular raises questions about the relationship between the state and elites in society. Poulantzas argues that (i) the state has 'relative autonomy' (i.e. independence) from the ruling capitalist class; (ii) the state aim is to maintain the unity of the ruling class and ensure its position as the politically dominant class; (iii) hence the state has autonomy from the bourgeoisie and negotiates between class 'fractions'; (iv) hence policy is not always clearly in the interests of the ruling class as it is a product of a balance of class forces – the state acts as a 'factor of cohesion'; and (v) none the less in the last instance the state acts in the long-term interests of capital.

There appear to be quite irreconcilable differences between these differ-ent perspectives. Pluralists see power in society as dispersed among many competing interest groups. Politics is an arena of negotiation – organisations operate as veto groups and the political process relies on negotiating alliances and compromises. The sources of power are widespread throughout society – power can come from economic wealth, political office, social status/prestige, or even personal charisma – and only exceptionally do all sources fall into the same hands. Hence in this view the state is either a neutral body concerned with the dispassionate arbitration of needs and the efficient and fair allocation of resources among individuals, or a broker between the various social classes and interest groups within its jurisdiction. The implication is that not even the most influential people always get their way and even the most disadvantaged are able to band together to ensure that some of their political interests are addressed.

Marxists tend to see economic power as the most important form of power in society and this is heavily concentrated amongst the wealthy capitalist class and the 'military-industrial-business' elite. There are a few interconnected centres of power with broad control over the rest of society. Instead of operating as 'checks and balances' the power centres share similar political interests. Few have power and the upper class dominates – wealth, status and power overlap. Voting whilst called 'democratic' involves choosing between two authorities acceptable to the elite. Rather than a pluralist democracy the more appropriate view is that society is an oligarchy – ruled by the wealthy few. The state is an agency that ultimately acts in the interests of the dominant social formation – although the exact relationship between the state and the ruling elite/class is debatable.

In recent years, however, it has become clear that Marxist and pluralist accounts of the state in action often overlap to a quite a considerable degree. In the next section we shall explicitly look at accounts of sport and the state to demonstrate this theoretical convergence.

Theories of the state and sport

British social historians and sociologists of sport and leisure have provided much of the fuel in the debate over which of these perspectives best explains the growth of state intervention in sport. Hence, whilst it is widely acknowledged that over the last two hundred years there has been an increase in central and local government involvement in leisure and sport (Malcolmson, 1973; Cunningham, 1980), there is disagreement as to the exact significance of this change (see Chapter 3). Historian Peter Bailey (1989) has noted that it is difficult to establish the precise motivations that lay behind state intervention in popular culture, including sport, in nineteenth-century Britain. To what extent was action taken in a deliberate conspiracy to control people's 'hearts and minds' and to what extent were the administrators and politicians of the day acting in a co-ordinated fashion? Has the growth in state intervention in leisure in the last two hundred years merely been a result of an increasingly sophisticated policy of 'bread and circuses'? Does sport and leisure policy and intervention enable the state to maintain an ideological hold on subordinate social groups? There is no one simple answer to these questions. As we have seen already, debates in sociology of sport often take place between writers who hold different theoretical points of view about what is appropriate evidence and what that evidence means. Theoretical perspectives are themselves related to, and influenced by, the changing social, political and economic environments within which theorising occurs. But it is worth bearing in mind what Haralambos and Holborn (1995: 259) state about pluralist and neo-Marxist perspectives on leisure in general. They 'offer quite different interpretations of this area of social life. Perhaps both tend to generalise and pay too little attention to evidence which contradicts their respective theories.' This is a useful way of considering pluralist and Marxist accounts of sport and the state as well. Let us look at examples of each perspective.

Pluralist accounts

Houlihan (1991) is critical of the two Marxist analyses of the state and state policy – the 'instrumentalist' approach of Miliband and the 'structuralist' account of Poulantzas. Houlihan argues that the instrumentalist account is too crude – it lacks the subtlety to analyse policy outputs. The structuralist account is tautologous – it is a circular argument, in which policies in the apparent interest of the working class are explained as ultimately in the interests of capital. Thus no realistic counter-example of the state acting against the interests of capitalism is permitted. Hence he argues that a more promising approach to understanding the macro level of the policy process is derived from a 'pluralist analysis of society' in which (i) power in society is viewed as dispersed among a politically active citizenry and a variety of elites, institutions and organisations; (ii) policy is the outcome of a process of competition between these interests; (iii) entry to the policy process is relatively open and no interest is assumed to be excluded or be in a dominant position; and (iv) the state in the pluralist model is 'value-neutral', has the role of a 'neutral adjudicator' between interests and has no inherent bias towards one set of interests. Thus pluralism has been defined as 'the study of the formation and intermediation of political interest groups as a precondition of competitive liberal democracy' (McLennan, 1995: 34). Few accept this model now, however.

Houlihan recognises several criticisms of and amendments to this 'ideal type' of pluralism: (i) citizens are not very politically active; (ii) agendas can be manipulated by powerful interests to avoid debate over matters that might threaten their fundamental interests; and (iii) capitalist businesses are privileged participants in the policy process – since governments are dependent on them for employment and growth. None the less Houlihan believes that 'neo-pluralism' describes political processes more accurately and accounts for the ambiguities and paradoxes in the policy process better than other accounts. In particular Houlihan recognises the growth and role of 'policy communities' in the creation of policy as vitally important. McGrew (1992: 95) describes this development as follows:

> the increasing specialization, technical nature and overwhelming volume of policy issues has encouraged the formation of functionally differentiated 'policy communities' e.g. health, social security, energy, defence, education, etc. Within these 'policy communities' officials and experts from the responsible state agencies concerned, together with representatives of the most influential or knowledgeable private organised interests, formulate public policy often with only very limited participation by elected politicians.

Hence most powerful organised interests are privileged within the policy process, and the less influential and those critical of the status quo are relegated to outsider status, for example the Department of Health, the medical profession (including the BMA) and commercial pharmaceutical companies often jointly determine health policies. Neo-pluralists see this privileging as a structural necessity (see Kingdom, 1991). Power is viewed as highly concentrated whilst corporate interests and economic issues dominate the agenda. Inequalities in the distribution of power resources and access to government decision makers undermine the idea of a highly competitive political process with no single interest dominating. The capitalist state has to be attentive to the needs of corporate capital above all others.

Additionally, Houlihan suggests that in practice 'incrementalism' is a common feature of policy making – piecemeal solutions are preferred over optimal solutions to problems (for example in the case of the development of policy on football hooliganism). Furthermore, government is best understood not as a homogeneous entity but fragmented, both internally with competition within state institutions and externally where:

> the institutions, such as local authorities, quangos and central government departments, that make up the state have interests and objectives of their own which frequently lead to competition between state institutions for access to and influence over the policy process.

(Houlihan, 1991: 157)

Thus he concludes that 'the pluralist analysis of political processes coupled with insights derived from organisational sociology, form the broad context for this study of the policy process for sport'.

How far is this approach shared by Ian Henry (1993, see especially pp. 76 ff.)? Henry is more concerned with the relationship between the state and the local state than Houlihan, but draws some similar conclusions about existing theories. He makes a useful distinction between theories of the state that may be prescriptive or normative – specifying how the state ought to operate – and analytic or heuristic theories that seek to illustrate or explain how the state does in fact operate. He also points out that theories develop in accordance with changes in social, economic and political reality – pluralism, managerialism, Marxism, 'dual state' and new right perspectives are just a few of the approaches to the state that have developed since the 1950s. Like Houlihan he regards conventional pluralism as beset with problems. Methodologically pluralism also leads to a form of 'descriptivism' that focuses on overt behaviour and political decisions, whilst ignoring underlying structural social realities (McLennan, 1995: 37). Most especially pluralist accounts do not locate the activities of interest groups in the context of the structural demands of capitalism. None the less Henry is critical of Marxist accounts for being structuralist and functionalist. The conclusions of much Marxist analysis are built into the premises that underpin any empirical work into the state (Henry, 1993: 80). Many arguments are functionalist in the sense that state activity is explained by reference to general principles (i.e. the need to reproduce labour power) – not how and why particular policies at particular points in time are developed. Yet, he argues, 'such explanations of detail must be a criterion of the adequacy of social theory, and in this sense also the marxist explanation is inadequate' (p. 80).

Henry's preferred approach is 'dual state' theory since it conceives of the state not as some monolithic entity but as a set of institutions and levels of operation. Henry argues that this neo-Weberian view captures the differential operation of the state machinery at different levels of government without collapsing into atheoretical, anecdotal, descriptive accounts.

Both Houlihan and Henry can be seen as representative of the neo- or 'critical' pluralist tradition, recognising defects with the original pluralist account, but critical also of theories such as structuralist Marxism that explain the actions of the state without any necessary reference to detailed empirical analysis. In recent years, however, neo- (or 'revised') Marxist analyses of the state and sport have developed that share these criticisms of Marxist analysis and go some way to avoiding them whilst retaining a Marxist perspective.

Neo-Marxist approaches to power and the state

We have stated that the debate between pluralists and Marxists has largely centred around the the relative importance of force or consent in the political process. The classic Marxist view of the state seems to imply it is an instrument for the dominant class. Pluralists see the state more as a value-free mechanism for balancing conflicting interests. More recent discussions derived from Gramsci in the neo-Marxist tradition suggest that political power is the product of a balance between force and consent. In the next section we shall briefly outline the distinctive features of this approach.

Gramsci considers the process of running a society to involve both force (coercion) and consent. His emphasis upon the importance of consent in mature parliamentary democracies leads to a focus on the attempt to rule by consent or *hegemony*. For Gramsci then the state is best understood as the institution central to the process of hegemony. Because it is a process it is also highly precarious. Both ruling and subject classes are fragmented, and the state always makes concessions in order to operate through consent and not force. Complete indoctrination is not possible because individuals possess *dual consciousness* – ideas and beliefs come from everyday life and cultural activities as well as dominant institutions.

Coates (1984) uses Gramsci's ideas to analyse the British state in the 1970s and 1980s. He argues that it is important to understand that the British state, like all others, operates within an international capitalist system in which multinational corporations and international transnational organisations restrict its power. In Britain finance capital – the City of London and allied institutions – has had a preponderant role in shaping government policy in the post-war period. Industrial capital has had less influence. Because there are divisions in the ruling class the state cannot be a mere 'instrument' of the ruling class since the ruling class is divided into different 'fractions' of capital, which compete. Hence conflicting demands derive from divisions within the ruling class and between classes. The existence of the capitalist system does not ensure that the state acts in the interests of the ruling class as a whole either (as in the 'structuralist' Marxist view).

Capitalism produces an economy and a civil society – private institutions such as the family and other social groups. These can make demands on the state. People can adopt dual consciousness in which they can both accept capitalism as legitimate and at the same time recognise its exploitative nature. The state tries to maintain hegemony despite the existence of this consciousness or contradictory beliefs. In order to do this Coates sees the state as an institution that tries to cement alliances, or historic blocs, of different sections of the population capable of maintaining hegemony. This involves concessions to certain groups – the ruling class do not monopolise power entirely. Most British governments maintain hegemony by getting most of the population to accept a 'national project' although how this is accomplished varies at different times – the Second World War, social democracy and the welfare state; Thatcherism and turning back the 'nanny' state; New Labour, New Britain.

This is a sophisticated theory that depicts a wide range of groups, institutions and processes through which power is exercised and the activities of the state influenced. Different groups are involved and no one group monopolises all social power, nor does power stem from wealth alone, but power is unequally distributed. The role of sport in the hegemonic project is to help construct a national popular culture.

Writers such as John Hargreaves (1986 and see also his essay in Allison, 1986) and John Clarke and Chas Critcher (1985) take a different view of state intervention in sport to the pluralists and conventional Marxists (see also Whannel, 1983: 88ff.). Whilst there are differences in emphasis between their views, the history of the growth of state involvement in sport and leisure is seen by them as part of the struggle between capital and labour in a capitalist economy. The state, in this neo-Marxist view, is not a neutral agent, acting as an impartial umpire in this conflict. Rather, the state co-ordinates the responses of capital and other bodies – such as the church, philanthropists and educationalists – to the wider capitalist socio-economic environment. Both the state and the market have gradually provided entertainments and sport in an attempt to shape the leisure habits of the working class so that they complement, rather than conflict with, the needs of capitalist production.

Hargreaves argues that sport has been utilised since the nineteenth century to integrate dominant groups and to fragment subordinate social groups – a division between the 'rough' and the 'respectable' working-class men, women and ethnic groups. The working class is reproduced socially in a divided way – it is stratified by occupational status, gender and racial characteristics. In turn sport socialises people into a form of repressive individualism, featuring disciplined self-control, personal self-advancement, deference and social deferment. Sugden and Bairner (1993) analyse the role of sport and the state in Northern Ireland largely using a similar theoretical framework.

The main criticism of Gramscian accounts of hegemony has been, how can the influence of hegemony be demonstrated? Abercrombie et al. (1980) argue that the emphasis on ideological control in Gramscian accounts is misleading. Little evidence for the existence of dominant ideas exists and the real sources of social control remain material forces such as the threat of unemployment, the risk of poverty and the possibility of imprisonment for 'innovative' (i.e. criminal) means of gaining wealth within capitalist relations of production. None the less a considerable amount of research does point to the importance of cultural activities, including sport, in providing symbolically influential resources for governments.

Beyond pluralist and Marxist accounts

The broad distinction between pluralist and Marxist theories of the state exists but as we have already noted there are rival analyses within each tradition. This confusion over the nature of the state is replicated in the literature concerning the relationship between sport and political institutions. Since the 1970s a 'new' debate over state power and the relationship of the state to civil society has produced a different distinction between approaches to analysing advanced capitalist states (McGrew, 1992: 94ff.). This is between 'society-centred' approaches, which see states as influenced by society, and 'state-centred' approaches, which see them as more influential in steering social development. State-centred approaches include the new right, corporatism and neo-Marxism. The state is seen by left-wing versions of this approach as a kind of 'power broker', constructing and sustaining political coalitions necessary for the success of its strategy for enhancing corporate profitability whilst marginalising societal resistance to its policies (for example, Jessop *et al.*, 1988).

Increasingly it has been recognised that it may not be necessary to choose which is most convincing since political scientists have formulated another distinction between 'strong' and 'weak' states. Japan and France are considered examples of the former, whilst the USA and Canada are examples of the latter. State-centred approaches may best explain the actions and policies of strong states whilst society-centred approaches may best explain those of weak states (McGrew, 1992: 106). In addition it may be possible to apply this distinction within states to different policy sectors and thus 'account for the very different styles of policy making which occurs in different policy sectors within the same state' (McGrew, 1992: 106). In some policy sectors the state may be considered strong whilst in others the state may appear weak. Hence both models may provide valuable insights into the infrastructure and power of the state. This balance may alter over time as well. They can complement as well as compete, just as Marxist and pluralist accounts appear to do.

Conclusions

In common with the authors of *Sport in Canadian Society* (Hall *et al.*, 1991: 85–87) we consider the role of the state in capitalist countries such as Britain, the USA and Canada to involve the following dimensions: to create or maintain conditions in which capital accumulation can take place; to create or maintain social order or harmony through legitimation; and to retain the monopoly on the legitimate use of violence or coercive force. Capital accumulation, legitimation and coercion summarise the threefold objectives of the state in Britain and underline the breadth of the latter notion compared with a narrow focus on government, which is the hallmark of some recent studies on politics and sport. In a recent review of the concept of pluralism Gregor McLennan (1995: 99) concludes 'we are all pluralists now' – in theory and in everyday life. This is part of the postmodern condition. As such he argues conventional political pluralism is 'owed an apology for the sometimes shabby way it gets treated by radicals' (p. 99). It is possible to be a theoretically 'radical' or 'moderate' left-wing or right-wing pluralist. Various efforts to manage a synthesis between elements of Marxism and critical pluralism have been attempted after the recognition of conventional pluralism's failures: (i) group interests are held prior to the political process; (ii) states and governments are important interest groups; (iii) the state's policy agenda is related to key business sectors; (iv) non-decisions in the political agenda are as important as decisions; and (v) conventional behaviourist and empiricist canons of investigation lead to 'descriptivism' focusing on overt behaviour and political decisions, whilst ignoring underlying structural social realities (McLennan, 1995: 36–37). There has been a move away from grand theory to the 'meso level' of social enquiry in which theories are applied to concrete institutional arrangements and organised collective actors (McLennan, 1995: 39). There is a recognition of the need to know how and why particular policies arrive at particular points of time. The notion of the state as 'monolith' is replaced with the state as a 'process', but in which power is unevenly distributed. This view informs the consideration of sports policy to which we shall briefly turn.

The politics of sport and sports policy

The following sections deal with the increased role of the state in sport in the last thirty years in Britain, rhetoric and reality in sports policy, the different dimensions of state intervention and involvement in sport, and the politics of sports policy.

The increased role of the state in British sport since the 1960s

With respect to sport (and leisure) the increasing role of government since the 1960s has been largely *ad hoc*, leading to the existence of many government departments having an interest and involvement. In 1973 the Cobham Report of the House of Lords' Select Committee on Sport and Leisure (1973: para. 114) noted 'the fragmentary nature of Government responsibility for sport' and not much has changed in the twenty five years since. Through a number of departments, notably the Department of Culture, Media and Sport (CMS, formerly the Department of National Heritage, DNH), the Department of the Environment, Transport and Regions (DETR formerly the Department of the Environment, DoE) and the Department for Education and Employment (DfEE), the government is able to exert influence on quasi non-governmental organisations (quangos) and voluntary bodies and trusts such as the Sports Council and the Central Council for Physical Recreation (CCPR) in England and Wales. Territorial responsibilities lie with the Welsh Office, the Department of Education for Northern Ireland (DENI) and the Scottish Office (see Houlihan, 1997, Chapter 3 especially).

As a result a coherent and systematic policy towards sport has never been produced in Britain. This is reflected in the fact that until 1997 there had never been a government ministry with 'sport' in the title, although since the 1960s there has been a Minister for Sport. For nearly twenty years he (there has not been a female in this position to date) was located in the Department of the Environment (DoE). In 1990 responsibility for sport moved briefly to the Department for Education and Science (now the DfEE). In 1992 the Department of National Heritage became the location for both the minister and the Sport and Recreation Division (SARD) – a group of civil servants responsible for most sport-related policy (Coghlan and Webb, 1990; Macfarlane, 1986). The current Minister for Sport's proper title – 'Parliamentary Under-Secretary of State' within the Department of Culture, Media and Sport – reveals the relatively junior, i.e. non-cabinet or 'third-level', standing of the position. All sports ministers under Margaret Thatcher (1979–91) held this status, whilst Dennis Howell, Labour's Sports Minister in the 1960s, held a second-level position as a Minister of State. Houlihan suggests that the creation of the Sport and Recreation Division (SARD) alongside the Sports Minister role rivalled the Sports Council for significance. Yet in 1990 SARD had a mere twenty staff out of the DoE's 6,488. It was small and further sub-divided into three sections (Houlihan, 1991: 32).

The first Minister for Sport, Lord Hailsham, summed up the prevailing ethos of his appointment in 1962 when he spoke of 'a need, not for a Ministry, but for a focal point under a Minister, for a correct body of doctrine perhaps even a philosophy of Government encouragement' (quoted in Sugden and Bairner, 1993: 96). The main function of the minister was to determine and administer the Sports Council's grant and establish a policy framework for the service. When Labour came to power in 1964, despite being committed to a sports council, a protracted period of negotiation followed. The main difficulty was in establishing the nature of the relationship between a statutory sports council and the Central Council for Physical Recreation (CCPR). Set up in 1935 as the Central Council for Recreation and Training, the CCPR had acted as the main forum for the many national governing bodies of sport and the medical and physical education professions.

The problems were a reflection of a typical desire on the part of the British state to prevent institutions appearing to be state controlled. A Minister for Sport would be answerable to parliament, whereas a quasi-independent council, even if appointed by the government, would be outside the parliamentary political process (Whannel, 1983: 91).

When a Conservative government eventually established a statutory and executive Sports Council by Royal Charter in 1971 the underlying tension between the needs of the national governing bodies (the 'elite') and the grass roots remained unresolved. The Sports Council took over many of the functions of the CCPR and most importantly the responsibility for the distribution of funding for sport. The CCPR became an independent forum of sports organisations, with democratic methods of appointment to its ruling body, whereas the Sports Council board was appointed by the Minister for Sport.

British sport policy: rhetoric and reality

Maurice Roche (1993) notes that the traditional rhetoric in British sports policy comprises two fairly widely espoused ideals that have come to be enshrined in the modern Olympic movement and international sports bodies in general. First, the idea that sport should be engaged in for the love of the game and not for money and, second, that sport ought to be above politics, or that politics should be kept out of sport. Since modern sport – in Britain from the 1960s especially (Whannel, 1986) – has become thoroughly pervaded with both commercialism and politics an alternative rhetoric about sport has been developed. This utilitarian rhetoric 'provides an alternative set of legitimating ideals concerned with the social utility of sport for promoting such things as public health, social integration and collective morality' (Roche, 1993: 72) – a clear continuation of the nineteenth-century concerns about rational recreation and the 'cult of athleticism'. It was when this second rhetoric was introduced that the associated notions of 'sport for the community' and 'sport for all' were developed as major themes in the development of sport policy.

The traditional rhetoric about sport had its roots in the educational uses of sport in the nineteenth-century British public school system, which was largely responsible for the creation of modern sport as a cultural form and set of institutions. The alternative utilitarian rhetoric, though with some roots in the education sphere, has its main roots in the health promotion of sport by government and the medical establishment in the 1920s and 1930s. The full blown rhetoric and promotion of sport for its social utility has really only occurred since the late 1950s. At times of apparent national and economic crisis - such as the 1920s and 1930s and the 1970s and the 1980s – the 'problem of enforced leisure' or unemployment has seen state intervention in leisure and sport move forward rather more quickly than at other times (Horne, 1986). As one of us once wrote – 'Nothing loosens the purse strings like panic' (Whannel, 1983: 92).

Roche (1993: 73–74) makes two observations about the sports 'policy community'. The first is that whilst sport has been presented, in a populist and thus quasi-democratic image, as being 'for all' in post-war campaigns, sports administration and sport policy making certainly have not been 'for all'. He argues that spectators and players have usually been either excluded or discouraged from involvement in the work of sport governing bodies and other policy-making agencies. Despite the rhetoric of 'consultation' and 'representation', in reality the sports policy community 'has been largely unresponsive to and untouched by democratic ideals and practices' (Roche, 1993: 74). The maintenance of the gentlemanly – amateur or elitist tradition remains reflected in the composition of many of the executive committees of the national governing bodies of sports and the leading forum for their collective voice – the Central Council for Physical Recreation (Hargreaves, 1986; Whannel, 1983).

Roche's second point is that the sports policy community has been consistently in a state of 'disorganisation'. None the less it has still tended to take for granted that it has a lot to offer the wider community. Roche argues that it might be better to adopt a more realistic appraisal of the limitations of sport as well as its vulnerabilities. In short, sport is one of the most 'divided, confused and conflictive policy communities in British politics' (Roche, 1993: 78). Roche makes a powerful case for seeing the sport policy community as an illustration of the tendencies in modern society towards internal over-complexity, in addition to external dependencies and vulnerability to external (especially economic) forces. Endemic system disorganisation and impotent policy making are the result (Roche, 1993: 77).

This is illustrated well by Houlihan (1991) in his study of the policy process in British sport. In particular he looks at three areas of sports policy in the 1980s in which conflict over fundamental aims and purposes was very noticeable – divisions within the sports 'policy community' over football hooliganism, drug use in sport, and school-aged sport. As many different organisations have an interest in sports, different attitudes and values exist which in turn create different definitions of the issues involved and the preferred solutions to them.

A good example of this is the official response to spectator violence at football matches, which has occupied centre stage as the English contribution to the world of sport for almost the past thirty years. There have been eight official and semi-official reports or inquiries into aspects of spectator violence and crowd control in Britain since 1923. Since the 1960s sociological research into the causes of football hooliganism has become quite extensive. Explanations are varied – ranging from the ritualisation of male aggression, historical accounts of working-class loyalty to the local club, and sociological explanations that draw attention to the socialisation of young working-class males into a sub-culture that emphasises toughness as a status symbol (Marsh *et al.*, 1978; Clarke, 1978; Dunning *et al.*, 1988). 'Solutions' suggested by the research carried out in the 1970s and 1980s point to the need to build closer links between the clubs and the local communities, upgrade the facilities for spectators, and make the stadia more attractive for women and children. The problem seems to be that most of the proposed solutions are long-term, relatively low key, expensive, complex to administer, or a combination of two or more of these. Governments prefer to be involved in solutions that promise an immediate impact, have a high public profile, are cheap and are simple to administer, possibly through a non-governmental body (Houlihan, 1991: 185). As Houlihan remarks, 'complex social problems rarely have simple solutions' (1991: 200).

Dimensions of state involvement/ intervention in sport

What factors account for the increased role of central government in British sport since the 1960s? James Riordan (1986) has observed that in contrast with the former communist states, western motives for promoting sport, especially sports excellence, have been much less easy to define precisely. This was because western sport has had a much more fragmented organisational structure, it has been underpinned by competing and sometimes conflicting aims and ideologies about the purpose of sport, and because the state has not been so formally integrated into sports institutions. None the less western nations have increasingly taken sport seriously, as was indicated in the quote from Wilson near the beginning of this chapter. Riordan cites the Sports Council Annual Report for 1982–83:

> The nation lifts its head when our national teams succeed. It also takes to the court, pitch or swimming pool when would-be champions have witnessed their idols demonstrating a high level of sports skill.
>
> (1986: 38)

So the inspirational value of sports success in terms of nation-building has generally been recognised in the west, if not to the same degree as in the former communist states. In the case of post-imperial Britain, with the loss of world-leader status since the 1950s, it has increasingly been assumed that international sports success would help generate patriotism.

Additionally Riordan noted the gradual transition from the traditional amateur-elitist ethos to a more commercial-professional one in western sport:

213

> The dominant credo of the former has been that sport should be divorced from politics, government interference and commercialism, professional coaches, sports schools, and the like, and that there should be a firm commitment to the Olympic ideal.
>
> (1986: 39)

In the UK an apolitical view of sport has affected the political left-wing for most of the twentieth century (Hargreaves, 1987). Amongst the mainstream political parties in the UK this view of sport has also held sway – and continues to do so in terms of public debates about a 'golden age' of sport (see Polley, 1998: 1–6 for a discussion of this). Sport was never fully mobilised by the political left in Britain at a time when it was being used in other parts of the world to do precisely that (Kruger and Riordan, 1996). But recognition that sport and politics are related has developed since the 1950s. From covert and informal relations overt and more formal relations have developed. Examples of the development of the relationship include the growth of the Sports Council.

Historical studies of the growth of state intervention in sport and leisure in Britain and other advanced capitalist countries suggests that governments have perceived sports policy as a means to an end, rather than an end in itself. A comparison with other countries suggests that national governments may have different goals that they wish to pursue through sports policy. They are none the less usually non-sporting goals – nation-building in Canada and the former GDR, and control of the young in France and Britain more generally (Houlihan, 1991: 40–50). The present 'state of play' in sport and leisure policy and institutions bears the legacy of dominant ideas in the nineteenth century as well as a 'conventional wisdom' as to the appropriate division of labour between the voluntary, the public and the commercial sectors of sport and leisure. From this stance it is possible to see the development of sport and leisure policy in Britain – from 'rational recreation' to the welfare state and 'recreational welfare', via the attack on popular culture and the growth of leisure in the nineteenth century and the development of a mixed economy of leisure in the twentieth – as underpinned by a number of key social concerns. Coalter *et al.* (1988) and Coakley (1998) have outlined the range of motives for state involvement in sport in both Britain and the USA (see Figures 7.2 and 7.3).

Four factors in particular stand out in explaining the change in the relationship – from informal to formal – between the state, at both central and local level, and sport in Britain since 1945. First, the growth of welfarism and collectivism as the dominant political policy ideology in the post-Second World War period led to calls for greater intervention. This period was to last until the mid-1970s. Second, the state has responded to trends – demographic, economic and social – which have encouraged greater involvement in the provision of sport and leisure facilities, especially for young people. Third, the state has responded

1 Urban deprivation.
2 Physical health.
3 Moral welfare.
4 Social integration, social control and the construction of 'community'.
5 Self-improvement.
6 Limits to public provision.

FIGURE 7.2 Key concerns of sport and leisure policy in Britain (nineteenth century onwards)
Source: adapted from Coalter *et al.*, 1988.

1 Safeguard public order.
2 Maintain and develop fitness and physical abilities of citizens.
3 Promote the prestige of a community or nation.
4 Promote a sense of identity, belonging and unity amongst citizens.
5 Emphasise values and orientations consistent with dominant political ideology.
6 Increase citizen support for a political leader and system.
7 Promote general economic development in the community and society.

FIGURE 7.3 Reasons for the the sports–government connection in the USA
Source: adapted from Coakley, 1998: 403

to a series of specific crises or events that have beset sport or Britain's sporting accomplishments in the period, for example a series of significant defeats in international football matches inflicted on England in the 1950s, the emergence of the anti-apartheid campaign using the sports boycott of South Africa as a key tactic in the 1960s and 1970s, and the decision formally to boycott the 1980 Olympic Games held in Moscow in protest at the Soviet Union invasion of Afghanistan. Finally, the growing economic and social significance of sport has ensured that the state will intervene in sport. In 1986 sport-related revenues were bringing central government £2.4 billion annually. By 1990 sport-related economic activity in Britain (according to the Sports Council, cited in Polley, 1998) constituted £8.27 billion (or 1.7 per cent of GNP), £9.75 billion of consumer expenditure and some 467,000 jobs. This growing economic significance of sport has also coincided with the transformation of sport brought about by the collapse of older sources of revenue and the growth of the sport/media/advertising nexus. These developments are discussed more fully in the next two chapters.

In an analysis of trends since 1945, Peter Bramham looks at the gradual shifts in rationale for sport intervention in the 1960s, 1970s and 1980s. He notes (1991: 140) that changing rationales for state involvement in sport in Britain 'reflect fundamental concerns about the nature of individual freedom and rights of citizenship'. Since the Second World War he has identified four predominant rationales:

1   'Traditional pluralism' – with the market and the voluntary sectors to the fore as the major providers of sporting opportunity, and the state in a residual role, stepping in where gaps or 'externalities' occur.
2   'Welfare reform' – with an emphasis on the proactive role of the public sector in meeting the needs of groups disadvantaged in the commercial and voluntary sectors. Sport and recreation came to be seen almost as a 'right of citizenship' – 'as the apex of the framework of the welfare state constructed since the war, with more basic needs having been provided for in earlier stages of development' (1991: 140).
3   'Managerialist critique of welfare reformism' – stemming from a critique of the approach adopted under 2 above to reach and meet the needs of disadvantaged groups. Alternative approaches to sports provision for example community recreation services starting from the grass roots and decentralising service provision, were attempted.
4   'Neo-liberal' – in which the political thinking of the new right informed a departure from the emphasis upon publicly funded provision towards voluntary and commercial sector investment.

Each of these rationales can be related to different stages in the development of sports organisation and sports policy in the UK. The movement from one to the next is best understood as a response to changes in socio-political and economic conditions, which can also be seen as tempering the full force of each rationale. The highpoint of welfarism came in the mid-1970s when the 1975 Government White Paper, Sport and Recreation, supported the notion of sport and recreation as a 'need' and a 'right' as a policy intention. As soon as the paper was published, however, economic developments overtook the Labour government. In order to avert a balance of payments crisis a loan from the International Monetary Fund (IMF) was negotiated. Public expenditure cutbacks were a central condition of the loan and the White Paper's recommendations were not delivered. Interestingly, in the same way the 'neo-liberal' rationale for reducing government support for sport and recreation in the 1980s was restrained by, on the one hand, the recognition of the role of elite sport in contributing to national prestige (Hargreaves, 1986) and, on the other hand, the continued disintegration of social order in the inner cities. Hence Bramham (1991: 142) concluded:

> in the late 1980s and early 1990s provision for mass participation is effectively being squeezed out of the public sector . . . while provision for elite sport is being manoeuvred towards private sector funding, leaving a residual public sector concern for physical health promotion and social order.

Sugden and Bairner (1993: 1–9) suggest that the state seeks to exert a degree of influence over sport because sport has come to play an influential part in an individual's socialisation and the construction of notions of community in modern life. They assert that 'the real link between sport and politics is a sociological one'. After Hoberman (1984), sport is seen to have no intrinsic value structure but rather it is a ready and flexible medium through which ideological associations can be relayed:

> despite the idealism of certain sports practitioners and administrators, who cling to the cherished belief that sport is or should be free from politics, historical evidence reveals that this is rarely the case.
>
> (Sugden and Bairner, 1993: 10)

It is for this reason that a major underlying reason for growing state intervention in sport in Britain since the 1950s has been the perennial 'youth problem'. The 'Wolfenden gap' identified in the 1950s was about how to get more young people participating in sport. This concern has re-emerged in every decade since although it has been couched in slightly different terms each time (see Kremer *et al.*, 1997 for a comprehensive discussion of youth and sport in Britain and Houlihan, 1997: Chapter 7 for a comparison of sports policy for young people in Britain and other advanced capitalist countries).

Conclusions

Rather than providing a coherent and unified policy for sport Maurice Roche (1993) argues that the sports policy community in British sport has been little short of a 'disorganised shambles' for much of the post-war period. In this he shares the conclusions of both pluralists Henry and Houlihan and the hegemony approach of Hargreaves. This situation reflects the influence of three associated ideologies and the lack of a central organising body for sport. The sports community in Britain has been, and remains, largely a very divided policy community. The three dominant ideologies attached to sport in Britain in the twentieth century – amateurism, welfarism and, since the 1980s, commercialism – all currently co-exist and compete for influence in British sports policy. Different sections of the state, quangos (such as the Sports Councils) and the national governing bodies of sport all provide different inputs into debates about sport and offer examples of these ideologies. Hence there has been no clearly articulated national sports policy in Britain. Increasingly this pluralistic debate is framed within the wider context of political internationalisation and economic globalisation. Hence there is diversity and no single policy model that best explains sports policy. The 'Task Force' for football announced shortly after Labour formed its government in 1997 seems to fit with the idea of sport as a product for consumers, the notion of developing 'sports academies' appears to fit with the demands of the sports elite for the technocratic production of champion athletes, and 'cultural conservatives' continue to bemoan the end of tradition and fight largely rearguard actions such as attempting to retain exclusive membership rights to sports clubs (for example the reluctance of a significant minority of the members of the Marylebone Cricket Club (MCC) to admit women members in 1998). As a result of this, policies for sport have had far less influence than might be imagined on sports development and trends in participation and involvement. Interest in sport is divided and reflects the social divisions of society along lines of class, gender, ethnicity, age and impairment. There is a wide gap between the rhetoric and reality of sports participation. A fuller appreciation of historical and sociological perspectives on sport, of the kind offered by this book, will enable a better understanding of this reality.

ESSAYS AND EXERCISES

Essays

Why has the state become more involved in sport in the late twentieth century?

Outline and critically assess the operation of the Sports Council in Great Britain since 1972.

'Sport is corrupted if used for political purposes by the state.' Discuss with reference to studies of sports 'mega events' such as the Olympic Games, the FIFA Football World Cup Finals and the Commonwealth games.

Exercises

Talk to an influential actor in the sports policy community and evaluate whether he or she has a clear policy for sport.

List ways in which 'State intervention in sport and physical recreation aims at normalising individuals' (Hargreaves, 1986). Discuss with reference to the notion of 'community' used in sports policies.

'Politicians have increasingly sought to associate themselves with the positive image of successful competition often delivered by sports men and women.' Find examples of this process from the print and broadcast media. How effective do you think it is in shaping public opinion of the politicians?

FURTHER READING

B. Houlihan, *Sport, Policy and Politics*, London, Routledge, 1997, provides a comparative overview of the state's role and government policy in sport in five countries.

M. Roche, 'Sport and Community: Rhetoric and Reality in the Development of British Sport Policy', in J. Binfield and J. Stevenson (eds), *Sport, Culture and Politics*, Sheffield, Sheffield Academic Press, 1993, is a concise and astute summary of phases and issues in British sports policy.

References

Abercrombie, N., Hill, M. and Turner, B. (1980) *The Dominant Ideology Thesis*, London: Allen & Unwin.

Allison, L. (ed.) (1986) *The Politics of Sport*, Manchester: Manchester University Press.

Allison, L. (ed.) (1993) *The Changing Politics of Sport*, Manchester: Manchester University Press.

Anthony, D. (1980) *A Strategy for British Sport*, London: C. Hurst.

Bailey, P. (1989) *Leisure and Class in Victorian England: Rational Recreation and the Contest for Control, 1830–1885*, revised edition, London: Methuen.

Bishop, J. and Hoggett, P. (1986) *Organising Around Enthusiasms: Patterns of Mutual Aid in Leisure*, London: Routledge/Comedia.

Borrett, N. (ed.) (1991) *Leisure Services UK*, London: Macmillan.

Bottomore, T. (1979) *Political Sociology*, London: Hutchinson.

Bramham, P. (1991) 'Explanations of the Organisation of Sport in British Society', *International Review for the Sociology of Sport*, Volume 26, pp. 139–154.

Canter, D., Comber, M. and Uzzell, D. (1989) *Football in its Place: An Environmental Psychology of Football Grounds,* London: Routledge.

Cashmore, E. (1996) *Making Sense of Sport*, 2nd edition, London: Routledge.

Clarke, J. (1978) 'Football and Working Class Fans: Tradition and Change', in R. Ingham (ed.), *'Football Hooliganism': The Wider Context*, London: Inter-Action Inprint.

Clarke, J. and Critcher, C. (1985) *The Devil Makes Work – Leisure in Capitalist Britain*, London: Macmillan.

Coakley, J. (1998) *Sport in Society: Issues and Controversies*, 6th edition, Boston: McGraw-Hill.

Coalter, F., with Long, J. and Duffield, B. (1988) *Recreational Welfare*, Aldershot: Gower.

Coates, D. (1984) *The Context of British Politics*, London: Hutchinson.

The Cobham Report (1973) *Second Report of the Select Committee of the House of Lords on Sport and Leisure*, London: HMSO.

Coghlan, J. and Webb, I. (1990) *Sport and British Politics Since 1960*, London: The Falmer Press.

Cunningham, H. (1980) *Leisure in the Industrial Revolution c.1770–c.1880*, London: Croom Helm.

Donald, D. and Hutton, A. (1986) *The Administration and Promotion of Sport in Scotland*, Edinburgh: Scottish Sports Council.

Dubin, C.L. (1990) *Commission of Inquiry into the Use of Drugs and Banned Practices Intended to Increase Athletic Performance*, Ottawa: Minister of Supply and Services.

Dunning, E., Murphy, P. and Williams, J. (1988) *The Roots of Football Hooliganism*, London: Routledge & Kegan Paul.

Edwards, H. (1969) *The Revolt of the Black Athlete*, New York: The Free Press.

Elvin, I. (1990) *Sport and Physical Recreation*, London: Longman.

Giddens, A. (1985) *The Nation-state and Violence*, Cambridge: Polity Press.

Giddens, A. (1989) *Sociology*, Cambridge: Polity Press.

Gratton, C. and Taylor, P. (1991) *Government and the Economics of Sport*, London: Longman.

Guardian, 3 November 1994; 24 March 1995; 1 April 1995; 9 May 1996; 4 October 1996; 31 May 1997.

Hall, A., Slack, T., Smith, G. and Whitson, D. (1991) *Sport in Canadian Society*, Toronto: McClelland & Stewart.

Hall, S. (1986) 'Popular Culture and the State', in T. Bennett, C. Mercer and J. Woollacott (eds), *Popular Culture and Social Relations*, Milton Keynes: Open University Press.

Haralambos, M. and Holborn, M. (1995) *Sociology: Themes and Perspectives*, 4th edition, London: Collins Educational.

Hargreaves, J. (1986) *Sport, Power and Culture – A Social and Historical Analysis of Popular Sports in Britain*, Cambridge: Polity Press.

Hargreaves, J. (1987) 'The Outflanking of Socialist Sport in Britain, 1880–1980', talk given at 'Images of Sport', British Society of Sports History Conference, South Glamorgan Institute of Higher Education, Cardiff, September.

Henry, I. (1993) *The Politics of Leisure Policy*, London: Macmillan.

HMSO (1975) *Sport and Recreation*, London: Her Majesty's Stationery Office.

HMSO (1995) *Sport: Raising the Game*, London: Her Majesty's Stationery Office.

Hoberman, J. (1984) *Sport and Political Ideology*, London: Heinemann.

Holt, R. and Tomlinson, A. (1994) 'Sport and Leisure' in D. Kavanagh and A. Seldon (eds), *The Major Effect*, London: Macmillan.

Horne, J. (1986) '"Enforced Leisure" and Compulsory Games in the 1930s: An Exploration of the Social Control of Spare Time' in F. Coalter (ed.), *The Politics of Leisure*, Eastbourne: Leisure Studies Association.

Houlihan, B. (1991) *The Government and Politics of Sport*, London: Routledge.

Houlihan, B. (1994) *Sport and International Politics*, London: Harvester Wheatsheaf.

Houlihan, B. (1997) *Sport, Policy and Politics*, London: Routledge.

Jessop, B., Bonnett, K., Bromley, S. and Ling, T. (1988) *Thatcherism*, Cambridge: Polity Press.

Kingdom, P. (1991) *Government and Politics in the United Kingdom*, Cambridge: Polity Press.

Kremer, J., Trew, K. and Ogle, S. (eds) (1997) *Young People's Involvement in Sport*, London: Routledge.

Kruger, A. and Riordan, J. (eds) (1996) *The Story of Worker Sport*, Champaign, Illinois: Human Kinetics.

Leaman, O. (1984) 'The New Sports Ideology', *Youth in Society*, no. 90, May, pp. 16–18.

Macfarlane, N. (1986) *Sport and Politics: A World Divided*, London: Collins Willow.

McGrew, A. (1992) 'The State in Advanced Capitalist Societies', in J. Allen, P. Braham and P. Lewis (eds), *Political and Economic Forms of Modernity*, Cambridge: Polity Press.

McLennan, G. (1995) *Pluralism*, Milton Keynes: Open University Press.

Malcolmson, R. (1973) *Popular Recreations in English Society 1700–1850*, Cambridge: Cambridge University Press.

Marsh, P., Rosser, E. and Harre, R. (1978) *The Rules of Disorder*, London: Routledge & Kegan Paul.

Marx, K. and Engels, F. (1973) (1848) *The Manifesto of the Communist Party*, Moscow: Progress Publishers.

Miliband, R. (1973) *The State in Capitalist Society*, London: Quartet Books.

Monnington, T. (1993) 'Politicians and Sport: Uses and Abuses', in L. Allison (ed.), *The Changing Politics of Sport*, Manchester: Manchester University Press.

Murdoch, E. (1987) *Sport in Schools*, London: Sports Council.

Observer 11 May 1997.

Orwell, G. (1970) (1945) 'The Sporting Spirit', in *The Collected Essays, Journalism and Letters of George Orwell*, Volume 4, Harmondsworth: Penguin Books, pp. 61–64.

Pieda plc (1991) *Sport and the Economy of Scotland*, Edinburgh: Scottish Sports Council.

Pierson, C. (1991) *Beyond the Welfare State*, Cambridge: Polity Press.

Polley, M. (1998) *Moving the Goalposts – A History of Sport and Society since 1945*, London: Routledge.

Poulantzas, N. (1973) *Political Power and Social Class*, London: New Left Books.

Riordan, J. (1986) 'Politics of Elite Sport in East and West', in G. Redmond (ed.), *Sport and Politics*, Champaign, Illinois: Human Kinetics.

Roberts, K. (1992) 'The Disintegration of Sport', in T. Williams, L. Almond and A. Sparkes (eds), *Sport and Physical Activity: Moving Towards Excellence*, London: E & FN Spon.

Roche, M. (1993) 'Sport and Community: Rhetoric and Reality in the Development of British Sport Policy', in J. Binfield and J. Stevenson (eds), *Sport, Culture and Politics*, Sheffield: Sheffield Academic Press.

Scottish Sports Council (1994) *Achieving Excellence*, Edinburgh: Scottish Sports Council.

Sports Council (1986) *The Economic Impact and Importance of Sport in the UK*, London: Sports Council.

Sports Council (1988) *Sport in the Community: Into the 90s*, London: Sports Council.

Sugden, J. and Bairner, A. (1993) *Sport, Sectarianism and Society in a Divided Ireland*, Leicester: Leicester University Press.

Tomlinson, A. (1996) 'Olympic Spectacle: Opening Ceremonies and Some Paradoxes of Globalization', *Media, Culture & Society*, Volume 18, pp. 583–602.

Tomlinson, A. and Whannel, G. (eds) (1984) *Five Ring Circus: Money, Power and Politics at the Olympic Games*, London: Pluto Press.

Torkildsen, G. (1992) *Leisure and Recreation Management*, London: E. & FN Spon.

Whannel, G. (1983) *Blowing the Whistle: The Politics of Sport*, London: Pluto Press.

Whannel, G. (1986) 'The Unholy Alliance: Notes on Television and the Re-making of British Sport 1965–1985', *Leisure Studies*, Volume 5, pp. 22–37.

Wilson, J. (1988) *Politics and Leisure*, London: Unwin Hyman.

Chapter eight

Sport and work

Suppose someone told you there was a regime in Europe where agents scour the country looking for talented young boys, who are taken from their homes and brought to camps to do menial jobs and train consistently – for whom, because of the intense competition for places, education is cursory. The lucky ones are kept on, bound under a contract system where they can be bought and sold by employers. The successful and the bright do very well. But many of the second-raters will find themselves, in their 30s, on the scrap heap and uneducated. Thus does Britain produce 'the greatest football league in the world'.

(Vincent Hanna, journalist, *Guardian*, 9 May 1996)

We may note in passing an additional peculiarity of sport. It would seem to be readily apparent that the occupation is one in which the work cycle differs from that of most other occupations. Specifically, the worker has a relatively short productive work life, and generally his occupational experience does not qualify him for any other skill.

(Stone, 1970: 20)

Introduction

Whilst the effort we expend in keeping fit, working out, or producing the match-winning serve on the municipal tennis court may have little of the innocently playful about it, for most of us – even those who are into 'serious leisure' – for most of the time, sport is a form of recreation or play. For a prominent, and growing, minority of people in Britain sport is also paid work. Over 450,000 people are employed in the provision of sports clothing, publicity, ground and club maintenance and other activities associated with sport. It has been estimated that £9,750 million is spent on sport annually in Britain (Central Office of Information, 1994: 3) and employment in sport-related occupations is above that in agriculture and the chemicals industry. The main focus of this chapter, however, is the relatively smaller number of professional sportsmen and sportswomen.

Ned Polsky (1985: 98) has commented that 'sociology has unduly neglected the study of people who engage in sports or games for their livelihood'. He suggests this has largely been because of the compartmentalisation of work and leisure. There has been little social research into 'the people who work at what most of us play at' (ibid.). This chapter will review attempts to correct this imbalance. It primarily concentrates on the working context of professional sport. It will examine careers, working conditions, rewards and costs in the competitive world of professional sport. It will also consider the influence of beliefs and values associated with high performance sport – such as 'no pain, no gain' – which grow out of the intensity of training now thought necessary to attain excellence. We will argue that workers in sport, and the 'leisure industry' more generally, experience conditions and exhibit strategies similar to other workers in a capitalist labour market.

Sport, work and the economy

It is important to situate our consideration of sports work within an understanding of the changes that have been affecting it for the last forty years. Most notably these transformations involve changes in the social and cultural background and assumptions of administrators of sport, the artificial depression of the costs of sport, the flow of income into mass-spectator professional sports, and the relationship between sports and the mass media, especially television. These changes and their impact on sport since the 1960s are discussed in more detail in the next chapter.

Studies of artistic and sport-related occupations, including full-time professional sport, suggest that entering them often requires the ability to break *in*. In order to do this you have to get yourself noticed – either through your teacher or coach at school if they have a contact with the professional game or local sports officials, or by writing directly to the regional branch of your sport's national governing body (Fyfe, 1992: 9). Whichever you do, and whether you play a team or individual sport, you will also have to join a *club*. Here is an illustration of an association footballer breaking into the English professional game:

From the age of 11 I had been visiting Luton Town for training and coaching sessions. My ambition was to play for my home town team, but even though I ended one season as leading scorer for the youth team, the club didn't keep me on as an apprentice. My dad advised me to get a job and play in my spare time, so I joined Chesham United in the Isthmian League and after leaving school took up an apprenticeship with a local firm as a toolmaker ... Dad was adamant that I should persevere with my engineering apprenticeship, but the thought that I was just not going to be good enough to earn a full-time living as a professional made me dreadfully depressed.

(Dixon, 1985)

Fortunately for Kerry Dixon he went on to be capped for England and play for Reading, Chelsea, Southampton and, eventually, Luton Town and Millwall after finishing his apprenticeship. His story reveals the steps that are still necessary to make it into professional football. If a professional club is interested in a young football player – normally aged about 12 or 13 – they will sign him on via Associated Schoolboy or 'S' forms. The agreement will enable him to train at the club two or three times a week but it will restrict the player from playing for any other team. At 16 the club will decide whether or not to sign the player on as a full-time trainee, often as part of Youth Training. As well as practising and playing, trainees have to carry out routine mundane chores, such as cleaning kit, sweeping out changing rooms, etc. At 18 the club will either ask players to sign on full time or ask them to leave.

There is a considerable amount of wastage at this stage. In his account of the life of Matt Busby and Manchester United Eamon Dunphy (1991: 180-181) recalls the success of United's youth team that had won the 1953 FA Youth Cup final first leg against Wolverhampton Wanderers at Old Trafford, 7–1:

The United team for this historic game makes interesting reading:

		Clayton		
	Fulton		Kennedy	
	Colman	Cope	Edwards	
McFarlane	Whelan	Lewis	Pegg	Scanlon

Eddie Colman, Duncan Edwards, David Pegg, Liam Whelan and Albert Scanlon became established first team players. Ronnie Cope played only a single first team game before the Munich Air Disaster (in 1958). Of others in that great youth side, football would hear very little. And that was a vintage year. The failure rate was high. United went on to win the first five FA Youth Cups. A glance through the teams shows that most who helped to win the prize never went on to play regular first team football.

A few years later when two 15- year-old Belfast boys arrived in Manchester for a two-week trial they were so alienated by the initial experience that they returned home after one night. Fortunately for Manchester United (and football) one of them – George Best – was persuaded to return for another try a few weeks later (Dunphy, 1991: 280-281). As the comment from Vincent Hanna at the beginning of this chapter suggests things have not changed fundamentally in terms of the employment relationship in high performance football in Britain since the 1960s.

Attempts have been made to calculate the chances of actually becoming a professional athlete in the USA. Some computations look at the chances of high school or college student athletes becoming professional; others attempt to rate the chances of people from different ethnic groups; still others attempt to calculate the chances of anyone becoming a professional athlete. Tables 8.1, 8.2 and 8.3 provide a guide to some of the findings.

Clearly, whichever method is used the chances of making it to the top in sport in the USA are extremely limited. That is why young athletes are increasingly encouraged to pursue other non-sports careers as well. A further problem is that professional sports careers can be very short-lived, leaving someone with a working life of 30 or even 40 years after their sports career is over. In American football, basketball and baseball average professional careers range from four to seven years in length, but 'this average is deceiving because it obscures the fact that the number of people who play for only 1 or 2 years is far greater than those who play for more than 5 to 7 years' (Coakley, 1994: 284).

In Britain opportunities for making the 'big time' are no more readily available and careers in sport are equally likely to be short-lived. Jobs in sport other than as an active professional sports player include coaching, PE teaching, recreation management, ground staff, sports medicine, sports business, and sports journalism and photography (Fyfe, 1992). These do not offer the immediate fame and fortune some professional players receive, but they are attractive occupations for those who want to be involved in sport in some way. The important thing to note is that most of them require the same academic and personal qualifications as many other non-sport related occupations.

TABLE 8.1 Chances of high school players making it to the top in (American) football, basketball and baseball in the USA (1992)

Sport	(A) High School	(B) Professionals	Percentage (A>B)
Football	1,000,000	1,400	0.14
Basketball	500,000	360	0.07
Baseball	400,000	730	0.18

Source: adapted from Coakley, 1994: 282–83

TABLE 8.2 Odds against making it among black high school (American) football and basketball players

Sport	School	Professionals	Odds Against
Football	350,699	80	3,897 to 1
Basketball	289,672	38	7,622 to 1
Combined	640,371	118	5,003 to 1

Source: adapted from Coakley, 1994: 282–83

TABLE 8.3 Odds of becoming a professional athlete by ethnicity and sport

Sport*	White	Black	Hispanic
Football	1:62,500	1:47,600	1:2,500,000
Baseball (18–39)	1:83,300	1:333,300	1:500,000
Basketball	1:357,100	1:153,800	1:33,300,000
Golf			
Men's	1:312,500	1:12,500,000	1:33,300,000
Women's	1:526,300	—	1:33,300,000
Tennis			
Men's (16–34)	1:285,700	1:2,000,000	1:3,300,000
Women's (15–34)	1:434,800	1:20,000,000	1:20,000,000

Source: adapted from Coakley, 1994: 282–83
Note: * age 20–39 unless otherwise indicated

When considering career opportunities in sport it is useful to refer to Coakley's discussion of the myths and realities behind careers in sport in the USA (1994: 281ff.). Whilst sport can provide satisfying and rewarding careers for some he argues that there are four important qualifications that need to be made.

1   The number of career opportunities for athletes is severely limited.
2   Career opportunities for athletes (as opposed to coaches, trainers, etc.) are short-term, seldom lasting more than five years.
3   Most career opportunities in sports do not bring much fame or fortune.
4   Opportunities for women, black and other ethnic minorities, older people and disabled people are extremely limited.

We will explore these ideas more in the following sections.

Rewards in sports work

A mythology about the amount of earnings that can be made from sport has developed out of the secrecy shrouding private employment contracts in professional sport and 'shamateurism' in high-performance amateur competitions. The basic wages of sports workers can be augmented by, amongst other things, bonus payments, prize money, endorsements, benefits and media appearances. Yet reports in the mass media may quite considerably exaggerate the sums involved by, for example, failing to consider the deductions from a lump sum payment (such as the manager's and agent's percentage cut).

High annual earnings also need to be put into the context of total career earnings. The chances of maintaining or improving on the level of income after retirement from a sport are very doubtful. Earnings and conditions vary greatly from sport to sport and within sports. Income, security, length of career and future prospects all differ. Substantial economic inequalities exist between sports workers. Some are at the level of semi-skilled workers, others are paid the same as professionals, better paid skilled workers and small businessmen, whilst the 'superstars' vie with the income of top company executives and employers.

The largest group of full-time professional athletes in Britain – full-time professional footballers – provide a good illustration of the differentials that now exist in earnings from the sport. Whilst it is a pervasive assumption that professional footballers are now an affluent, relatively homogeneous, occupational group the reality is quite different. Until the 1960s professional football operated a maximum wage system. It was also underpinned by a code of loyalty to the team almost unthinkable in the present day. So Tom Finney, one of the greatest English players of all time, who spent his whole career at Preston North End, earned £14 a week (£12 in the summer), with a £2 bonus for a win and £1 for a draw throughout the 1950s. Even in 1952 when he was approached by the president of the Italian club Palermo and offered £10,000 to sign for them, with wages of £130 per month, plus bonuses, a villa on the Mediterranean and a car, Finney was persuaded by the club chairman not to leave Preston out of loyalty (Dunphy, 1991: 159). At the same time Manchester United players were earning about £750 per year including bonuses. Compared to the rest of the world, wages in British football were very poor and relied upon what Dunphy (1991: 158) calls 'the extraordinary psychological confidence trick the Masters had played on their Slaves'.

After the abolition of the maximum wage in 1961 the differentials between different players and teams widened. Fulham was the first club to pay a player (Johnny Haynes) £100 per week. During the 1970s and 1980s players in the English 3rd and 4th Divisions at the lower end of the earnings scale were on wages similar to semi-skilled manual workers. There was a big earnings gap between players in Division 1 and the rest and within Division 1 between the 'stars' and the rest. During the 1970s and 1980s Kevin Keegan regularly made £200,000 per year from salaries, advertising, bonuses, media work, etc. In short, a minority of professional football players can earn a great deal of money each season; the majority far less, although still a solid middle-class standard; the rest may be 'comfortable' earning average industrial wages. Chas Critcher (1979: 164) provided a four-part typology of soccer players in relation to the class structure which is worth considering in assessing these changes:

1   Traditional/located – part of the respectable working class
     (e.g. Stanley Matthews, Nat Lofthouse, Albert Finney).
2   Transitional/mobile – upwardly mobile working class
     (e.g. the Charlton brothers, Bobby and Jack).
3   Incorporated/embourgeoised – small-scale entrepreneurs
     (e.g. Bobby Moore).
4   Superstars/dislocated – showbiz/*nouveau riche*
     (e.g. George Best).

How far these distinctions still apply can be seen from research carried out by Craig Gurney (1997). Whilst top players in the 1990s, such as Ryan Giggs and Eric Cantona, have been 'commodified and produced as an iconography', most professional footballers have also been subject to the twin processes of what Gurney (1997: 7 and 13) calls 'Shearerisation' and 'Gascoingnisation'. Footballers are presented in the mass media as either an undeserving rich elite group or a bunch of notorious, if talented, buffoons, and sometimes both. The result is to project an image of homogeneity in experience and destroy any empathy for football players as *workers*. Gurney used unpublished English Football League data on the average basic weekly wages of players in the four divisions to show the extent of salary differentials in the 1990s. Most of the 3,800 professional footballers in England and Wales only earn a little above the average national professional wage. There is a clear divide between players in Premier League teams and the First Division, and between those in the First Division and lower divisions. Up-to-date information about the earnings of Premier League players was not available for Gurney's survey, but in the 1995/96 season basic earnings in Division 1 were twice that in Division 2.

In most other professional team sports in Britain the pattern is similarly a small minority at the top securing vast amounts of money a year, some being quite well off, and quite a few struggling. County cricketers, for example, were poorly paid up to the mid-1970s. Now the 230 or so top class players, with benefits every ten or fifteen years, selection for winter tours, writing and advertising, can bring in up to £30,000 per season. The exceptional star player (such as Brian Lara) is obviously able to improve on this through endorsements and promotional activities. Minor county and league cricket players make considerably less.

Even gaining an FA Cup Final Winners' medal in football is no guarantee of riches as the following examples illustrate. Kevin Beattie, who played for the successful Ipswich Town cup-winning team in 1978, was injured and forced to leave the game prematurely. In the mid-1980s after labouring and sales representative jobs he was made redundant and offered his cup-winners' medal to the local council in order to meet a rates demand and save his family's furniture. Likewise a few years later when Peter Osgood organised a charity dinner for Southampton's 1976 FA Cup winning team the guest list included an oil company executive, a publican, a self-employed builder, a grocer, a TV celebrity and racehorse trainer, a chef, and only one football club manager (*Guardian*, 3 November 1990).

A professional footballer's playing career is short, it is mobile and earnings are variable. The average length of a professional footballer's career is calculated to be eight years. Over this limited time the exchange value for the player's 'physical capital' will fluctuate. As Gurney concludes: 'unless players make investments of cultural, social or economic capital whilst they are playing then their 'retirement' will be a difficult one' (1997: 11). Table 8.4, comparing the condition of two clubs at the extremes of British football, is indicative of the continuing inequality in the sport.

TABLE 8.4 Professional football in Britain – Manchester United and Albion Rovers compared

	Manchester United	*Albion Rovers*
Division	English Premier	Scottish Third
Ground Capacity	43,500	1,238
Record transfer fee	£7 million (Andy Cole, 1995)	£7,000 (Gerry McTeague, 1989)
Average home attendance (1993–94)	44,245	339
Highest paid employee	Andy Cole: £24,000 per wk (including signing on and bonuses)	Jim Crease: £100 per wk (manager)
Financial position	Pre-tax profits to July 1994 = £10.8 million	Need £1,000 per wk to break even; £0.25 million in debt
Most capped player	Bobby Charlton, 106, England	Jock White, 1, Scotland

Source: *Guardian*, 7 March 1995

Equal opportunities in sport?

Sarah Gilroy (1997: 109) has suggested that Pierre Bourdieu's notion of 'physical capital' is useful when examining the gendered nature of the body and sport. She argues that 'the exchange value of women's physical capital is very limited' and this helps explain the greater participation rates of men over women in professional sport. Just as female prostitutes have a limited time-span before their bodies lose their 'exchange rate value', she writes, 'in a similar way, it could be argued that female gymnasts have a limited currency' (ibid.).

Despite the popularity of the film *A League of Their Own* – which portrayed the professional women's baseball leagues in the USA in the 1940s – the reality today, as yesterday, is that opportunities to take part in professional sports for women in the USA, as well as the UK, are very limited. Women who really want to play professionally have to consider moving abroad. In the USA there are no professional volleyball or basketball leagues and hence despite its popularity in North America women have to come to Europe where professional leagues do exist. The same applies to British women who want to play professional (association) football, although some find opportunities in the North American professional leagues. In many sports, however, the chances for a full-time career are next to nothing as there are no women's events, teams or leagues.

Jennifer Hargreaves (1994: 203–207) points out that apart from a small number of sports – athletics, golf, gymnastics, horse-riding, skiing and tennis – sponsorship deals for women's sports are unusual and in any case are nowhere near as lucrative as those for men's sports. Career opportunities remain concentrated in a few sports, notably golf and tennis. Disparities in comparisons of the earnings of individual men and women athletes are evident. Of the twenty highest paid athletes in 1992, only three were women (Theberge and Birrell, 1994: 336). Tennis player Monica Seles earned $3 million from winnings and bonuses, but only (!) $6 million from endorsements. In the same year basketball star Michael Jordan and boxer Evander Holyfield had incomes of $25 million. Steffi Graf made $2.2 million from winnings and bonuses and $5.5 million from endorsements, but was only 15th in the list (ibid.). In golf the 1991 'Volvo' Order of Merit winner (Ballesteros) earned £545,353, in comparison with the 'Woolmark' Order of Merit winner (Dibnah) who won £89,058 (Hargreaves, 1994: 205). Gender issues related to salaries in professional sport are further highlighted by the fact that, according to the American current affairs magazine *Forbes* which publishes an annual 'Top 40' of highest-paid athletes, there was not one woman athlete from any sport on the list in either 1996 or 1997. For example, the average salary of women playing in the ABL (American Basketball League) during the 1996–1997 season was about $70,000 whilst the average salary for men in the National Basketball Association (NBA) was $2.2 million.

TABLE 8.5 *Forbes* magazine 'Top 40' athletes list in 1997 in $million (per cent)

	Endorsement	*Salary*	*Total*
1 Michael Jordan (basketball)	47.0 (60%)	31.3 (40%)	78.3 (100)
2 Evander Holyfield (boxing)	1.3 (2.4%)	53.0 (97.6%)	54.3
3 Oscar De La Hoya (boxing)	1.0 (2.6%)	37.0 (97.4%)	38.0
4 Michael Schumacher (F1)	10.0 (28.6%)	25.0 (71.4%)	35.0
5 Mike Tyson (boxing)	0.0 (0%)	27.0 (100%)	27.0
6 Tiger Woods (golf)	24.0 (92%)	2.1 (8%)	26.1
7 Shaquille O'Neal (basketball)	12.5 (49.2%)	12.9 (50.8%)	25.4
8 Dale Earnhardt (motor racing)	15.5 (81.2%)	3.6 (18.8%)	19.1
9 Joe Sacik (ice hockey)	0.1 (0.6%)	17.8 (99.4%)	17.9
10 Grant Hill (basketball)	12.0 (70.6%)	5.0 (29.4%)	17.0
11 Greg Norman (golf)	13.0 (80.2%)	3.2 (19.8%)	16.2
12 Arnold Palmer (golf)	16.0 (99.4%)	0.1 (0.6%)	16.1
13 Horace Grant (basketball)	0.4 (2.7%)	14.5 (97.3%)	14.9
14 George Foreman (boxing)	4.5 (30.6%)	10.2 (69.4%)	14.7
15 Pete Sampras (tennis)	8.0 (55.2%)	6.5 (44.8%)	14.5
16 Andre Agassi (tennis)	14.0 (99.3%)	0.1 (0.7%)	14.1
17 Cal Ripken Jr. (baseball)	6.5 (49.2%)	6.7 (50.8%)	13.2
18 David Robinson (basketball)	2.0 (15.2%)	11.2 (84.8%)	13.2
19 Ken Griffey Jr. (baseball)	4.2 (32.3%)	8.8 (67.7%)	13.0
20 Alonzo Mourning (basketball)	3.5 (26.9%)	9.5 (73.1%)	13.0
21 Michael Chang (tennis)	9.5 (79.2%)	2.5 (20.8%)	12.0
22 Naseem Hamed (boxing)	2.5 (20.8%)	9.5 (79.2%)	12.0
35 Lennox Lewis (boxing)	0.2 (2.1%)	9.5 (97.9%)	9.7

Source: adapted from *Forbes*, Volume 158, no. 14, December 1997

The *Forbes* magazine 'Top 40' list in 1997 also featured two British boxers – Prince Naseem Hamed in 22nd position and Lennox Lewis in 35th place (see Table 8.5).

Women's sports often survive through much unpaid labour and various fund raising activities. Hargreaves (1994: 204) provides the example of the first Women's Rugby World Cup held in Wales in 1991:

> Hundreds of applications were made to a range of sponsors, including corporations which support the men's game: refusals were based on traditional ideas about masculine and feminine appropriateness – 'But it's a men's game' and 'They don't drink lager'! The twelve competing countries as far as possible paid their own expenses, but the event ran into a deficit for which those who organised it were legally responsible (The Sports Council and the men's Rugby Football Union between them were eventually persuaded to pay it off).

Outside of full-time professional playing, jobs in sport do exist for women. Again, however, there are barriers. West and Brackenridge (1990: 10-12) provide some good illustrations of these. Whilst British Sports Council statistics have shown that more women than ever before engage in some form of sporting activity, West and Brackenridge argue that 'no commensurate increase has been registered in the numbers of women in positions of power'. Those with the most influential positions in sport tend to be men:

> whilst the proportion of female athletes attending the Olympic Games increased from 30% in 1980 to 33% in 1988, the number of female officials fell from 33% to 25% . . . In 1988 women constituted just 12% of full members of the British Association of National Coaches (BANC) and 20% of associate members.
>
> (West and Brackenridge, 1990: 10)

Despite equal opportunity legislation in the USA there has been a noticeable decline in the number of women coaches in the American university system. Few women coaches have been in charge of men's athletic programmes in universities, whereas men are often in charge of coaching women. Where sports have expanded it has been male coaches who have benefited (West and Brackenridge, 1990: 11). Women in sports work face the same barriers that other women face trying to enter a 'male domain'. They are often seen as unusual and possibly not as competent for no other reason than their gender.

The increasing visibility of black athletes in North American and, especially over the last fifteen years, British spectator sports gives the impression that sport provides many career opportunities for black people. In the *Miller Lite Report on American Attitudes Toward Sports* (1983) 70 per cent of adults in the USA agreed with the statement that 'there are more opportunities in sports than in any other field for the social advancement of blacks and other minorities' and over 50 per cent agreed that 'athletics is one of the best ways for blacks to advance their social status'. If a similar survey were carried out in Britain today it is likely that a similar set of findings would result, yet there is no objective data to support these assumptions. In fact the extent to which job opportunities in sports exist for black and minority people in Britain and in the USA has been greatly exaggerated by the coverage in the mass media of individual success stories. The reality is that hardly any black women are able to make a professional career in sport whilst the number of black men is fairly negligible in comparison with white men – except in England where black (Afro-Caribbean) footballers now account for about 20 per cent of professionals in the four leagues (Cashmore, 1982, 1996; Parry and Parry, 1991).

Despite the rise to fame of Tiger Woods in golf – and large sponsorship and endorsement deals that have come with the success – there are very few blacks in the most lucrative individual sports such as golf, tennis and auto racing, or in ice hockey in North America. Track and field athletics offer some opportunities but the rewards for most athletes are relatively small. Even in boxing many of the most successful black fighters have not been able to retire in comfort or use their sports careers as a stepping stone to others. Yet none of this information appears to influence the career aspirations of many white and especially black school students. One research project with American high school students found that:

> As they near (possible) entry into the job market, young blacks are becoming more aware that the rhetoric that 'you can become anything you want to be in America' is, for them, a myth. As the doors for the conventional means of occupational advancement close, many turn to the one industry which has an open door policy with regard to 'good, talented' blacks – the entertainment industry. The many rags-to-riches stories, the testimonies of athletes who now own fine cars, furs and homes, and the (visibility) of super heroes . . . encourages many young men to abandon dreams of success in traditional arenas for a life of basketball, football, or baseball.
>
> (Harris and Hunt, 1984, quoted in Coakley, 1994: 290)

In Britain sports such as football, boxing, rugby league, horse-racing and speedway continue to offer a possible route of social mobility for white working-class men, whilst male black athletes tend to be involved in football, boxing and track and field athletics. The largest minority ethnic groups in Britain, Indian, Pakistani and Bangladeshi, continue to be under-represented in most of these team games, prompting some research into the reasons why they are not involved to the same extent (Fleming, 1995).

The next sections of this chapter seek to reveal the reality of work in sport today. What *social class* do sports workers belong to? What is the *labour process* like in sport? What are the distinctive features of sports' *occupational communities?*

The labour process and professional sport

Professional football has most of the characteristics of a vast capitalistic industry. It is on the lines of big business that the clubs are organised, with their boards of directors, their managers, their shareholders, and their employees. The monopoly of the means of satisfying the demands of the consumers (the spectators) is for the most part concentrated in the hands of comparatively small groups of industrialists and financiers ... The driving force, the overriding motive, of professional football clubs is not the satisfaction of public demand, but the acquisition of profits.

(Professor E.W. Hunt, 'Karl Marx versus the Stretford End', *Guardian*, 13 February 1981)

Most economists would disagree with this – football has not been run along business lines at all, even if the control of the game has been in the hands of a small number of men. In the 1983–84 football season, for example, a survey carried out by *Labour Research* (September 1983: 238–242) found that in nine of the twenty-two English First Division clubs, directors owned more than 40 per cent of the shares; in a further three clubs outside stakes held by one or two individuals or companies lead to control by the few; and fifty men controlled half the First Division clubs.

Ten years on, however, football was hitting the headlines of the non-sports pages of daily newspapers for reasons other than crowd trouble or hooliganism. The financing of football, especially Premier League football, has been affected by three main developments in the 1990s. Gate receipts have continued to go down in terms of their relative importance as new sources of income, notably television revenue and income from merchandising have increased. For example, in May 1995 Manchester United announced the following turnover figures for the year ending 31 May 1995:

Gate receipts and programme sales	£19,648,000
Television	£6,758,000
Sponsorship, royalties and advertising	£7,363,000
Conference and catering	£3,365,000
Merchandising and sales	£23,488,000
	£60,622,000

Source: Manchester United Annual Report and Accounts 1996

Another change is that the ownership structure of clubs has been altering. It is increasingly likely that boards of directors will treat their clubs as business operations and have the experience and occupational background to do so. Third, many more clubs have followed the lead taken by Tottenham Hotspur in the 1980s to issue shares via their supporters. January is thought to be one of the worst months in stocktaking terms for gaining new investments. When Glasgow Celtic put out a share issue in January 1996, however, it was oversubscribed by 1.8 times and eventually raised the club £10 million in the month. Purchases of stocks and shares in football teams have been driven largely by the sentiment of the supporters for their team. This is beginning to change as more financial institutions become involved (for example the British Coal Pension Fund has invested in Manchester United) and the acceptance in 1998 by the Manchester United Board of Directors of Rupert Murdoch's bid is likely to be followed by similar takeovers in the near future. One accountant acquaintance has pointed out that perhaps the 'FT' (the *Financial Times*) is really better understood now as the 'Football Times' given the extensive coverage of the performance of the shares of football league teams listed on the Alternative Investment Market (AIM)!

Role specialisation and the division of labour in team sports

Alongside these changes, how far can professional sport be analysed using the same approaches as those adopted to examine other forms of work in a capitalist society? Critiques of sport that attempt to do so have been presented by writers such as Jean-Marie Brohm (1978) and Bero Rigauer (1981 (1969)). Brohm considered the work world of sport to be a reflection of industrial capitalist society:

> Sport, as an activity characteristic of bourgeois industrial society, is an exact reflection of capitalist categories. And as Marx explained, economic categories reflect the structures and principles of organisation of the capitalist mode of production. The vertical, hierarchical structure of sport models the social structure of bureaucratic capitalism, with its system of competitive selection, promotion, hierarchy, and social advancement. The driving forces in sport – performance, competitiveness, records – are directly carried over from the driving forces of capitalism: productivity, the search for profit, rivalry and competitiveness.
>
> (1978: 49–50)

In *Sport and Work* Bero Rigauer (1981 (1969)) argued that whereas sport had originally served as a counter-agent to work in capitalist society, in the course of the twentieth century it has increasingly taken on more and more of the characteristics of paid employment. According to Rigauer, modern sport has been shaped in both its organisational arrangements and content by the industrial division of labour, mechanisation, rationalisation and bureaucratisation also evident in modern work. He argues that modern sport and work complement each other in six ways:

1   Gruelling training techniques, necessary for the achievement of excellence in modern sport, mirror the alienating and dehumanising character of the factory floor assembly line.

2   The individual is swamped by whole teams of 'experts' and – especially in team sports – is expected to comply with a prescribed tactical plan and fit into a fixed division of labour that he (and sometimes she) has played no part in working out.

3   As in paid work, he or she has minimal scope for the exercise of initiative (the American 'gridiron' footballer performing set 'plays' called by the coach is a concrete example).

4   The bureaucratic administration of sport means that full-time officials, not athletes themselves, decide on sports policies (Rigauer admits that room for exercising initiative is actually greater in sports than in most forms of paid work, but argues that the gap is constantly narrowing).

5   The effect of these changes is to turn sport into a demanding, achievement-oriented and alienating area of human activity. Consequently sport loses its potential for relieving the strains and tensions of work.

6   The belief that sport can fulfil this function is a 'masking ideology', hiding from participants the real function of sport in modern society – which is to reinforce, in the sphere of leisure, an ethic of hard work, achievement and group loyalty, necessary for the operation of an advanced industrial capitalist society. For Rigauer sport helps maintain the bureaucratic-capitalist status quo and bolster the dominance of a ruling class.

Brohm's and Rigauer's critiques of contemporary sport stimulated other writers to respond with arguments about the *relative autonomy* of sport. Allen Guttmann's *From Ritual to Record* (1978) is the most widely cited response to their analysis. Guttmann adopted what he claimed was a Weberian perspective (see Chapter 3). He wanted to examine the ways in which modern sport reflects features of modern society, but without reducing an explanation of the growth of sport to it being fully dependent on the growth of capitalism.

Guttmann produced a list of seven characteristics of modern sport in order to outline what distinguishes modern sport from sport in previous historical periods and to demonstrate that sport reflects modern society, but not completely. The seven characteristics were:

- secularism;
- equality;
- role specialisation;
- rationalisation;
- bureaucratisation;
- quantification;
- the quest for records.

The concept of 'role specialisation' – similar to the notion of the 'division of labour' used by Emile Durkheim and Norbert Elias – is important for Guttmann in explaining the nature of work in modern team sports. The division of labour refers to 'the process whereby productive tasks become separated and more specialised'. It also refers to 'the process of occupational specialisation in society as a whole, and the separation of social life into different activities and institutions, such as the family, the economy and the state' (Jary and Jary, 1991: 168–170).

For Dunning and Sheard (1979: Chapter 1) role specialisation is a distinctive feature of modern as opposed to folk football. In 'folk football' there were no sharply defined roles – the men, women and children of entire villages would play against each other, for example as 'up-streamers' versus 'down-streamers'. Sports were unspecialised and undifferentiated in three ways – from other games, between players roles and between players and spectators. On the contrary modern team sports are increasingly dominated by players in specialist positions and spectators who watch. High performance athletes have to dedicate themselves to exclusive participation in a single event or a single position within an event or a sport.

The death in April 1997 of Dennis Compton – who played cricket for Middlesex and England and football for Arsenal and England – marked for some the end of an era. He joined Arsenal as a 17 year old in 1935 and made his first-class debut for Middlesex a year later, scoring 1,000 runs in the season. The following year he made his debut for England in a cricket Test Match. Positions within team sports now have clearly defined roles, distinguished from each other in terms of skills and responsibilities. American football teams have players in offense and defense – twenty-two positions in all – plus 'special teams' restricted to place kicks, kick-offs and kick-off receptions. Whilst role exchange in this game is possible – a defensive lineman may occasionally intercept a forward pass – quick return to position is expected. Baseball, founded in 1845 and based upon a division of labour into nine separate playing positions has increasingly moved towards offensive teams of 'designated hitters' and defensive teams of pitchers. Specialisation on the field of play is mirrored by the development of supportive personnel off it: owners, managers, coaches, trainers, scouts, doctors, recruiters, referees, umpires, schedulers, linesman, groundsmen, ticket-takers, popcorn sellers, spectators, journalists and disciplines like sports medicine, sport psychology and physiology, sport administration, management and sport sociology!

Guttmann considers specialisation and professionalisation to be the same thing – about the amount of time in one's life one dedicates to the 'job' of achieving athletic excellence, not whether or not you get paid for doing it. Since athletic achievement in a variety of sports is increasingly incompatible with high-level performance in any one of them, specialisation becomes narrower and narrower. For Guttmann (1978: 39) 'Specialisation results from the characteristically modern stress on achievement.'

Rationalisation, bureaucracy and 'McDonaldization'

Guttmann argues that two additional features of modern sport are rationalisation and bureaucracy. Rationalisation is present in modern sports through the complex rules and strategies that are utilised to play them. Rules specify the goals (the end, or purpose, of the sport) and the means to achieve these ends. Rules also regulate equipment, playing techniques and the conditions of participation. Strategies provide the basis for training and for defining the experience of involvement. Specialised equipment is produced as a result – racquets are used in tennis, the pole in pole vault, the javelin, etc.

Bureaucracy is derived from the French word 'bureau', meaning office, and hence literally means 'government by office holders' (officials). It is referred to in a pejorative manner when called 'red tape' but social scientists use it in a more neutral way to describe a way or 'ideal-type' of organising administration. The central importance of rules in governing behaviour and the priority of contractual relations over personal relations are key features of bureaucratic organisations. Modern sports are controlled through the establishment of complex organisations at international, national and regional and local levels. Governing bodies, associations and unions oversee and sanction athletes, teams and events – they make up the rules, implement rule changes and enforce them, organise events and certify records.

In many ways Guttmann's ideas have been relabelled for the 1990s as 'McDonaldization'. George Ritzer (1993) argues that this is 'the process by which the principles of the fast-food restaurant are coming to dominate more and more sectors of American society as well as the rest of the world'. The five principle dimensions of 'McDonaldization' according to Ritzer – efficiency, quantifiability and calculability, predictability, control, and technology – are equally applicable to modern sport as Guttmann's original list of characteristics. It can be agreed that work in sport is more than a reflection of capitalist society but it is also necessary to look in more detail at the working lives of professional athletes.

The sports labour process – the social position of sports workers

A large amount of trivial knowledge about professional athletes is provided by the popular press, television and the numerous sports 'autobiographies', which are usually 'ghosted' by sports journalists. Much less is known about them as *sports workers* (Beamish, 1993; Lenskyj, 1986). John Hargreaves (1986: 122–130) provided a useful set of arguments about the social position of sports workers. They are a small occupational group, the majority of whom are men since opportunities for women in professional sport are limited. In the major British sports in the mid-1980s there were 2,800 professional footballers plus 900 apprentices in England and Wales, 2,500 golf professionals plus 1,000 trainees, 450 licensed jockeys plus 450 apprentices, 475 professional boxers, and around 230 first-class county cricketers (Hargreaves, 1986: 122).

Since the work tasks, the pay and conditions at work, the social origins of the entrants and the social milieu and status of different sports vary so much it is difficult to conceptualise sports workers as a coherent group. A few generalisations are possible, however:

1   Like manual work sports work involves physical labour. Top-level sport demands so much physical fitness and ability that sports careers are considerably shorter than those of average industrial workers.

2   Competitive sport is highly specialised and requires an elaborate *division of labour.* Team sports such as hockey, football and cricket provide perfect examples of the division of labour on the field of play. In hockey and football players can specialise as goalkeepers, defenders, midfield players or attackers, whilst in cricket players usually specialise in batting, bowling or wicket-keeping, even though they may be required to perform more than one of these tasks in the course of a match. Off the field of play the division of labour exists where sports workers employ managers to negotiate contracts on their behalf and solicitors when they go to court.

3   Sports workers' performance is analysed and developed with the aid of time and motion techniques – 'the scientific programming of labour power in sport has advanced beyond that in industry' (Hargreaves, 1986: 122). Jean-Marie Brohm (1978) refers to this as the 'Taylorisation of the body' and John Hoberman (1992) as the production of 'mortal engines'.

4   The division in industry between mental and manual labour, which sees a large technical and administrative structure used to control and co-ordinate the labour process, is paralleled in sports work by the growth of specialists and officials – managers, coaches, trainers, medical experts, sports psychologists, etc. (Davies, 1985).

5   As in much manual work, injuries and other hazards are an accepted part of the job – specific sports have their own typical injuries and ailments, and injury can result in permanent disablement and even death.

6   'Sweated' labour and unhealthy and dangerous conditions at work can be found in sport. The lack of adequate medical safeguards in boxing and the use of drugs, to kill pain as much as directly enhance performance, are testimony to that.

But here the contrasts begin to appear with manual work. Sports work has high prestige, provides opportunities to acquire and use skills and abilities, and permits professionals the opportunity to play at their occupation. Furthermore:

1   The physical health of sports workers is better than the average industrial worker's health, simply because it is attended to more systematically by the individual athlete and the relevant institutions. Physical health is a condition of the efficient performance of the job.

2   Those sports that are tests of skill rather than physical fitness (darts, golf, bowls, snooker) are not especially hazardous or physically stressful, although mental strain is possible.

3   Even if the 'deskilling' thesis is accepted to apply in the wider world of paid employment (Braverman, 1974), it does not apply directly to sports work even though narrow specialisation has long been the case and knowledge and planning is monopolised by specialists and administrators. In sports work there is a greater opportunity to exhibit and develop skill; sports work produces a spectacle of entertainment via the display of talent. A deskilled, less talented work-force would be counter-productive; it is more difficult to routinise creative work, especially entertainment work: 'this type of work has in-built limits beyond which it can not be readily deskilled or its productivity rationalised' (Hargreaves, 1986: 123).

In sum Hargreaves suggests that:

> The retention of skill gives sports workers more control over their work tasks and they are, therefore, not only in a better position in relation to the exercise of authority than at first appears to be the case, but work satisfaction is also likely to be greater.
>
> (1986: 123)

Hence studies of the working lives of professional athletes often find them generally content with their work (Davies, 1985; Brookes, 1978; Wagg, 1984). These satisfactions go some way to explaining the lack of strong reactions to the tight control kept over them in the labour process. Athletes are routinely admonished for rule infringements and subsequent punishment is very much part of the spectacle. Suspension and banning from a sport is the usual punishment for transgressions of the rules, with the consequent loss of earnings and livelihood. In British football the frequent use of the phrase 'bringing the game into disrepute' in charges brought against a player is especially difficult to refute as the charge is so vague.

Competition and control at work and play

Adequately to answer the question, what is the production process in sport, would require more detailed consideration of the relationships between employers, management and employees, in short the *sports labour process*. The labour process refers to the way in which work is systematically organised and conducted so as to produce a useful article, service or, in the case of sport, result. Of great importance in terms of the latter is the *production of consent* on the part of athletes to accept certain social relations in production. Co-operation is required for the production of goods and services, just as much as for a good team effort, but it is often argued that management and labour have different and competing interests.

An important dimension of this is what Beamish (1993: 208) calls the age of entry into competitive sport and the 'long "apprenticeship"' that athletes serve as they win their way through the feeder system. Beamish continues:

> The product that athletes produce is, for them, directly related to the pursuit of the linear record so that they can win championships and progress toward the provincial, national and finally international level. The ideological experience of this activity is overwhelmingly dominated by concerns related to the acquisition and refinement of the skills and strategies involved in the sporting activity and how science and technology can assist performance enhancement . . . In terms of political relationships – the social relations in production – the athletic experience for many high performance athletes involves some nationalist sentiments such as the importance of winning for their country or beating certain athletes/countries, but it is predominantly local in focus. That is, the political dimension of high performance sport at the site of production – training and competition – is narrowly focused on the production of superior performances and does not tend to extend to a complete understanding of the entire structure of the high performance sport system and its global political significance. Because winning is paramount, and the entire developmental process and experience of working one's way through the feeder system select only certain winners, the dominant ideology of scientific experts combines with the long-standing residual tradition of a coach's authority to create a set of political relationships in which the athlete is rendered substantially less powerful than his or her supervisors . . . for the athlete the product has a very narrow meaning and significance . . . the 'bottom line' of results.

In economist's terms both employers and employees want to 'maximise their utility' – gain higher profits on the one hand and higher wages on the other. Workers in, for example, a car factory have been regarded as adopting an *instrumental* approach to work (Beynon, 1973). Not all workers adopt this approach, however. Roy (1973), writing in 1960, considered that workers who face a relatively monotonous job may adopt a *consummatory* approach instead. These workers are interested in little more than themselves and their work-mates. Alan Tomlinson (1983) has suggested that the lives of professional footballers can be understood in a similar way. Amongst footballers an *occupational culture* is evident which has the following characteristics:

- Informal controls and interaction stemming from authoritarian controls over their time and lives off the pitch and simple boredom.
- 'Mucking about' is directed inwards – 'getting a laugh out of life' – rather than outwards towards the authority structure.
- *Resentment* exists, but not in the form of outright opposition to the structure of authority. Hence responses to authority sometimes take the form of juvenile giggles or pranks, rather than any more serious opposition.
- Players are *dominated* and *controlled*, but they are also *dependent* upon the shared success of the managed and the managers. This can contribute to the extended adolescence and even *infantalisation* of the professional athlete.

In many ways the contemporary football manager and other sports managers share similar relations with players as the early capitalist entrepreneurs did with their workers (e.g. Brian Clough in football, Barry Hearn in snooker). These employment relations do not apply uniformly throughout European football clubs, however (Kuper, 1994: 93–99). In the following extract the control exerted by the coach over the players in American football in the USA provides another illustration of employer–employee relations in sport.

> I believe in everything being well planned in my work. I believe that no stone should be left unturned. I want to gather all the facts and get all the answers. I relate this information to my coaches and then they relate it to the players. I want to be sure they understand the total picture. I don't want any loose ends that could cause a player to fail.
>
> In our defensive system everybody has to work together. We rely on planning, preparation, systems, drill and logic, and not much on emotions. In defense, we don't strive for flair, but consistency and logic. We emphasise purpose, planning and excellence in execution. On offense, we try to use more flair to achieve a surprise and the unexpected. The

innovations, such as the shotguns and motions, are not done for innovations' or changes' sake. They're done for a logical purpose. Our competitors will see what the Cowboys do on offense as 'wide-open', 'daring', 'gambling', perhaps. Sure there's a lot of show to it, but there's a purpose to the show. We're trying to bring about the result of the opponent's defeat by means of the unexpected, the bold move, the unanticipated surprise stroke. Let's say that we are preparing to play the Pittsburgh Steelers. A given Cowboy player is preparing to play them. The coach reviews the player's job with him, exactly what he's to do. He has precise objectives. He must do these certain things to bring results. If he isn't prepared, he'll do the job in an imperfect way that will fail to achieve results. We do not want any player to fail. He must feel secure to succeed. If he fails to feel secure, he won't do his best. All our coaches use computer printouts. Hundreds of them. Every pattern, every stat of every team we play is on the computer. Each coach has one and uses it. It's analysis every step of the way. Football is a game of objectives. The Dallas Cowboys play football by objectives. We set team objectives, our offensive objectives, our defensive objectives, our game objectives, and our play objectives. Every player has his own objectives.

> (Tom Landry, Coach, Dallas Cowboys,
> quoted in Hellriegel and Slocum, 1983: 126)

One response to the 'scientific management' approach in sport is summed up in the following comment by Eric Nesterenko, a Canadian ice hockey player.

> You know they're making an awful lot of money off you. You know you're just a piece of property. When an older player's gone, it's not just his body. With modern training methods you can play a long time. But you just get fed up with the whole business. It becomes a job, just a shitty job. (Laughs)
>
> (Eric Nesterenko, Toronto Maple Leafs/Chicago Black Hawks,
> in Terkel, 1977: 319)

Similar to Roy's (1973) workers in 1960, professional athletes may adopt a *consummatory* approach to their working conditions. Sports workers are normally interested in little more than their own performance and possibly that of their work-mates, not with issues such as the 'rate for the job', conditions at work, or in engaging in collective action such as strikes. As Hargreaves (1986: 128) says

> The isolated position of the sports worker from the working-class, the differential reward structure, the power of the owners and controllers and the

individualist ethos, mutually reinforce each other to produce a group, which as a whole is scarcely trade union conscious, let alone class conscious in any real sense.

This was well illustrated in the second edition of *The Glory Game*, Hunter Davies's superb account of a year in the life of Tottenham Hotspur (Davies, 1985). Only seven players in the first team squad of nineteen completed the section of his questionnaire on political behaviour. Glenn Hoddle, formerly England's team coach, had voted Liberal, Miller voted Conservative and Galvin and Hazard voted Labour in the 1983 General Election.

Labour relations in sport

It is not always the case, however, that professional athletes are reluctant to act collectively in order to secure an improvement in their working conditions and salaries. Perhaps as commercialisation in sport increases players will adopt a greater 'worker consciousness' and the number of strikes and disputes over wages and conditions between management and players will increase. As sport becomes increasingly designed to generate revenues, when people pay to watch them live, or television companies pay to broadcast them, athletes become part of the entertainment industry (Coakley, 1994: 317ff.). This has consequences for their legal status and rights, which has been the most controversial issue in professional team sport in Britain and North America since the 1960s (Beamish, 1993). Here are two examples, from North America and Britain, of struggles over the *social relations of sports production*.

The reserve system and free agency in North America

Until the mid-1970s professional athletes in team sports in the USA and Canada had little or no legal power to control their own careers. They were subject to a set of employee restrictions known as the *reserve system* which began in baseball in 1879. It virtually bound a player to one team in perpetuity:

- They could play only for the team drafting (selecting) them.
- They could neither pick the team they wanted to play for, nor control when and to whom they might be traded (transferred) even when their contracts expired.
- They were obliged to sign contracts forcing them to agree to forfeit rights to control their careers.

Basically professional athletes in team sports in the USA in the 1960s and 1970s were the property of who ever owned the team. It enabled owners to set salaries relatively low and prevented players from being able to sell their abilities to the team that would give them the best deal in terms of money and playing/working conditions. The owners had a greater degree of control over their players/workers than in any other business in the USA.

Professional athletes had often objected to the reserve system, but in the 1970s players' unions and organisations were established which helped to challenge the system through the courts. In 1976 the courts ruled that players had the right to become free agents – to accept contracts from other teams when their contracts expired. This led to a great increase in the salaries of baseball and basketball players in the 1970s and 1980s. In the NFL (football) and NHL (ice hockey) team owners managed to avoid the effects of the legal change through negotiating restrictions on free agency with the players' associations. In 1992 these restrictions were challenged, with hockey players gaining some concessions and the NFL agreeing to let football players become free agents after being in the league for five years.

The growth of players' unions and associations since the 1970s has given them a collective strength that previously only the team owners possessed. They have been able to gain greater control over their salaries and working conditions – with the latter being more at issue than money. It has not been easy to keep players organised (Beamish, 1988). Owners have not looked kindly upon players who act as union representatives. A strike, which could last for a whole season, might cost a player 20 per cent of his or her total income as a professional player. During the 1987 NFL strike owners signed non-union players to take the place of those taking part in the action.

The issue of incomes in sport is confused by the attention that the highest paid athletes receive. Salaries actually vary widely within and between sports in the UK and in the USA. Many professional athletes in the USA do not receive incomes much greater than those of other workers. Coakley (1994: 321) cites figures that show that in 1993 the salaries of players with the 158 minor league baseball teams ranged from $1,200 to $3,000 (£750–£1,880) per month. As their jobs are seasonal they do not always get paid for twelve months of the year. This pattern is similar for other professional sports including men's and women's basketball, American football, ice hockey, soccer and volleyball. Of course since the 1970s some athletes have been able to draw enormous salaries. A few established baseball players have signed contracts worth around $7 million per year (£4.38 million) in the 1990s and some young basketball players have signed contracts worth several million dollars. Current average salaries in the NBA, NFL, NHL and MLB can compare favourably with those paid to other entertainers in the television, film and music industry.

The football labour market in England

The labour market in British sport is equally distinguished from other markets for labour by the special restrictions imposed on the sale and mobility of labour. As in the USA the freedom of labour to chose its own employer is restricted and professional athletes face increased dependence on the owners and controllers of sport. So, for example, county cricketers must obtain permission to register with another county, whilst in football, rugby league and speedway, players can be bought and sold by their employers. Employers are in a position to choose the next employer of a current employee!

The English Football League Clubs used to operate a *retain and transfer system* similar to the reserve system in the USA. In 1963 the retain and transfer system was dramatically modified following the successful claim for damages made by George Eastham against his club Newcastle United. Under the retain and transfer system that then operated a professional footballer signed a contract with his club for one or two years. At the end of the contract the players were not free to move to another club under the jurisdiction of the Football League or the FA unless the directors of the club gave permission. When a contract came to an end under the retention system either a player could register again with the same club or the club might give notice of retention with an offer of a minimum wage of £418 a year. There was no maximum period of retention and the player remained a member of his club and could not play for any other.

In June 1960 George Eastham had refused to resign the contract that Newcastle offered him. He was supported in his legal action by the players' 'union', the Professional Footballers' Association. The retain and transfer scheme was found to be in restraint of trade and was modified in the players' favour. At the end of a contract a player is either given a 'free transfer' or retained on terms that are as good as in his previous contract and put on the transfer list at some negotiable fee.

Before 1961 the footballers' market was also governed by a maximum wage regulation. The threat of a strike (led by Jimmy Hill and the Professional Footballers Association – PFA) removed this restraint and changed the whole shape of the league. Those clubs in large centres of population could now exploit their economic power and induce the most talented players to their sides (Corry, Williamson and Moore, 1993). An interesting exception to this rule, at least until the 1980s, was Manchester United. Five years after the abolition of the maximum wage, in 1966, no Manchester United player was close to earning the £100 per week Tommy Trinder, the chairman of Fulham, had awarded to Johnny Haynes. 'The going rate at Old Trafford was half that amount, the club's renewed preeminence notwithstanding' (Dunphy 1991: 301).

Until 1995 players could still only move from one club to another if a transfer fee, or at least terms for the transfer, had been agreed. Those who wished to leave a club against its wishes were at a disadvantage. Transfer requests made in writing lost a player approximately 5 per cent of the agreed fee, which was his by right if he was transferred at a club's behest. On the other hand, a player's refusal to comply with a transfer might hinder his chances of selection for the team. A manager might decide to transfer a player but not always to the highest bidder – especially if a transfer to a rival in the same division might rebound upon their chances of promotion or a championship (Dunphy, 1991: 297). The virtual abolition of the old style retain and transfer system saw the rise of agents negotiating terms of employment and salaries for the top players and the practice of sales of players just at the end of their contracts. This was given yet another boost in December 1995 by the Bosman judgment.

The Bosman judgment refers to a ruling made by the Court of Justice of the European Communities (the 'European Court') on 15 December 1995 in proceedings between the former Belgian football player Jean-Marc Bosman, the Belgian Football Association, RC Liège, US Dunkerque and the Union of European Football Associations (UEFA) about the interpretation of Articles 48, 85 and 86 of the EEC Treaty. It enforced two changes which have affected all professional European football players. First, it abolished the legality of all foreign player restrictions or 'nationality clauses' on European Union (EU) citizen players anywhere within the EU. Second, it confirmed the right of an EU citizen player to move free of any transfer fee to another country within the EU on the expiry of his contract.

As with the example from North America it would seem that sportsmen only go on strike when they become free agents. In the USA, up until the mid-1970s, baseball players were tied to their clubs even when out of contract. Until the Bosman ruling made the practice illegal European footballers were tied to their clubs in the same way. When the judgment was made nearly every national football association in the EU enforced tight restrictions on the use of foreign players. The judgment's impact has been made more rapid by the growth of television's interest in football and the increased spectacularisation of the game. The ruling has enhanced quality at the highest club level but may be enforcing less enthusiasm and skill at the national team level. Clubs in Italy, Spain, England and Germany can now pack their squads with limitless numbers of foreign players which may have a detrimental affect on the national team. At the time of the ruling former Spurs and German international Jurgen Klinsmann said: 'The Bosman verdict is great for the superstars but I'm not sure how good it is, in the long run, for the run-of-the-mill professionals' (quoted in World Soccer, February 1997, p. 20). Another effect of the Bosman case is that players with the big clubs can demand more pay in return for committing themselves to longer contracts. In 1996, for example, the Brazilian World Footballer of the Year, 20-year-old Ronaldo, was able to secure a contract worth £2.5 million a year for nine and a half years with Barcelona. Figure 8.1 summarises the situation in a number of European football associations.

If the Bosman judgment has enhanced quality at the highest club level and the showbiz aspects of football, at the lower reaches of the game the only certainty seems to be that there will be more uncertainty. Bosman has won his fellow players freedom of movement between European clubs. Any player at the end of his contract is entitled to a free transfer to any club in Europe who wants to sign him. As at September 1998, if a player moved to a new club in the same country a transfer fee could still be demanded. Support remains for the argument that a modern form of slavery still exists in British football.

United Kingdom
Domestic transfer system remains intact; lifting of restrictions has seen a greater influx of foreign players; the English Premier League has the largest 'foreign' contingent in Europe – with over 250 players under contract, 227 from the EU (which includes Scots, Welsh and Irish) according to UEFA figures. There is a maximum of three non-EU players per English team. Few British exports.

France
75 contracted foreign players, only 24 from the EU. The French have a system where clubs sign young players on long contracts up until age 24 – possibly restrictive.

Holland
125 foreign players, 50 from EU countries. Discussions about longer contracts for young players; no restrictions on non-EU players; domestic transfers scrapped.

Germany
A clause in German contracts stated that if the transfer system changed mid-contract the club had the right to extend the agreement by one year – now challenged and overruled. Fourth largest foreign contingent with 93 of 106 overseas players from the EU.

Austria
Domestic transfer system scrapped and no limits on non-EU players since the beginning of the 1996/97 season. Exodus of players to bigger clubs overseas.

Italy
87 foreign players in Serie A, with 44 from the EU; domestic transfer system still in place, but restrictions on non-EU players.

Portugal
Third highest number of foreign players with 24 of the 137 coming from EU countries.

Spain
Over 140 foreign players in the First Division, 33 from the EU. Number of non-EU players allowed per team limited to six, with four on the field at any one time. Very few Spanish exports.

FIGURE 8.1 European football associations after Bosman
Source: *World Soccer*, February 1997, p. 21

Individual sports

Athletes in individual sports, such as boxing, tennis, track and field athletics and golf, seldom share a common legal status with those in team sports, and seldom share one with other individual athletes. Their situation depends upon what they must do in order to train and qualify for competition in their sport. Few sports people can pay for the training needed to attain professional level skills without outside assistance. In boxing a fighter must have a recognised agent or manager. Participation in golf and tennis tournaments usually requires prior membership of a professional organisation. Track and field meetings often have an official selection committee that issues invitations to take part. In these ways the legal status of individual athletes is shaped by the particular agreement they reach with their sponsor or other persons or groups needed for participation.

In the UK the top five earners in sport from sponsorship in 1994 were all men, and were all individual athletes rather than team-game players (*Guardian*, 30 January 1995):

Golf	Nick Faldo
Auto racing	Nigel Mansell
Track and field	Linford Christie
Boxing	Frank Bruno
Boxing	Lennox Lewis

Because most people who want to work in sport do not possess the income necessary to attain the skill levels required to engage in it full time they usually have to enter into a contractual relationship which requires them to give up some control over their lives and future rewards from the sport in return for the help needed to become professional. This is another way in which *class relations* enter into the work world of sport. Athletes pass a degree of control over their lives to another person or group of persons in order to continue their sport beyond amateur performance levels.

Yet this leads, as Hargreaves (1986: 127) puts it, to the situation where most sports workers are in a *contradictory class position*:

> In common with working-class people they are employees selling their labour, experiencing insecurity and subject to the authority of employers and officials. But in terms of levels of earnings, work satisfaction, autonomy in the work task and future prospects, most are clearly closer to the middle and upper levels of society.

Another way in which top sports workers appear to join the social and economic elite is in their support of the capitalist ideal through their function as heroes and role models. The star system turned George (Best) into 'Georgie' in the 1960s, and Paul Gascoigne into 'Gazza' in the 1990s (Dunphy, 1991: 299; Hamilton, 1993) and in so doing they are made to perform:

> the role of sales staff, not only for particular products and organisations, but for a way of life as such. When stars' performances and appearances endorse products and business organisations they simultaneously endorse the system of production and consumption and the ideals associated with it.
>
> (Hargreaves, 1986: 129)

Whilst there are risks attached to the use of certain sports celebrities to endorse products, sporting performance usually outweighs any problems associated with traditional considerations of marketability. Hence manufacturers Nike have used McEnroe, Agassi, Ian Wright and Eric Cantona to sell sports shoes. Through association with such 'rebels', 'bad boys' and 'anti-heroes' the link between the company's slogan to 'Just Do It' and the footwear was actually enhanced.

Increasingly, in high-performance athletics the product is judged by the results. Writing about North America Beamish (1993: 207) suggests, however:

> High-performance sport has changed remarkably since the introduction of the modern Olympic Games. As marked as the changes have been, they have been equally uneven. Virtually every aspect of contemporary, international, high-performance sport is dominated by the ethos and practices of the bureaucratically controlled, instrumentally rational market society in which sport exists and thrives. The major exception is the relationship between high-performance athletes and sport administrators. Labor relations in high-performance sport are still dominated by the residual notion of the amateur athlete and the continued refusal of both groups to recognize that high-performance sport has become an overt employee/employer relationship. Once that emergent reality is recognized and accorded legal status, labor relations in high-performance sport will undergo revolutionary change as they are brought into the reality of the late 20th century.

Professionalisation

One development associated with these changes in high performance sport is the professionalisation – and unionisation – of sport workers. The rise of player militancy and the recognition of the need for collective organisation vis-à-vis owners and controllers has seen the growth of professional associations amongst sports workers, such as the Professional Footballers Association, the Cricketers Association, the Professional Golfers Association, the Association of Lawn Tennis Professionals, the Jockeys' Association and the International Athletes Club. The emergence of these organisations, and professionalisation in general, can be understood 'as a strategy designed, amongst other things, to limit and control the supply of entrants to an occupation in order to safeguard or enhance its market value' (Parkin, 1979: 54).

Six characteristics have been identified with an occupational claim to be a profession: a body of theoretical knowledge, education and training, examinations, code of conduct, 'service to the public', and the existence of a professional association. Yet sport workers are not professionals in the conventional sense – they exercise virtually no control over entry to their jobs, they have no monopoly over knowledge, they cannot lay down standards of work, and they cannot control the labour process. In this respect the market for sports labour remains close to the capitalist ideal of a free market, and with freedom of movement secured players' thoughts have turned to what they might achieve from collective action. As journalist David Runciman (1996) puts it:

> Free agency meant that what had once been a highly artificial market in baseball players' salaries became a truly competitive one, with the top performers able to command undreamt of sums and the journeymen pros merely unheard of ones. To meet this demand, the clubs had to find new sources of income, which they duly did, in merchandising and multi-million-dollar (and eventually multi-billion-dollar) TV deals. But far from making everyone happy, all this money made everyone extremely insecure.

Along with insecurity comes the transformation of relationships between sport workers and their employers, and sport workers and their fans. The taking of industrial action, as in Italy's Serie A in 1996 – and the threat of doing so in the English Premier League in the same year – risks destroying the credibility of the game amongst its supporters. Shortly before the England friendly against South Africa at Old Trafford in May 1997 when the South African players demanded a larger slice of the proceeds from the fixture they were accused of greed by their Football Association. It is not difficult to imagine more situations such as this developing in the future as the stakes get ever higher.

Conclusions

Jay Coakley (1994: 445) argues that:

> dominant sports in Western societies, including the United States and Canada, have traditionally been grounded in the values and experiences of

men concerned with military conquest, political control, and economic expansion. These sports fit what might be called a *Power and Performance Model* . . . some people have maintained or developed other sports grounded in values and experiences related to their connections with each other and their desire to express those connections through playful and enjoyable physical activities. These sports fit what might be called a *Pleasure and Participation Model*.

The power and performance model seems to be quite a good stereotype of elite, high performance-oriented 'business sports'. The kind of sport captured in the so-called 'jock-raker' exposés of the late 1960s and 1970s in the USA and Europe (e.g. Hoch, 1972; Meggyesy, 1971; Rigauer, 1981). As high performance sport becomes more business-oriented in the rest of the world outside of the USA and amongst its leading world-wide organisations, such as FIFA and the IOC, concern begins to grow about the impact of these developments on the integrity of high performance sportsmen and women. Inglis (1985) recounts the many scandals in the game of association football and demonstrates that these are not just recent occurences. Dunphy refers to the match fixing scandal in 1963 involving Swan, Kay and Lane (Dunphy 1991: 270-271) and the controversy over Manchester United's former manager Tommy Docherty ('the Doc') and FA Cup tickets in the 1970s (Dunphy, 1991: 375). With increasing amounts of money in the game the lifestyles of elite athletes have been subject to increasing scrutiny. Comparisons between famous football players of the 1950s and 1960s, for example Tom Finney, Stanley Matthews and Billy Wright, and those of the present, such as Paul Merson, Gazza and Bruce Grobbelaar, have been inevitable. In 1995 the *Guardian*'s (3 June 1995) account of Chelsea captain Dennis Wise's successful appeal against a prison sentence for assault and criminal damage was illustrated with two fantasy football teams: 'Guilty United and Innocent City'. In 'goal' for the latter was Bruce Grobbelaar who, with John Fashanu and Hans Segers, has since been involved in court cases over allegations of involvement in a match result-fixing syndicate.

It can be argued that the first column in Figure 8.2 reveals the attraction of top level performances to sports spectators, whereas the second expresses the virtues of participation. Although it is difficult to measure with great precision, since participation data rarely enables the distinction to be made between the dedicated and the casual participant, Ken Roberts (1989) believes that the expert and committed minorities in most sport and leisure activities are growing in size. Sales of specialist magazines have risen and membership of leisure-based voluntary associations has been growing (Bishop and Hoggett, 1986). Among the mass of sports participants there remain dedicated minorities who, with great commitment, set about developing their skills and personal bests (PBs)

through routine training and preparation. Serious leisure appears capable of providing some of the social psychological functions of full-time employment –
structuring time, providing interest and social relationships, bestowing social
status and personal identity. But for most of us, most of the time, the central

Power and Performance Model	*Pleasure and Participation Model*
Strength, speed, power	Personal expression, enjoyment, growth, good health
Aggression	
Domination of opponents	Mutual concern and support for team mates and opponents
Victory and winning	Empowerment
Excellence equals competitive success	The body is to be experienced and cultivated, not treated as a machine to be repaired when broken
Success is achieved through dedication, hard work, making sacrifices and risking personal well-being	Inclusiveness
Emphasises setting records, pushing human limits, using the body as a machine, using technology to supplement the body	Playing not winning is the important thing
The body is to be trained, controlled, monitored	Differences in physical skill are incorporated informally or formally through handicapping systems – competition can take place between players with different skills
Sports are exclusive – for those with the requisite physical skills and abilities	Sports organisations are democratic decision-making structures, co-operative, power sharing
Sport organisations and teams are hierarchical authority structures, athletes are subordinate to coaches and coaches are subordinate to owners and administrators	Players and coaches enjoy a give-and-take relationship
Coaches can humiliate, shame and derogate athletes to push them	Sponsorship is motivated by the idea that participation is socially useful – not by the achievement of performance excellence
Sponsorship of sports is associated with the pursuit of winning – either to make money or to establish a favourable public relations profile	

FIGURE 8.2 Models of sport
Source: adapted from Coakley, 1994: 445–447

place of sport in contemporary popular culture – and mainly gained through domestic consumption – 'is as a marketed product and media discourse' (Philips and Tomlinson, 1993: 25). The following chapter looks at developments in the commercialisation of sport, to help understand these transformations more clearly.

ESSAYS AND EXERCISES

Essays

How are bureaucratic characteristics manifested in sports clubs and organisations?

To what extent are professional sportsmen and sportswomen members of the working class?

Outline and analyse the occupational culture of any one professional sport using different theoretical perspectives on sport as work discussed in this chapter.

Exercises

Re-read the passage outlining Tom Landry's management style (pp. 243–244). What do you think it would be like to work in the Cowboys' organisation? Do you think Landry's management style would be effective? What alternative management approaches are used in sport?

Prepare a five-minute debating speech on the following motion, either for or against it: 'This House believes that whether a football team remains in the Premier League or not now depends more on the club's bank balance than the club's team balance.'

Outline the division of labour in a non-professional sports club or society that you are familiar with. Compare this with the division of labour in a professional sports club. What functions do the officials serve? Who is responsible for upholding the rules and/or punishing offenders? Is anyone in the organisation irreplaceable? Where does the power lie?

FURTHER READING

John Hargreaves, *Sport, Power and Culture – A Social and Historical Analysis of Popular Sports in Britain*, Cambridge, Polity Press, 1986, considers 'The Social Position of Sports Workers' in a subsection of Chapter 6.

Gary Nelson, *Left Foot Forward*, London, Robson Books, 1997, offers a telling account of a journeyman's experiences in the lower echelons of professional football.

References

Bale, J. and Maguire, J. (eds) (1994) *The Global Sports Arena: Athletic Talent Migration in an Interdependent World*, London: Frank Cass.

Beamish, R. (1988) 'The Political Economy of Professional Sport' in J. Harvey and H. Cantelon (eds), *Not Just a Game – Essays in Canadian Sport Sociology*, Ottawa: Ottawa University Press.

Beamish, R. (1993) 'Labor Relations in Sport: Central Issues in their Emergence and Structure in High-performance Sport', in A. Ingham and J. Loy (eds), *Sport in Social Development*, Champaign, Illinois: Human Kinetics.

Beynon, H. (1973) *Working for Ford*, Harmondsworth: Penguin Books.

Birrell, S. and Richter, D. (1987) 'Is a Diamond Forever? Feminist Transformations of Sport', *Women's Studies International Forum*, Volume 10, pp. 395-409.

Bishop, J. and Hoggett, P. (1986) *Organising Around Enthusiasms: Mutual Aid in Leisure*, London: Comedia/Routledge.

Braverman, H. (1974) *Labor and Monopoly Capital – The Degradation of Work in the Twentieth Century*, New York: Monthly Review Press.

Brohm, J.-M. (1978) *Sport – A Prison of Measured Time*, London: Ink Links.

Brookes, C. (1978) *English Cricket – The Game and its Players Through the Ages*, London: Weidenfeld and Nicolson.

Burn, G. (1987) *Pocket Money: Bad-boys, Business Heads and Boom-time Snooker*, London: Pan Books.

Cashmore, E. (1982) *Black Sportsmen*, London: Routledge & Kegan Paul.

Cashmore, E. (1996) *Making Sense of Sport*, 2nd edition, London: Routledge.

Central Office of Information (1994) *Sport in Britain*, London: Her Majesty's Stationery Office.

Coakley, J. (1994) *Sport in Society: Issues and Controversies*, St Louis, Illinois: Mosby.

Corry, D. and Williamson, P. with S. Moore (1993) *A Game Without Vision: The Crisis in English Football*, London: Institute for Public Policy Research.

Critcher, C. (1979) 'Football since the War', in J. Clarke, C. Critcher and R. Johnson (eds), *Working Class Culture: Studies in History and Theory*, London: Hutchinson, pp. 161–184.

Davies, H. (1985) *The Glory Game*, Edinburgh: Mainstream Publishers.

Dixon, K. (1985) *Kerry – The Autobiography*, London: Macdonald/Queen Anne Press.

Dunning, E. and Sheard, K. (1979) *Barbarians, Gentlemen and Players: A Sociological Study of the Development of Rugby Football*, New York: New York University Press.

Dunphy, E. (1991) *A Strange Kind of Glory – Sir Matt Busby and Manchester United*, London: Heinemann.

Fleming, S. (1995) *'Home and Away': Sport and South Asian Male Youth*, Aldershot: Avebury.

Forbes (1997) Volume 158, no. 14, December.

Fyfe, L. (1992) *Careers in Sport*, London: Kogan Page.

Gilroy, S. (1997) 'Working on the Body: Links between Physical Activity and Social Power', in G. Clarke and B. Humberstone (eds), *Researching Women and Sport*, Basingstoke: Macmillan.

Guardian, 13 February 1981; 3 November 1990; 30 January 1995; 7 March 1995; 9 June 1995; 9 May 1996.

Gurney, C. (1997) *'Football(er)s coming Home*: A Case Study of Housing Histories, Labour Market Histories and Propinquital Relationships of Male Professional Footballers', unpublished paper, presented at the British Sociological Association Annual Conference, University of York, April.

Guttmann, A. (1978) *From Ritual to Record – The Nature of Modern Sports*, New York: Columbia University Press.

Hamilton, I. (1993) 'Gazza Agonistes', *Granta No. 45*, London: Penguin Books, pp. 9-125.

Hargreaves, Jennifer (1994) *Sporting Females: Critical Issues in the History and Sociology of Women's Sports*, London: Routledge.

Hargreaves, John (1986) *Sport, Power and Culture – A Social and Historical Analysis of Popular Sports in Britain*, Cambridge: Polity Press.

Harris, O. and Hunt, L. (1984) 'Race and Sports Involvement: Some Implications of Sports for Black and White Youth', paper presented at the AAHPERD Conference, Anaheim, CA, cited in Coakley, 1994.

Hellriegel, D. and Slocum, J. (1983) *Organizational Behaviour*, 3rd edition, New York: West Publishing.

Hoberman, J. (1992) *Mortal Engines: The Science of Performance and the Dehumanisation of Sports*, New York: The Free Press.

Hoch, P. (1972) *Rip Off the Big Game – The Exploitation of Sports by the Power Elite*, New York: Doubleday Anchor.

Inglis, S. (1985) *Soccer in the Dock*, London: Willow Books.

Jary, D, and Jary, J. (eds) (1991) *Collins Dictionary of Sociology*, Glasgow: Harper Collins.

Kuper, S. (1994) *Football Against the Enemy*, London: Orion Books.

Labour Research (1983) 'Footballers' Lives and Attitudes', Volume 72, September, pp. 238–242.

Lenskyj, H. (1986) *Out of Bounds: Women, Sport and Sexuality*, Toronto: The Women's Press.

Manchester United (1996) Annual Report and Accounts 1996.

Meggyesy, D. (1971) *Out of their League*, New York: Coronet Paperback Library.

Miller Lite (1983) *The Miller Lite Report on American Attitudes Toward Sports*, Milwaukee: Miller Brewing Co.

Parkin, F. (1979) *Marxism and Class Analysis: A Bourgeois Critique*, London: Tavistock.

Parry, J. and Parry, N. (1991) 'Sport and the Black Experience' in G. Jarvie (ed.), *Sport, Racism and Ethnicity*, London: The Falmer Press.

Philips, D. and Tomlinson, A. (1993) 'Homeward Bound: Leisure, Popular Culture and

Consumer Capitalism', in D. Strinati and S. Wagg (eds), *Come on Down?: Popular Media Culture in Post-war Britain*, London: Routledge.

Polsky, N. (1985) *Hustlers, Beats and Others*, New York: Doubleday Anchor.

Rigauer, B. (1981) (1969) *Sport and Work*, New York: Columbia University Press.

Ritzer, G. (1993) *The McDonaldization of Society*, London: Sage.

Roberts, K. (1989) 'Great Britain: Socioeconomic Polarisation and the Implications for Leisure', in A. Olszewska and K. Roberts (eds), *Leisure and Life-style: A Comparative Analysis of Free-time*, London: Sage.

Roy, D. (1973) (1960) 'Banana Time: Job Satisfaction and Informal Interaction' in G. Salaman and K. Thompson (eds), *People and Organisations*, London: Longman.

Runciman, D. (1996) 'Striker Force', *Guardian*, 20 August.

Stone, G. (1970) 'American Sports: Play and Display' in E. Dunning (ed.), *The Sociology of Sport*, London: Frank Cass.

Terkel, S. (1977) *Working*, Harmondsworth: Penguin Books.

Theberge, N. and Birrell, S. (1994) 'Structural Constraints Facing Women and Sport', in D. Margaret Costa and S. R. Guthrie (eds.), *Women and Sport: Interdisciplinary Perspectives*, Champaign, Illinois: Human Kinetics.

Tomlinson, A. (1983) 'Tuck up Tight Lads: Structures of Control Within Football Culture', in A. Tomlinson (ed.), *Explorations in Football Culture*, University of Brighton, Eastbourne: Leisure Studies Association (Publication No. 21).

Wagg, S. (1984) *The Football World: A Contemporary Social History*, Brighton: Harvester.

West, A. and Brackenridge, C. (1990) *A Report on the Issues Relating to Women's Lives as Sports Coaches in the United Kingdom* – 1989/90, Sheffield City Polytechnic: PAVIC Publications.

World Soccer, February 1997.

Chapter nine

Commercialisation and the political economy of sport

As a social practice, sport occupies a contradictory position. On the one hand, it is associated with spare time, leisure, exercise and doing things for fun. On the other, it has become a multi-million dollar industry, with huge rewards for top performers, and a branch of both the entertainment and leisure industries. Clearly sport is part of the economic system and a potential means of generating profit. Yet so many of its key institutions, still marked by the formation of modern sport in the nineteenth century, are not simple examples of capitalist entrepreneurship. One striking feature of much sport is precisely the way that it is not organised as a business. Even the most potentially profitable English sport, football, has been, until very recently, largely owned and run by people who do not necessarily have profit as their main motive.[1] Sport does, however, provide means by which significant profits can be generated in peripheral activities (sport agencies, the clothing industry, etc.) and clearly aids the process of profit generation (advertising and sponsorship). One common means of making sense of this is to distinguish between state, commercial and voluntary sectors of sports provision. While this can be of analytic value, it has to be remembered that in most lived sports practices there is a complex combination of all three.

This chapter contains an account of the economic development of sport and its transformation since the 1960s, a review of analytic perspectives upon this development, and an analysis of economic processes and relations in sport.

The economic development of sport in Britain

Before the 1860s sporting practices could not be said to have involved the systematic and regularised institutionalising of economic relations. Certainly there were plenty of instances of the exchange of money. Working-class cricketers were rewarded for their performance by country squires, boxers, pedestrian runners and jockeys could gain from their excellence, and substantial sums changed hands in gambling. The aristocracy and the squirearchy played a significant role as patrons (Malcolmson, 1973). Cricket, golf and horse-racing all developed institutional bodies, aristocratic in form and style, that were formed in the eighteenth century and functioned as *de facto* governing bodies (the Marylebone Cricket Club, the Jockey Club and the Royal and Ancient Club of St Andrews – see Cousins, 1975; Brookes, 1978; Mortimer, 1958). However, the public performance of sport did not typically involve the regular and routinised exchange of money.

From the 1840s, as Chapter 1 has demonstrated, the new public schools became the seed bed of a cult of athleticism. Traditional team games were appropriated, transformed and codified, and an ideology of fair play developed (Mangan, 1981; Dunning, 1971; McIntosh, 1979). Yet there was still no organised form of professionalised sport that we would recognise as such.

1860–1890

From the 1860s a complex process of transformation began, which saw the emergence of nationally agreed rules, governing bodies, competitions and trophies, spectator sport, professional sport and the amateur/professional distinction. The growth of rail travel and inter-school competition required nationally agreed rules and governing bodies. The amateur/professional distinction emerged from the need of the middle class to mark social distinctions, and the working class became marginalised from sport organisation (Whannel, 1983; Mason, 1988). This transformation took place under very particular conditions, which ensured that during the period when everyday leisure cultures of the subordinate classes were being undermined by industrialisation, the men from upper and middles classes were able to establish the distinctive institutional forms of modern sport.

By 1860 the old rural traditions of sporting events at local fairs and festivals, sustained by squirearchical patronage, had been in decline for several decades. The enclosure of common land and other agricultural change, industrialisation and rural de-population, and a retreat into insularity amongst the rural gentry all played a part in this decline (Malcolmson, 1973). Living conditions in the new industrial towns left little space, time or resources for informal leisure cultures to flourish, although the very existence of such cultures was a tribute to the resilience of subordinate classes in the teeth of brutal exploitation. The long working week, lack of public open space, Sabbatarianism preserving Sunday as the Lord's Day, and the clamp-down on cruel sports during the first half of the nineteenth century constituted major limitations on the leisure of popular classes (Cunningham, 1980; Bailey, 1978; Holt, 1989). From the 1860s a whole series of governing bodies came into being, consolidating the power of the male Victorian middle class to define the shape that sport was taking (Figure 9.1).

New competitions such as the Open Golf Championship (1860) were established. Cricket's County Championship was started in 1873 as a compromise between the country house game, dominated by the socially exclusive rural gentry, and the professional touring teams seen as too vulgar and commercial (Brookes, 1978). The Football Association established its Challenge Cup in 1871. Boxing's Queensberry Rules were established in 1867 (Brailsford, 1989; Butler, 1972; Carpenter, 1982) and the first Wimbledon championship was in 1877 (Robertson, 1977; Brady, 1959).

The growth of working-class sport, and resultant pressure for broken time payments put pressure on the ethos of amateurism. The Football Association compromised to retain control, allowing the establishment of a professional Football League in 1888; whilst in refusing any compromise, the Rugby authorities precipitated a split, the northern clubs breaking away to form Rugby League in 1895 (Dunning and Sheard, 1976). Other sports like tennis and athletics were successful in outlawing and marginalising professionalism. The last decades of the nineteenth century saw the emergence and development of regular entry-fee paying spectator sport, and in effect the commencement of commercialisation in the modern sense.

Football	1863
Swimming	1869
Rugby	1871
Cycling	1878
Rowing	1879
Skating	1879
Athletics	1880
Boxing	1881
Hockey	1886
Tennis	1886
Skiing	1903

FIGURE 9.1 Formation of national governing bodies of British sport

1890–1914

Between 1890 and 1914 a number of developments contributed to a growing commercialisation of society and a more sophisticated commodification of cultural forms was underway. Spectator sport was becoming established as a significant element in the national culture (Dobbs, 1973).

There was a considerable consolidation and development of retailing, with the establishment of department stores and chain stores. The launch of the *Daily Mail* in 1896 ushered in the era of the mass circulation popular press. Advertising grew rapidly. In sport, there was substantial investment in the construction of sports stadia (Inglis, 1983), the sporting press emerged and thrived (Mason, 1993), and sporting goods and equipment businesses began to develop. International governing bodies (IOC, FIFA, IAAF, ILTF, etc.) were established and the number of regular international competitions grew. A sport star system began to become more central, with W.G. Grace, in his later years, one of the biggest figures, in every sense. Regardless of the amateur code, sport at its elite level was already taking on some of the characteristics of business. It had an income, and an eye to the balance sheet. Most sport organisations were decisively not businesses in form, structure or aspiration. However, around the cultural activity of sport, a wide variety of entrepreneurial activities were beginning to develop.

1918–1939

The inter-war era saw a continuation of this commercialisation process, with significant developments associated with the growth of the cinema and the emergence of the new mass media, radio and television (Scannell and Cardiff, 1991; Richards, 1984). Clarke and Critcher, in *The Devil Makes Work* (1985), argue that in this period leisure was moving from a peripheral to a central place in the economy, but leisure experiences were sharply divided by access to the leisure market and not all people could participate as equal consumers. Nevertheless, the development of the cinema, spread of motor cars, emergence of broadcasting and growth of gambling all played a role in the growing commercialisation of sport.

The inter-war period was an era of economic upheaval, substantial unemployment, a growing gap between rich and poor, and significant recomposition in class structure. The 1920s saw the start of a real decline in manual labour, especially in the south, and the growth of the professions, civil service and middle management. The salaried class had already grown from 12 per cent to 22 per cent between 1911 and 1921 (Jones, 1986). The Wall Street Crash of 1929 triggered a world-wide recession. Britain, already losing its share of world trade throughout the 1920s, was hit especially hard by the drop in world prices and trading volumes, and by the cessation of American aid. Economic crisis led to political crisis in 1931, with the formation of a National Government, with both Labour and Liberal parties split over the issue. Unemployment, which was above 1 million throughout the 1920s, peaked at 3.75 million in 1932 and stayed above 2 million till the mid-1930s. The cultures of consumption that developed in the inter-war period were structured by these profound divisions between rich and poor. In particular, cinema became the major form of leisure for the working class in general, and football became the major leisure form for working-class men.

The characteristic imagery of the period features hunger marches and industrial graveyards. But, despite the economic recession, real value of average wage rose steadily throughout the inter-war years, partly because of decline in cost of living, so those in work had a sense of growing affluence. There were dramatic regional differences with unemployment in parts of the north over 20 per cent compared with around 6 per cent in the south-east. When the economic recovery began in the mid-1930s the new technologies of leisure, radio and the car played a significant role (Jones, 1986). The 'frontiers of exclusivity' broadened a little with the expansion of the consumer-conscious suburbs (Howkins and Lowerson, 1995).

The major elements of leisure cultures were dance halls, cinema, radio, spectator sport, greyhound racing and the pools, hiking, rambling and cycling, and the growth of excursions and holidays (Tomlinson and Walker, 1990). The rise of the *nouveau riche*, young financially secure and mobile young people, after the First World War helped fuel a growth in the culture of cabarets, night clubs and cocktail bars, whilst at the cheaper popular end, dance halls flourished. Between 1918 and 1924 11,000 dance halls and night clubs opened (Jones, 1986).

By 1919 half the population was already in the habit of weekly cinema visits. Between 1924 and 1931 1,000 cinemas were built and another 300 between 1932 and 1934, and annual admissions grew from 364 million in 1914 to 1,027 million in 1940 (Walvin, 1978). There was a substantial increase in investment in cinemas, and a concentration of cinema ownership into three giant circuits, Gaumont British, ABC and Odeon. Cinema was a major form of working-class entertainment for both sexes and its cheapness enabled it to thrive amidst poverty. Newsreels were a regular feature and so for the mass audience cinema was the first time that they were able to see major sporting events in moving pictures as opposed to newspaper and magazine stills. The spectacle of media sport was itself integral to media experimentation and expansion.

The first regular radio broadcasts started in 1922, when six radio and electrical companies combined to form the British Broadcasting Company and the Post Office gave them an exclusive licence to broadcast. The vested interests of newspapers prevented the new company covering sport until 1927 when on the recommendation of the *Crawford Report* (1925) it was decided that broadcasting should be conducted by a public corporation, after the fashion of the Forestry Commission or the Port of London Authority.

The shape of public service broadcasting was massively shaped by the first Director General, John Reith, who insisted that it should be a non-commercial, national monopoly with high standards. Reith's own combination of middle-class ethics, a rather severe Christianity and a patrician attitude to culture was a major influence. In the words of Scannell and Cardiff (1991), Reith installed not simply a business monopoly, but a cultural dictatorship, with the BBC as arbiter of tastes and definer of standards. As the first major domestic medium, radio brought live sport into the home and enabled the establishment of new shared national rituals, such as the Christmas Message, Cup Final Day, the Boat Race and Last Night of the Proms. The percentage of households with radio rose from 10 per cent in 1924 to 71 per cent in 1938.

Car ownership grew from 500,000 in 1920 to 3 million in 1940, helping to trigger the ribbon development of suburbs along major roads, the emergence of motor sports and the beginning of traffic congestion. It was the era of charabanc trips and other day trips – 7 million annually went to Blackpool alone. Rail travel grew threefold during the 1930s. But as well as day trips, people increasingly expected to have holidays. By the late 1930s some 15 million people had at least one week away from home. The 1938 Holidays with Pay Act instituted a statutory right to holidays and the first Butlin's Holiday Camps were opened (Walvin, 1978). Leisure was acquiring a more significant place in the life of the nation.

Gambling grew rapidly, fuelled by the introduction of greyhound racing in the late 1920s and football pools at the start of the 1930s. The introduction of greyhound racing was a great popular success. Sixty-two companies were set up in 1927 alone and the following year a governing body, the National Greyhound Racing Association, was established. By 1931 there were around 18 million admissions. The launch of football pools was an even bigger success with around 6 million punters by the mid-1930s. Illegal off-course betting may have had a turnover of as much as £400 million annually in the inter-war period.

For sport it was a time of expansion. New sports like greyhound racing and motor sport emerged and women's sport began to acquire its first proper organisational forms, such as the establishment of the Women's Amateur Athletic Association in 1922. The Football League founded a Third Division in 1921, and this Division became regional with north and south sections the next year. Wembley stadium opened in 1923. Average First Division crowds, which had been around 16,000 before the First World War, had risen to over 30,000 by 1938.

Sport became more commercialised in the period. There was a growth in spectatorship, investment in stadia, the launch of new sports, and with cinema newsreels and radio broadcasting, the emergence of media sport coverage as a significant factor. However, compared to other cultural leisure forms like cinema, sport was still comparatively uncommercialised and indeed its distinctive institutions often exhibited a striking resistance to commerce. They functioned as organisational bureaucracies, with a redistributive function, but had less entrepreneurial dynamism than many other elements of the leisure industry.

1945–1962

At the end of the war the troops were gradually demobilised and there was a period of enormous appetite for public entertainment. Cinemas, dance halls, public houses and sporting attendances all peaked in this period, with abnormally high crowds. However, the post-war boom was soon replaced by the 1950s slump. All the old communal public forms of entertainment – pubs, cinemas, dance halls and sporting venues – suffered from competition from the growth of television and other forms of domestic entertainment (hi-fi record players etc.) and activity (DIY etc.). The increase in car ownership, while enabling greater mobility, seems to have largely benefited other activities – day trips to the countryside, seaside or relatives – rather than sport.

Three processes were striking: a growing affluence, the rise of private, familial and domestic spheres as sites of consumption, and the break up of traditional working-class communities. Consumer durables (irons, vacuum cleaners, washing machines, fridges, televisions, cars) spread to more sectors of society. The old communal public forms of leisure (pubs, dance halls, cinema and football) all began to decline in popularity. Private leisure activities – watching television, listening to records – grew.

The traditional working-class community, characterised by extended kinship networks, mutual interdependence and a local economy, was disrupted by the development of new estates, high rises and slum clearance, which destroyed the integrative function of the street (Cohen, 1972).

Ironically, in the very period when television was growing to the point that it could become the economic saviour of major sports, it was seen largely as a threat and a nuisance. There was a continued resistance of sport to entrepreneurship. In many sports there was a slump in attendances throughout the 1950s and early 1960s (e.g. football, cricket, athletics, rugby, horseracing). Voluntary administration was typically inefficient, untrained and non-entrepreneurial. Within the context of the affluent society and the emerging strength of the leisure industry, sport remained comparatively isolated. Yet sport had its well-established calendar of major events, and its stars, who in this period were often still in the noble amateur tradition – Roger Bannister,

Edward Hilary – or alternatively were humble, modest chaps like Stanley Matthews.

There was, however, the beginning of an increase in the tempo of commercialisation, which was most visible in football. Charles Critcher argues that a transformative trend commenced in the 1950s, at least in football, in which the major factors were the growth of professionalisation, spectacularisation, internationalisation and commercialisation (Critcher, 1979). It was a trend that was to become bigger and more dramatic during the next two decades.

Transformation: 1962–present

Critcher is plainly correct about the developments that he sketches. However, the processes of commercialisation that begin to develop in the 1950s in my view reach a crucial watershed in the early 1960s. The impact of the technological improvements in television, the addition of a second BBC channel, BBC2, in 1964, and the banning of television cigarette advertising in 1965 combined to trigger a revolution in which sponsorship revenue became crucial, and television coverage became a prerequisite for obtaining such sponsorship (Whannel, 1986).

Briefly, it has been argued that the transformation of sport by television and sponsorship between 1965 and 1985 was as dramatic as that earlier transformative period between 1860 and 1900. Television at the start of the 1960s provided a grainy black and white image. By 1985 we had come to take for granted the provision of high quality live colour pictures relayed around the world by satellite, augmented by slow motion action replay. Sponsorship had become a major source of revenue for the elite level of sport. Sports agents had become rich and powerful by intervening to manage relations between stars, managers, governing bodies, promoters, television executives and sponsoring companies.

In the television era, sport had become an international spectacle, producing vast earnings for elite performers and strengthening the power of sports agents, and in the process traditional authority had been undermined (Gruneau, 1997). Amateurism was heading for terminal decline, as the brakes came off commercialisation. Made for television and tailored for television events proliferated, the sports shoe, clothing and equipment businesses mushroomed. The 1968 Copyright Act enabled the patenting of distinctive shirt designs and triggered the extraordinary growth of the replica clothing business (Chaplin, 1991).

Sewart (1987) said that in being subsumed to the needs of capital, sport was being standardised and commodified. Goldlust (1987) argued that from the 1960s onwards, television increasingly colonised sporting cultures and undermined communal control of sporting institutions. Lawrence and Rowe (1987) argued that television cricket promoted capitalist ideology by legitimising capitalist social relations of production; socialising viewers to accept the values of capitalism; limiting the acceptance of what is fair, normal and desirable; promoting the myth of upward mobility; and diverting people's attention from the problems of life under capitalism.

It was not the governing bodies of sport who were the main force in commercialisation. Much of the impetus for the transformation of sport came from opportunist and maverick entrepreneurs who established themselves as sports agents, and who constituted the mediation point between sport organisations, sport stars, television, sponsors and advertisers (see Wilson, 1988; Stoddart, 1990; and Aris, 1990). Jack Kramer, Kerry Packer, Mark McCormack, Horst Dassler of Adidas and Rupert Murdoch of News Corporation are key figures in this process. Kramer's professional tennis circuit sowed the seeds of professionalisation in tennis. McCormack's skilful handling of the earning power of the three top golfers of the 1960s and 1970s, Arnold Palmer, Jack Nicklaus and Gary Player, provided the foundation of his business empire, International Management Group, with its television subsidiary TWI. Packer had the economic power to challenge the previously cosy relationship between cricket and television, and his own World Series Cricket ushered in floodlit cricket, coloured clothing, hard-sell advertising, more cameras, more close ups and more replays (see Bonney, 1980; Haigh 1993). Dassler taught the leading world governing bodies, like FIFA and the IOC, how to exploit television advertising and sponsorship, through his company ISL. Murdoch's Sky Television has been the driving force behind the transformation of football in England.

The commodification process seeks to maximise sponsorship, advertising and merchandising revenue. Snooker capitalised on its television success during the 1980s with new tournaments, new sponsors and expansion into new markets (see Burn, 1986). Television was the shop window that allowed for the promotion of sporting spectacles like American football to new markets (see Maguire, 1990c). The global reach of television and the economic power of the USA encouraged an Americanisation of the form, content and styles of sport television around the world (McKay and Miller, 1991). However, the process of bringing together an audience for new, imported or Americanised sporting spectacle was complex . Long-established sporting cultures are embedded in lived experiences with their own histories, rooted in national cultures. Transplanting cultural experiences is a problematic and uneven process, as the short history of professional basketball in Britain suggests (see Maguire, 1988a).

Sport organisations could often be slow to respond to the process of commercialisation. A Sports Council report on sponsorship expressed concern at the power of sports agents, whilst being somewhat cautious about the revenue potential for sport that sponsorship offered (Howell, 1983). Another Sports

Council report on the impact of cable and satellite showed British sport relatively unprepared for the revolution to come (Jones, 1985). Satellite sport in the United Kingdom grew slowly at first, hampered by slow dish sales and competition between two providers, BSB and Sky (see Chippendale and Franks, 1991). However, once Sky Television, into which BSB was 'merged', had the field to itself, the rapidly growing revenue from the pay-per-channel services began to give satellite television enhanced scope to obtain the rights to major events. Barnett (1990) has drawn attention to the rising power of satellite television, and to the shift from broadcasting as a public service towards broadcasting as a commodity to be chosen and purchased. The launch of digital television and growth of pay-per-view transmission of major football matches and other big events is about to provide a significant new impetus to the commodification of sport.

Perspectives on the economic development of sport

There is a substantial degree of agreement that commercialisation is a striking feature of modern sport, and broad agreement as to the main features of the subsequent transformations of sport, which have been well documented (Aris, 1990; Barnett, 1990; Hofmann and Greenberg, 1989; Wilson, 1988) There are various interpretations that can be offered, from the perspectives of modernisation, conservatism, functionalism and Marxism. Guttmann's Weberian argument in *From Ritual to Record*, about the nature of modern sport, stresses the role of specialisation, rationalisation, quantification and the quest for records. The implication of this argument is that commercialisation of sport is a logical outcome of the development of a modernised rationalised society (Guttmann, 1978).

A functionalist variant of this argument would stress the functionality of the commercialisation of sport in boosting facilities, providing a means of entertainment and integration, a model of reward for achievement and a system of incentives (Coakley, 1978; Gratton and Taylor, 1986, 1987, 1991). Certain features of modern sport, such as drug taking, violence, and excessive competitiveness, might be seen as disfunctional. Within this framework debates can be had about the rational allocation of resources or means of regulating market forces (Coalter, 1993; Lamb *et al.*, 1992).

In opposition to both the 'inevitability of modernisation' and functional pragmatism, a conservative perspective contrasts the 'corruption' of modern sport with the supposed greater purity of sport and its more Corinthian and amateur ideals. This form of cultural conservatism usually involves establishing a contrast between a generalised decline of the present and a superior past (see

Allison, 1986, 1993; Lasch, 1980). Indeed, this tradition of anti-commercialism, etched deeply into English cultural debate, is a significant influence on contributions to public debate from both right and left. In January 1995, Labour leader Tony Blair attacked the growing commercialisation of football, citing high transfer fees and wages, their effect on seat prices, and falling standards of behaviour both on and off the pitch. While Blair denied that he was calling for a return to Corinthian idealism, he did refer to the erosion of values embodied by the Stanley Matthews era. Critiques of commercialism are often articulated, consciously or unconsciously in golden age nostalgia (*Guardian*, 16/1/95).

From a Marxist perspective the commercialisation of sport provides another rich example of the tendency of capital to seek out and penetrate new areas of society in which profits can be generated. One can distinguish between some early Marxist inspired critiques which were interesting and provocative, whilst also being somewhat one-dimensional and prone to a crude reductionism (Brohm, 1978; Hoch, 1972; Vinnai, 1976) and the greater sophistication of some more recent accounts (Gruneau, 1979, 1983; Hargreaves, 1986).

Jean-Marie Brohm (1978) argues that modern international sport is an imperialist phenomenon, an assertion that patently has a degree of truth. Brohm argues that sport is directly linked to the interests of imperialist capital. He cites the links between early Olympic Games and trade fairs, and suggests that sport, as an activity characteristic of bourgeois industrial society, is an exact reflection of capitalist categories. One problem with this argument is that from the 1950s sport in communist societies increasingly took a similar form. Brohm says this is because such societies were not genuinely communist but rather state capitalist, but this is an over-simple explanation for a complex phenomenon in which sport developed a globalised character.

Brohm rightly draws attention to the ways in which sport is governed by the principles of competition, and record, and by the precise measurement of space, time and output. For Brohm, sport is the rational organisation of human output, and in a most useful formulation he calls sport the Taylorisation of the body;[2] in other words the scientific means for producing maximum output from the human body. This gives him a means of applying the principle of labour power and surplus value to athletic performance.

While there is much of value in this analysis, it is worthwhile remembering that until recent decades the institutions of sport had a striking resistance to penetration by capital, and that the forces of tradition remain a strong force within sporting institutions. More recent analysis has been marked by a greater degree of sophistication and sensitivity to the complexities and contradictions immanent in the complex economic processes underlying lived cultural practices.

In *Sport, Power and Culture*, John Hargreaves (1986) sketches five different forms that the relation between sport and capital can assume within commercialisation. The first is profit maximising, with examples being professional boxing and horse-racing. However, as Hargreaves points out, many sports have no real aspirations to make profits and simply hope to break even. Thus the second form of relationship is the attempt to remain financially viable through various survival strategies such as fund raising. The third form of relationship sees sport stimulating the accumulation of capital indirectly, providing a market for goods and services. So sport helps to produce the sports equipment, clothing and gambling industries. In the fourth relationship, sport aids capital accumulation indirectly, by offering opportunities for advertising and sponsorship. Finally, sport attracts a degree of investment for non-economic reasons. Directors of football clubs are often motivated by prestige, desire to have local influence or to use the club for corporate entertaining. Of course, economic and non-economic motives often overlap and in practice several of these relationships can be at work simultaneously.

Hargreaves (1986) argues that during the transition to and early phase of industrial capitalism rational recreation was resisted by elements of the working class. A tension developed, with links between the religious and radical respectable working class and the dominant class element supporting reform and rational recreation on the one hand, and links between the disreputable working class and dominant class elements defending popular culture and traditions on the other.

The successful achievement of bourgeois hegemony in the mid-Victorian era helped produce the ideology of the gentleman amateur, whose institutional networks aided a male ruling class unity. The growth of spectator sport and a demand for sport as entertainment, fuelled by the greater disposable income and free time workers had in the latter part of the century, provided an impetus for the development of professionalism, and a threat to the amateur-gentleman hegemony. Gentlemanly amateurism saved itself by conceding fresh ground, restricting the effects of commercialism and retaining control.

Hargreaves sums up the process whereby through commercialism sport has become a central component of national culture in the following terms:

- Without the cult of athleticism there would be no organised sports.
- Without rational recreation and athletic missionising, organised sport would not have penetrated and become a part of working-class culture.
- Without the popularity of sport among sub-groups, and their move into some amateur-gentleman controlled sports, the commercial development of sport could not have happened.
- Without mass sport, the political elite would have not had this field for articulating the national interest.

Economic relations

While there has been a fairly extensive debate about the nature of commercialisation in sport, it has tended to focus on the issue of commodification of elite sport. A full and comprehensive political economy of sport has yet to be elaborated. Such analysis would need to attend to a range of aspects of the economic process – the question of ownership and control, the nature of economic relations within the sports business, the process of production and relations of production, sports labour power and the production of surplus value. We need to clarify what in modern sport constitutes the product, who are the workers, who the owners, who are the customers, what precisely are the relations between them, and what is the nature of sport consumption. In the following section we map out some of the key questions, concerning ownership and control, the process of production, labour relations, and commodity exchange.

Ownership and control

What is the 'sports business'? Clearly this term now denotes a wide range of economic activities and institutions, many of them only connected by sets of economic relations. Television companies, sponsors, agents, promoters, governing bodies and performers are all part of the sports business but occupy distinctly different places within it. Who owns it, who controls it, and what distinctions can be made between owners and controllers? How much consolidation, vertical integration, horizontal integration has there been? How much diversification?

The label 'sport' covers complex sets of cultural practices and institutions, and the ownership of sport is therefore no simple question. The infrastructure of sport – tracks, courses, pitches, pools and stadia – has the character of a mixed economy. Public ownership, predominantly at local level, and private ownership are both common. The competitions and organisational forms of sport could be said to be the 'property' of the various governing bodies, but only by virtue of authority vested in them by their constituent members. Individual performers are, in some sports, the property of their clubs, in others the property of managers, and in still others they are free agents. The so-called 'Bosman' ruling, by the European Union, has set a precedent that prevents clubs retaining players who wish to move. In many cases, but not all, clubs also own their venue. To take one example to illustrate the complexities – Chelsea FC is owned by its directors and shareholders, but the stadium is owned by Chelsea Village. There are overlapping shareholdings but the two are legally distinct entities. The Premier League is owned by the Premier League, and the FA Cup by the Football Association. The players could be said to be owned by Chelsea, but only for as long as their contracts run.

As in other forms of business, ownership and control are not the same. Owners do not necessarily exert sole control and enterprises can be, in part, controlled by those who have no share in ownership.

Governing bodies notionally control their sports, but such control can only be exerted if it reflects the wishes of their constituent parts, or members. The interests of such members can diverge and, where possible, governing bodies have to engineer compromise. On occasion this is impossible. Smaller football clubs have an interest in the continued redistribution of television revenue, the major clubs would prefer to retain it for themselves. It was the inability of the Football League to produce a compromise formula that led to the break-away Premier League. Television, advertisers and sponsors all exert powerful influences on the ways in which sports are controlled. Horse-racing provides an example of the complexities. Racecourses have a variety of owners, most of whom are limited companies. Horses are predominantly in the hands of affluent individuals. They are looked after by training establishments, also private businesses. Television companies and the betting industry exert a significant influence on the organisation of racing, without having any ownership stake in it. Not surprisingly then, tensions between those who notionally own sport and those who seek to control it are common.

Such tensions thrive on the striking lack of consolidation in sport. There is surprisingly little vertical or horizontal integration compared to other elements of the leisure industry (see Figure 9.2). In sports like tennis and golf, while a few agents play a dominant role, promoters and venues around the world compete to attract the stars. There are a few exceptions. The Grand Prix circuit is tightly controlled by the governing body and operates, in many ways, as one integrated concern. The European athletic circuit has within it a four-site cartel with the power, backed by TV money, to outbid the others. British boxing has tended to be dominated by one or two groups which link a promoter, a television company, venues, managers and boxers in relationships that exclude outsiders. There is some horizontal integration in horse-racing – United Racecourses owns three of the major racecourses.

However, the majority of sporting venues in Britain are owned by private clubs (as in golf courses), local associations (as in county cricket grounds) or small limited companies (most football grounds). Horizontal integration is both rare and discouraged by governing bodies. Municipal ownership of stadia, which are then leased to clubs, while common on the continent is rare in Britain.

It should be noted that from this perspective the sports business is still relatively undeveloped when compared with some other sectors of the leisure economy or the culture industries. There is far more integration in the music and cinema industries than there is within the field of sport. For example, in 1965, when the sports business in its current form barely existed, the hugely lucrative British record market was dominated by EMI, Decca, Philips and Pye who

Consolidation
The acquisition of an interest in several elements or sub-units of a market sector. This can involve vertical or horizontal integration.

Vertical integration
An organisation that owns studios and production facilities, distribution companies and cinemas is an example of vertical integration. (Historically, there have been restrictions on companies acquiring too much power at several levels of the business.) A sporting example would be the ownership of a major American football or baseball franchise, the television company that broadcasts its games, and the clothing firm that produces its replica shirts.

Horizontal integration
An organisation that owns large numbers of cinemas or has acquired several studios is an example of horizontal integration. A sporting example would be the ownership, by United Racecourses, of Epsom, Sandown Park and Kempton Park. In football, there are restrictions limiting the acquisition of shares in more than one club.

Diversification
A company or individual seeks to develop business interests by expansion into new areas. The acquisition by Tottenham Hotspur of clothing company Hummel, and the later acquisition of Tottenham Hotspur by Alan Sugar (boss of Amstrad, manufacturer of satellite dishes) are examples of diversification.

FIGURE 9.2 Ownership structures

between them produced 90 per cent of all Top Ten records. During the period 1960–72 the proportion of pubs owned by the big six breweries rose from a quarter to more than a half. Murdock and Golding (1974, 1977) have demonstrated the process of consolidation, integration, diversification, share ownership and interlocking directorships within the media industry. Compared with this integration and consolidation, the sports business was small, fragmented, disorganised and under-capitalised. Even now, the nearest sport organisations have got to diversification is the development of the highly profitable replica kit and club-linked merchandising. Promoter Barry Hearn, who added boxing promotion and football club ownership (Leyton Orient) to his snooker empire, is one of the few British promoters with cross-sport interests.

Not surprisingly, then, as sport became more commercialised, it was the highly organised leisure conglomerates that were best placed to move into the more profitable aspects of sport, such as gambling and the clothing and equipment market. If you gamble, there is a good chance you have dealings with Ladbrokes, Littlewoods or the Rank Organisation. In 1994 the Ladbroke Group owned Jack Solomon (betting shops), Vernons Pools and Vernons Mail Order, Greyhound Racing tracks (e.g. Perry Barr), as well as Hilton Hotels, Texas Homecare and assorted casinos and holiday centres.[3] Littlewoods Pools has diversified, using the profits made from football pools to establish its own empire. It includes the Universal Sporting Press, as well as Burlington Warehouses, Dorchester Holdings, Harrogate Hotels, Brian Mills and Shopping Mail. The Rank Organisation owns Mecca betting shops in addition to, among many other businesses, Odeon cinemas, the Hard Rock Cafe, Pinewood studios, Top Rank, Prima Pasta, Pizza Piazza and Pleasurama amusement arcades.

In the shoe business, when the trainer moved from being an athletes' shoe to an item of high street fashion Sears was well placed to benefit, as it owned the British Shoe Corporation (which in turn owned Curtess, Dolcis, Freeman and Lilley and Skinner), Manfield and Saxone. And as high street clothing fashion increasingly borrowed from sport, Sears benefited through its ownership of Foster Brothers, Millets, Freemans, Hornes, Selfridges, Miss Selfridges and Wallis. The prestigious Lillywhites sports shop is owned by Trusthouse Forte, which also owns hotel chains, Jermyn publications, London Coin Machines, Mister Whippy, Puritan Maid, the Savoy Hotel and Fortes.

When it comes to media coverage too, the process of integration has played a role. Sky Television, and the *Sun*, both organisations that have benefited from their sports coverage, are owned by Rupert Murdoch's News Corporation. It also owns *The Times*, *Today*, *The Sunday Times*, the *News of the World*, and 20th Century Fox. If you want to buy a sports book, it also owns Hatchards, Claude Gill, Grafton, Granada publications, Hart Davis, Mayflower and Panther.

If the process of conglomeration is so visible on the periphery of sport, why has it not become more central to it? Why hasn't this process affected sport more? There are a number of possible answers. Much of British sport is still effectively controlled by organisations that are not set up to be profit making – they are administrative and redistributive rather than commercial or rapacious. Cricket clubs are run by committees elected by members. Football clubs, which have historically had a range of restrictions on their ability to pay dividends or fees to directors, are in the process of transformation, with a few having become public limited companies. The huge revenues promised by digital television have encouraged an enthusiastic rush to flotation. Up till now, given the enormous re-capitalisation involved in the massive reconstruction of stadia, it is slightly surprising that so little speculative capital has been attracted. There must be economic opportunities for at least one modern multi-purpose stadium that would be hired to a major football club but also used for pop concerts and other activities.

Labour and profit

There clearly are relationships between management and labour involved in the sports business. Substantial areas of work are poorly paid and involve relatively low levels of skill – ticket collecting, stewarding, shop workers. Other tasks –

groundsman, stable girl – involve possibly greater skill but are still low reward. At the core of sporting practice the sports performer may be rewarded massively, modestly or, in amateur sport, not at all. As a work-force, workers in the sports industry are poorly organised – there is a broad and divisive division of labour with little in common between the roles. Top stars, on the other hand, in conjunction with their agents can now wield substantial power. However, managers and owners in sports like soccer still exert considerable power to hire and fire in abrupt ways that would not be possible in many other industries (see Beamish, 1988, 1993; Maguire, 1990c; and Bale and Maguire, 1993).

If the performance, once commodified, becomes the product, then it has been produced by sports labour power and, in Marxist terms, surplus value has been created. The product can be sold for a sum greater than the investment required to produce it. Yet this is certainly not the case for much sport, which still requires all sorts of economic support in the form of sponsorship patronage or membership fees. It is essential to remember that sport is an umbrella term that embraces the most highly capitalised of activities (e.g. football's World Cup) and the most voluntaristic (e.g. village green cricket). At the level of the elite globalised spectacle in the Olympic Games, enormous sums can be generated in revenue in the form of television advertising, yet the performers are paid nothing directly (they greatly increase their earning power) and the event is staged in part by voluntary labour mobilised in the name of civic and national pride. Such labour generates a large amount of surplus value.

At the elite level, employers may be clubs, governing bodies, local county associations or promoters. Elite performers may receive a salary, with bonuses, prize money, appearance fees and other benefits. The performance is sold to spectators, to television, to advertisers and to sponsors. The income from this includes surplus value produced by the performance, where such income is greater than the cost of producing the spectacle. Such profit may go to a promoter, a club or a governing body, or be shared between them. In a sport like football, whose owners typically (at least up till now!) put success ahead of profit and whose star players are much in demand, much or all of the profit is re-invested. Even in rigidly amateur sports elite sport inevitably generates surplus value and profit somewhere. The stiff defence of amateurism maintained by Rugby Union until its almost complete capitulation in 1995 merely meant that profits were made by the Association, television companies, shirt-sellers and others at the expense of the star performers at the heart of the spectacle.

The production process and the product

Analysis of the sports process of production, reveals a contradiction. The sports performance is transient, and unpredictable, and this is precisely what gives sport much of its appeal. Paradoxically, though, it has to be turned into a product, an object, in order to be marketed. In turning it into a commodity, there is the need to guarantee its quality. Inevitably some of the uncertainty must be sacrificed. The process of commodification threatens the very value of the performance precisely as it tries to cash in on the value (Whannel, 1994b). So if the sports performance is the product, who is the producer? To what extent is it merely the athletes, or is it also the coaches, the promoters, the agents and the television producers? More systematic analysis is needed of the cash nexus here – who is paying who to do what?

Commodity exchange

There is no doubt that commodification is at the heart of this process, and that, in as much as sport has increasingly been penetrated by capital, the market value of the sporting event has assumed a key importance. The major new source of income is sponsorship, which in the British context alone has risen from less than £1 million in 1966 to around £320 million in 1998. As is well known, most of this money goes to televised events. So one set of customers for sport are the major companies who provide the bulk of sponsorship revenue. And they are buying, not the sports performance itself, but the audience watching it. So we could argue, following Dallas Smythe (1977), that the real product of sport is the television audience, which is produced by televised sport performance, and the consumer who is paying for it is the sponsor. In other words, television companies sell us to advertisers. There are, of course, problems with this argument. It applies to advertisement revenue-funded television channels like ITV, but is less help in analysing licence-funded channels like the BBC, or subscription channels like Sky Sports. As dominant programme forms and conventions are largely similar across channels, Smythe's analysis doesn't seem to offer a way of accounting for the content of television. It does, however, provide a suggestive way of conceptualising the whole process which helps to reveal some of the underlying economic dynamics.

Globalisation and postmodernity

In the context of the last three decades of the twentieth century, the economic process cannot be understood without some examination of the supposed impact of globalisation and postmodernity.

Globalisation denotes a broad process in which markets, trade, labour relations and culture itself have attained global dimensions, that is, the forms of organisation that connect them have a global character. In the course of this process the influence of nation-states has declined. In the field of sport it has been the combination of the emergence of a world media system and an international sport system that has given the sports business its global character. As far as globalisation in sport is concerned, the crucial take-off period is between 1870 and 1930.

1861	First English cricket side to tour Australia
1877	First cricket Test Match
1894	International Olympic Committee formed
1896	First modern Olympic Games, in Athens
1904	FIFA, world governing body of football, formed
1909	Imperial Cricket Conference formed
1912	Formation of International Amateur Athletic Association
1913	International Lawn Tennis Federation formed
1930	First football World Cup staged

International sporting contact developed rapidly between the wars, but just as the spread of the railways helped produce national sport in the mid-nineteenth century, so it was jet travel that gave a major boost to international sport in the post-war period. The growth of sport internationally in turn helped the growth of the sport clothing and equipment industry, led by firms like Slazenger, Lillywhites, Dunlop and Wilson. The development of the sports business from the 1970s required a whole new category of professionals – international lawyers, corporate accountants, financial advisers and management consultants. These developments served to further weaken traditional amateur paternalism and fostered the growth of entrepreneurship.

Modern international sport is a product of the jet, television and corporate capitalism. In 1950 there were 5 million TV sets world-wide and only Great Britain, the USA and the USSR had television. By 1970 there were 250 million sets in 130 countries, and since the early 1970s television has spread rapidly to Africa, Asia and Latin America. The media system was increasingly prompting international exchange in sport. This partly retained the traditional character of cultural imperialism. American television had a massive advantage in that the high production values and spectacular appearance of a sport like American football could make an economic return in the North American market alone. This meant that American football, like much of American television, could be sold very cheaply around the world, undercutting local production whilst still making a profit (Whannel, 1985). However, sport from other countries now contributes to the export trade – Australian Rules, sumo, and the Tour de France have all found their space and their audience on British television (see also Boyle and Blain, 1991).

American television has assumed an awesome cultural and economic power, with its companies bidding astronomic sums for the rights to the Superbowl and the Olympic Games. The American television rights for the 1992 Winter and Summer Games cost American television more than $600 million. US television pays for the Olympics, and plays a major role in influencing how it is run, exerting a subtle, indirect, but major influence on the layout of the site and stadia, the nature of ceremonies and the choice and timing of events.

The spectacularisation of top level sport on television, enabled by the growing technological command of image production and distribution, is a key part of the commodification process (Morris and Nydahl, 1985). Major sporting events win and hold enormous audiences, and have become global events. They serve to condense complex symbolic systems – of politics, nationalism, gender, race and aspiration (see Real, 1975; Wenner, 1989). The ceremonies and rituals surrounding the Olympic Games are in themselves a rich and complex field, juggling the needs of television for a comprehensible spectacle, the desire of Olympics organisers to demonstrate their munificence, the pressure to advertise a national culture, and the need to draw on aspects of the history, heritage and traditions of the host country, not necessarily easily read by the TV audience (Tomlinson, 1996). The production of spectacle on this scale is necessarily laden with ideology. (See Gruneau, 1989b; Tomlinson, 1989; Wren-Lewis and Clarke, 1983; Whannel, 1994a; for more broad ranging collections on the Olympics and the media, see McPhail and Jackson, 1989 and Moragas *et al.*, 1996.)

The International Olympic Committee has the benefit of an instantly recognisable and highly marketable symbol, which signifies internationalism, excellence and the purity of Greek idealism. Perversely, the prohibition of advertising in the Olympic arena gives the symbol the aura of being above commerce and hence greatly increases its commercial value. This gives a clue to the resolution of a paradox at the heart of sport. Sport is capable of generating substantial profits although the key institutions were not formed as commercial endeavours. Yet, increasingly, beneath the cloak of traditional amateurism, they are reshaping themselves according to the nature and opportunities of the market-place.

Gruneau (1997) charts this re-shaping in the context of Canadian sports, emphasising the re-alignment between public, private and voluntary subsidisation of the spectacle of sport and the market. His examples include

- budget cuts in government-funded community recreation programmes, leading to contracting out and partnerships;
- commercial sponsorship of sports programmes in the voluntary sector;
- cuts in school sports programmes and reliance on fund-raising;
- erosion of state funding to national amateur sports, and the need to search for corporate sponsorship.

Throughout, government policies were guided more and more by a new rhetoric of privatisation, deregulation and economic 'competitiveness'. Gruneau states that 'the market has responded by infusing sport at virtually all levels with the spectacular promotional logic of a media-based and increasingly trans-national, consumer culture' (1997: 4).

North American leagues are attempting to expand globally in various ways:

- Satellite and cable channels relay American sport to Asia and Europe.
- Merchandising team logos and the global products of teams.
- Global marketing of sportswear, shoe retailers.
- Staging of exhibition games outside North America.
- Sponsorship of other professional teams trans-nationally.

Gruneau (1997) asserts that 'In today's society of the spectacle, virtually every cultural event indeed every public communication, has come to have promotional messages and public relations purposes built into it'.

Like the Olympics, Wimbledon tennis is efficient at trading upon its image. Ticket sales are only 20 per cent of income, with 60 per cent coming from television, and 20 per cent from other sources (Wilson, 1988). Rejecting title sponsorship, competition sponsorship and arena ads, which could be worth £5–10 million, the Wimbledon authorities accepted the prompting of agent IMG to concentrate on marketing and licensing the name and the logo. They now market clothes, shoes, wallets, belts, luggage, bone china, preserves, sheets, blankets, towels, stationary and calendars with the Wimbledon brand (Wilson, 1988).

Exporting sports has become a significant trend in the 1980s. American football, Australian Rules, sumo, and even cricket have been targeting new potential markets. Baseball has a long-term strategy for marketing the game in Europe, snooker is established in Thailand, Hong Kong, Malaysia, Singapore, Brazil and China. Attempts continue to establish a European American Football League and FIFA, having staged a successful World Cup in the USA, now wait for signs that the game has caught on more fully in North America (Sugden and Tomlinson, 1998).

There is general agreement that globalising processes are at work. Some regard this as a new phenomenon transcending the established structures of nation-states, seen as of declining relevance. Others see the process as a continuation of established patterns of cultural imperialism. For many analysts, globalising processes in sport are closely linked to Americanisation (Maguire, 1990a). Whannel (1985) regards international television sport as a form of western cultural imperialism. Jean Harvey and François Houle (1994) argue that globalisation is an alternative to Americanisation and imperialism, not a form of it. Maguire (1990c) in discussing the spread of American football to England, points out, with reference to soccer, that cultural exchange is not always a one-way process. US dominance has been challenged by Europe and Japan. Guttmann (1991) says globalisation is just part of modernisation, whilst McKay and Miller (1991) and McKay *et al.* (1993) say that the globalisation of capital is a key part of the process. Rowe *et al.* (1994) also remind us of the complexities of international cultural exchange:

> In order to comprehend the reach of international images and markets it is necessary to move beyond the simple logic of cultural domination and towards a more multi-directional concept of the flow of global traffic, in people, goods and services.

Postmodernity is a more contentious term, assuming different connotations in different contexts. Broadly it refers to the centrality of information and image, the ways in which culture has become increasingly self-reflexive, juxta-positional and parodic; the growing irrelevance of a stable conception of 'reality' and the undermining of established certainties of progress and development. Surface appearances have become central, with substance and authenticity impossible to identify. Postmodern theorists argue that in such a world, the old totalising grand narratives of modernity such as Marxism no longer have explanatory force. In opposition to this view other theorists (see Giddens, 1990) argue that this period is better characterised as late modernity. However theorised, it is undoubtedly the case that the spread of, not only American football, but also Australian Rules Football and sumo, around the world, via television, indicates significant new cultural processes that demand new modes of theorisation.

According to postmodern theory, the last two decades have seen the emergence of a world characterised by the rapid exchange of information, the saturation of images and a concern with consumption and identity. This world is characterised by fragmentation, by the dominance of surface appearance over substance, by a growing self-conscious self-reflexivity permeating all areas of cultural and social life, by pastiche, parody, irony and playfulness. In this context sporting exchange can be seen as another form of cultural playfulness. The television programme *Gladiators* is a good instance of this process, juxtaposing the formal structure of sport, the setting of show business and the iconography of the comic book. The fact that one of its presenters, John Fashanu, was, during 1997, on trial accused and subsequently acquitted of fixing the results of football matches, rather punctures the playful postmodern carapace, with its disturbing reminder of the contrast between Corinthian idealism and crude profiteering, or even sordid immorality. The passing popularity of sumo in Britain highlights the transient character of much popular culture in the postmodern era.

It is notable that sumo has spawned its own bar-based pastiche in which men don fat belly costumes to compete with each other in sumo rings, presumably with ironic quote marks suspended above. Whether one accepts the main precepts of postmodern theory or not, it is clear that the commercialisation of sport has developed to the point that wholly synthetic pseudo-sport events like *Gladiators* can be positioned in the mainstream of popular culture.

Notes

1 Football, as this book was completed, was in the midst of a period of dramatic transition and reorganisation. It is clear that developments in digital television will enable the Premier League clubs dramatically to increase their revenue. Clubs are increasingly seeking to join Manchester United, Millwall and Newcastle United in floating shares on the open market and becoming plcs. This brings them more closely in alignment with other capitalist enterprise – they will be owned by shareholders who will expect to remove some of the surplus from the game in the form of profit.
2 Taylorisation involves the application of principles of time and motion analysis to the work process. It was introduced first in the United States of America as a means of increasing productivity and reducing labour costs. A Marxist analysis interprets this as one of the strategies adopted by the capitalist class to counteract the systematic tendency, described in Marx's *Das Kapital*, for the rate of profit to decline.
3 I am grateful to Ian Wellard for compiling this information in 1994. Readers should be aware that this information rapidly dates, but that they can easily do their own research – key sources are *Who Owns Whom* and the *Directory of Directors*.

ESSAYS AND EXERCISES

Essays

In what senses can it be said that the commercialisation of sport has corrupted the essence of sport?

Sponsorship: sport's bane or saviour?

Discuss the nature of the political economy underlying the globalisation and spectacularisation of sport.

Exercises

Note, at a live sports event, the nature, profile and prevalence of sponsors' names and logos.

On the internet, search for the website of, say, a prominent Premier League football club. Find out all you can about its annual turnover and consider its main sources of income.

Look at some prominent television adverts featuring sports stars and celebrities. What are they being used to sell, why and how?

FURTHER READING

J. Goldlust, *Playing for Keeps: Sport, the Media and Society*, Australia, Longman, documents media-led commercialising influences on sport.

J. Sugden and A. Tomlinson, *FIFA and the Contest for World Football – Who Rules the Peoples' Game?*, Cambridge, Polity Press, 1998, Chapter 4, provides an account of the global media and market penetration of UEFA's European Champions League and FIFA's World Cup.

References

Allison, L. (ed.) (1986) *The Politics of Sport*, Manchester: Manchester University Press.

Allison, L. (ed.) (1993) *The Changing Politics of Sport*, Manchester: Manchester University Press

Aris, S. (1990) *Sportsbiz: Inside the Sports Business*, London: Hutchinson.

Bailey, P. (1978) *Leisure and Class in Victorian England – Rational Recreation and the Contest for Control 1830–1885,* London: Routledge & Kegan Paul.

Bale, J. and Maguire, J. (eds) (1993) *The Global Arena: Sports Talent Migration in an Interdependent World*, Leicester: Leicester University Press.

Barnett, S. (1990) *Games and Sets: The Changing Face of Sport on Television,* London: BFI.

Beamish, R. (1988) 'The Political Economy of Sport', in J. Harvey and H. Cantelon (eds), *Not Just a Game: Essays in Canadian Sport Sociology*, Ottawa: University of Ottawa Press, pp. 141–158.

Beamish, R. (1993) 'Labour Relations in Sport: Central Issues in their Emergence and Structure in High-performance Sport,' in A. Ingham and J. Loy (eds), *Sport and Social Development*, London: Human Kinetics

Bonney, B. (1980) *Packer and Televised Cricket*, Sydney, Australia: NSW Institute of Technology.

Boyle, R. and Blain, N. (1991) 'Footprints on the Field: TV Sport, Delivery Systems and National Culture in a Changing Europe', paper at 'International Television Studies' conference London: Institute of Education, University of London.

Brady, M. (1959) *The Centre Court Story*, London: Sportsmans Book Club.

Brailsford, D. (1989) *Bareknuckles: A Social History of Prizefighting*, Cambridge: Lutterworth Press.

Brohm, J.-M. (1978) *Sport – A Prison of Measured Time*, London: Ink Links.

Brookes, C. (1978) *English Cricket – The Game and its Players Through the Ages*, London: Weidenfeld and Nicolson.

Burn, G. (1986) *Pocket Money – Bad Boys, Business Heads and Boom-time Snooker*, London: Heinemann.

Butler, F. (1972) *A History of Boxing in Britain*, London: Arthur Barker.

Carpenter, H. (1982) *Boxing – An Illustrated History*, London: Collins.

Chaplin, D. (1991) 'History of English Football Equipment', unpublished 3rd year dissertation (SPS 110), London: Roehampton Institute of Higher Education.

Chippendale, P. and Franks, S. (1991) *Dished: The Rise and Fall of British Satellite Broadcasting*, London: Simon & Schuster.

Clarke, J. and Critcher, C. (1985) *The Devil Makes Work – Leisure in Capitalist Britain*, London: Macmillan.

Coakley, J. (1978) *Sport in Society: Issues and Controversies*, St Louis, Illinois: Mosby.

Coalter, F. (1993) 'Sports Participation: Price or Priorities?', *Leisure Studies*, Vol. 12, pp. 171–182.

Cohen, P. (1972) 'Sub-cultural Conflict and Working Class Community', *Working Papers in Cultural Studies,* no. 2, Spring, Birmingham: Centre for Contemporary Cultural Studies, University of Birmingham.

Cousins, G. (1975) *Golf In Britain*, London: Routledge & Kegan Paul.

Crawford Report (1925) *Report of the Broadcasting Committee*, London: HMSO (Cmd 2599).

Critcher, C. (1979) 'Football Since the War', in J. Clarke, C. Critcher and R. Johnson (eds), *Working Class Culture – Studies in History and Theory*, London: Hutchinson.

Cunningham, H. (1980) *Leisure in the Industrial Revolution c.1780–c.1880* London: Croom Helm.

Dobbs, B. (1973) *Edwardians at Play: Sport 1890–1914*, London: Pelham Books.

Dunning, E. (1971) 'The Development of Modern Football', in E. Dunning (ed.), *The Sociology of Sport*, London: Cass.

Dunning, E. and Sheard, K. (1976) 'The Bifurcation of Rugby Union and Rugby League', *International Review of Sport Sociology*, Vol. 11, pp. 31–72.

Giddens, A. (1990) *The Consequences of Modernity,* Cambridge: Polity Press.

Goldlust, J. (1987) *Playing for Keeps: Sport, the Media and Society*, Melbourne, Australia: Longman.

Gratton, C. and Taylor, P. (1986) *Sport and Recreation: An Economic Analysis*, London: E & FN Spon.

Gratton, C. and Taylor, P. (1987) *Leisure in Britain*, Letchworth: Leisure Publications.

Gratton, C. and Taylor, P. (1991) *Government and the Economics of Sport*, London: Longman.

Gruneau, R. (1979) *Class, Sport and the Modern State*, Ontario, Canada: Sports Studies Research Group.

Gruneau, R. (1983) *Class, Sports and Social Development*, Amherst: University of Massachusetts Press.

Gruneau, R. (1989a) 'Making Spectacles: A Case Study in Television Sports Production,' in L. Wenner (ed.), *Media Sports and Society*, Newbury Park, California: Sage.

Gruneau, R. (1989b) 'Television, the Olympics and the Question of Ideology', in T. McPhail and R. Jackson (eds), *The Olympic Movement and the Mass Media – Past, Present and Future Issues*, Calgary, Canada: Hurford.

Gruneau, R. (1997) 'Canadian Sport in the Society of the Spectacle', presented at 'How Sport Can Change the World', annual conference of the Japanese Society for Sport Sociology, Kyoto, Ritsumeikan University, Japan, March 27/28.

Guttmann, A. (1978) *From Ritual to Record – The Nature of Modern Sports*, New York: Columbia University Press.

Guttmann, A. (1991) 'Sport Diffusion: A Response to Maguire and the Americanisation Commentaries', *Sociology of Sport Journal*, Vol. 8, pp. 185–190.

Haigh, G. (1993) *The Cricket Wars: The Inside Story of Kerry Packer's World Series Cricket*, Melbourne: Text Publishing.

Hargreaves, J. (1986) *Sport, Power and Culture – A Social and Historical Analysis of Popular Sports in Britain*, Cambridge: Polity Press.

Harvey, J. and Cantelon, H. (eds) (1988) *Not Just a Game: Essays in Canadian Sport Sociology*, Ottawa: University of Ottawa Press.

Harvey, J. and Houle, F. (1994) 'Sport, World Economy, Global Culture and New Social Movements', *Sociology of Sport Journal*, Vol. 11, pp. 337–355.

Hoch, P. (1972) *Rip Off The Big Game – The Exploitation of Sports by the Power Elite*, New York: Anchor Books.

Hofmann, D. and Greenberg, M. (1989) *Sport$biz,* Champaign, Illinois: Human Kinetics.

Holt, R. (1989) *Sport and the British: A Modern History*, Oxford: Oxford University Press.

Howell, D. (1983) *Howell Report on Sponsorship*, London: Central Council for Physical Recreation.

Howkins, A. and Lowerson, J. (1995) 'Leisure in the Thirties', in A. Tomlinson (ed.), *Leisure and Social Control*, Leisure Studies Association Publication No. 19 (new edition), pp. 79–99.

Inglis, S. (1983) *The Football Grounds of England and Wales*, London: Willow.

Jones, E. (1985) *Sport in Space: Effects of Cable and Satellite Television*, London: Sports Council.

Jones, S. (1986) *Workers at Play: A Social and Economic History of Leisure 1918–39*, London: Routledge & Kegan Paul.

Lamb, K.L., Asturias, L.P., Roberts, K. and Brodie, D.A. (1992) 'Sports Participation – How Much Does it Cost?', *Leisure Studies*, Vol. 11, pp. 19–30.

Lasch, C. (1980) *Culture of Narcissism*, London: Abacus.

Lawrence, G. and Rowe, D. (1987) 'The Corporate Pitch: Televised Cricket Under Capitalism', in G. Lawrence and D. Rowe (eds), *Power Play – The Commercialisation of Australian Sport*, Sydney, Australia: Hale and Iremonger.

McIntosh, P. (1979) *Fair Play – Ethics in Sport and Education,* London: Heinemann.

McKay, J. (1973) *My Wide World*, New York: Macmillan.

McKay, J., Lawrence, G., Miller, T. and Rowe, D. (1993) 'Globalisation and Australian Sport', *Sport Science Review*, Vol. 2, no. 1, pp. 10–28.

McKay, J. and Miller, T. (1991) 'From Old Boys to Men and Women of the Corporation: The Americanisation and Commodification of Australian Sport', *Sociology of Sport Journal*, Vol. 8, pp. 86–94.

McPhail, T. and Jackson, R. (eds) (1989) *The Olympic Movement and the Mass Media – Past, Present and Future Issues*, Calgary, Canada: Hurford.

Maguire, J. (1988a) 'The Commercialisation of English Elite Basketball 1972–1988', *International Review for the Sociology of Sport* Vol. 23, pp. 305–321.

Maguire, J. (1988b) 'The Quest for Excitement or Exciting Signficance: A Revision of the Elisian Perspective on a Theory of Sport, Leisure and the Emotions', in D. Botterill (ed.), *Leisure Participation and Experience: Models and Case Studies*, Brighton: Leisure Studies Association.

Maguire, J. (1988c) 'Race and Position Assignment in English Soccer: Ethnicity and Sport,' *Sociology of Sport Journal*, Vol. 5, pp. 257–269.

Maguire, J. (1990a) 'The Media-sport Production Complex: The Case of American Football in Western European Societies', *European Journal of Communication*, Vol. , pp. 315–335.

Maguire, J. (1990b) 'The Commercialisation of Sport and Athletes' Rights', in F. Kew (ed.), *Social Scientific Perspectives on Sport*, Leeds: BASS, pp. 24–29.

Maguire, J. (1990c) 'More Than a Sporting Touchdown: The Making of American Football in England, 1982–1990', *Sociology of Sport Journal*, Vol. 7, pp. 213–237.

Malcolmson, R. (1973) *Popular Recreations in English Society 1700–1850*, Cambridge: Cambridge University Press.

Mangan, J.A. (1981) *Athleticism in the Victorian and Edwardian Public School – The Emergence and Consolidation of an Educational Ideology*, Cambridge: Cambridge University Press.

Mason, T. (1988) *Sport in Britain*, London: Faber and Faber.

Mason, T. (1993) 'All the Winners and the Half Times', *The Sports Historian* (The Journal of the British Society of Sports History), no. 13, pp. 3–12.

Moragas, M. de, Rivenburgh, N.K. and Larson, J.F. (eds) (1996) *Television in the Olympics*, London: John Libbey.

Morris, B.S. and Nydahl, J. (1985) 'Sports Spectacle as Drama: Image, Language and Technology', *Journal of Popular Culture*, Vol. 18, pp. 101–110.

Mortimer, R. (1958) *The Jockey Club*, London: Cassell.

Murdock, G. and Golding, P. (1974) 'For a Political Economy of Mass Communications', in R. Miliband and J. Savile (eds), *The Socialist Register*, London: Merlin.

Murdock, G. and Golding, P. (1977) 'Capitalism, Communications and Class Relations', in J. Curran, M. Gurevitch and J. Woollacott (eds), *Mass Communication and Society*, London: Arnold.

Real, M. (1975) 'Superbowl: Mythic Spectacle', *Journal of Communication*, no. 25, pp. 31–43.

Richards, J. (1984) *The Age of the Dream Palace: Cinema and Society in Britain 1930–39,* London: Routledge & Kegan Paul.

Robertson, M. (1977) *Wimbledon 1877–1977,* London: Arthur Barker.

Rowe, D., Lawrence, G., Miller, T. and McKay, J. (1994) 'Global Sport? Core Concern and Peripheral Vision', *Media Culture & Society*, Vol. 16, pp. 661–676.

Scannell, P. and Cardiff, D. (1991) *A Social History of British Broadcasting V1 1922–39*, Oxford: Basil Blackwell.

Sewart, J. (1987) 'The Commodification of Sport', *International Review of the Sociology of Sport*, Vol. 22, pp. 171–191.

Smythe, D. (1977) 'Communications: Blindspot of Western Marxism', *Canadian Journal of Political and Social Theory*, Vol. 1, pp. 1–27.

Stoddart, B. (1990) 'Wide World of Golf', *Sociology of Sport Journal* Vol. 7, pp. 378–388.

Sugden, J. and Tomlinson, A. (1998) *FIFA and the Contest for World Football – Who Rules the Peoples' Game?*, Cambridge: Polity Press.

Tomlinson, A. (1989) 'Representation, Ideology and the Olympic Games: A Reading of the Opening and Closing Ceremonies of the 1984 Olympics', in T. McPhail and R. Jackson (eds), *The Olympic Movement and the Mass Media – Past, Present and Future Issues*, Calgary, Canada: Hurford.

Tomlinson, A. (1996) 'Olympic Spectacles: Opening Ceremonies, and Some Paradoxes of Globalisation', *Media, Culture & Society*, Vol. 18, pp. 583–602.

Tomlinson, A. and Walker, H. (1990) 'Holidays for All: Popular Movements, Collective Leisure and the Pleasures', in A. Tomlinson (ed.), *Consumption, Identity and Style – Marketing, Meanings and the Packaging of Pleasure*, London: Routledge/Comedia.

Vinnai, G. (1976) *Football Mania*, London: Ocean.

Walvin, J. (ed.) (1978) *Leisure and Society 1830–1950*, London: Longman.

Wenner, L. (1989) 'The Super Bowl Pre-game Show: Cultural Fantasies and Political Subtext', in L. Wenner (ed.), *Media Sports and Society*, Newbury Park, California: Sage.

Whannel, G. (1983) *Blowing the Whistle: The Politics of Sport*, London: Pluto.

Whannel, G. (1985) 'Television Spectacle and the Internationalisation of Sport', *Journal of Communication Inquiry*, Vol. 2, pp. 54–74.

Whannel, G. (1986) 'The Unholy Alliance: Notes on Television and the Re-making of British Sport 1965–1985', *Leisure Studies*, Vol. 5, pp. 22–37.

Whannel, G. (1994a) 'Profiting by the Presence of Ideals: Sponsorship and Olympism', in *International Olympic Academy: 32nd Session*, Olympia, Greece: International Olympic Academy.

Whannel, G. (1994b) 'Sport and Popular Culture: The Temporary Triumph of Process over Product', *Innovations*, Vol. 6, pp. 341–350.

Wilson, N. (1988) *The Sports Business*, London: Piatkus.

Wren-Lewis, J. and Clarke, A. (1983) 'The World Cup – A Political Football?', *Theory Culture & Society*, Vol. 1, pp. 123–132.

Index